Modern Japan

A Social History since 1868

J. E. THOMAS

LONGMAN
London and New York

Addison Wesley Longman Limited
Edinburgh Gate,
Harlow, Essex CM20 2JE, United Kingdom
and Associated Companies throughout the world.

*Published in the United States of America
by Addison Wesley Longman, New York*

First published 1996

ISBN 0 582 259614 PPR

British Library Cataloguing in Publication Data

A catalogue record for this book is
available from the British Library

Library of Congress Cataloging-in-publication Data

Thomas, J. E., 1933–
    Modern Japan: a social history since 1868/J.E. Thomas.
        p.   cm.
    Includes bibliographical references and index.
    ISBN 0–582–25962–2. – ISBN 0–582–25961–4 (pbk.)
    1. Japan – History – 1868–   I. Title.
DS881.9.T496   1996   95–51035
952 – dc20   CIP

Transferred to digital print on demand 2001
Printed and bound by Antony Rowe Ltd, Eastbourne

Contents

List of Illustrations and Maps

Whilst every effort has been made to trace the owners of copyright material, in a few cases this has proved to be problematic so we take this opportunity to offer our apologies to any copyright holders whose rights we may have unwittingly infringed.

Acknowledgements

It is a truism that the writing of a book is accompanied by a need for help and advice: and so it has been in my case. I wish to express my gratitude to those people who so freely gave me information, and admonition, and to those who went to so much trouble to read sections of the book. I begin by thanking Mr Hasegawa Haruo, Counsellor and Medical Attaché at the Embassy of Japan, and Miss Kakinuma Mika of the Japanese Centre for Intercultural Communication, both of whom helped with difficult specialist information. I am grateful to two representatives of campaigning organisations in Japan for giving me permission to use their material. These are Mr Arai Junji of the National League for Support of The School Textbook Suit in Tokyo, and Mr Nakamura Seiji of the Buraku Liberation Research Institute in Osaka. Next I would like to thank experts in Japan, who commented on the draft text. These are Professor Uesugi Takamichi of Kyoto University, Professor Shimada Shuichi of Chuo University, Professor Yamaguchi Makoto of Ryutsu Keizai University and Professor Hirasawa Yasumasa of Osaka University. Others who read chapters, and gave of their valuable time were Mr Simon Thomas, to whom I am particularly obliged, because of his critical and unfailing help, Mrs Michiko Homma Thomas and Ms Judith Cherry. I am grateful to Maurice Vinden who was a prisoner of war on the Burma railway. He brought alive for me the horror which he and others suffered. Finally I owe more than I can express to Ms Nakamura Keiko of the Information Section of the Embassy of Japan in London. For many years she has been indefatigable in sending me material on Japan which she identifies as being of interest to me, and has always replied promptly to any request I make, however weird it might be. I owe her special thanks. To my typist, Mrs Heather Blackburn of the Department of Adult Education in the University of Nottingham I am most grateful. Her patience, speed, and relentless cheerfulness were a delight. Thanks also go to Mrs Kate Booth for help with typing. Thanks too to Longman for giving me the opportunity.

All of these people helped. But in the usual way I must absolve them from supposed error, of fact or of analysis. This book is my responsibility.

This book is dedicated to:
(in order of appearance)

Olwen, Simon Gerard, Colleen Teresa,
Philip Owain, Michiko, Joseph Matthew McDonnell,
Henry Takashi Homma, Emily Caitlin McDonnell,
and those as yet unborn.

Celebrating their rich heritage.

J.E. THOMAS

Overleaf ▶
A Tokyo street today

Introduction

This book arose out of the experience of teaching Japanese history to a variety of students from undergraduates to those attending adult education classes. Especially with history students, it became clear that the modern history of Japan is a subject with a lot of appeal. There are many reasons for this, ranging from the novelty of the subject which is refreshing to those whose historical palate has become rather jaded by more traditional areas of history, to the intrinsic, and increasing, fascination of Japan. It also became clear that younger people especially are interested in the nature and evolution of Japanese society, rather than the rather exclusive focus of some years ago on military and political history. This book attempts to cater for this interest in social structure, organisation and dynamics.

Naturally, the major features of the evolution of modern Japan, such as the role of militarism, must be, and are addressed. The form is that a chapter on a major period is followed by a chapter identifying an aspect of society which was, or is highlighted by that period. Thus, the period from 1912 to the 1930s raised questions of political freedom which were as important to women as to men. The discussion of this Taisho democracy is therefore followed by a long account of women in Japan. In the same way the belief that education was perhaps the major reason why the Japanese accepted their government's imperial policy, necessitates a longer assessment of education as a formative influence than is usually found in introductory texts. When dealing with such specialist areas, for the purpose of coherence I have brought the account up to the events of the present day.

It will be clear that this is a book for people who know little or nothing about the history of Japan. It seeks to go into only as much detail as is necessary both to inform and to encourage further study. It is not therefore a text for experts.

Note about names and spellings

When Japanese names are written in Latin script, several systems are used. Sometimes a letter will be accented, as in *daimyō* for example. I have followed the practice of italicising Japanese words, and have also included a glossary of such words. The Japanese custom is to put family name before given name, and I have done so. There is also a problem arising from changes of name, or alternative spellings. Thus 'Peking' can be either that, or Peiping or Beijing: the Chinese province of Shandong can be written Shantung. Even Tokyo occurs as Tokio. I have spelt words consistently, based upon practice and advice, and where a place has more than one name, I have chosen the one which was used at the time being discussed, or the one which is the most intelligible in context. Thus, Formosa is used instead of Taiwan, and the Liaotung peninsula at the tip of Manchuria is written as the Kwantung peninsula – the name used in Japanese history. Outcast(e)s is spelled both ways – I use the more common 'outcaste'.

CHAPTER ONE

Out of Isolation

Overleaf ▶
*Japanese beating a foreign seaman
(Nishaka-e print by Ipposai Hoto)*

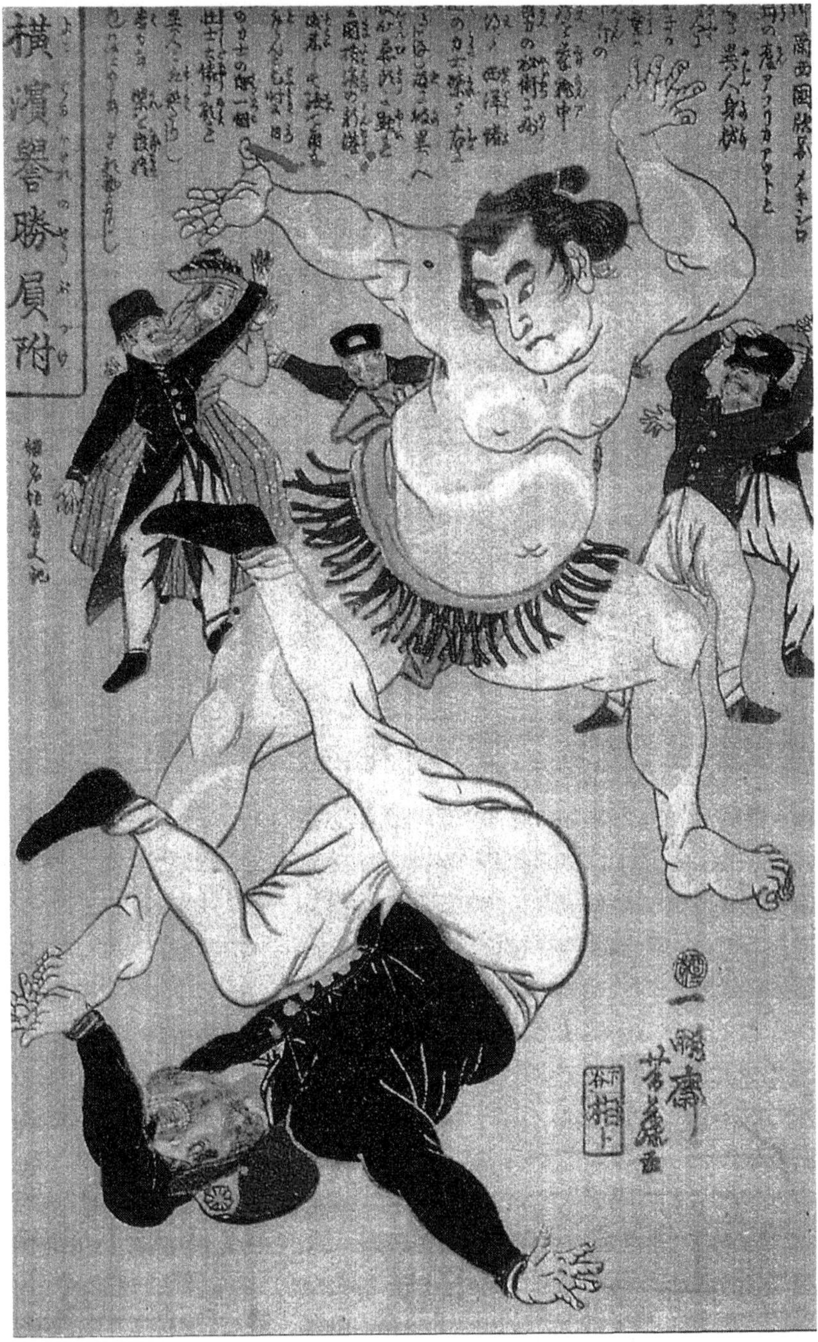
横濱譽勝負附

Out of Isolation

On 3 January 1868, the emperor of Japan was 'restored' to what was claimed as his rightful position in society. This is accepted as the point and the event from which the modern history of Japan begins. Although the circumstances were turbulent and violent, this was by no means a sudden change, even though for the Japanese today it is perhaps the most important event in their history. They regard the years after the Restoration with awe, and attribute the phenomenal 'catching up with the west' exemplified by economic and military success, as due to the wisdom and power of the restored emperor. Quite how much real power or even influence modern Japanese emperors have had, it is impossible to know: But the question is important, and we shall return to it. What is certain though is that like most major upheavals in societies, the Restoration was the culmination of a complexity of events. To understand this complexity, it is necessary to be aware of the nature of Japanese society and its nineteenth-century inheritance.

From 1185, if there was an individual who was most powerful in Japan, it was the *shogun*, whose full title means 'barbarian-subduing generalissimo'. In that year the famous Kamakura shogunate was established, and the emperors' power, over succeeding centuries, was reduced, and sometimes eliminated. Although there is some truth in the commonly held belief that the *shogun* had absolute power, we shall go on to see that his authority was moderated both by the presence of powerful clans who often usurped power for themselves, and by the refusal of some emperors to be compliant. The battles for power by the aristocracy led to very destructive civil wars, which came to a peak and to an end in the closing years of the sixteenth century. It was then, in 1598, that Hideyoshi, to whom we shall return because of his Korean adventures, died.

His followers were beaten in a famous battle at Sekigahara in 1600

3

by Tokugawa Ieyasu, who, despite the fact that he was a guardian of Hideyoshi's heirs, prompted the suicide of most of them, and the execution of the last, an eight-year-old boy. Because of his lineage – he claimed he was of the house of Minamoto, the founders of the Kamakura shogunate – he was appointed *shogun* in 1603. Then began a remarkable period in Japanese history, noted for its peace, stability and isolation from the rest of the world. This period, in which the Tokugawa *shoguns* reigned supreme, is called the Edo (or sometimes, in more antiquated language Yedo) Era, Edo being the name of the capital city of Tokyo before the restoration of 1868. Immediately after Edo was established as the shogunal capital, it seems to have become a grand city where 'money flowed like water'.[1] A European visitor to the castle in 1609 observed that at the first gate there were 2,000 armed guards, at the second another 400, and at the third 300. The armouries, he reported, contained enough equipment to arm 100,000 men.[2] The administration of the regime was known as the *bakufu*, meaning 'field government'. Within the *bakufu*, power was exercised by a handful of men appointed by the *shogun*. But below them was created an elaborate and powerful bureaucracy, a phenomenon which made their administration as slow as it is under their bureaucratic heirs in modern Japan.

Ieyasu is one of the most important figures in Japanese history. His achievements, notably bringing peace to a country desperate for it, derived from remarkable personal characteristics, many years of experience and, especially a capacity for introspection which both controlled and directed his behaviour. In his advice to his heirs he wrote:

> The strong manly ones in life are those who understand the meaning of the word Patience. Patience means restraining one's inclinations. There are seven emotions, joy, anger, anxiety, love, grief, fear and hate, and if a man does not give way to these he can be called patient. I am not as strong as I might be, but I have long known and practised patience. And if my descendants wish to be as I am ... they must study patience.[3]

1 Yamazaki Masakazu, 'Reexamining the era of national seclusion' in *Japan Echo*, Vol. XII, No. 4, Winter 1992, p. 75.

2 Ratti, Oscar and Westbrook, Adèle, *Secrets of the Samurai: A Survey of the Martial Arts of Feudal Japan* (Rutland, Vermont, 1973), p. 66, quoting Cooper, Michael, *They Came to Japan: An Anthology of European Reports on Japan* (London, 1965).

3 Storry, Richard, *A History of Modern Japan* (London, 1960), p. 60, quoting Sadler, A.L., *The Makers of Modern Japan* (London, 1937), pp. 389–90.

In the next forty years the Tokugawa *shoguns* established a regime which was to last for some two hundred and fifty years. Their overriding concern was to ensure the stability of Japan, and concomitantly their power in it.

A key factor was the relationship between the *shogun* and the imperial court which remained in Kyoto, and would continue to do so until 1868. The attitude of the Tokugawa *shoguns* to the emperor was respectful, since there could be no possibility of a *shogun* usurping the throne, because of the acceptance of the tradition of the singularity and purity of the imperial lineage. But the *shogun* was aware of the fact that the emperor could validate the authority of a new shogunate, and thus unseat the Tokugawa clan, a process which had happened before, would happen at the time of the Restoration, and in power politics generally, afterwards. So the court was tightly controlled by such devices as requiring imperial appointments to have the approval of the *shogun*, and the placing of family members in key posts. As well as such coercion the *shoguns* increased the wealth of the emperor and his court, a wise tactic for obvious reasons, especially since in the previous history of the dynasty, some emperors were impecunious to the point of beggarhood.

It was natural that the *shoguns* should take steps to increase their own wealth, and they did so by the reallocation of resources, notably of course land. Such tactical redistribution was used as a means of penalising those great lords called *daimyo*, literally 'great name', who had fought against the Tokugawa house, and rewarding their allies, which reinforced the latter's loyalty. However, the *shoguns* were well aware that the power of the *daimyo* was still a reality, and that the loyalty of their retainers could soon be deflected for an assault upon their newly established authority. The *daimyo* were therefore restricted by a network of constraints on their ambition. They had to seek the agreement of the *shogun* to a marriage, for example, and they had to take an oath of support upon accession. Again, as required, they had to bear the costs which were often crippling, of public works. But the most important, and probably most effective weapon of control was a requirement of domicile. This meant that all the *daimyo* had to spend every other year in Edo, the *shogun*'s capital, and when they were absent, their wives and families had to do so.

Despite such curbs on behaviour, the *daimyo* remained very powerful and retained a good deal of independence in the administration of their domains, in an arrangement with which successive *shoguns* appeared content. Apart from the kinds of restrictions discussed above, *daimyo* had autocratic power in their own territories. Those in western Japan, especially the domains of Choshu, Satsuma, Tosa and Hizen, were notably powerful and were to remain a threat to shogunate power, a threat which was to become reality in the events leading up to the Restoration.[4]

The perceived internal potential for instability was matched by a belief that foreign influence too could threaten the new regime. Traders and missionaries from Portugal first arrived in Japan at the end of the sixteenth century, to be followed by Spanish friars. In the early years of the Tokugawa, first the Dutch, and then the British arrived. Many Japanese were converted to the Christian religion, and the several trading arrangements seemed to be felicitous, operating to the advantage of all. But from the beginning the situation was potentially explosive. The Europeans brought all their rivalries and hatreds with them. The Portuguese Jesuits and the Spanish friars recreated a microcosm of their deadly sectarian and national antagonism. All nationalities engaged in vicious commercial competition, and in the middle of all the resultant attempts by the foreigners to gain credence at the expense of each other, appeared the remarkable character Will Adams, a shipwrecked English seaman, in the 1980s the subject of a best-selling novel, *Shogun* by James Clavell. Adams for a variety of reasons, not the least being his considerable knowledge of seamanship, was acceptable to Ieyasu, to their mutual profit.

The Japanese authorities though had never quite come to terms with the behaviour of the foreigners, nor were their suspicions allayed about their motives, or how Japan figured in their plans. At first Nobunaga, the ruler displaced by Hideyoshi was tolerant, and even favourable. Hideyoshi was equally tolerant, except when he issued a decree, never enacted, expelling the missionaries. On another occasion suspecting that the missionaries were the vanguard of an invasion force, he ordered the execution of twenty-six Christians, including six Spaniards in 1597, just before his own death in 1598. Ieyasu, although he had abdicated in favour of his son only two years after becoming *shogun*, became more and more concerned about the behaviour and intentions of the Europeans and their increasingly large body of converts. This included an allegation of a plot by both to overthrow the government. In 1612 and 1614 proclamations were made which, on the face of it, were

4 For a more detailed account of the organisation of the state in the nineteenth century, see Beasley, W.G., *The Meiji Restoration* (Stanford, California, 1972), especially Chapter 1.

severe. In them Christianity was prohibited, foreign priests were to leave Japan, and churches were to be demolished.

But it was Ieyasu's son, Hidetada, upon his father's death in 1616 who began a serious campaign against Christians, which for the next twenty years included torture, armed struggle, and massacre – a process which produced a home-grown list of martyrs. The shogunate was certain that there were clear links between foreigners, especially the Portuguese, missionary activity and subversion. Not only was there ample contemporary evidence that they were right, as in a revolt dominated by Christians at a place called Shimabara in 1637, but Christian missionary work must, intrinsically, be subversive. Much encouragement in repression came from the emperor, and indeed the latter considered that the *shogun* Iemitsu was not sufficiently determined, a matter to which we will return in a consideration of the role of the imperial institution.

As a consequence of negotiation between emperor and shogun, in 1634 it was ordered that all foreigners were to be expelled, except for a small Dutch trading post, strictly supervised, in Nagasaki. The Japanese people were forbidden to leave the country. Any foreign ships trying to re-establish links were turned away if they were lucky, and in the case of the crew of a Portuguese ship in 1640, executed if they were not. The effects of the isolationist policy were manifold. It effectively eliminated the possible collusion of Japanese dissidents with foreign imperialists, as indeed it was intended it should. But as well as excluding subversive political ideas, all the new industrial innovation and expertise which began to burgeon in Europe soon afterwards were similarly kept out. Storry points out that the policy contained what might have been Japanese expansion in Asia, during the very period when such expansion was being undertaken by nations whose energy and imagination were no greater than that of the Japanese.[5] Above all though, events in the nineteenth century were to show that the ambitions of the western nations in Asia were not easily to be contained, and the 'sacred' nature of Japanese social religious and political life, much enhanced and emphasised during the Edo Era, was to be one of the battlefields upon which the shogunate which had promulgated exclusion, was to fall.

Since this book focuses upon the nature and evolution of Japanese social structure, institutions and relationships, one aspect of Tokugawa consolidation is of special significance. This is the division of society into hierarchical groups and clans. The latter 'was the

5 Storry, *A History of Modern Japan*, pp. 65–6.

sum of the Japanese soul'. The Japanese subject was 'throughout his
long history "essentially a clansman, with all the group feelings
which a clan organization implies"'.[6] The clan was firmly located in
an area which, because of the relationship of the Japanese to
territory, was deeply significant. Indeed, 'the old domains still live in
the Japanese consciousness. In fact, there are some who say the
modern prefectures never really took hold'.[7] The whole society was
strictly hierarchical. Naturally, at the top were the emperor, court
aristocracy, *shogun* and *daimyo*. The rest, in a pristine, and therefore
much oversimplified form were the *samurai*, the farmers, the
artisans and the merchants. Below all of these were minority groups,
of which the most important were the outcaste people known at the
time as *eta*. In this account of social history they will receive more
discussion than is general in mainstream historical accounts.

Within each of these strata there were subdivisions. In the case of
the *daimyo* position depended for example on the size of the estate,
and the relationship with the Tokugawa family. The *samurai*, literally 'one who serves', the group which has captured the imagination
and interest of the west, notably through the cinema, were similarly
ranked. Although the *samurai* class, including families, numbered
'as much as 5 or 6 per cent of a total population in the nineteenth
century of something like thirty million people',[8] the variations in
their status, power and wealth were considerable. Beasley, marshal-
ling existing evidence uses the categories 'upper', 'middle' and
'lower', but goes on to admonish that 'the subject remains full of
pitfalls'.[9] Which category an individual could claim is not only
debatable in historical analysis, but was contentious at the time. It
would depend on whether or not he had a right of audience with
the *daimyo*, his wealth, or whether or not in battle he was a foot
soldier. Upward mobility was difficult, and movement into the
samurai class from below was rare, but as time went on, and farmers
became wealthy, there were various avenues which led to elevation
including marriage, and judicious financial help to the right people.
Such elevation gave the right to bear arms and to adopt a family
name. Position in the hierarchy might mean adoption of the code of
bushido, which was of great significance because of its influence on

6 Ratti and Westbrook, *Secrets of the Samurai*, p. 129, quoting Seligman, C.G.,
'Japanese temperament and character', *Transactions and Proceedings of the Japan Society*,
Vols 28–9 (London, 1930–32), p. 129.

7 Yamazaki, 'Reexamining the era of national seclusion', p. 74.

8 Beasley, *The Meiji Restoration*, p. 24.

9 Ibid., p. 25.

social behaviour, especially in the conduct of the armed services in the wars of the late nineteenth and twentieth centuries.

Bushido meaning the 'Way of the Warrior' was the dominating code of the *samurai* for hundreds of years, and its central tenets still affect Japanese behaviour even, or more correctly especially, in modern corporate activity. Exactly what the code embraces is difficult to define, since not only have definitions varied at different times, but the very ideas of which it consists, are ethereal. This is expressed by a Prince Mitsukuni of the Tokugawa family, in his statement as to the use of the *samurai*: 'The people of the other classes deal with visible things, while the *samurai* deal with invisible, colourless and insubstantial things.'[10] More practically, *bushido* calls for both personal excellence and a social commitment in the form of loyalty of an ultimate quality. Personally the *samurai* had to possess military skills of a very high order, and were enjoined to lead an ascetic, or at least restrained life, above all avoiding excess. The personal aspect above all emphasises the rejection of the fear of death. These are broadly the Japanese constituents of the code, while from Confucianism comes the ideal of filial piety which, while very much a precept for family behaviour, in *bushido* extends to the lord, and ultimately by extension to the emperor. There could be no disobedience; instead there was total subordination of self, and the hope and expectation of the great glory of dying for the lord. This was expressed simply by the author of *Hagakure*, an especially highly regarded commentary on the complexity of *bushido*: 'Being a retainer is nothing other than being a supporter of one's lord, entrusting matters of good and evil to him, and renouncing self interest.'[11]

A quintessential and true story which demonstrated the ideals, and which is known to every Japanese, is that of the forty-seven *ronin*, the Japanese word meaning masterless *samurai*. It began in Edo castle in 1703 where a *daimyo*, Asano, wounded another *daimyo*, Kira, as a consequence of an insult by the latter. To wield a weapon so near to the *shogun* was deeply offensive and Asano, as ordered, killed himself. His retainers vowed revenge, and eventually they saw their opportunity and killed Kira, placing his head on Asano's tomb. This presented the *shogun* and his advisers with a difficult problem, since already there were efforts to curb traditional behaviour

10   Bellah, Robert N., *Tokugawa Religion: The Values of Pre-Industrial Japan* (Glencoe, Illinois, 1957), p. 90.

11   Yamamoto Tsunetomo, *The Book of the Samurai: Hagakure* (Tokyo, 1983, translated by W.S. Wilson), p. 20.

however honourable, which so blatantly breached the peace. Eventually they were sentenced to suicide, an act which they welcomed, since it was a natural consequence. Their tombs became, and remain, a popular shrine for the Japanese. Although the episode symbolises virtue, it may have had another very important aspect. The advice given to the *shogun* that the offenders should die 'signalled a shift from the rule of virtue to the rule of law' – a critical stage in the maturation of society.[12] This episode is an almost perfect expression of key elements in *bushido*. The code itself, while it has been profoundly influential, like all codes is an 'ideal type' in the sense used by Max Weber; that is something to which aspiration can be directed, but which is unlikely to be achieved. Throughout the history of commentary on *bushido*, *samurai* are exhorted to mend their ways, and are often accused of failure even to try to behave as they should.

A warrior tradition which lies uneasily in a code dominated by concepts of honour is that of *ninja*, which means roughly 'secret person'. These were warriors mainly from the areas of Iga and Koga who were used as assassins and spies, and in furtive murderous night attacks in which they developed special expertise. With their legendary black clothing, they have become part of Japanese folklore. But at the time of the pre-Tokugawa civil wars, their treacherous methods of fighting, even though much utilised by the powerful, were hardly in the tradition of 'noble' fighting. The great *daimyo* Nobunaga, who played a major part in bringing to an end the civil wars of the sixteenth century, paving the way for the Tokugawa regime, is made to say in one account:

> The Iga rebel fellows grow daily more extravagant and presumptuous, aggravating our patience. They make no distinction between high and low, rich or poor, all of whom are part of carrying out this outrageous business. Such behaviour is a mystery to me, for they go so far as to make light of rank, and have no respect for high-ranking officials. They practise disobedience and dishonour both my name and ancient Court and military practices.[13]

As this extract shows the *ninja* ignored all precepts of *bushido*, but their effectiveness was such that when Tokugawa Ieyasu formed a personal bodyguard, it was three hundred *ninja* men of Iga and Koga whom he recruited.[14]

---

12 Yamazaki, 'Reexamining the era of national seclusion', p. 73.
13 Turnbull, Stephen, *Ninja* (Dorset, 1992), p. 68.
14 Ibid., p. 79.

The farmers were, of course, the backbone of the country for it was they who provided the food. For them the immediate advantage of the Tokugawa regime was that it brought peace, and a world in which they could plant and harvest their crops free from the rapacious marauding bands and armies which had harmed not only them, but their forebears. Yet such contentment as they felt was not to last in the uncertain times ahead. It was the artisans, and especially the despised merchants, who were to be the cause of the changes which were, relatively soon, to begin the long process culminating in the downfall of the shogunate. Their position in the theoretically rigid, idealised hierarchy began to challenge that hierarchy, because of their place in an economic system which had its own momentum, independent of tradition, law, or religious dogma.

The power of religious codes is an important theme in Japanese history, and was much deployed in the Edo Era. But because the Japanese attitude generally towards religion is pragmatic, and free of the proselytising extremism of Christianity or Islam, three codes have been used at different times as supports for regimes rather than as bases upon which social structures are built. The common denominator of the three major codes, *Shinto,* Buddhism, and Confucianism, is that like all religions, they restrained radicalism. At the beginning of the Tokugawa shogunate, it was to Confucianism, or more precisely Neo-Confucianism, that those who formed political and social policy turned.

Although Neo-Confucianism had been studied in Japan for several hundred years before Tokugawa, it was especially attractive to the new authorities both because it was consonant with the *bushido* code, and because one element in it emphasised the parent–child relationship, which could be extended to all hierarchical relationships. The exhortation to achieve such virtues as sincerity, truth and restraint were complementary to *bushido.* The difference between the Chinese mandarin seeking these ideals, and the *samurai,* lay in the fact that for the latter everything was to contribute to a military end. In respect of 'filial' duty, the obligations of the child to a parent were extended to those of the *samurai* and his lord, and later were to be employed as part of the apparatus to establish 'emperor worship'. These beliefs were inculcated through the extensive network of schools for the families of the *samurai* which were an important feature of Tokugawa Japan. The effect of the network of duties and obligations deriving from Neo-Confucianism on Japanese society was, and remains, profound.

Awareness of its significance is of great importance in understanding that society.[15]

Ieyasu's wish to establish a social structure and social and economic relations which would last for ever, is a wish which has always been shared by usurpers and revolutionaries. It is the weakness of all utopian political creeds that they suppose that society can reach, by prescription, a stasis where everybody is content. Such faith is easily dismissed by reference to the simplest historical evidence. Yet the causes of the downfall of the shogunate are a matter of controversy, not so much in the identification of the several events which were detrimental to the ruling interest, but in the relative importance which should be ascribed to each. What is not disputed though is the importance of economic change in the configuration. Perhaps the basic change arose from the very nature of Tokugawa society, since it achieved one of its chief aims through the pacification of Japan. This created an environment in which commerce and trade flourished, at the same time as society itself was changing. At the heart of the changes was the position of the *samurai*, which was deteriorating. The *samurai* were supported by income in rice, which, of course, had to be produced by the farmers. As society began to change, for obvious reasons rice gave way to currency, a process which benefited the emerging merchant class, since it was to this class that the *samurai* turned to trade rice for cash. But a turbulent factor was that the relative values of rice and cash, as well as the amounts given to individual *samurai* varied throughout the country.

Such events were exacerbated because of the traditional position of the *samurai*. He was a warrior, and as such was usually unproductive in terms of agriculture, nor, with rare exceptions, would he consider working as a merchant. Furthermore, he had in any case become increasingly distanced from the land, because large numbers had to live in *daimyo* castle towns, which were expanding, and developing the changes in economic and social structure concomitant with such growth. The lifestyle, especially in Osaka, by the early nineteenth century a great commercial city, and Edo was becoming increasingly expensive. *Daimyo* and *samurai* now began to find that they were in debt to an increasingly complex community of merchant and finance houses. Attempts by the *bakufu* to curb the extravagance of *daimyo* or *samurai* failed, in part because like warrior castes elsewhere they had no wish, nor could they see any reason, to

15 For a fuller account of Japanese religion see the text by the Agency for Cultural Affairs, *Japanese Religion: A Survey* (Tokyo, 1981).

change their lifestyles. And, as has been pointed out, there was in any case a structured attempt by the shogunate to prevent the accumulation of wealth by the *daimyo*, through the residence rule – often a huge expense – and forced contributions to public works. If to these are added the changes in the economic pattern, the potential for serious instability can readily be seen. The farmers suffered at least as badly as anyone. They were the people who suffered from the economic variation in rice prices, and although they were the producers of wealth, when *daimyo* or *samurai* were in trouble, the farmers often had to take the strain.

There were a number of ways in which this happened. There could be a simple demand for a bigger tax contribution, or stipends could be reduced. Although there is much expert debate about the amounts of tax farmers had to pay – predictably it varied from time to time and place to place – it is agreed that they had a bad time, especially from the beginning of the nineteenth century. There were bad harvests, and natural disasters of all kinds, which led to years of famine. There followed the classic results, including infanticide, together with a high death rate, which made the population static in the eighteenth century, but caused it to drop in the middle of the nineteenth. Some of the more imaginative and flexible of the farmers began to grow cash crops, other than rice, or used fertiliser, and thus were able to reduce the proportion of the yield which had to be paid in tax. Such devices did not shield the many, and their resentment was expressed in demonstrations and violent assemblies, and attacks on those they believed responsible for their misery, such as rice dealers. There were almost four hundred such protests between 1813 and 1868.[16]

The economic changes described affected the shogunate as well, although the impact was delayed because of the scale of the shogun's resources. Partly because of extravagance and mismanagement, from the middle of the eighteenth century the *bakufu* accounts were in deficit and remained there.[17] It appears that the government found it beyond their capability to change the system of taxation to one which would be consonant with the new situation. But they did engage, as did the *daimyo*, in a number of initiatives to try to put their financial position in order. One of these, by the *bakufu*, was debasing the currency through the issue of new coins. The government and the *daimyo* also forced the wealthy to lend

16 Beasley, *The Meiji Restoration*, p. 57.
17 Ibid., p. 51.

them money. And, like impecunious rulers at other times and in other places, they instituted a system of monopolies which were given to merchant groups. This restriction fell especially hard upon farmers, whose activities and initiative were consequently curtailed. It was also a target in the unrest of the period.

From time to time the *bakufu* tried to be systematic in addressing such problems. An especially noteworthy example are the reforms of 1841–43, called the *Tempo* Reforms. The title derives from the name given to the years 1830–43 in the Japanese calendar. Although the period of Tokugawa rule is described as the Edo Era, within it there are subdivisions and *Tempo* is one of these. The reforms are associated with the senior member of the *bakufu*, Mizuno Tadakuni. He tried to implement policies which would regularise the supply of food, thus eliminating farmers' grievances, attend to the supposed deterioration in the behaviour of the *samurai*, and reduce apprehension about foreign intervention by improving military capability.

As may be expected, most of these policies were authoritarian and negative. He forbade farmers to leave agriculture, and ordered those living in Edo to return to the countryside. Commercial activity was restricted, merchants were ordered to make financial gifts to the government, and tax collection was tightened up. Turning to the *samurai*, Mizuno instructed them to show more restraint in their consumption, and to practise military arts. Not all his initiatives merely curbed activities; for example he engaged in land reclamation. On the whole they proved deeply unpopular, and in 1843 he resigned. Since the *daimyo* ruled their domains with a large degree of independence, many of them tried similar ways of dealing with the crises. These too were, overall, unsuccessful. As can be seen from the content of policies, these were hardly reforms in the usual sense, which carry a connotation of change and forward-looking development. They were rather an attempt to halt development by restoring a value system which was not only obsolete, but which was in part responsible for the very crisis in which society found itself.

As well as economic turmoil a second major cause of instability which was to lead to the demise of the shogunate, was the behaviour of western nations in Asia. During the previous hundred and fifty years, India had become part of the British empire, while other nations, notably the French, German, Dutch and Portuguese had made steady inroads into the countries of south Asia. During the late eighteenth century they had turned their attention to the north, and it was the particular experience of China which alarmed both Korea and Japan. At the beginning of the nineteenth century, Korea was isolated, was a vassal of China, and was, by western standards economically and socially backward. These facts, combined with a realisation that it was a country of great natural resources, made it an interesting prey for imperialist ambition. At the same time as they made their appearance in Japanese waters, western vessels tried to 'open up' Korea. A British merchant ship appeared in 1831, followed by the French, and in 1854 especially persistent Germans. In subsequent years there was fighting, some of it savage, as Koreans objected to invasion, and especially the brutality which accompanied the assaults on their sovereignty. The crew of an American ship, the *General Sherman*, were killed in 1866, but only because they had seized food and kidnapped women. In 1871 there was a battle on Kangwha island between Koreans and Americans, caused in part by the latter plundering royal tombs. The same debate which was taking place in Japan about how to react became the central issue in Korea too. Like the Japanese, the Koreans were divided into two broad groups, those who wished to come to terms with the foreigners and those who wished to resist. Korea's solution, which was to be hopelessly ineffective in the event, was to establish a policy of isolation, in 1871. Apart from all other considerations this seemed essential if the country was not to suffer the fate of China.

The treatment of China by the western powers, especially Britain, must rank as among the most shameful in recent colonial history. This is not a view which rests on the benefit of hindsight, but was commonly, and forcibly held at the time. There had been a long history of trade between several countries and China, but the latter had always been concerned about the dire consequences of allowing 'barbarian' culture to sully the purity of their own Confucianism upon which their society was structured. And so, again as in the Japanese case of Nagasaki, foreign trade was confined to one city: Canton. For a combination of reasons, the British in particular at the end of the eighteenth century needed to expand its trade with China, and this had to be preceded by a more open relationship. It was this that led to the remarkable expedition in 1793, led by Lord Macartney and comprising nearly seven hundred men, which sought the agreement of the emperor of China to British expansion. This failed largely because of the leader's very British refusal to 'kowtow' to the emperor. This meant kneeling and touching the forehead on the floor in a complex ritual which was an absolute prerequisite to an audience. Eventually, there was a compromise, but Macartney's refusal doomed the chances of negotiation, and the emperor ordered the immediate expulsion of the expedition.[18]

But it was the Opium War of 1839 which both alarmed China's Asian neighbours, and seemed to them proof of the intentions of the foreigners. Opium had been used in China for centuries, and was used, legally, in Europe. Because of concern by the government, it was banned in China in 1729, including imports in 1796. The East India Company which exported it to China, excited competition and production so that despite the law, China's imports went from some 1,000 chests in 1767 to 30,000 chests in 1836.[19] By this time the Chinese government had tried to take action, but the extent and profit of the trade had made so many people from traders to pirates to revenue officers dependent upon it, that it corroded huge tracts of Chinese society. The British government depended upon it for the purchase of Chinese goods.

Despite such obstacles, the Chinese attempt to suppress the trade in 1836 received widespread support, including from the British at home and in Canton. The situation quickly became confused. An Imperial Commissioner ordered the surrender of opium in the foreign factories. This was not done, so he confined the foreigners, and they eventually surrendered their stock, understanding that they would be compensated by the British government. After a number of incidents, a good deal of canvassing in London, and a fair share of misunderstanding, the British government decided on war in 1839. The upshot was the Treaty of Nanjing signed in 1842, which apart from allowing the opium trade to continue, increased the power of the British in China. Among other things Hong Kong was ceded, 'extra territoriality', to which we will return, was established, and more ports were to be opened up. Yet although this treaty was to be regarded as a classic 'unequal' treaty between the west and the east, there is a view that at the time, in context, and in outcome, it was 'very mild'.[20] It was though the first of many such – France and the United States signed in 1845 – and the whole period, rightly as it turned out, caused deep concern in the two northern countries. Despite its isolation, Japan was well informed about such events in China. The latter had been of the most profound influence culturally, and news of outside events came

18 For a fascinating account of this remarkable expedition see Peyrefitte, Alain, *The Collision of Two Civilisations: The British Expedition to China in 1792–4* (London, 1993).

19 Gray, Jack, *Rebellions and Revolutions: China from the 1800s to the 1980s* (Oxford, 1990), p. 26.

20 Ibid., p. 50.

through the Dutch traders in Nagasaki, who had to prepare reports for the *shogun* as a condition of their operation. It is against this background of increasing belligerence by western nations, that the debates which so confused the last *bakufu* should be understood.

This leads to the question as to how complete Japan's isolation was. The commonly accepted view is that it was not as rigorously enforced as was once assumed. Nagasaki was a point of intercourse, and in general trade 'was regulated, not cut off' but was 'managed'.[21] The same Japanese authority goes on to wonder 'whether *sakoku* (closed country) was ever a reality.[22] Further, he claims that 'the country was far more open to new currents during the *sakoku* period than it is now'.[23] Another Japanese commentator agrees that:

> the country wasn't really walled off. You might say it was surrounded at most by a bamboo blind or a silk curtain that let the breeze in and allowed the administration to maintain a balance between internal and external pressures in both the economic and cultural spheres ... it was brilliant.[24]

The transition from the Edo to Meiji Era is now accepted as much more gradual than has been supposed, even by the Japanese who 'in modern times have put too much emphasis on the Meiji Restoration'. This was 'an important political event. But in economic and cultural terms, the elements of continuity from Edo to Meiji are far more significant.'[25] The policy of seclusion had been most firmly enforced in the first century of Tokugawa rule, but in 1716 *shogun* Yoshimune allowed the import of foreign books, especially those in Dutch. A measure of how limited this source was to prove can be seen in the scholarly career of a man called Fukuzawa Yukichi, who will be mentioned several times in this book. In 1854, as a young man of about twenty, he went to a college in Osaka which taught Dutch culture, and in 1858 he founded his own college which eventually became a university. In spite of all of his study, it was not until he met some foreigners in Yokahama in 1859 that he realised that Dutch was not as widely spoken as English.[26]

21 Yamazaki, 'Reexamining the era of national seclusion', p. 71.
22 Ibid., p. 72.
23 Ibid., p. 75.
24 Haga Toru, in the discussion 'Reexamining the era of national seclusion', p. 73.
25 Yamazaki, op. cit., p. 76.
26 See the entry under his name in Thomas, J.E. and Elsey, B. (eds), *International Biography of Adult Education* (Nottingham, 1985).

The final stages of 'opening up' were dominated by the Americans, notably of course in the person of Commodore Matthew C. Perry. In fact, other nations had tried earlier to dent the exclusion policy. The most important of these was Russia, an unfriendly neighbour in the nineteenth century and most of the twentieth, a neighbour moreover who was a good deal nearer than most, and possessed of vibrant expansionist ambition. Russian envoys arriving at the end of the eighteenth century and beginning of the nineteenth were promptly dismissed, but Russia persisted, and during the period when Perry eventually made his mark on Japanese history, Russian ships and would-be delegations continued to try to establish a foothold in Japan. There were clashes and incidents involving British ships from the beginning of the century, while in 1844 advice from the Dutch king pointing out the inevitable consequences of continuing seclusion was rejected. So was the overture by the American Biddle, who sailed into Edo Bay in 1846.

Such events, together with the insights provided by the study of foreign texts, even though these were confined to Dutch, led to a good deal of debate, some of it radical. Despite the fact that the writing was limited to a small group of Japanese and was clandestine because of the nature of the regime, it gives some indication of the awareness of key Japanese figures of the need to reassess the seemingly eternal framework of Japan. In such writing it was advocated variously that officials should be chosen on merit, that Japan should catch up with the west in military capability, and that, like the west, it should accrue an empire. It was proposed, ominously, that such an empire should begin with the never-ending symbol of Japanese ambiguity, China. As always in regimes which perceive themselves to be in decline, there was a vein of utopianism which sought the reestablishment of long-lost, probably mythical, agrarian communities and values, and the restoration of the legendary skills of the *samurai*. At the same time there were serious attempts to understand why China was collapsing, and the role of the imperial institution in that collapse. These debates were well timed, since it was already incumbent upon Japan to address the reality that its 'sanctity' was to be assailed. The issue was to move from a debate to a cause for dying.

The inevitable happened in July 1853, one of the turning points in the history of Japan. Commodore Perry, of the United States navy arrived in Edo Bay with his four 'black ships of evil mien'. At a small town called Uraga which was near Edo, he delivered a message. Quite what would have happened had it not been Perry, or in 1945 had another American than MacArthur been the leader, is an interesting question. Perry had a quality which appealed to the Japanese at the time. He was belligerent, and throughout his contact with the country, he made it clear that he would not countenance the indignity and duplicity with which previous foreigners had had to cope. He laid out a list of demands, which included a guarantee of protection for shipwrecked seamen, the crews of American whaling ships having been treated badly. But his demands for this humanitarian provision, which could easily be met, were accompanied by others which included access for provisions and coal. In the expansionist mood in east Asia at the time, in the new steamer age, access to what was called 'coaling' was crucial, and it was known that Japan had good resources. Throughout his statement, and specifically, was the demand for a right to trade. Perry said he would be back in a year.

Perhaps an indication of a new realism in Japan is the unprecedented action by a key figure in the *bakufu*, Abe Masahiro, who solicited the opinions of the *daimyo* about Perry's demands. The replies were a reflection of the variety and intensity of the debates in the country. Some wanted to accede, variously because there were trade opportunities, or because resistance would be futile. Some said they would follow the *shogun*, whatever his decision. Others advised procrastination, a classic Asian response to the west. And predictably a number, following the lead of the Mito domain whose *daimyo* was Tokugawa Nariaki, proposed resistance, placing their faith in the antique Japanese trust in the loyalty of the people. The several positions were so firmly committed that Abe could no longer adjudicate. The inability of Japanese politicians to take decisive action is an important step in the understanding of how Japanese government has always operated. As a result of the impasse Abe gave way to Hotta Masayoshi, who was also a reformer. He managed to persuade the *bakufu* that they must have a policy which accommodated the foreigners and served the best interests of Japan. In the end, Hotta had also to stand down, in large part because of opposition from the imperial court in Kyoto. It was in the court that conservative ideology developed. Although their opposition had proved futile, the court officials had enough power to topple a key statesman. The emperor himself was an active participant in the matter, and his role will be discussed later. In the background to increasingly angry discussion was the return, as promised, of Perry in 1854, with an enlarged fleet. This consisted, in one account of many, of nine ships including three sailing ships carried by three steamers.[27] Negotiations began in March, and on the last day of the month the Treaty of Kanagawa was signed. Remarkably, Perry accepted ambiguity about commercial trade, but he gained some important concessions. He rejected the proposal that Nagasaki should remain as the sole open port, and it was agreed that Shimoda and Hakodate would be available for provisioning and a limited amount of trade. A very remarkable clause allowed the presence of a consul in Shimoda, and a less contentious one ensured the well being of shipwrecked seamen. The historical judgement must be that Japan had marshalled its best skills – pragmatism and realism. Japan's leaders knew what they were doing, they knew that Perry was only the beginning of a process, and that some deeply rooted traditional forces would not be assuaged.

In late 1854 Perry's initiative was followed by an agreement with Admiral Sterling of Britain, enabling ships to anchor at Nagasaki and Hakodate. The Russians, who had never left Japanese waters, while continuing their Chinese ambitions, met with success in 1855, with the signing of a treaty with Japan which allowed them to call at Nagasaki, Shimoda and Hakodate, and settled, at least for the moment, the vexed question of ownership of the Kurile islands, and Sakhalin. The parties also agreed on Russian extraterritoriality. The issue of extraterritoriality was of the greatest significance to relations between Europe and Asia in the nineteenth century. In effect, it meant that foreigners who committed offences, whether local or universal, whether serious or not, were not subject to local law. The especially insulting aspect of this was the implication that the system of criminal justice in the indigenous country was unsafe. In north Asia the issue was to be a focus, and an unanswerable grievance, for many years. The historic relationship with the Netherlands was consolidated in an agreement, along familiar lines, in 1855, the year in which the Netherlands gave Japan its first steamship. In 1856 the first American consul, Townsend Harris, set up his office in Shimoda. In the next year he established the right of American extraterritoriality, and went on to secure the right to permanent residence in Shimoda and Hakodate. In 1857 he had an audience of the *shogun*.

The successor to Hotta was Ii Naosuke, who was determined to persist with the reforming programme. So much so that in 1858 he defied the emperor's will, on this occasion a remarkably strong emperor, by arranging a series of treaties with America, Russia,

27 Barr, Pat, *The Coming of the Barbarians: A Story of Western Settlement in Japan 1853–1870* (London, 1967), p. 27.

Britain and France which demolished much of the historical paraphernalia upon which, traditionalists believed, Japan survived. The
essence of the treaties were provisions to allow cities, including Edo,
to be 'opened', low import duties, and extraterritoriality; the usual
agreements which were familiar to people who had no choice. They
added to the tradition of 'unequal treaties' and because of his
compliance Ii was assassinated, as he was entering Edo castle in
1860. He takes his place in a long list of Japanese public figures who
were to die because of their perceived treachery and disregard of
Japanese sanctity.

In the midst of this instability the emperor issued an order in
1862 instructing the *shogun* to expel all foreigners by the summer of
the following year. Aside from the action of some famous western
clans, to which we will return, there was little organised response,
but there was some harassment, and worse, of foreigners which has
a place in the evolution of events. There were several murders of
foreigners which caused anger and fear. In November 1864, two
British officers, Baldwin and Bird, when returning from a visit to
Kamakura were attacked and killed. In this case the Japanese
government caught and executed those responsible. They may have
done so because of an earlier assassination, the consequences of
which were very serious. In September 1862 Charles Richardson, an
Englishman, was riding with companions on the Tokaido, the
famous highway linking Edo and Kyoto. They encountered a large
party of Satsuma retainers accompanying their lord to the far west
after a formal visit to the *shogun.* Because the retainers believed that
the foreigners were not showing respect, they set upon them, and
Richardson was killed. His death outraged the British and they
demanded compensation, and reprisals against Satsuma. The *shogun* paid the amount demanded of him, but the clan refused. By
August 1862 a small fleet was in position off Satsuma and after an
unsatisfactory answer to demands for reparation and the punishment of the assassins, the British attacked with gunfire from their
ships. The Japanese had heavy guns, and did a good deal of damage,
killing and wounding some sixty-three British,[28] while the town too
suffered badly from the shelling. The day after the first exchanges,
the British fleet returned to Yokohoma. The indemnity remained
unpaid and the assassins went unpunished.

The next major outbreak of violence arose from the emperor's
edict that the foreigners should be expelled in June 1863. The

28 Ibid., p. 166.

Choshu territory dominated the Shimonoseki strait, and following the edict, in June the Choshu shore batteries fired on an American steamship. In July a French ship and a Dutch ship were attacked, both by the guns on shore, and by three warships which had recently been bought. In July an American warship and French warships retaliated with a bombardment of the Choshu forts, followed by a landing which resulted in the destruction of houses and removal of armaments. This was not the end of the matter, for in the autumn of 1864, persisting attacks on shipping led to an attack on Choshu by a combined fleet of eighteen British, Dutch, French and American ships. The bombardment and the subsequent landing ended large-scale resistance, but not only because of the defeat itself. A few Japanese had already visited the west – Ito Hirobumi is a famous example – and realised, as the Imperial Navy was to do before 1940 – that the west was simply too strong to take on. Yamagata Aritomo, the founder of the modern Japanese army, took part in the fighting,[29] and like other far-sighted members of the clan, understood that defeat should be turned to advantage. That advantage was to learn from the west how to create an army, and how to build ships and command fleets, matters which were to become central in the evolution of the new state.

In the face of such evidence of the strength of the westerners, key powerful people in Japan began to realise the futility of any attempt to expel them. Nevertheless the issue still caused instability. The emperor resisted pressure on him to engage in a full-scale war with the compromising *bakufu*, and instead accepted the advice to try conciliation. This he did by marrying his sister to the young *shogun*. A new destabilising factor now arose with the death of the same *shogun* in 1866, and the death – Bergamini claims murder – of the Emperor Komei in the following year.[30] The new emperor was a fifteen-year-old, Mutsuhito, whose reign was to be given the name Meiji meaning 'enlightened rule'. The beginning of the end of the assassinations, skirmishes and harassing of foreigners including a murderous attack on the party of the British envoy Sir Harry Parkes in the very act of going for a first audience with the new emperor in 1868, was heralded by a crucial three-day battle. This took place in January 1868, in the month in which the new emperor issued a Rescript restoring imperial rule. The battle was between the forces of the emperor and the *shogun* in the area between Osaka and

29 Hackett, Roger F., *Yamagata Aritomo in the Rise of Modern Japan, 1838–1922* (Harvard, 1971), pp. 22ff.
30 Bergamini, David, *Japan's Imperial Conspiracy* (London, 1971), pp. 248ff.

Kyoto. This did not end resistance. There was further fighting around Edo and when beaten there, the rebels went north to what was then the island of Ezo, now Hokkaido. One oddity was that some of the rebel ships were commanded by French officers. Originally the French supported the *shogun*, support which was to diminish their credibility especially in Japan, where misplaced loyalty is rarely forgotten. These deserters were naturally a great embarrassment to the French government.

The rebels then petitioned the emperor to be allowed to settle in Ezo, cultivating the land and employing 'hitherto useless people in useful work'[31] by whom they presumably meant the poor Ainu people, the original inhabitants of the island. The new government would not agree and the situation was finally resolved in April 1869 when the imperial fleet attacked the last stronghold, the rebels surrendered, and were allowed their freedom. Already in November 1868 the emperor had visited Edo, and it was announced that the imperial court would move to that city which was then renamed Tokyo, 'Eastern Capital'. The former *shogun*'s castle became the imperial palace.

As to the last *shogun* Tokugawa Keiki, he was allowed to settle down peacefully, although it was to be some thirty years before he was to be received by his emperor. The persistence of power is well illustrated by the career of his would-be heir, Iesato. In 1890 he became a member of the upper chamber, the House of Peers, and was its presiding official from 1903 to 1933, a very traumatic period, and was in other ways a key public figure. But the surrender of the *shogun*'s powers to the emperor in November 1867, and the January 1868 Rescript restoring imperial rule, quickly became a reality. The dictatorship of the Tokugawa shogunate was over. Now began one of the most remarkable periods in modern Japanese history.

31 Barr, *The Coming of the Barbarians*, p. 218.

CHAPTER TWO

Racism

Overleaf ▶
Ainu people on Sakhalin Island in the 1890s

Racism

The previous chapter described the remarkable transformation of Japan. But apart from the changes which have caught international attention, there is the less proclaimed effect these changes have had on ordinary people in Japan. The Japanese are usually regarded as a racially homogeneous group, and there is indeed justification for such a view. But whilst there is a remarkable homogeneity, there are minorities, in some cases comprising substantial numbers of people. As we shall go on to see, they have been and still are the victims of discrimination and prejudice. This chapter will begin with a review of the position of these groups, their origin, their treatment in the past, and their present state in Japanese society. They tend to be marginalised, or even left out of accounts of Japan, because of the naturally greater emphasis given to the two giant concerns of historians, militarism and economic success. Discrimination against minorities is of course common in all societies, so Japanese attitudes are not aberrant or unusual. But there are some particular components of Japanese beliefs which will be highlighted in this discussion. The first stage is to set out the characteristics of minority groups as commonly perceived by the majority of Japanese, and to consider how far these stereotypes are found in some other societies.

The first firmly held, common belief is that minority groups are socially inferior. This is of course a matter of fact. It is rarely considered though that their position could be the result of an artificially created social stratification, which is illogical and which could be moderated. The best known example of such stratification, famous because of its rigidity, is the caste system of India which, in any discussion on stratification acts as an ultimate reference point. This central belief about natural social inferiority is so immutable that even the apparent educational advances, and claimed enlight-

27

enment of this century have done little to dent it, even in a country such as Japan, which has a notably highly educated population.

Edward Norbeck, in a discussion of fieldwork he carried out, provides an excellent example of the seemingly immutable nature of prejudice, despite the manifest 'advances' of the twentieth century. In the 1950s he was working in a small village in Okayama prefecture. In this village, although physically separate, was a community of fisherpeople, members of an historic, identifiable group called *sokobiki*. Outwardly, relationships were good. All children attended the same schools, and adults were involved in the many communal activities which are the hallmark of the Japanese village or district. Yet intermarriage was discouraged, and the term *sokobiki* itself was not used in public because it was regarded as insulting. Norbeck was visiting an 'ordinary' member of the village when a woman from the fishing community came to the house. She was invited in, and normal etiquette was observed. Then the hostess saw two villagers approach, and the fisherwoman was hurriedly hidden away in another part of the house for half an hour. When the two visitors had gone, she emerged from hiding, and normal conversation carried on. The hostess explained that she and the fisherwoman had been friends since school, but their contact had to be clandestine since if the villagers knew of their friendship 'life would be very hard for me here'.[1]

This episode, though minor, illustrates several features of deep prejudice which seems to be immanent in Japanese society. The first is that such historic prejudice continues to exist, in this case in a context which is socially reasonably affable. Secondly, and this is very distinctive in Japanese society, this prejudice is held against a group which is distinguished not by race, but by occupation, since the *sokobiki*, like other groups described by Norbeck, are ethnically Japanese. In the same way one of the largest minorities, the *burakumin* against whom is displayed virulent prejudice, are racially the same as the majority group, although the latter persist in maintaining the historical fiction that they are alien. Because the *burakumin* are such an important group in Japanese society, they will be discussed at some length. This insistence upon racial difference when there is none whilst rare, is not unique. The parallel with the Indian attitude to outcastes and 'tribal' people is striking.

Where there *are* racial differences, then the Japanese, in common

1 Norbeck, Edward, 'Little-known minority groups of Japan' in De Vos, George and Wagatsuma Hiroshi, *Japan's Invisible Race: Caste in Culture and Personality* (California, 1966), pp. 13ff.

with many other societies, seek to justify discriminatory behaviour by the ascription of a link between race and inferiority. This is a justification which is widely employed, and increases in vigour as the racial differences become more marked. It was the basis in colonial Africa not only of social attitudes, but of legal barriers to inter-marriage, overt sexual relationships, employment, or use of public facilities. There are in Japan non-Japanese minorities, in the ethnic sense. The most notable of these are the original inhabitants of northern Japan – the Ainu – and the Koreans, the Chinese, and the Okinawans.

Naturally, a belief in racial distinction and inferiority leads to disapproval of intermarriage, and occasionally, as in the case of South Africa when the apartheid policy existed, to its being defined as criminal. Despite this, except when unlawful, inter-racial and inter-group marriages do take place, whilst there is invariably interbreeding but outside the formal institutions: a process which was called in the days of strong disapproval, miscegenation. South Africa again provides an example where three hundred years of interbreeding has created the considerable group classified as 'coloured'. In the same way prolonged racial mixing of the Japanese and the Ainu, especially since the expansion of the Japanese northward in the Meiji Era, has created a situation where the very definition of Ainu is problematic. Generally, those of mixed race in Japan, by which is meant the offspring of Japanese and non-Japanese are regarded as outsiders, and are described as *konketsuji*, meaning literally 'mixed blood child', although the less derogatory word 'hafu' (half) is also used.

Okinawa is the largest of the Ryukyu islands, and is of great significance in Japanese history. The Okinawans, like other minorities, are distinguished by low educational achievement, low income and high unemployment.[2] There are a substantial number of people of mixed race, largely because of the long post-war occupation by the Americans. For these the Japanese have a galaxy of abusive terms: america, *kurombo* (nigger), *chijiru* (curly hair), *heejar-mie* (goat's eyes) and others.[3] That the Japanese feel so strongly about interbreeding that they have a fairly elaborate vulgar vocabulary to describe them is a measure of the degree of racial superiority they feel, and which it is commonly agreed they possess. Nor is this a

2 Minority Rights Group, *Japan's Minorities: Burakumin, Koreans, Ainu, Okinawans* (London, 1983), p. 13.
3 See Murakoshi Sueo and Yoshino, I. Roger, 'Minorities' in *Kodansha Encyclopedia of Japan* (Tokyo, 1983).

new phenomenon. As part of the isolation policy of the Tokugawa *shogun* it was decreed that the children and grandchildren of foreigners born to Japanese women should be exiled, which prompted sad reflection by what was no doubt a representative voice, in a letter: 'Ah, beloved Japan, how I long to go home, how I want to see you, to see you, to see you'.[4]

Nor is the creation of verbal categories confined to other races and mixtures of races. After the atomic bombing of Japan, there were many disabled survivors. These suffer varying degrees of ostracism and are known as *hibakusha*. This is given added poignancy because Hiroshima and Nagasaki were heavily populated with Koreans and *burakumin*, whose survivors are thus doubly labelled. The *hibakusha* have found it difficult to get work, because they are supposed to be poor and diseased. This is not only something which the Japanese find difficult to tolerate, but causes employers to be reluctant to employ them, for the singularly heartless reason that they are likely to die prematurely. It is not only these victims of physical abnormality who suffer. People with physical or mental disability are kept apart, and facilities to enable them to cope are notoriously rare. There may even be a new category of outsiders which also is a consequence of the events of the Pacific War. In the confusion in the last stages of the war many Japanese children were lost or deserted in the imperial colonies, such as Manchuria. With increasing contact between China and Japan substantial numbers of these have returned to Japan, where they have been recognised as ethnic Japanese. In every social sense, by language and custom, they are Chinese, and the degree of difference may well cause them to be sufficiently different to be defined and treated as a special but inferior group.

A common device to create distance between majority and minority is to allege that people are more like animals than people. The allegation that an individual is the child of an animal – as in 'son of a bitch' or 'son of a camel' – is common. Of Africans in colonial territories it was commonly said that they were no better than animals. The same trait is found in Japan. In the case of the *burakumin*, as we shall go on to see this is very deeply rooted. It is given expression by the raising of four fingers at the mention of, or in the presence of, members of the group. This implied that they walked on all fours. This insult has in recent times led to conflict which has sometimes become serious. With regard to the Ainu, the

4 Ben-Dasan, Isaiah, *The Japanese and the Jews* (New York, 1991), p. 64.

insult centres upon a play upon words. The word Ainu in the language of those people means man. But in Japanese there is a word *inu* which means dog. Thus '*Ainu da*' (it's an Ainu) easily becomes '*Ah, inu da*' (it's a dog).[5] It is of course possible to dismiss such behaviour as harmless fun, even if puerile. The victims regard it as much more socially significant, leaving aside the humiliation and indignity it signals.

Groups which are regarded as inferior generally have ascribed to them undesirable and anti-social characteristics. A very common allegation for instance is that they are promiscuous, or possessed of excessive sexual urges which are uncontrolled and uncontrollable, and which are particularly directed at the dominant group, especially the women in the group. The African, whether dispossessed in colonial Africa, or slave in the New World, has always had a particular place in this fantasy. The literature about the *burakumin* records the same belief. It is also generally assumed that minorities are physically dirty. No account is taken of the difficulty of keeping clean in slum conditions, and it is rare that common brave attempts to do so are witnessed by the majority who rarely visit such areas, or even, in Japan, know of their existence. In any case like all of the pejorative assumptions about minorities, these are predicated upon a belief that like the virtue to be found in the dominant group, the vice of the minority is wilful and the consequence of studied choice.

An especially serious belief and one which admirably demonstrates the complex nature of inter-group relationships is that the members of minority groups are criminal. Accepting this as a fact, the conclusions of debate in the majority as to why this should be so merely reinforce the depravity they recount, and the inevitability of the status quo. These conclusions are that either criminality is inherent in such people, or that once again criminal and deviant behaviour is a path which has been consciously chosen. The complexity of criminal behaviour cannot be admitted because of the threat to stability and the simplicity of the beliefs which sustain it. And so there can be no discussion about how certain acts come to be defined as criminal, or how the visible juxtaposition of wealth and poverty might shape attitudes, or how people might seek to redress the imbalance of opportunity by resorting to anti-social behaviour.

There is much argument amongst criminologists about the pre-

5 Minority Rights Group, *Japan's Minorities*, p. 13.

ponderance of certain categories of people in criminal statistics: members of lower classes, of certain areas, or of minority races. It is a commonplace, for example, that the Maoris of New Zealand, or the Aborigines of Australia are overrepresented in such statistics, and even more so in the numbers in penal institutions.[6] In contrast to the assumption that this happens because of vice which is either congenital or deliberately chosen, theories have been developed in recent years which claim that members of depressed groups, by subtle and not so subtle processes, are identified and 'labelled' as deviant because of their membership of those groups. Once this process has begun, their bad behaviour becomes persistent and they are soon in a circle of events from which it is impossible to break away. Furthermore, it is argued that much of what is defined as deviant or criminal behaviour is not deviant at all, although the consequences of such definition will fall upon certain groups. A stark example would be political protest, which might be defined as illegal, with a resultant penalising of those engaged in it. Indeed the evidence for this is plentiful in Japan, both in the 1920s and 1930s when left-wing dissent was put down, but not right-wing dissent even if murderous, and in the stormy historical relationships between the several authorities and the *burakumin.*

There is, in part, a simple explanation for the seemingly disproportionate numbers of minority people who engage in criminal behaviour, but it is an explanation which can be applied only to relatively few. These are people who engage in professional crime, exemplified by the Mafia in the United States, and the *yakuza* in Japan. This phenomenon indicates that the belief of the majority group that a minority group is slothful and unintelligent is not only intrinsically wrong, but is manifestly wrong. In the ranks of important criminal fraternities there are to be found members of minorities who, having found the legal avenue to advancement blocked because of prejudice, apply their considerable talents to illegal alternative means of upward mobility. We will see that there is some evidence that a small number of Koreans in Japan have done so. Not that such 'success' improves their image in the eyes of the majority. On the contrary it merely confirms what has always been accepted by them as self-evident: that their minorities are degenerate.

Minorities, including those of Japan, are poor, often living in conditions of extreme poverty and squalor. This is explained simply

6 For an illustrative account in Australia see Thomas, J.E. and Stewart, A., *Imprisonment in Western Australia: Evolution, Theory and Practice* (University of Western Australia Press, 1978), especially Chapter 6, 'The Imprisonment of Aborigines'.

by the more prosperous observer. It is because they are unwilling to work, are shiftless and feckless. Perhaps the only element of truth in such a massive overgeneralisation is that if people are unable to obtain work, a culture can develop which is inimical to the social pressures and incentives which combine to make work appear a desirable activity. Poverty is linked to a host of factors which combine to produce inferior social conditions. These include discrimination in employment practice, a tradition of poor educational achievement resulting from third-rate provision, ill-health caused by malnutrition and insanitary environments, poor housing and so on. Such factors have always been found in the minority communities of Japan. It requires a high degree of maturity and empathy on the part of the majority to accept that the dynamics of society are complex. So high indeed that it is hardly surprising that it is rare. From the gypsies of Europe to the *burakumin*, the disadvantaged are held responsible for whatever position they find themselves in. We shall go on to see that in the exemplary case of the *burakumin*, such a view is intellectually untenable, but that it is nevertheless generally and firmly held.

An especial charge levelled against minorities in Japan arises from what are generally agreed to be strong feelings of national identity. Thus to all of the generic prejudices felt by majorities in human society, there is the added suspicion in Japan that especially in times of crisis, minority groups are not to be trusted. This feeling is notably aroused by the Koreans. They have been suspected at various times of fomenting rebellion, or exploiting natural disasters, notably the great Tokyo earthquake of 1923. Some Koreans were involved in a plot to kill Emperor Hirohito, but Japanese have also made such attempts; more inflammatory perhaps because their target was Meiji. The Ryukyu islands, which has an indigenous population, although now mixed, of about one million, periodically demonstrates its distaste for, or disloyalty to, the Japanese. In 1993, for example, an order that schoolchildren should do obeisance to the Japanese flag led to the burning of the flag on Okinawa. Such actions do indeed illustrate the lack of subscription to the national Japanese identify. What is remarkable is that a majority group actually expects the same enthusiasm as it feels for national values, from groups who are excluded from, or penalised by, those same values and what they represent.

Minority groups usually have to take menial, unpleasant or demeaning work. The Indian caste system is based upon religious mythology, but an important manifestation of its structure lies in the division of labour which is central to it. In the same way the interrelationship of status and work can be found in Japan, especially in pre-Meiji times. Then there were several identifiable groups who were ethnically Japanese, practised endogamy, were confined to certain occupations, and can be regarded as minority and of course, inferior groups. Some examples described by Norbeck were *ebune*, who lived and worked on sea-going boats, *kijiya* who were specialist woodworkers, *sanka* who worked on rivers, *matagi* who were professional hunters selling meat and skins, and the iron-working *tatara*, whose high quality products were much valued.

Such groups, in such definitive forms, were already beginning to disappear by the Meiji Restoration, because of changes in the needs of the community, or because of the difficulty of obtaining materials. This trend was hastened by the tighter control, with further restriction on their traditional activity, which was a concomitant of the years after the Restoration.[7] The group which remains in the social configuration, and which had lower status than any of those described above were the *eta* or *burakumin*. This, the largest of the ethnic Japanese minorities will be discussed in detail. At this point it should be noted that they are an excellent example of the relationship between status and occupation. Their lowly status was reflected by the fact that they worked with animals and with the dead. As a consequence they suffered another social blow, which was that they were labelled as ritually unclean. The significance of the effect of occupation on status can be judged by a comparison with the Ainu. Although the latter are a depressed minority, and regarded as outsiders – the Japanese still call them *gaijin*, foreigners – because their occupations are not specific, they are not regarded as ritually unclean. The association of the *burakumin*, and for that matter the *matagi* with animals and the eating of meat was an important factor in their social isolation. The Buddhist disapproval of eating meat naturally led to the conclusion that those who did ought to be regarded with contempt. The rehabilitation of meat-eating after the restoration did not lead to any reconsideration of the status of the *burakumin*, which was based, at least in part, upon the practice.

The only minority which has not been mentioned so far in this introduction is the Chinese. The cultural debt owed by Japan to China is immense, although in the time since the Restoration, relationships between the two countries have been hostile and belligerent. Nevertheless, from time immemorial small numbers of

7 For a more detailed description of such groups see Norbeck, 'Little-known minority groups of Japan'.

Chinese have lived in Japan, and continue to do so. In 1990, there was an estimated population of 150,000, mainly concentrated in the cities, some in 'Chinatowns' in cities like Yokohama. They pursue the classic immigrant Chinese occupations such as restaurant ownership. Historically and generically the Japanese regard the Chinese as inferior and, for example, disapprove of intermarriage. But they do not ascribe to them the anti-social or degenerate characteristics applied to other minorities. As in other countries with a small Chinese population, they adjust to the rules of the majority and are not driven by religious or ideological beliefs which might bring conflict. This pragmatism, together with their characteristic maintenance of distance in the community, leads to a high degree of tolerance of the Chinese in Japan, as elsewhere. This general outline of the nature of minority groups, and the sources and forms of the invariable discrimination which they suffer will help to put into context the specific examples of Japanese minorities. The three most important of these are the Ainu, the Koreans, and the *burakumin*. The Ainu is numerically a small community, but it deserves consideration because of its importance in the history of Japan as the original inhabitants, and because it exemplifies some aspects of relationships which other groups do not: notably, the classic effects of invasion and colonisation of a small community.

The Ainu people, in the last several hundred years at least, lived on the northernmost major Japanese island of Hokkaido, the Kurile Islands, Kamchatka Peninsula, and southern Sakhalin Island. Since their situation was altered dramatically by the policies following the Restoration, this is an appropriate chronological point to consider their place in Japanese society. The Ainu – the word means man or person – have always been a puzzle for scientists trying to identify racial links and connections with other groups. In the long disappeared 'pure' form they were of medium height, with a fairly heavy skeletal structure. Their facial characteristics have led to a generally accepted belief that they are not Mongoloid, but are of Caucasian origin. Some of the evidence for this is adduced from the fact that they do not have the characteristic mongoloid eye pattern, their faces are relatively flat, their noses are broad, their lower jaws are broad and heavy, the skin colour is light, and eyes are dark brown, and occasionally grey or blue. The most obvious physical feature which marks them out from the Japanese and other Asians is the amount, and sometimes the colour, of the body hair. They have moustaches and beards as well as hair on the rest of the body which, while usually black, can be tinged with red. This distinctive pattern has given rise to the nickname by which they have been commonly known, 'the hairy Ainu'.

Since the advent of sophisticated linguistic sciences, racial origins and links have been discovered through language patterns. These patterns have solved the mystery of the origins of many people, for example the gypsies of Europe, who it has been established through linguistic evidence, are of Indian origin. The application of linguistic techniques to the Ainu however has led only to further speculation. It is speculation which suggests links with Polynesia, Gilyak (another minority living on Sakhalin), Eskimo, and perhaps the most arresting of all, with Welsh and Cornish. But in the complex world of linguistics the conclusion seems to be that: 'Ainu is best described as a language-isolate.'[8]

The history of the lands in which they lived in the last two hundred years was turbulent, notably because of the unceasing quarrels between Russia and Japan about territory and boundaries. Indeed the Kuriles, a string of fifty-six volcanic islands covering seven hundred and fifty miles from the Kamchatka Peninsula to Hokkaido, are still a matter of critical political debate. The islands were divided between Japan and Russia in 1855, and in 1875 Russia agreed to relinquish her share, in return for sovereignty over all of Sakhalin, the southern part of which had until then been under Japanese influence. In 1951, as part of the Treaty of San Francisco, the Kuriles were given to the USSR, and at the present time the Japanese demand for their return has led to serious blockages in political relationships between the two countries.

Sakhalin too has changed hands several times. Its history has been of little interest to the west, but in the context of Russian–Japanese hostility, has been a flash point. After the settlement of 1875 when Russia assumed control, the position was stable until 1905. In that year as part of the Treaty of Portsmouth which concluded the Russo-Japanese war, south Sakhalin was returned to the Japanese. In 1925, in diplomatic negotiation Japan formally acknowledged Russian authority over north Sakhalin. After 1945 the Japanese were expelled, and the whole territory was formally returned to the USSR, again as part of the Treaty of San Francisco. When the writer Chekhov visited Sakhalin in the 1890s, the Ainu claim that it had always been their land must have sounded pitiful in the light of its focus for international barter by powerful nations. That the Ainu crossed these modern national frontiers to engage in their most

---

8 Shibatani Masayoshi, *The Languages of Japan* (Cambridge, 1990), p. 5.

important task, hunting, is commented upon by Kayano Shigeru in his moving autobiography when he recalls that at the beginning of the twentieth century, his father went to Sakhalin for a long period to hunt bears.[9]

The heartland of the Ainu people has always been in Hokkaido, also the target of Russian ambitions, quickly curbed, in 1945. The name Hokkaido which literally means Northern Sea Road was coined in 1869, heralding a new expansionist colonial policy under the Meiji regime. Before the Restoration the island was called Ezo, and was very much Ainu territory, which is made clear by the periodic battles between them and the Japanese on their borders. To the Ainu, the island was known as Ainu Mosir, 'a peaceful land for human beings'. Japan proper was called Wa, and the Japanese were called, in the Japanese form *wajin*, and in the Ainu *shamo* which was derogatory or *sisam*, which was rather more polite.[10] By the time of the Restoration a Japanese enclave had been established in the south-west corner of the island, which was called the Matsumae domain. This had been established in the very early years of the Edo Era, but there had been regular Ainu resistance. A particularly forceful rebellion in 1668 led by a man called Shakushain led to heavy punishment by the Japanese.

One of the aims of the newly established Japanese regime of 1868 was the 'development' of a large and very rich island, and the thwarting of Russian ambitions. To achieve this there was set up the Hokkaido Colonisation Office which, as well as building railways, opening coalmines, and other predictable means of exploitation, encouraged Japanese settlers. This initiative, quite by chance, was to lead to an important development in the political evolution of Japan. In 1881 the director of the Colonisation Office proposed to sell its properties for a very low sum, to a trading company headed by a friend. The resultant outcry was an important contribution to a demand for a representative national assembly. Because of the scandal it was promised in an Imperial Rescript that the assembly would be realised by 1890. For the Ainu this northward expansion was to lead, inevitably, to the corrosion of their culture. This culture centred upon a mystical relationship with the natural world, in which the bear played an especially significant part. It also led to a familiar clash between the culture of the stronger, who were farmers, and that of the weaker, who were hunters. Such culture

9 Kayano Shigeru, *Our Land was a Forest: An Ainu Memoir* (Boulder, Colorado, 1994), p. 61.
10 Ibid., p. 166.

conflict has usually only one outcome which is the victory of the farmers. The Ainu had also been weakened by disease introduced by the Japanese, and against which they had little resistance. An important stage in the colonial process was reached when in 1899 a law was passed to 'protect' the Ainu. This was the Hokkaido Former Aborigine (*kyudojin*) Protection Law, and introduced into official discussion and documents a term – *kyudojin* – to which Ainu people take great exception.[11] Kayano explains that:

> We are no 'former aborigines'. We were a nation who lived on the national land called Ainu Mosir ... The 'Japanese people' who belonged to the 'nation of Japan' invaded our national land ... Ainu Mosir beyond a doubt was a territory indigenous to the Ainu people. Not only are the high mountains and big rivers graced with Ainu names, but so, too, is every creek and marsh, no matter how small.[12]

The Japanese takeover followed a familiar colonial pattern. Occupations such as salmon fishing were outlawed, and there was forced labour, which was not only alien to the Ainu, but brutally carried out. Of 116 villagers in one area, 43 men and women were taken for forced labour.[13]

There is contemporary evidence that by the end of the nineteenth century the warlike qualities and cultural dignity of the Ainu, who had in earlier times kept the Japanese at bay, were in decline. That demoralisation which is usually found in indigenous people after prolonged contact with 'advanced' people was by then well established. In the early 1860s the first British consul visited the then Ezo, and wrote a report about the Ainu. There was much in it about these 'cowed aimless, half savage people, one of those pathetic remnants of humanity who get heedlessly trampled over in some great stampede by a more aggressive race'.[14] Perhaps it was awareness of this demoralisation which led, as in the infamous example of the Australian Aborigines, to some unspeakable behaviour by anthropologists and their agents. This was the robbing of Ainu graves, and the removal of skeletons variously to find 'missing links' or perhaps to be certain of the evolutionary ascendancy of the Caucasian. Whatever the British thought of the Ainu, this was intolerable. Sir Harry Parkes, the British Minister, dismissed the British Consul who had colluded with them, and sentenced the

11 Minority Rights Group, *Japan's Minorities*, p. 12.
12 Kayano Shigeru, *Our Land was a Forest*, pp. 59–60.
13 Ibid., p. 28.
14 Barr, Pat, *The Coming of the Barbarians: A Story of Western Settlement in Japan 1853–1870* (London, 1967), p. 113.

grave-robbers who were European, to imprisonment in Hong Kong. A remarkable act, in the best of the Victorian colonial tradition, by a man of great principle.[15] Kayano gives a first-hand account of the persisting insensitivity and cultural brutality of the scientists:

> There were a number of reasons why I hated them. Each time they came to Nibutani, they left with folk utensils. They dug up our sacred tombs and carried away ancestral bones. Under the pretext of research, they took blood from villagers and, in order to examine how hairy we were, rolled up our sleeves, then lowered our collars to check our backs, and so on.[16]

The deterioration in Ainu life is recorded by Chekhov. When he visited Sakhalin in the 1890s it was a Russian penal colony. He wrote a vivid and detailed account of life there, including that of the Ainu, and of another people of mysterious origins called the Gilyaks, described by him as 'neither Mongols nor Tungus'. Before south Sakhalin became Russian in 1875, Chekhov was told that the Ainu were: 'virtually Japanese serfs ... it was so much the easier to subjugate them because they are meek and timid, and because there were hungry and could not live without rice'. He went on:

> The Ainu are as dark as gypsies. They have tremendous beards and moustaches, and thick wiry black hair. Their eyes are dark, expressive and gentle. They are of medium height and have a strong stocky physique ... chest hair, and his heavy beard and thick wiry head of hair, is so rare in aboriginals that it astounded travellers who returned home and spoke of 'the hairy Ainu'.[17]

With regard to the numbers of Ainu, these have never been large. In 1804 it was recorded that there were 23,797 on Hokkaido and Sakhalin, but by 1873 the numbers were down to 18,644. A census on Sakhalin in 1935 reported a population of only 1,512. In 1940 a census indicated the Hokkaido population stood at 16,170. Most of those on the Kuriles, and some on Sakhalin were relocated to Hokkaido when the islands were occupied by the USSR in 1945, and it is unlikely that any remain on those northern islands.[18]

There is today a problem of definition which makes enumeration difficult. The population was badly affected by introduced diseases, as Chekhov, being a doctor, is interested to note. Of more sig-

15 Ibid, pp. 184–5.
16 Kayano Shigeru, *Our Land was a Forest*, p. 98.
17 Chekhov, Anton, *The Island of Sakhalin* (London, 1989), pp. 133–4.
18 These figures are taken from Minority Rights Group, *Japan's Minorities*, Shibatani, *The Languages of Japan*, and *Kodansha Encyclopedia* under 'Ainu'.

nificance is the increase in the numbers of Japanese in Hokkaido. In 1873 there were 151,786 and this steadily increased until there are about 6 million today. The consequent interbreeding is compounded by the fact that the Japanese policy is one of assimilation, and one expression of that policy is the absence of separate counting of Ainu in censuses. Paradoxically, the Japanese classify the offspring of a Japanese–Ainu liaison as Ainu, which springs from their concern about racial purity. The general view is that there are some 16,000 on Hokkaido today, of whom only about 10 per cent are 'pure'. One definition of this is: 'Ainu whose lineages have not involved majority Japanese as far as can be remembered by surviving elders'.[19]

Yet a survey carried out in Hokkaido in 1979 reported that 24,160 people identified themselves as Ainu.[20]

Perhaps the gloomiest prognosis is provided by the evidence of language, that most important cornerstone of cultural identify. The claims that are made range from an assertion that it is dead, to an estimate that: 'It is true that while Ainu is no longer used as a means of daily communication ... it is remembered only partially by a handful of people of advanced age.'[21] The whole process has been expedited by the fact that the language had no indigenous written form.

In recent years, in common with minorities inside and outside Japan, the Ainu have sought to assert their rights. Being an indigenous, and ethnically a different people from the Japanese, one dimension of that assertion is the attempt to retrieve and preserve aspects of a very distinctive culture. There is in existence an Hokkaido Ainu Association whose Director has said: 'At least some of our people have got to the point where they can say with pride – I am an Ainu. But it took us years to reach even this point. The next step is to preserve our culture.'[22]

At a meeting of the Association in May 1984, the dismal history of the Ainu was rehearsed and demands made for legislation to try to put right some of the damage which has been done. The meeting recorded that the process of incorporating Ainu territory into the Japanese empire took place without discussion or negotiation. It may be noted that the same happened when aboriginal land was

19 Minority Rights Group, *Japan's Minorities*, p. 12, quoting Suzuki Jiro, 1973.
20 *Kodansha Encyclopedia*, under 'Ainu', p. 35.
21 Shibatani, *The Languages of Japan*, pp. 3–4.
22 Minority Rights Group, *Japan's Minorities*, p. 13, quoting *International Herald Tribune*, 24–25 October 1981.

seized in Australia. Furthermore, all the perennial negotiation with Russia over territory took no account of Ainu entitlements. The occupation of Hokkaido was accompanied by restriction of traditional means of living when 'hunting deer or fishing salmon became poaching, while collecting firewood became theft'. Reservations were established, and far from the post-Pacific war land reforms helping, the small Ainu farmers' position remained the same or deteriorated.

What the meeting demanded was a redressing of all such adversity, to be enshrined in legislation and set out in a programme. The first would recognise the distinctiveness of the Ainu and would ensure their possession of those very rights which were established in the post-war Constitution for all the people of Japan. Recognition of their difference and of past discrimination could be expressed by designated seats in all levels of government. The proposed programme would maintain Ainu culture, increase holdings in agriculture, ensure fishing rights, encourage involvement in forestry, and remove discrimination in employment. All the legislation and activity of government bodies concerning the Ainu since the Meiji Era have been restrictive and discriminatory, and should be repealed and abolished, and replaced by an Ainu Independence Fund, directed towards the fulfilment of the programme set out.[23] Since the 1984 meeting pressure has been maintained upon local authorities in Hokkaido and on the central government. As a result committees have been set up, the most recent in March 1995 to consider the issues. The March committee, chaired by a judge, is supposed to report after a year. One interesting development was the election of the first Ainu member, Kayano Shigeru, to the upper house of the Diet.

In recent years minorities throughout the world have formed international associations which seek to give mutual support, and to bring pressure upon powerful bodies and governments. One of these, which will be mentioned again in this book, is the 'International Movement against All Forms of Discrimination and Racism' (MADR). The Chief Director of the Hokkaido Ainu Association is one of the Directors of this organisation. The analysis set out in the 1984 'Proposal' is difficult to fault. Nor can the Ainu, or any other peoples in their position be blamed for agitating. In fact, the patience of many minorities is a matter for wonder. Yet the future of the Ainu people is questionable, both socially and cultur-

---

23 Privately printed document, 'A proposal for legislation concerning the Ainu People', trans., Lie, John J. and Hideaki Uemura.

ally, apart from all other considerations, because of the small numbers remaining. As with other disadvantaged groups, in all such areas Ainu standards remain well below that of the mainstream Japanese, and they 'are economically among the poorest groups in Japan'.[24] On a practical level, because of pressure, the government has given subsidies to improve living conditions, to raise standards of economic activity, and to encourage children to stay on at school. It is generally agreed that such measures have met with some success. The role of tourism in the maintenance of a sense of cultural difference is a matter of great controversy, but its defenders see no harm in its support in the transmission of traditions. A realistic projection must be that the Japanese policy of assimilation in respect of such small numbers, which has been steady and successful for a long time, must inevitably succeed.

---

24 Murakoshi Sueo and Yoshino, Roger, 'Minorities' in *Kodansha Encyclopedia.*

CHAPTER THREE

Towards a New Japan

Overleaf ▶
Emperor Hirohito performing the fertility ritual of planting rice

Towards a New Japan

The decision to move the imperial court from Kyoto to Tokyo was of profound significance, not only because of the physical removal of the *shogun* from his castle and his replacement by the emperor, but because of the momentous break with the past it represented, on a scale which is rare in Japanese history. Kyoto had been the imperial capital since 794, and upon the establishment of the Tokugawa shogunate, the latter, while observing formal respect for the emperors, nevertheless curbed their freedom of movement. As a consequence between 1632 and 1863 the emperors never left the palace except in emergency.[1]

Everyone concerned recognised the significance of the move. For some time during the Restoration process, consideration had been given to this central means of proclaiming change. Osaka, as one of the two most important cities, was considered, but the powerful court officials were divided, not only about the desirability of the move, but about the best place for relocation. The emperor himself led a party to inspect Osaka, but finally Tokyo was chosen, in 1868, perhaps by Meiji himself since Kido Koin records the choice as a result of 'imperial decision'.[2] Naturally, opposition to any move came from the traditional courtiers who recognised that there would be no hereditary or automatic position for them in the new system. Some were to enter what the sociologist Vilfredo Pareto called in a definition of history 'the graveyard of aristocracies'. After the court had visited the new Tokyo in November of 1868, it returned to Kyoto in early 1869. In the spring of that year, the final step was taken, and the emperor left Kyoto for good. In 1873 the *shogun*'s castle was designated the imperial palace.

1 Maki, John M., under 'Emperor' in *Kodansha Encyclopedia*.
2 Muramatsu Takeshi, 'The Emperor as Priest-King' in *Japan Echo*, Vol. XVI, No. 1, 1989, p. 53.

All the events of these turbulent years had created a situation where traditional authority and power was undermined, and had to be redistributed in ways which would fulfil the expectations which had been built up. These included the wish to modernise Japan, to cope with insistent western demands, and yet to maintain a stability which, despite the previous thirty years, had been a hallmark of Tokugawa rule. The central theme had been the 'restoration' of the emperor, in the new period known as the Meiji, or 'enlightened government' Era. The designation led to a common belief that the emperor was active, powerful and personally responsible for modernising Japan. The question as to the real power of Meiji and his successors is not only of interest to historians, but it was to be a critical political issue in 1945 at the end of the Pacific War. Then there was a widespread demand, inside and outside Japan that Emperor Hirohito, known since his death as *Showa*, his era name, should be tried as a war criminal. Generally, for the Japanese advocating such a course, he represented those forces which had halted the Japanese movement towards western style democracy, his ability to do so finding its authority in the constitution of his grandfather Meiji. Some Western powers wished to put him on trial because, they perceived, he was an autocratic ruler, whose decisions were directly responsible for aggression at Pearl Harbour, and for the appalling behaviour of the imperial forces in Asia. How fair is it to ascribe the direction of Japanese history, especially between 1867 and 1945, to the exercise of power by emperors? This is a question of considerable political significance.

Meiji was the one hundred and twenty-second emperor, in a lineage which contains several mythical figures, since the foundation of the dynasty by Jimmu in 660 BC, a date which is variously regarded as too early or mythical. In the years before 1945, as part of the campaign to mystify the monarchy, Japanese schoolchildren had to undergo the formidable task of learning all the names of the emperors. The early years of the dynasty owed a good deal, as did much Japanese culture, in this case of imperial form, to China. But gradually the autocratic power which was immanent in the Chinese model gave way in Japan to a more symbolic and religious role. A very ancient example was the offering by the emperors of freshly harvested rice to the gods at their accession, which together with other rice festivals were both to thank them, and ask for continuing fertility. The annual, very important rice festival was abolished by the Occupation forces in 1945, 'but the traditional rituals are still carried out privately by the imperial family'.[3] An indication of the emperor's submission to the exercise of power by others, lies in the fact that the westerners arriving in the mid-nineteenth century, including Perry, thought at first that the *shogun* was the emperor. The question remains though as to the existence or extent of imperial power.

There are generic difficulties in trying to discover the nature of power, even in an analysis of contemporary society. Much of the discussion and machination which goes on in any powerful arena is not susceptible to public scrutiny, an impediment which is greater in Japan because of the formidable Imperial Household Agency and its predecessor, the Imperial Household Ministry. Both have always been extremely reluctant even to deliver matters of simple fact about the imperial family, never mind engage in controversy. The Agency was founded in 1947, as successor to the Imperial Household Ministry. The Agency and the Ministry which preceded it managed, and still does, the state affairs of the emperor down to every detail, such as maintenance of the imperial tombs. Inevitably therefore there can only be deduction and suggestion based upon scant evidence about the imperial institution. This includes the imperial family in this century, which is, as in previous centuries subject to rumour, some of it wild, much of it outrageous, but commonly accepted by the people. One such rumour is that the deranged Emperor Taisho, son of Meiji, was murdered.

There is another source of confusion for western observers, which derives from western tradition: this concerns the use of the title 'emperor'. In the west 'emperor' connotes an all-powerful ruler, examples of which are plentiful, ranging from the Romans to the kaisers and tsars of more recent years. It is this tradition which makes some commentators, some Americans especially, insist on the autocratic power, and therefore the personal accountability of Meiji, and Showa in particular.[4] As one writer points out one problem lies in the translation of the Japanese title. This title is *tenno* which is literally translated as 'heavenly sovereign' or 'ruler of the heavens'. It is first recorded in the sixth or seventh century AD, was probably taken from the Taoist name for the north star, and was used to distinguish the Japanese from the Chinese emperors.[5] The point that Robert J. Smith makes is that in the early years of the

3 Ibid., p. 57 and p. 59.

4 See, for example, Bergamini, David, *Japan's Imperial Conspiracy* (London, 1971), *passim*, and Hoyt, Edwin P., *Japan's War: The Great Pacific Conflict* (London, 1986), pp. 20–1, and *passim*.

5 Ueyama Shunpei, Umehara, Takeshi, and Yano Torin, 'The Imperial Institution in Japanese History' in *Japan Echo*, Vol. XVI, No. 1, 1989, p. 48.

Restoration the term *tenno* was used to refer to the head of state. But when it was translated 'the unfortunate choice was "emperor" rather than "king". As a consequence, the nature of the position has long been obscured.'[6]

Despite all such complications, there are some generally accepted examples of emperors who were determined to be more active in the use of what they believed was imperial power. A notable example is the early fourteenth-century Emperor Go-Daigo. When he ascended the throne in 1318 he plotted to overthrow the *shogun*. For this he was banished to an island, but he escaped and continued his revolt. So that he could become *shogun*, the commander of the *shogun's* army supported the emperor, and the latter was able to establish direct rule, albeit for only about three years. At the end of that time, after complex struggles for power caused in part by Go-Daigo's refusal to appoint a *shogun*, fighting led to the emperor fleeing and the eventual re-establishment of the shogunate. Even the powerful Tokugawa *shoguns* had to take account of the views of the emperors, especially at the beginning. Ieyasu faced the same problem as all *shoguns* and their successors, the political and military oligarchies of the post-Meiji Restoration. This was to persuade the emperor to do what they wished, constrained as they were, especially in the twentieth century, by the reverence with which he was regarded, a reverence enhanced and exploited by them. They all needed the validation which would in a real sense sanctify their actions.

The particular issue at the beginning of the seventeenth century was the entry into Japan of foreigners, especially missionaries, a process which the Emperor Go-Yozei, wished to see halted and reversed. Ieyasu's first tactic, a common resort of aristocracies in troubled times, was that the emperor should marry one of Ieyasu's daughters. As a protest against inaction the emperor abdicated for three years. In 1614, the marriage was agreed, and the war against Christianity began. Even though the new emperor, Go-Mizu-Noo, fulfilled the contract by marrying into the *shogun's* family in 1620, he still thought that insufficient had been done to clear the country of foreign influence, despite the fact that the *shogun* had met with considerable resistance by Christians and allies disaffected with the new shogunate. In 1629 the emperor abdicated, and was succeeded by a young girl. The occupation of the throne by a female was not without precedent, especially much earlier in the monarchy. She

6 Smith, Robert J., *Japanese Society: Tradition, Self and the Social Order* (Cambridge, 1983), p. 13.

was one of the two female emperors in the three hundred years to the ascension of Meiji. In 1634 *shogun* Iemitsu, the grandson of Ieyasu met the ex-emperor, and after negotiation, an agreement was concluded which added to Iemitsu's fame, and was to be a landmark in Japanese history. It also gives some indication of the influence, if exercised, of imperial power. The order was given that all foreigners should be expelled, except for a small Dutch trading post, and the Japanese were forbidden to leave the country. And there took place the final and bloody slaughter of Christians. Only then was the emperor content.

It was the same issue which divided the *shogun* and the emperor in the mid-nineteenth century. The pressure to open up the country has been described in a previous chapter, but aspects of the matter provide further illustration that some emperors on some issues could not be ignored. When Perry presented his demands in 1853, the *shogun* consulted the Emperor Komei, who held the same opinion about foreigners in Japan as his ancestor Go-Yozei in the previous century. The reply was not helpful. For the emperor and his supporters the issue was simple: the foreigners should be expelled. Despite this treaties were drafted by the *bakufu*, with the United States, Britain and Russia, parts of which included 'extra-territoriality'. This meant that foreigners who committed offences were not subject to Japanese jurisdiction but, it will be remembered, were to be dealt with by their own people. The implication that the Japanese criminal justice system, like the Chinese, was barbaric, was especially annoying for the Japanese, and there was the certainty that crimes might go unpunished. Such clauses were deeply resented, as they had been in the Chinese ports, and with good reason. The emperor's continuing resistance led to one of the famous slogans of the time 'Revere the emperor: expel the barbarian'. Eventually, in 1865, under pressure from moderates at court, after extremists had been subdued, the emperor approved the group of treaties known as the Ansei Commercial Treaties.

In the middle of these difficult times in the late 1850s the *shogun* died, to be succeeded by a twelve-year-old. In 1860, the year in which a delegation went to America to discuss treaties, the strongest, most determined, of the *shogun*'s party was killed because of his pursuit of policies to collaborate with the foreigners, as was mentioned in an earlier chapter. Ii Naosuke was murdered in an especially savage attack at the very entrance to the *shogun*'s castle. In 1866 the next *shogun* died suddenly. A critical event in early 1867 was the death, after a short illness of Emperor Komei from 'either smallpox or melancholy fever'. Bergamini goes so far as to allege suicide or murder, referring to the famous statesman Iwakura as Komei's 'assassin'.[7] A more restrained view is that he died of smallpox and that although 'it was rumoured that he had been poisoned ... this was never substantiated'.[8]

Emperor Meiji thus began his reign from Tokyo with some formidable problems. Unlike his father and some of his more uncooperative ancestors, he did not have to deal with the hostility of the *shogun* and the *bakufu*; in other words he should have been in a much more powerful position than any emperor for almost a thousand years. Before considering the scale of the changes in Meiji Japan, we will review his constitutional position, and try to identify events where his view was paramount.

According to one authority,[9] the beginning did not look promising. He was not much interested in public affairs, but after a while and a rebuke from his advisers, he began to engage in the machinery of state. His formal position was set out in the new Constitution of 1889, a position that was to remain unchanged until 1945. The opening Articles are formidable, noting that the empire 'shall be reigned over and governed by a line ... unbroken for ages eternal', that the emperor 'is sacred and inviolable', 'exercises legislative powers', 'has the supreme command of the Army and Navy', 'declares war, makes peace, and concludes treaties': and much else besides. There has always been discussion about Article 55, which is marshalled when an emperor has acted unwisely, or failed to act at all, since it appears to exonerate him:

> The respective ministers of state shall give their advice to the emperor and be responsible for it. All laws, imperial ordinances and imperial rescripts of whatever kind, that relate to the affairs of the state, require the countersignature of a minister of state.

On the face of it, it would appear that emperors under this Constitution could not be wrong. Certainly, with the exception of attempts to assassinate them by political radicals who regarded them as the source of social dysfunction, blame for mistakes was generally attributed to advisers who had given them 'bad' advice. When affairs were going badly in the late 1920s, criticism of ministers was severe, while the emperor was exonerated. As a result, at that time there was

---

7 Bergamini, *Japan's Imperial Conspiracy*, pp. 248–54.

8 Entry under 'Komei, Emperor (1831–67)' by Miki Seiichiro in *Kodansha Encyclopedia.*

9 Maki, John M., under 'Emperor' in *Kodansha Encyclopedia.*

a demand for another 'restoration'. The point has been made above that it is impossible to discover, perhaps especially from those who recorded events at the time, how much influence or pressure an emperor may have exerted in debate. However, in the case of Meiji and Showa, there is a strong measure of agreement about decisions which were made at their insistence, usually against a background of irreconcilable differences between advisers.

The probability is that Emperor Meiji made at least three important political decisions. The first of these, already mentioned, was to move the court to Tokyo, traditional opposition to which was immense. The next concerned the rejection of the advocacy of some powerful *daimyo* to invade Korea, a matter which was to lead to a serious rebellion. The background detail of this will be discussed in Chapter Six. It was a question which divided the Grand Council of State, the chief minister of which was Sanjo Sanetomi, who supported the idea of invasion, but became ill in the middle of the debate. He was replaced by Iwakura Tomomi, one of the most important political figures of the period, who took the opposite view. In what was probably an unprecedented act he decided to present the arguments to the emperor, and ask him to decide. This angered the pro-invasion group, because they regarded such a course as a break with tradition.

As a result, in 1873 the emperor ordered that the debate about invading Korea should cease: there would be no invasion. Having made this decision, he made his third which was still part of the same controversy. He resisted the inevitable demands for the dismissal of Sanjo.[10] In a society where age is the most important factor in the award of respect, one of the more remarkable features of the actions of Meiji was his age at the time. The decision to move to Tokyo was taken when he was seventeen, and the orders both to cease debate about Korea, and that Sanjo, despite his mistake, should stay in office, were issued when he was twenty.

Although these decisions, however personal, were very important they hardly add up to an autocratic rule. These may be regarded as isolated examples, perhaps made all the more dramatic by their rarity. Thus, they are compatible with a Japanese summary of imperial power.

After the (Pacific) war, the historian Tsuda Sokichi made the point that the imperial institution had managed to survive over the centuries precisely because it refrained from ruling directly and building

10 Ueyama *et al.*, 'The Imperial Institution in Japance History', pp. 55–6.

up an independent power base. He was refuting the argument that under the Meiji constitution the emperor exercised direct rule, an interpretation shared by the post-war leftists and the war-time nationalists.[11]

This comment illustrates the continuity of the debate from the Restoration to 1945. The much more important role of Showa (Hirohito) in the Pacific War will be discussed later, but the difficulty of arriving at any measure of imperial power can be illustrated, finally, from the debate about the marriage of Emperor Showa to Princess Nagako. This provoked a political crisis, but one eastern and one western writer give totally different assessments of the role of the crown prince, as he then was, in the affair. Doubt was expressed about the suitability of Nagako, because it was alleged there was colour blindness in her family. This developed into serious argument, but the two writers differ as to the influence of the crown prince. Kawahara states that 'Hirohito was not involved in the selection of his prospective wife ... it would be two years before he himself would be told about the choice'.[12] Hoyt, on the contrary, writes that 'Hirohito, however, wanted to choose his own bride, a matter unheard of in Japanese history ... after a good deal of manoeuvring, it was announced from the palace that the prince would be betrothed to Nagako ... the *genro* had been outmanoeuvred with the connivance of the prince himself.'[13] Even about very recent times, incontrovertible evidence is difficult to obtain. This discussion about imperial authority is important because it illustrates an especial problem in the understanding of events, major and crucial events in Japanese history: how decisions are taken.

As the account of Meiji's reign develops, the question of involvement in decisions is never far away. What is difficult to deny is the dominating presence of the emperor for forty-five remarkable years, even allowing for the hyperbole and reverence which Japanese popular tradition accords him. One succinct summary, which is a valuable background to the transformation of Japan is offered by Maki:

> During his reign of forty-five years emperor Meiji developed from a youngster with inadequate training and little concern for the affairs of state into a dignified figure who looked and acted the role of a

11 Ibid., p. 49.
12 Kawahara Toshiaki, *Hirohito and His Times: A Japanese Perspective* (Tokyo, 1990), p. 26.
13 Hoyt, Edwin P., *Hirohito: The Emperor and the Man* (New York, 1992), p. 38.

national symbol of Japan's newly found dignity as a great power ... the reign of Meiji did illustrate the remarkable adaptability of Japan's imperial institution. What must have been regarded in Western eyes as an important, cloistered, and archaic institution had by 1912 been made the axis of Japanese polity.[14]

The dramatic change in the position of the emperor in the state was a symbol of the fact that new forms of government had to be developed, since the feudal structures which had been in place for so long were now an anachronism. This realisation had been at the heart of the Restoration, and it is a realisation which marks an important stage in the transition to the modern state. In a simple or pre-modern society, such as Japan had been, complex and restrictive social structures are maintained by a belief that the existing generation of exercisers of power at various levels will produce a succeeding generation, possessed of the inherited ability to exercise the same power. This is, of course, something of an oversimplification, but in essence it is true that such societies, built upon rigid caste and class divisions, typically linked to degrees of power or powerlessness, restriction of occupation, and limited mobility, cannot sustain the operation of a modern industrial state. Such a state needs to be able to facilitate political, educational, and social movement so that the best talent of whatever kind is exploited. A stagnant society cannot be sure that required qualities are inherited, because they are not, as the very uneven quality of the Tokugawa *shoguns* shows very well. Nineteenth-century Japanese critics realised this in their slogan about the need to look for 'men of talent': 'Since the regulations insist that administrators be chosen from among persons of high rank, it is natural that there are few men of ability among them'.[15]

Initially power fell into the hands of those who had supported the emperor. Notably, but not exclusively, these were the clans of Choshu, Satsuma, Tosa and Hizen. From this group there emerged an oligarchy dominated by talented men, free from the restriction imposed upon them by birth. Eventually they became known as the *genro*, meaning 'the original elders', the first two being appointed in 1889. They were appointed by the emperor, although there was no constitutional basis for their position. Nevertheless their power was considerable during the Meiji Era, and well into the twentieth

14 Maki under 'Emperor' in *Kodansha Encyclopedia*, p. 206.
15 Beasley, W.G., *The Meiji Restoration* (Stanford, California, 1972), quoting Keene, D., *The Japanese Discovery of Europe: Honda Toshiaki and Other Discoverers 1720–1798* (London, 1952).

century. They were not only the closest advisers to the emperor, but to them was given the right to select and recommend prime ministers. The first seven original *genro* were from Choshu and Satsuma, and all were middle or lower *samurai*, the newly emancipated class whose talents were to mould the new Japan. To modern eyes the *genro* group seem to be the antithesis of democratic government, which indeed they were. But the argument has been made that against a background of continuing unrest and uncertainty, they were a force for stability, that they took a broad view, and tried to act in the best interests of Japan.[16]

Their internal stability as a group persisted because of several shared beliefs, primarily in the supremacy of the emperor and distrust of 'democracy'. They maintained their domination over national affairs by restrained rivalry, concessionary skills, and agreeing the allocation of areas of power and influence. So it came about that soon the Choshu controlled the army, and the Satsuma the navy. And with the same techniques between 1885 and 1918, the premiership with a couple of exceptions was held by Choshu and Satsuma clansmen. But the power of these original seven was maintained not only because upon the death of one of them, power was transferred to people they had selected, but because sometimes one of the original seven, as a very old man, was still at the centre of national affairs. An example is Yamagata Aritomo, about whom we shall hear a lot, who when he was over eighty, became embroiled in the matter of the marriage of Crown Prince Hirohito to which reference has been made. Despite the traditional respect for age which pervades Japanese tradition, society began to grow impatient with the old men. Those who wanted more democracy had in common with a new generation of young military officers a feeling that the *genro* tradition should be ended. The last of the *genro*, Saionji, died in 1940 at the age of 91; but not before he had issued a warning. It was, interestingly, 'against over aggressive policies', but his warning was 'largely overlooked'.[17]

From the policies of the *genro* it is clear that the divisions between the oligarchy were based upon their ancient clan loyalties, not upon rival political beliefs in any commonly understood modern sense. The struggles were about which groups would inherit the disintegrated authority of the shogunate. The notion of 'groups' is important since it is integral in Japanese social structure. As in the

16 See, for example, the entry under *genro* by Sheldon, Charles D. in *Kodansha Encyclopedia.*
17 Ibid.

code of *bushido*, the individual is subordinate to the group, and the upheavals in Japanese society in the last one hundred and fifty years have not altered this central fact. Because of the absence of rigid, 'alien', politically held beliefs, with the exception of the events leading to Saigo's rebellion over Korean policy, it was possible for there to be a remarkable flexibility in the formation of alliances and allegiances in the oligarchy's commonly agreed determination to exercise power.

In an important sense therefore, the Restoration left some things unchanged. As it had been important for the *shogun* to secure the sacramental validation of the emperor, so the new rulers would need the support of Meiji. But one crucial difference was that the 'new *shoguns*' were not hampered by the faltering traditions of latter shogunates, nor did they have to cope with all of the historical lumber which had made the functioning of those governments impossible. Despite their backgrounds, they addressed major problems of impediment to change, and from the beginning there was astonishing determination about the directions which Japan should take.

Despite the overwhelming, yet informal power of the *genro*, from the beginning of the Meiji Era organs of government were established. Often re-creations of antique bodies, and not in any sense representational, they nevertheless pioneered the movement towards some degree of broad representation. Very soon after the Restoration such a body, first established in the early eighth century, was put in place. It was called *dajokan*, a Grand Council of State, and the term was perhaps resurrected to underline the newly restored power of the emperor. It consisted of a grand or chief minister, two ministers and councillors who were also ministry heads. But it was not adequate for the complex needs of a society which was, to put it mildly, different from the Japan of some eleven hundred years before. The Grand Council was abolished in 1885, and replaced by cabinet government partly because of dissatisfaction on the part of those who wanted more democracy, and partly because Japan was turning to the west for models. Although it was abolished, it was the same membership of seven imperial counsellors who were to become the *genro*. In 1875 a *genroin*, chamber of elders was established, but this had no connection with the *genro*. This too was a body to which the emperor appointed people. Although it had some administrative functions, it seems to have had little purpose, and in 1890, upon the establishment of the Diet, it was abolished.

Although the movement to what the Japanese perceived to be

western-style government was sometimes punctuated by the failure
of systems and of administrative initiative, the movement can also be
seen to have been characterised by progress, even if slow, and
despite the clever opposition of some of the most powerful of the
genro. This progress is marked by statements of intent, laws, and the
establishment of new structures. An early example in the era was
what is commonly called 'The Charter Oath', which as Spaulding
points out, is more correctly translated as the 'Imperial Oath of Five
Articles'.[18] There has been considerable controversy about the
language, meaning, significance and translation of this short document. Translation is always a problem and nowhere more so than
from the Japanese language, where argument and misunderstanding are rife. The problem is exacerbated if, as is commonly the case
in Japanese official documents, ambiguity is inbuilt.

Article One announces the convening of an assembly, and that all
'matters shall be decided by public (open) discussion'. Despite the
scholarly controversy about the meaning of public, or the nature of
an assembly, the central core seems to be that there should be
consultation. The second Article proclaims that all groups or classes
'high and low' should unite, probably to the end that the national
economy should be strengthened. In his commentary on this Article
Spaulding[19] states that this is an especial exhortation to accept some
of the unpopular financial and economic measures which the
government was introducing; a reminder that there was still great
instability and apprehension in the country. Article Three seems to
advocate that everybody's potential should be realised, to the end
that people would not feel frustrated or discontented; but Spaulding cautions that this is 'probably the most obscure' of the Articles.[20]
The next Article is usually agreed as intended to arrest the persisting anti-foreigner activity, and to urge that differences should be
settled diplomatically. The last Article is the best known and most
intelligible. In its proclamation that 'knowledge shall be sought
throughout the world', with the purpose of strengthening the
empire, it is clear that isolationism is over, once and for all, and that
Japan will set out to learn from other countries. This was to become,
and remains, the most notable characteristic of every facet of
Japanese behaviour. The ability to pursue this aim and, at the same
time, to maintain cultural integrity is an important difference

18 'The intent of the Charter Oath' by Spaulding, Robert M. in Beardsley, Richard
K. (ed.), *Studies in Japanese History and Politics* (Ann Arbor, 1967), p. 3.
19 Ibid., p. 9.
20 Ibid., p. 10.

between Japan on the one hand, and China and Korea on the other. It is a difference which has coloured the history of all three.

Whatever the debates about the Charter Oath, it is attended by an irreducible significance. It announces potentially important changes in the structure of government, it adds to the assault on the moribund social structure, and it indicates that Japan is moving into the world. Its place in the historical culture of Japan is perhaps indicated by the fact that in the chaos of 1945, it was to the Oath that leading Japanese turned for a clue as to how reconstruction could be achieved. It is significant too that the Imperial Rescript of 1946, which renounced the divinity of the emperor, quoted the Charter Oath in full.[21]

It should be stressed again that all of this political activity, even if in so modest a form as a statement of intent, took place against a background of considerable social and administrative problems. Yet the fact that the country was ruled by a new, seemingly conservative oligarchy, did not mean that there was a brake on development. On the contrary, immense change took place. One of the most dramatic of these was the signal ending of feudalism by the abolition of the *samurai* class in 1870. This was followed by a kind of *coup de grâce* in 1876, when the wearing of swords was banned. In 1870, at the time when the inadequacies of the *samurai* as a military force were recognised by their abolition, conscription was introduced in the creation of a modern army. Another significant step was the establishment of compulsory education in 1872. Both are so important, and were so controversial at the time that they will be treated separately in later chapters. Other revolutionary acts, such as the emancipation of the outcastes, will similarly be discussed in appropriate context.

One of the most difficult problems in the early years of the Meiji Era concerned the authority over the feudal domains of the *daimyo*. Before Meiji, Japan was divided into areas, variously called *han* or domains, the supreme head of which was a *daimyo* who, even under the shogunate, had almost unfettered authority over the area. The question now was whether this authority was consonant with the restoration of the land to the emperor. Initially, in this matter the authority of the *shogun* was simply transferred to the emperor; that is the *daimyo* were restricted in the same way as they had been under the *shogun*. They had to obey imperial decrees, but in essence their power remained. It seemed to some of the interested parties that

21 Ibid., p. 3.

this situation was perfectly satisfactory. But others, especially those who had some knowledge of the power exerted by some of the more authoritarian western monarchs, believed that the perpetuation of this antique relationship was incompatible with the enhancement of imperial authority.

The difficulty for the reformers was finding a way of restoring imperial authority over the domains, which would not alienate the *daimyo* to a degree where civil war might again break out. Two important figures in Meiji Era politics, Kido Koin and Ito Hirobumi, both of Choshu, are usually credited with the proposals which moved the matter forward.[22] Critically, they were supported by both Satsuma and Tosa leaders. All agreed with Kido's contention that unless authority in the domains were invested in the emperor, Japan would consist of a number of 'little *bakufus*',[23] which would forever prevent the cohesion of a Japan which would be a world leader. As often in Japanese politics the discussion dragged on in the hope of reaching consensus, but this was an issue of such magnitude that it was eventually realised that consensus would never be achieved. However, there was sufficient agreement in the four dominant clans for a memorial to be presented to the emperor in 1869, offering the lands of the four. They surrendered everything 'so that state affairs, both great and small, may be in the hands of a single authority'.[24]

This action, while it provided leadership and offered direction, did not immediately resolve this dangerous situation. Not only were the leaders of each of the clans possessed of a considerable range of opinions, but so were their subjects, many of whom either wanted the status quo upheld, or wanted it demolished. They recognised that the abolition of the domains would be the final curtain on the feudalism which had variously perpetuated or denied them privilege. The predictable outcome was fighting and assassination, not only about the activities of the central government, but about the local government attempts at reform. Throughout the country the arguments proliferated; the need for a central army, which in turn was a prerequisite for dealing with the outside, the increasing impecuniousness of some of the domains, and centralisation as a means of ending internal strife.

The end came by the judicious distribution of key posts amongst the leaders of the four clans, replacing most of the nobility by

22 Beasley, W.G., *The Meiji Restoration*, pp. 25–6, quoting Kicho Koin Monjo (ed.), *Nihon Shiseki Kyokai* (Tokyo, 1932–33).

23 Ibid., p. 330, quoting F/0410/12, pp. 337–8, Memorandum by Mitford.

24 Ibid., p. 331, quoting *Iwakura Kojikki* (Tokyo, 1927).

samurai as heads of ministries, and the award of generous income to the *daimyo*, who were all to be given titles in a new peerage, based upon European practice, and which lasted until 1945. These inducements seem to have been sufficient, and there was resistance only from a few diehards. At the same time the moves were backed up by the positioning of reliable troops in Tokyo, when the *daimyo* were informed in an imperial audience in August 1870, that the network of domains, over which they had authority, was to be replaced by a prefectural system over which the emperor and the government would have complete authority. There were many important consequences. The *daimyo* mostly lost their institutional power, although if they were 'men of talent', they could share in the new power structure. This did not lead to anything approaching a breakdown in traditional social structure, but it did lead to some flexibility in the upper echelons. The *samurai* in particular were affected. They dominated the new bureaucracy, encouraged interest in the west, and became governors of the new prefectures in place of their own *daimyo*, now paradoxically confined to Tokyo. But the most important outcome was that the change cleared a major, perhaps the major organisational barrier to the creation of a strong central government. The final step was that in 1872 the 302 domains were reduced to 72 prefectures and mostly given new names.

Another illustration of the speed of events is that in 1871, the very same year in which the domains were abolished, and three years after the Charter Oath announced that 'knowledge shall be sought all over the world', a remarkable expedition left Japan for exactly that purpose. Not only was this a quite extraordinary act of implementation, but the leadership of the expedition or mission as it is usually called, illustrates well the shift in authority in the few years since the Restoration. The head, Iwakura Tomomi, a senior minister in the new government, born in 1825, was the son of a low-ranking courtier in Kyoto. Iwakura had been a chamberlain to Emperor Komei, was active in the Restoration movement, and was involved in the formulation of both the Charter Oath and process leading to the Constitution of 1889. Because he belonged to neither Choshu nor Satsuma, he was able to mediate between them. The leading people who went with him represented what was becoming a stereotype of the new people in government. Two of these were Okubo Toshimichi and Ito Hirobumi, and balanced in that the former was Satsuma, the latter Choshu, and both were middle-level samurai, Ito in fact by promotion from a farming background.

The party comprised some fifty people from a wide variety of backgrounds and included three girls, one of whom, Tsuda Umeko, was only five. She was to become a famous figure in women's education in Japan. More will be said about her in the later chapter on women. The mission had a variety of aims. Japan had concluded treaties with a number of western countries, and they were to carry the greetings of the emperor to the heads of those countries. These ranged from the American President Grant to Tsar Alexander II of Russia. In discussions they hoped to convince these countries that the Japanese were civilised, and in the process to discover the conditions under which the hated treaties could be revised, especially the vexed question of extraterritoriality. Next, although contact with the west was increasing, for instance by the recruitment of foreign experts, and the translation of texts, this expedition was to discover systematically wherein the success of the west lay, and which components of that success could be translated to Japan.

The scale of the operation was enormous. Apart from the travelling, the numbers of countries visited, the range of visits, and discussions in every kind of institution and organisation, the speed at which they accumulated and integrated information in the eighteen-month visit, must make the operation one of the most remarkable missions in not only Japanese, but world history. They refined opinions on industrial production, free trade, educational practice, the need for governmental intervention in industrial and commercial activity – which remains a key factor in Japanese economic success – and above all assessed the military strength of the west and the causes of the relative power of one country as against another. On their return they encountered the unrest associated with that stumbling-block to progress which must dominate accounts of the period: Saigo and his demand for an invasion of Korea. But this only increased Iwakura's determination to press ahead with reforms, and in the process to eliminate those in power who disagreed with him.[25]

One of the doubts about the west which Iwakura brought back to Japan concerned the matter of broadly based democracy, even in the rudimentary form in which it existed in the west at the time. Nevertheless, short of a broadly based elected assembly, or any transfer of power to ordinary people, he approved of a Constitution. Nor was he unusual in the high ranks of Japanese government in believing that power should not be shared. Furthermore, a representative of a great and successful nation, retired President Grant,

25 For a more detailed account of the mission and further references, see under *Iwakura Mission* by Mayo, Marlene J. in *Kodansha Encyclopedia.*

on a visit to Japan at about the time of the end of the Saigo rebellion, confirmed their fears. In discussion with the emperor and his councillors, he cautioned against democracy and power sharing.[26] The Japanese had to be impressed by such views from such a famous politician, especially since they were in tune with their own.

Despite such concerns, in 1885 there was another important political change. A cabinet system was instituted, headed by a prime minister. But they were not, as in modern democracies, accountable to an assembly. The prime minister was appointed by the emperor on the recommendation of the *genro*. Thus, they were accountable in theory only to the emperor. This was the system until 1945. The first prime minister was Ito Hirobumi, he who had been on the Iwakura mission, one of the *genro* who was to be an important influence in the formation of governmental structures and party politics for the rest of the Meiji Era.

Much of the political agitation at the time was about the question of a Constitution, and one of the chief spurs to action was Okuma Shigenobu, who was from a *samurai* family in Hizen, a fact of significance in his dealings with the two increasingly dominant clans of Choshu and Satsuma. He was a councillor, and in the early years of the restoration he built up great experience and skill in a wide variety of public appointments; for example he established the national mint, and negotiated a loan for Japan's first railway. In 1881 he published a paper on constitutional government, in which he advocated speed, that the Constitution should be modelled on that of Britain, and that it should be organised around parties. All of these views were anathema to his colleagues, but his public revelation of a scheme to sell government property in Hokkaido much below their value, to which reference was made in Chapter Two, and his consequential leaving of the government, created such turmoil that these events have been given a name in Japanese history; the Political Crisis of 1881. The relevance of these events lies in the fact that his actions, while they infuriated his colleagues, made the latter extremely unpopular. To placate the public, the government promised that there would be a National Assembly by 1890.[27]

The next step was the promulgation of a constitution, and to this end as one of his last acts before his death in 1883, Iwakura sent Ito Hirobumi to Europe, as usual, to look for models. Ito was head of an

---

26 Hoyt (1986), *Japan's War*, p. 19.
27 For a detailed account of Okuma, see his entry in *Kodansha Encyclopedia* by Lebra, Joyce C.

office to draft a constitution, but as Storry points out, this vital matter was not open to public debate. Ito's office was made part of the Imperial Household Ministry. The secretive nature of this body and its successor has already been described, and so as Storry points out, the 'entire venture' was enveloped 'in an aura of almost sacred dignity'.[28] The delegation spent most of its time in Germany, and came back with the palatable view, at least for the authoritarians, that an elected assembly should have limited powers, and that the executive should be accountable to the ruler. Storry's conclusion is that 'in the event – and not for the last time – it was Germany that exerted a baleful effect upon the course of Japanese history'.[29]

The Constitution was proclaimed in 1889. It was a composite of ideas from Ito's group, and decrees which had already been issued. The first chapter sets out, at length, the position of the emperor, and these clauses have been discussed earlier in this chapter. The second sets out the rights and duties of the emperor's subjects. These include the obligation to serve in the military, freedom from house search, and 'liberty of speech, writing, publication', 'but within limits of law'. The third chapter established an assembly. This would consist of a House of Peers and a House of Representatives. It was modelled upon a European system where the upper house would consist of the new nobility, and the lower would be elected. Next came the establishment of ministers of state, a privy council, and an independent judiciary. Finally, there were provisions regulating the organisation of finance.

Viewed from hindsight some commentators have been critical, or even dismissive, of the first Japanese Constitution. It is certainly the case that neither the prime minister, nor the cabinet were to be elected, and that there seemed to be little promise of an erosion of the authority of the Imperial Household Ministry or the *genro*, to name but two powerful groups. In fact, at the same time as the promulgation, the oligarchy announced their intention 'to remain aloof from party politics by adhering to the principle of non-party or "transcendental" cabinets'.[30] Another criticism arises from the fact that because of the property qualification, only somewhere over 1 per cent of the population could vote. But even in the most advanced western democracies at the time, there was nothing approaching universal suffrage.

A more sympathetic view would be to regard this as another

28   Storry, Richard, *A History of Modern Japan* (London, 1960), p. 116.
29   Ibid., p. 115.
30   Kodansha International, *Japan: Profile of a Nation* (Tokyo, 1994), p. 64.

important step towards political maturity. The Constitution did at least establish an Assembly, and there was always the hope that, as with any Assembly, it would act as an ultimate brake on excess. And such an assembly would be likely to provide an opportunity for a broadening of popular influence. Above all, and with all its hesitation, the Constitution should be seen as a radical act in a country which in twenty years had seen a complete upheaval of the established order, and where the leadership, however experienced, and whatever had been learned from the west, was very nervous of giving power to the people. In reflecting upon the event some years later, Ito made a significant point: 'At that time, we had not yet arrived at the stage of distinguishing clearly between political opposition on the one hand, and treason to the established order of things on the other'.[31]

The oligarchy hoped that the Constitution would dampen an emerging interest in government in Japan, since by 1889 it was clear that 'parties' were being formed. In the matter of creating a new Japan, the oligarchy regarded this as tiresome and obstructive. But they were to be disappointed. The issuing of a Constitution far from discouraging the development of party politics, excited interest. The powerful in Japan were now faced with a dilemma which is a permanent theme in the history of many non-European countries: How could Japan remain unchanged and unaltered and still be 'modern'? How could she adopt the forms of western democratic institutions, and not the substance? And, precisely, how could she establish an Assembly which would be powerless, satisfy the ambitions of those without power, and prevent further change? The oligarchy were to find it difficult to persuade people that they were the best judges of how Japan should be governed.

Japan had always been a place where intellectual ideas had been discussed and developed. Historically these had usually been concerned with religious, ethical, or mystical questions which often affected social and state structures. After the Restoration, in part because of exposure to the west, the debates became more focused on political questions, and quickly led to the formation of groups who disagreed with each other. This was a development which occurred in part because the Choshu–Satsuma axis not only excluded other groups, but increasingly excluded the other major clans who had assumed power, the Tosa and the Hizen. These new groupings have become known as protoparties. One such set up in

31 Storry, *A History of Modern Japan*, p. 118.

1874 was called the Public Society of Patriots, and its originators were Itagaki Taisuka and Goto Shojiro, who were councillors, but had been on the losing side in the Korean quarrel. They resigned from the government, and sent what is called the Tosa memorial which called for a democratically elected assembly. In 1881 this political initiative was to give birth to the Liberal Party, the first national party, with Itagaki as its head. Appealing to the mainly rural community of landowners and former *samurai*, it was to emerge from the maelstrom of early political alliances as the Friends of Constitutional Government, one of the two parties which were to be the most serious in pre-Pacific War Japan.

Its main rival in these early years was a party called the Constitutional Reform party, or sometimes the Progressive Party. This was established in 1882 by Okuma and two colleagues, was less radical than the Liberal Party, and appealed more to an urban constituency. Its heir was the Constitutional Democratic Party which continued until the Pacific War to be the second contender for power. Both parties expended considerable energy in attacking each other, but in the first Diet in November 1890, they were sufficiently united to oppose the oligarchs' parties, such as the National Association. The oligarchy had realised that one of the ways in which they could restrain these emerging parties was to field their own.

Another more physical response to social unrest was the enactment of the Peace Preservation Law in 1887. Public awareness of the latest proposals to tackle the problem of the unequal treaties was a reason for political activists to hold demonstrations in Tokyo. The Law was drafted by Yamagata Aritomo, who was prime minister and one of the most important people in recent Japanese history. It set out to curb political activity, prohibit secret societies, and forbid anything which interfered with public peace, for example through publication. It gave the police wide-ranging powers to stop meetings, and most severe, the power to expel from Tokyo for three years anyone judged to be a threat to public order. Five hundred and seventy prominent members of the Freedom and People's Rights Movement were so expelled.[32]

Despite such measures, political activity, and the formation of political groupings were sustained. The first Diet met, after elections in November 1890, and after a crisis occasioned by Diet opposition to increased taxation in 1898, Okuma and Itagaki joined forces and

32 Hackett, Roger F., 'Peace Preservation Law of 1887' in *Kodansha Encyclopedia*.

formed the first party cabinet with Okuma as prime minister. The coalition did not last, but by 1900 the oligarchy finally realised that they could not remain aloof from party politics. In that year Ito formed the Friends of Constitutional Government which was a coalition of the Liberal Party and bureaucrats, and won a majority. Over the succeeding years the ageing *genro* and the apparatus which sustained them lost to the parties, and the battles were less between the oligarchy and the parties than between rivals in the latter.

All of these political groupings shared the same basic values, which is to say there were no violent disagreements about the sanctity of the emperor, the need to industrialise, or the expansion of the empire. Their disagreements vary about pace, intensity, or most importantly, gaining access to power. There were people who were much more radical, whose beliefs had been imported as part of the paraphernalia of rapid industrialisation. The western antagonism between capitalist and worker, which was such a core political issue was transported into Japan, along with morally neutral techniques of engineering. However, faced with these views, the oligarchy acted quickly. In 1901 the Social Democratic Party was formed, only to be banned on the same day. The Japan Socialist Party formed in 1906 lasted longer: it was banned in 1907.

There was also extreme right-wing political activity which until 1945 was tolerated by the government, even though it was not formal public activity, and was often overtly violent and destructive. Such behaviour was the policy of secret societies, who often were not at all secret, especially to bodies like the military police, the *kempei-tai*, one of the most efficient of their kind. From the time of the Restoration these ultra-right-wing groups were present and influential in Japanese society. An exemplary figure in such a context is Toyama Mitsuru. Born in 1855, son of a *samurai*, he was involved in some of the most dramatic acts of violence for more than half a century. He was, for example, implicated in the 'Dark Ocean' Society bomb attack on Okuma Shigenobu in 1889, but like many of his kind was released after arrest. He was an *agent provocateur* in Korea before the war with China in 1894, and he was the founder of at least one of the violent secret societies which kept radicalism at bay during three imperial reigns, Meiji, Taisho and Showa. This was the Amur River Society, also called the Black Dragon. Since revolutions bring together odd allies, he was an adviser to the new Chinese republican government of Sun Yat-sen in 1911, a significant indicator of his status, which was clearly more than that of an organiser of slum dwellers. People like Toyama, able to organise, popular in poorer circles, supported by the right wing, and above all ruthless, are an important component of the modern Japanese political spectrum; as are the societies which cloaked them. As to the activities of Toyama, there is an agreed body of knowledge, which is surrounded by evidence of varying degrees of reliability: which is to be expected in any analysis of a secret society.[33]

While there were people in the new Japan who were anxious to maintain stability, and others who wanted a share in government, there were also those who were involved in the prime reason, or so it seemed to them, for interacting with the west. These were the businessmen and industrialists, who had felt most frustrated with the inelasticity of the shogunal government. The Meiji Era was a period of remarkable industrial growth, with the establishment of factories, and the building of railways and ports to service their products. This growth was helped a great deal by foreigners, some of whom like Adams in the seventeenth century, have become respected historical figures in Japan. The period also witnessed the origins of yet another singularly Japanese phenomenon, the *zaibatsu*.

Zaibatsu means something like wealthy estate. What it came to mean was a small number of companies which were so powerful and wealthy that they were a major force in society. Their importance can be gauged from the fact that the Occupation forces after 1945 determined to dismantle them, and in the event failed to do so. There is considerable debate about what constitutes *zaibatsu*, and the period from which the term should be used, but the central facts are that they certainly include the Mitsui, Mitsubishi, Sumitomo and Yasuda companies; that they were controlled by families; and that their wealth was founded upon the buying of state-initiated companies at very low cost. They dominated every part of the financial, commercial and industrial structures of Japan, attracted opprobrium, and influenced politicians. From the infancy of Japanese political parties they supported those which might further their interests. After the foundation of the several parties, Mitsui was associated with the Liberal Party and Mitsubishi with the Constitutional Reform party. There is nothing unusual in this alliance with political parties on the part of companies, in Japan or anywhere else. What distinguished the *zaibatsu* was their size and their consequent influence on the direction of Japanese affairs. Their most visible effect was in the production of goods, and in particular

33 See the entry under 'Toyama Mitsuru' by Harada Katsumasa in *Kodansha Encyclopedia*, and Bergamini, *Japan's Imperial Conspiracy, passim.*

armaments which helped to enable Japan to win two spectacular wars.[34]

The issue of extraterritoriality was finally settled in a new treaty with Britain in 1894, and soon afterwards other nations followed suit. The conclusion of these treaties was of ultimate significance in Japan. Rightly or wrongly, the Japanese had regarded the issue as being a clear indication of their inferiority. The importance of the change cannot be exaggerated. Okuma, in addressing the problem of extraterritoriality, had made proposals which resulted in his being the victim of a bomb attack in which he lost a leg. Now, in the judgement of the Japanese authorities, their country was accepted by the European powers, and they were now in the club which was entitled to create empires.

Also in 1894, the time appeared to be ready for the long-cherished takeover of Korea. In that year in Korea there was a rebellion by a group called the Tonghak. China, which had always regarded Korea as one of its subject states, sent the military to support the Korean king. Japan then sent troops, recognising the weakness of the Chinese and the strength of the opportunity. In July 1894 the Japanese attacked the Korean royal palace, and forced the king to expel the Chinese. The violence escalated a few days later when the Japanese navy sank a Chinese troopship, and after more warfare, by early 1895 they had occupied Korea, the Liaotung, which we will call the Kwantung, peninsula in Manchuria, and Port Arthur at its tip. The Japanese navy also commanded the seaways.

The Japanese felt triumphant. The popular foreign writer Lafcadio Hearn, resident in Japan at the time, describes the delight with which the returning soldiers were greeted, and how he shared in that delight. 'Japan' he wrote 'has neither fears nor doubts'.[35] He made a good point. The Treaty of Shimonoseki of April 1895 consolidated Japanese pride. Under it Japan would possess Formosa (Taiwan) the nearby Pescadores islands, the Kwantung peninsula, and Port Arthur. These were considerable acquisitions, so considerable indeed that western powers began both to take Japan seriously and to worry about the potential she displayed for intrusion into what seemed, evidently, European spheres of influence.

There then occurred one of the western actions which added to the stock of distrust and resentment felt by Japan about the west. It was the 'Triple Intervention' by Russia, France and Germany, which

---

34 For an indication of the complexity of *zaibatsu* see the entry in *Kodansha Encyclopedia* by Hadley, Eleanor M.

35 Lafcadio Hearn, *Kokoro* (Tokyo, 1972), Chapter VI *passim.*

cautioned, or as the Japanese believed instructed, Japan about the excesses of the Shimonoseki treaty. Despite the anger felt and displayed in Japan, the amended treaty was still a considerable triumph for Japan. It guaranteed the 'independence' of Korea, which meant that the way was open for Japanese conquest, a huge indemnity from China equal to about three times the Japanese national budget of 1894, and still the possession of Formosa and the neighbouring Pescadores islands. But Japan had to give up its claim to the Kwantung peninsula and Port Arthur.

The effects of this war in Japan, and in the world, were transformative. The west began to take Japan seriously, and to take into account strategies to deal with what the German kaiser called 'the yellow peril'. The western powers' response was to increase ambition in China, a notable, but not singular, example being the German target of the rich province of Shandong. This multi-nation interest in China saved that country, at least in the short term, from total domination by both Japan and Russia; a prospect which in the light of more recent experience is fanciful indeed. Again, in the short term Russia benefited because China had to agree to the building of a railway across the Kwantung peninsula, and Russian control of Dairen and Port Arthur. This was an arrangement which promised to solve a perennial Russian, and later Soviet, problem which was the need for access to ice-free ports.

In Japan, when the anger over the amelioration of the treaty had subsided, there was still national pride. It was a pride which, combined with the classic isolation of Japan, was to lead to an erroneous evaluation of Japan's invincibility. It created a conviction that the Japanese, because of their racial, religious and physical inheritance were invincible. It was the route to the Pacific War, and the next war after the 1894 China war set a new standard of conviction in national, racial excellence. Most damaging was a belief that the victory over China proved that the Japanese military were unstoppable, and so, logically, those in government who demanded a strong army were right. And so, the powerful people in Japan considered what to do next. At the end of the nineteenth century, apart from confusion about China, and contempt for Korea, the natural foe seemed to be, and remained until the downfall of Communism, Russia.

The historic explosive relationship between Japan and Russia, anxiously monitored by China and the western powers did not diminish after the Treaty of Shimonoseki. On the contrary the building of the railway, and the takeover of Port Arthur by the

Russians, and the continued build-up of troops by the latter, ostensibly because of continuing instability in China, notably the Boxer uprising, made the situation more volatile than ever. Japan was especially anxious over supposed Russian ambitions towards their prize, Korea. Because of the situation, Japan began to realise the need for an anti-Russian ally, and it was to Britain, also in need of allies, that she turned. An alliance was signed in 1902, which recognised Japan's special interest in Korea, and very importantly, if war broke out between Japan and Russia, provided no other country supported the latter, Britain would remain neutral.

The combination of Russian intransigence about their rights in Manchuria and in Korea, and growing Japanese confidence, together with wide popular support made war inevitable, and in February 1904, negotiations were broken of, and hostilities began. It turned out to be a most spectacular affair. The Russians moved into Korea, and the Japanese did likewise. The Japanese navy began the action which was to make it world famous by attacking Russian shipping in Chemulpo harbour and Port Arthur. The focus of the war rapidly became on land Port Arthur, and at sea the need to stop the Russian Baltic Fleet. In the land battles, the casualties were huge. The army commander Nogi Marasuke who was an important architect of the system which deliberately brutalised the Japanese soldiery, was determined to win whatever the cost. The cost was some 60,000 Japanese casualties,[36] including, famously, Nogi's two sons. But Port Arthur was taken.

Meanwhile at sea, another Japanese commander was in the process of becoming a legend. Admiral Togo Heihachiro was already a hero because of his exploits in the Sino-Japanese war. He was yet another excellent example of learning from the west. As a young man he had served on a 1,200 ton steamer with six guns, wearing *kimono*. In 1871, some five years later he went, with other naval officers, to the British nautical college on the Thames, and thence to sea on a British warship. At the beginning of the war with Russia, he was the commander of the imperial fleet. His flagship was the 'Mikasa', British built and the biggest warship afloat. He was in command of about one hundred ships, many built in Britain, ready to face the Russians, who had the third largest fleet in the world. The Russians were disadvantaged because they had the limp backing of an inefficient government. They were compelled to sail from the Baltic round the Cape of Good Hope, because the British would

36 Storry, *A History of Modern Japan*, p. 140.

not let them use the Suez Canal. This journey took from October 1904 until May 1905. Togo guessed correctly that they would steam through the Tsushima Straits, between Korea and Japan, and it was there that in a most unconventional, seemingly risky piece of seamanship, he sank or captured some thirty-eight vessels. Two escaped, and Togo lost three torpedo boats. This victory was no doubt a final indication that the Satsuma clan, personified in Togo and many of his officers who had rebelled against their emperor, were now amongst his most loyal subjects.[37]

President Theodore Roosevelt was asked to negotiate a peace, for which both countries were very ready. This was settled in the Treaty of Portsmouth, New Hampshire in the autumn of 1905. The Russians conceded Japan's 'interests' in Korea, and transferred the Kwantung peninsula, a section of the Manchurian railway and the southern half of Sakhalin island to Japan. The Japanese public regarded this as very unsatisfactory. They had of course been encouraged to believe that Russia had been virtually destroyed, and when indemnities were not included, the Japanese public demanded the resignation, and even the deaths, of the politicians. When it became clear that the Americans had supported the Russians, fuel was added to the xenophobia, deeply rooted in the Japanese historical consciousness, and heightened by the western reaction to paramount Japanese military success.

The dramatic victories of the Japanese over the Chinese and the Russians, while they astonished the world, for good reason increased the credibility of the military in Japan. The nascent or active political parties joined in the rejoicing, and for the most part advocated further imperial advance. Such success was to provide proof that the ancient beliefs, put forward as an explanation for Japan's new dignity, were enough. It was the military 'spirit', the persistent theme, which was the only acceptable proven way. Such major political developments occupied the powerful, as they have occupied mainstream historians. But the common people were affected by such great change, and not always to their advantage.

---

37 For an account of this famous event see: Busch, Noel F., *The Emperor's Sword: Japan versus Russia in the Battle of Tsushima* (New York, 1969).

CHAPTER FOUR

Japan's Outcastes: Discrimination Then; Discrimination Now

Overleaf ▶

Japan's Outcastes:
Discrimination Then; Discrimination Now

The term outcaste is both ugly and offensive, but it is an accurate description of a group of people in society who are set apart and not accepted, often for no rational reason, other than the fact that the majority group creates myths and social fabric which keeps the relationship unchanged. Outcaste groups are commonly found in Asian societies. The best known is that of India, but they exist in, among other countries, China, Tibet and Korea. They have several common denominational features, such as association with unclean or lowly occupations; disposing of the dead is just one example. It is also commonly believed that outcastes have alien ancestry which reinforces the belief of the majority community in their own racial purity and superiority. In such respects the Japanese outcastes are very typical. The history of this group provides something of a case study of the scale of social change after the Restoration, and the upheaval which accompanied it. This history shows too that economic circumstances may change radically while tracts of social life can stay intact. It also illustrates that Japanese society in the Edo Era was more complex than the received account indicates; that is the division into four classes, *samurai*, peasants, artisans and merchants. Even the lowest group was fractionised, containing at least two major groups.

The first group is called *hinin*, which means literally non-person. In this category could be found people such as beggars, prostitutes, and former members of more respectable groups. In historical times it was possible for such people to gain, or regain status in those respectable groups. They did not carry the stigma of hereditary pollution with which the group at the bottom of the society was burdened. This stratum historically was called *eta*, which means roughly 'much filth'. It was an official term in Tokugawa times, and is still used in informal conversation at the present time, as are racist terms of abuse in many parts of the world. In historical times the collective term for *hinin* and *eta* was *semmin*, which means 'base people'.

The existence of a group such as the *eta*, and its persistence in modern times, albeit with a less offensive title, is notable because of an especially irrational phenomenon. Generally, discrimination is based upon clear physical differences. The low status of people of African origin and indigenous people in the Americas, the typical demarcations of now-defunct European empires, the contempt displayed towards aboriginal people in Australia, and many other examples are based, however foolishly or unjustly, substantially on appearance. Even in Japan the Ainu historically, and even it is claimed today, can be distinguished, as can to some extent Koreans. The latter in any case can be identified in a variety of ways. The curiosity in Japan is that there was no physical difference between the *ippan* – commonly a term used for the majority – and the *eta*. The difference was not, and is not, one of race, but of hard social division. The nearest parallels might be with India, where it is not easy to distinguish outcastes from most Indians, or with Tibet.

Another curiosity of the Japanese situation is that despite the absence of physical difference, in all important respects the attempts in the last hundred years to demolish barriers have failed. Later, we shall see what action has been taken. Even more curious is that present day Japanese, especially in urban areas, for the most part not only do not have personal contact with the sub-group, but often do not know of their existence. A remarkable example is that of one of the most eminent of authorities on the subject, Wagatsuma Hiroshi, himself a Japanese, knew nothing of their presence in Japanese society until he was eighteen.[1] The existence of what were called, until the Meiji Era, the *eta*, is first recorded in the thirteenth century, but it is likely that the group existed before then.[2] Even if the precise term was not used, there is evidence of the existence of social groups which performed 'unclean' tasks, such as street cleaning and work with animals, and animal products, notably leather. There may well have been a diversity of backgrounds of the people who came to be *eta*. They may have included people from

1 Strong, Kenneth, Translators' Introduction, Shimazaki Toson, *The Broken Commandment* (Tokyo, 1974), p. ix.

2 Early and highly regarded work on the *eta* was carried out by Ninomiya Shigeaki. 'An inquiry concerning the origin, development, and present situation of the *eta* in relation to the history of social classes in Japan', *Transactions of the Asiatic Society of Japan*, Vol. 10, pp. 47–154, 1933. See De Vos, George and Wagatsuma, Hiroshi, *Japan's Invisible Race: Caste in Culture and Personality* (California, 1967).

the families of *samurai*, farmers and merchants who had encountered bad times or bad luck. Further, as Professor Hirasawa has pointed out to the writer, in a private letter, the 'processes of outcaste group formation differed from one area to another'.

Important consolidatory changes were introduced upon the establishment of a new shogunate by Tokugawa Ieyasu in 1603. This brought to an end over two hundred years of civil war and anarchy. A first priority was to establish a style of government notably authoritarian and intrusive, which would ensure that there would be no resurrection of that anarchy. Such intrusion necessitated the detailed regulation of life at all levels of society, and part of that process was the formalising of a rigid class/caste system. In the case of the *eta* their position was defined, fixed and immutable, and as has commonly happened in authoritarian societies, it was a position justified on grounds of birth, degeneracy, race or alien origin.

All such factors, at different times and to varying degrees, have been used to justify the treatment of the *eta*. It was believed, and is still believed, that their ancestors were not Japanese at all. Attempts have been made, amongst others, to prove that they are the descendants of Korean prisoners, or immigrants from somewhere in the lands surrounding Japan. The intellectual standard of such claims can be compared with the attempt to find the legendary lost tribe of Israel. Put shortly, serious investigation has never found a shred of evidence to support the theory of alien ancestry.

Some religions, notably Christianity, have been able to provide powerful force from biblical and other sources for discrimination against people of different race. Such support was and remains, a crucial integrative factor in the pattern of social relations in South Africa, or some American states. The major religions of Japan, except for some minority Christian sects in this century, are not prone to the kind of dogma which affects social relationships. But whilst religion in Japan has not added to the tribulations of *eta* life, it has not been active in encouraging change. The *eta* were as religious as their *ippan* neighbours, and were, substantially members of the True Pure Land Sect of Buddhism. Indeed in the novel by Shimazaki Toson *The Broken Commandment*[3] the outcaste hero lodges in a temple of the sect. Despite the claims of universal values which are a central feature of most religions, this Buddhist sect meant, for the *eta*, segregated temples. Yet, in the way that such groups manage to

3 See note 1.

do, the *eta* seem to have accepted the contradiction between religious claims and practice.

Throughout the Tokugawa shogunate the position of the *eta* seems to have been stable, and disadvantaged. From time to time new abuses would be enacted, often by local authorities. Commonly, they had to wear distinctive clothing, or were not allowed, for example, to use umbrellas unless it was raining, or were not allowed to cross the entrance to an *ippan* household. Visible demarcation by clothes is both common and pernicious, and has been used widely, from the red hats of the Jews of medieval Italy to the Star of David emblem in Nazi Germany. Other restrictions were firmly in place. They had to live in their own communities, and could not leave during the hours of darkness. They had to marry within their own group, and were not allowed into the shrines or temples of the *ippan*.[4] Most important in many respects was their restriction to certain occupations, generally unpleasant, and commonly regarded as unclean or polluting, definitions which arose from religious doctrine. And one of the most clear-cut of these was the slaughtering of animals. This had two dimensions.

The first was to do with religious belief about animals. Both *Shinto* and Buddhism disapproved of the eating of animals. The Japanese population did not commonly eat meat, apart from that of some wild animals, until encouraged to do so in the Meiji Era. The *eta* did – another source of contempt. In addition, traditional *Shinto* belief is that matters associated with death are unclean. In the case of humans, even the washing of a corpse was work for the *eta*; a striking parallel with the work done by the lowest in Tibetan society, which is the dismemberment of corpses and the feeding of them to vultures. Add to such inhibition Buddhist condemnation of the killing of animals, and the low status of working with animals can be appreciated. The *eta* seem also to have been confined to work for which there was no such 'rational' explanation. An example is that of making weapons, although it has been suggested that perhaps the fact that leather was often a component of weapons was a reason.

So during the Edo Era, the *eta* were labelled, identifiable, and hedged about with restrictions. Prejudice was accepted as a social norm, and discrimination was enshrined in law. However obedient people were to the rules of social order, in a situation where privilege and powerlessness faced each other, there was bound to be friction. And so there was, in some episodes which were to become

4 These and other examples are set out in Hane Mikiso, *Peasants, Rebels and Outcastes: The Underside of Modern Japan* (New York, 1982), pp. 142–3.

legendary. One of these occurred in the closing years of the Edo Era. In 1859, an *eta* youth tried to enter a *Shinto* shrine in Edo (Tokyo) and fighting broke out. He was beaten to death. The leader of the *eta* community, who carried the hereditary title *Danzaemon*, appealed to the magistrate for justice. In a complete and timeless summary of the injustice meted out to the powerless, the official ruled that seven *eta* were worth one ordinary citizen. It followed that justice demanded that the guilty party would have to kill another six *eta* if he was to be punished.[5]

The position of *Danzaemon* is interesting in the context of *eta* life. The title seems to have become hereditary in the early years of the Edo Era, perhaps as another piece in the consolidation of social structure. The *bakufu* seems to have approved, and until the Restoration he was often a man wielding considerable power. At that time he lived in a large mansion, with a shoe factory within the large garden surrounding the mansion, and a monopoly on the production and sale of leather goods. He controlled thousands of households in the Tokyo area, and beyond, organised their work, taxed them and had legal jurisdiction over them. It was altogether a remarkable position.[6] It is some indication of the fact that the structure of the Japanese outcaste community is not monolithic. Like any other it has hierarchies, and roles within it.[7] It also demonstrates, and there is evidence to support the fact, that financial success was possible for individual members of the community. Yet however prosperous a man might be, or however large his estate, it was located in the *eta* area of the town or village, and all the usual restrictions remained firmly in place.

The final collapse of the shogunate and the restoration of the emperor led to major upheaval in Japanese traditional society. For the *eta* people there was a major reform, which was the passing of the Edict of Emancipation in 1871. On the face of it, this could only bring benefit to the 281,311 *eta* enumerated in the national census of that year, which listed a population in Japan of some thirty million people. The *eta* figure did not include *hinin* and other fringe groups. It was a legal statement from an authoritarian government that the *eta* were not slaves but full members of a new Japanese state. Although the Edict was part of Japan's awareness of the process

5 Ibid., p. 142, quoting Tsuchikata Tetsu, *Hi-Sabetsuburaku no Tatakai* (Tokyo, 1973).

6 De Vos and Wagatsuma, *Japan's Invisible Race*, pp. 28–9.

7 Ibid., where several chapters deal with the complexity of the social structure of the community.

whereby a state appeared modern, it also indicated that discriminatory behaviour would no longer receive official support. As in the
United States at about the same time, the Edict was an important
statement of intent. But as in the United States, emancipation
brought disadvantages since, paradoxically, like black slaves the *eta*
had derived some benefits from their status. The fact that they were
confined to certain occupations meant that *ippan* would not do such
work. Often indeed they had an effective or real monopoly as in the
rather spectacular case of *Danzaemon* over leather work. Now the *de
facto* monopoly was broken, and one of the first casualties was
Danzaemon himself, whose social and economic power quickly
disappeared. As well as this, emancipation brought another economic blow. The *eta* had always been exempt from the taxes paid by
the *ippan*, probably because of the wretched nature of their lives.
Now, like all other Japanese they had to pay taxes. De Vos and
Wagatsuma suggest some unprincipled reasons for emancipation.
These include a general wish by the new oligarchy to destroy the old
regime, and replace it with one of their own. The Edict also meant
that the former *eta* could now be taxed to the advantage of the
state.[8] Finally, although the term *eta* was no longer acceptable, the
community was given a new name, *shin heimin* – new commoners.
Although this was not as offensive as the old, it nevertheless labelled
people and continued to make them identifiable.

Despite the legal change of status, which again should be emphasised as a significant political act, the relationship of the 'new'
commoners with 'old' did not change, except for the worse. They
bore some of the brunt of the resentment of people about major
disruption in a society which had in theory, and substantially in
practice, remained unchanged for two hundred and fifty years. Like
the dispossessed, degraded and disarmed *samurai*, commoners saw
these changes as undermining their privilege, and posing a general
threat to the fabric of society. This resentment often led to violent
confrontation and even '*eta* hunts' which are reminiscent of the
hunting and killing of aboriginal people by Australian settlers, or
the rewards offered for the heads of Indians by Argentinian authorities at the close of the nineteenth century. There are many
examples of riots over the newly accorded freedom in Japan. In
1872, a year after the Edict, the new commoners in a village in Nara
announced to their neighbours that as they were now free, they
would no longer do the village's dirty work. The villagers retaliated

8 Ibid., p. 34.

by forbidding them to collect firewood, and during the escalation, four new commoners were killed. Angry at the new prefectural government's arrest of the ringleaders, the villagers attacked again. But the authorities were firm, and three of the ringleaders were executed.

In the next year in the region of Okayama prefecture, which had had a substantial number of *eta* there occurred what is generally known as the Mimasaka riot. This started with a rumour that a stranger dressed in white was wandering about. The villagers believed that he was in some way connected with the *eta*, and failing to find him attacked several *eta* villages. The upshot was that a mob of about 26,000 destroyed fifteen school buildings, three hundred *eta* houses, and official houses. They killed at least eighteen *eta* and wounded eleven. No doubt the rioters blamed the officials for their association with the changes. Eventually, after seven days of killing and destruction, the mob was subdued. It took troops, officials and three hundred ex-*samurai* to achieve this. The *samurai* who were in plentiful supply since their class had just been abolished, drove the rioters away from the government buildings.[9] That three hundred could fend off a mob of thousands is a telling comment on the power of the *samurai*. Nor was this an isolated case.

Sometimes a local authority would show its reluctance to accept the new society. In 1870, a year before the Edict, when in any case *Danzaemon* and several other important figures had already been emancipated, thus adding to the certainty that legislation was nigh, the Wakayama region issued a statement. In one of the last autonomous acts of an old regional authority, it sought to add to the restrictions of *eta* life. Such people had to walk 'at the edge of one side of the street', could only wear sandals, and could not use umbrellas or headwear, except in the rain. Of particular nastiness in the context of Japanese tradition was that they were not allowed out after nine o'clock on New Year's Eve, even inside their own communities. The reasons for the imposition of these and other restrictions were that their morality 'was not good' and that 'they often act viciously'.[10] In 1880 the Ministry of Justice, no less, published a 'Handbook of Japanese Customs and Folkways' which described the *eta* and *hinin* as 'the lowliest of all people almost like

9 Ibid., pp. 36–7 sets out a detailed account.
10 Donoghue, John D., 'An *eta* community in Northern Japan: A study of intra group relations' unpublished Ph.D. dissertation, University of Chicago, 1956, p. 43 quoted De Vos and Wagatsuma, *Japan's Invisible Race*, p. 24. However, a Japanese expert has informed me that this episode 'is not recognised as important by *buraku* historians'.

animals',[11] thus providing a good example of the tension and discrepancy over the speed of official social change and the reality of social feeling.

Any hope that matters might improve, as Japan continued its phenomenal growth in the Meiji Era, were soon dashed. Examples are not difficult to find. In 1916 a village in Gifu prefecture decided that it had had enough of what were coming to be called the *burakumin*, meaning 'hamlet dwellers'. The term has long been used as a euphemism for the historically outcaste group. Clearly, it identifies them as unmistakably as the ancient term. In that year the *ippan* section of the village put out a notice which referred to the people living at the edge of the village as 'of a low and vulgar race of people known as the new commoners formerly called *eta*', who 'recognised the fact that they were odious people'. But since the restoration of imperial authority, their conduct 'has become haughtier with each passing day'. What seems to have upset the villagers was that a *burakumin* had bought land from an *ippan*, and intended to build a house. A pledge was drawn up, with seven rules, emphasising that there were to be no friendly relations, no sharing of food or drink, and a host of other conditions designed to restore the old relationships. One part of the pledge pointed out that the village would hire someone to look after animals: an interesting comment on the erosion of *burakumin* occupational monopoly. As Hane points out: 'Sixty-three households signed the pledge, designed to repress a small group of about ten *burakumin* families.'[12]

The human dimension behind such bold facts is well documented. There are first hand accounts by labourers who were treated in a manner which would normally be regarded as repugnant in a society which is famed for its courtesy:

> When we used to go to work for farmers, we were given tea in chipped bowls on the dirt floor by the kitchen. If we asked for a match to light our tobacco, they would throw it to us from the house. We weren't treated like human beings at all.[13]

An especially moving account of the world of the new commoners is given in *The Broken Commandment* which was written in 1906.[14] The fact that it has been in print ever since is a perplexing comment on

11 De Vos and Wagatsuma, *Japan's Invisible Race*, pp. 37–8.
12 Hane, *Peasants, Rebels and Outcastes*, p. 145.
13 Ibid., p. 147, quoting Shibata, *Hi-sabetsuburaku no Densho to Seikatsu*, pp. 200–1.
14 See note 1.

Japanese attitudes. Based upon fact, it is the story of a new commoner teacher who spends his life trying, and ultimately failing, to conceal his origins. As part of the narrative, the fate of the hero is reflected in the misery of the one boy from the same background. The writer observes the commonplace: that no one would speak to him or play with him, a situation which has often been related by real people who spent years of profound unhappiness as children in school. Apart from the fact that the book has become a classic of Japanese literature, it is a quintessential account of the relentlessness of mass discrimination, in this case in Japan. Especially noteworthy is the fact that the novel exhibits the irrational nature of prejudice, since relationships are normal before the revelation of the teacher's origins.

The ambiguity of the place of the *burakumin* in Japanese society, and the ambivalence of majority Japanese to that place is summed up well by their position in the military. One of the most important aspects of modern Japanese history, as we shall see, has been the rise of the military. Modern forces, especially the army, reflect the power of traditional hierarchies which may be in a process of decay or disintegration. The post-Restoration army was soon dominated by the ancient and powerful Choshu clan. But a modern army cannot fight and win on a basis of privilege alone. Those that try to do so in the twentieth century lose wars. There is a need for talent, skill, intelligence and numbers which elites cannot provide.

Japan, as we have seen, from 1894 onwards was engaged in a number of spectacular wars, often suffering appalling casualties. The answer to the question as to whether or not lower classes or ethnic groups should be allowed to fight and die for their country, was answered in Japan as elsewhere: they should. The position of the *burakumin* was classic. Although subject to the appalling social disability described, and despite being held in such contempt, like Koreans they were permitted to serve the emperor. Having been recruited to do so however, their position in the military was restricted. The ever pragmatic Yamagata Aritomo had assigned them to shoe repair, but this did not diminish the fury of lower-class people at the idea of the former *eta* being recruited, with consequent violent reaction in a number of cities.[15] There is no record of numbers of any size serving in the navy, which is generally the elite service. In the army, they did not serve in the Imperial Guards. They were put into second grade units, and even then there was

15 Hackett, Roger F. *Yamagata Aritomo in the Rise of Modern Japan, 1838–1922* (Harvard, 1971), p. 68.

minimal promotion.[16] Official lists of servicemen had the word *toku*, meaning special, against their names.[17] Added to such familiar indignities was the notorious physical brutality of the Imperial Japanese Army, which would have been directed at them both as junior ranks, and as *burakumin*.

It was in the army that an early significant, and because it was in the army famous, protest about discrimination took place. The new *burakumin* pressure group the Levellers had, in 1926, protested about discrimination and brutality in the army. This led to the arrest of the protesters who were charged with plotting sabotage.[18] The next event took place in 1927, when a regiment with a large proportion of *burakumin* paraded before the emperor. The soldier involved in the incident was called Kitahara Taisaku, a twenty-year-old who later gave an account of what happened. As the emperor approached he rushed from his place in the ranks, knelt down, and held up a petition protesting about the treatment of the *burakumin* in the army. He was quickly removed, but the concomitant and consequent fury may be imagined. One pathetic effect was that Kitahara's brother-in-law learned through these events that his wife came from a *burakumin* family, and he deserted his family.[19] Finally, we will see how the request of the Korean community to erect memorials to their dead at Hiroshima and Nagasaki have been denied. Similarly, the names of *burakumin* who were killed in action did not appear on war memorials.

Such events, and the persistence of institutionalised discrimination challenged the manifest intention of the rulers of Japan to be a 'modern' state. The difficulty lay in the fact that for at least one hundred and fifty years the countries of north Asia have been caught in a dilemma: the wish to change nothing, and the need to change everything. China notably is still unable to develop a means of coping with this. As we have seen Japan has been more successful, although the tension is clear even in political debate at the present time. In the context of the present discussion, the post-Meiji advocacy of change necessitated not only an improved industrial base, but as an accompaniment a loosening of all kinds of cultural and social barriers.

16 Hane, *Peasants, Rebels and Outcastes*, p. 150.
17 Minority Rights Group, *Japan's Minorities: Burakumin, Koreans, Ainu, Okinawans* (London, 1983), p. 5.
18 Hane, *Peasants, Rebels and Outcastes*, p. 151.
19 Ibid., p. 148, quoting Kitahara Taisaku, *Senmin no Koei* (Tokyo, 1974). A series of extracts from this autobiographical account appears in Hane, *Peasants, Rebels and Outcastes*, pp. 163ff.

It was some awareness of this which led to occasional government action to make the 1871 Edict an agent of change. It should be stressed that the enactment of the Edict was an important demonstration of intent. Such a measure was the establishment in 1913 of the Imperial Path of Justice Association. The Ministry of Internal Affairs helped *burakumin* leaders to establish this body to coordinate the several attempts being made to deal with the problems. In the prospectus there was talk of equality and removal of 'all evil customs', all of which was justified by 'our wish to observe the holy Imperial will of the late Emperor Meiji'.[20] Again, after the Kitahara incident described above, although some powerful figures sought to ascribe selfish motives for his action, others, including very conservative figures, made it clear that they wanted a change in the attitude to the *burakumin* in the armed services and in civilian life. But one factor may have been the awareness of revolutionary events in Europe, which Japanese authorities observed in the policies of some Japanese organisations.

The question always arises as to what a government can do, even if unanimously agreed, to reduce discrimination. They can outlaw racist acts, or engage in 'reverse or positive discrimination' where preference is given to minorities. Such policies, notably in India, often lead to resentment and violence, but they are an important demonstration. The truth is that such legislation can only hope to curb excess. Certainly in Japan the *burakumin* seem to have learned very early that agitation, and indeed aggressive behaviour, would do a good deal to improve their situation.

The first notable *burakumin* organisation was modest. In 1902 a small group established a Common People's Association in Okayama prefecture. In the next year another group was organised in Kyoto, another area with a large *burakumin* population, called the Great Japan Fraternal Conciliation Society. The beginning of government interest has already been mentioned in its encouragement to set up the Imperial Path of Justice Association. Naturally, these and other small groups wanted to eradicate discrimination. But their programmes for doing so assumed that the fault lay with their own people: That is to say they accepted the image held by the majority as justified, and so their several programmes advocated the plethora of reform and self-help which was so common in European nineteenth-century organisations of the kind.[21] By 1919 the mood

20 De Vos and Wagatsuma, *Japan's Invisible Race*, pp. 39–40.
21 Details of such *burakumin* organisations can be found in De Vos and Wagatsuma, *Japan's Invisible Race*, Section 11.

was rather different. In that year a Sympathetic Reconciliation Congress was held attended by *burakumin* leaders, members of both Houses of the Diet, military officials, and a wide cross-section of Japanese society. Out of this came demands for equality in employment, abolition of discriminatory language, and economic aid. One result was that in 1920 the government gave a subsidy to improve conditions for the first time.

A lot had changed during the previous ten years to make the *burakumin* more demanding and the government, as least ostensibly, more helpful. There were, firstly, the lessons of the First World War, one of which was that systems, and the distribution of power within those systems, were not immutable. The increase in the size of the Japanese Empire was clear proof. But the war had given hope to minorities, and the expectations of both the *burakumin* in Japan, and the people of colonised Korea, were raised on that account. The second, and consequent factor was the March First Movement in Korea, which alarmed the Japanese colonial government. But above all the successful revolution in Russia provided powerful lessons, some optimistic, some pessimistic, for everyone. Japan itself was experimenting, albeit modestly, with democratic institutions. This experiment continued despite, or perhaps because of the famous rice riots of 1918. The scale of these shocked the government, especially since, with the shortages and high prices affecting everybody, the whole community was in a state of turbulence. And: 'in all of these riots the *burakumin* were particularly active, often taking the initiative and leadership.'[22]

It was within the context of continuing discrimination, and these world events, that in Kyoto in 1922 the most important organisation so far was initiated. About 2,000 *burakumin* met to form the National Levellers Association, whose programme set a forceful tone, with demands for economic and occupational freedom. A declaration was read and accepted, which announced that they had had enough of insults. There was talk of unity, and the need for unity, and of the ruling class, indicating the emerging political maturity of these younger, mostly poorer *burakumin.* A flag was raised which symbolised the martyrdom of Christ, and the flagpole was a spear. Perhaps the most belligerent statement of intent was to 'denounce thoroughly and strictly those who insult us with derogatory words and deeds'.[23] Later children's and women's associations were formed. Although milder organisations continued to exist, it was the Lev-

22 Ibid., p. 41.
23 Ibid., p. 44.

ellers who were foremost in the various struggles until the Pacific War. They became well known for their confrontational tactics, and individuals who insulted them had to apologise, in writing, and often in a newspaper. From time to time, in the absence of action to redress injustice, there was violence. The establishment of the Levellers, in the words of Professor Hirasawa Yasumasa, 'marked the most important turning point in the history of the *buraku* movements'.[24]

But much of the energy of the Association was spent on factional fighting. This is not especially a characteristic of the *burakumin* or of the Japanese, but it seems to be a chronic feature of radical organisations. And so the political debates in a highly charged political era took place in the Association. There were communists, socialists of several persuasions, anarchists, religious adherents – Buddhism was a special issue – and moderates. A critical issue related to such debates was whether or not their people should ally with *ippan* people who were working class, farmers, or other similarly placed economic groups.

Despite the inevitable political differences, the Levellers made an impact and progress. At the fourth convention in Osaka in 1925, Matsumoto Jiichiro was elected Chairman. He was one of the most remarkable people in the emancipation movement. During the protests about treatment in the army, to which reference has been made, he was arrested in 1926, charged with plotting to destroy a barracks, and sentenced to three and a half years. During his time in prison the first general election, under the new electoral rules, for the House of Representatives took place. The Levellers put up three candidates, including Matsumoto, without success. But he was to prove, as we shall see, something of a political phenomenon.

By the end of the 1920s the brief flirtation with democracy was drawing to a close. In response to the growth of leftist and protest movements, which had surged as economic conditions began to deteriorate, the government carried out arrests of leaders and members of 'subversive' organisations, resulting in the collapse of some of them. But such persecution, together with the adverse economic conditions which affected the *burakumin* as much as anybody, led to reconciliation of disparate interests, and a new unity, at least for a few years. New petitions reiterating old demands were made to governments, and notorious cases were targeted. One of these was in 1933[25] when a *burakumin* man married an *ippan* girl.

24 Private comment to the author.
25 See De Vos and Wagatsuma, *Japan's Invisible Race*, pp. 58ff for details.

Later he and his brother were charged and convicted of not having told the girl of their background. They were sent to prison. The outcry was enormous. There were meetings and marches, and Matsumoto himself led delegations to the appropriate authorities. The consequence was that the men were released, and the bulk of Japanese society appears to have accepted the fact; perhaps because a lot had happened, and attitudes had moderated in the sixty-two years since the Edict of Emancipation.

The year 1936 witnessed a great victory, because in that year Matsumoto became the first from his community to be elected to the House of Representatives, a feat he repeated in the next year. Such a signal success, as well as the election of large numbers of socialists received a crippling blow with the Japanese invasion of China in 1937. This most disastrous of acts meant that the deeply felt nationalist instincts of the Japanese dominated sectarian interests. For a variety of reasons, and with differing degrees of enthusiasm, the several factions in the Levellers Association agreed that country must come first. It was even suggested in 1940 that the Association should be dissolved because of the war, but Matsumoto stopped that happening. In fact, during the war, it was moribund. Nor did the threats of the formidable Tojo government frighten him. Told in 1942 that it would not recommend him as a candidate for the Diet unless he abolished the Association: 'he replied that the organisation had come into existence because of a natural need and could not go out of existence until that need disappeared.'[26] Matsumoto was to remain a powerful political symbol.

The defeat of Japan in 1945 created high expectations amongst those millions of Japanese, sickened by the excesses of the military government, who hoped for fundamental change. The numbers, and suffering, of the opposition to that government amongst the Japanese are still not properly understood in the west. Apprehension at what the Occupation forces might do was quickly dispelled as it became clear that the primary task seemed to be to eradicate all traces of the old regime. In theory the Occupation force was a joint allied command. In practice the Supreme Commander Allied Powers, General Douglas MacArthur was in sole charge, and established himself as the most important westerner in Japanese history. The ways in which he set about destroying the old regime will be dealt with elsewhere. For the purpose of this discussion, it should be

---

26 Ibid., p. 60, quoting Matsumoto Jiichiro, *Buraku Kaiho e no Sanju Nen* (Tokyo, 1948).

noted that the principle of universal suffrage for the first time, and allowing hitherto proscribed organisations to form and reform raised the expectations of many, not least the *burakumin*. By 1946 representatives from pre-war groups, including the Levellers, had organised the National Committee for *Buraku* Liberation. In the next year the first general election was held under the new regime and the results were remarkable. Five *burakumin* were elected to the House of Representatives and two, one of whom was Matsumoto, were elected to the Upper House, the House of Councillors. Not only this, but he again made social history by being the first of his people to become Vice-Chairman of the House. This meant that he would also be the first to have an audience of the emperor which, to the horror of many, he declined. He also refused to bow in the classical manner to the emperor at the opening of the Diet in 1948. These were gestures which were to have serious repercussions.

The Prime Minister of the day was Yoshida Shigeru, a very conservative figure, and like many of his colleagues he regarded Matsumoto's attitude to the emperor as quite unacceptable. His revenge was a classic piece of Japanese manipulation of the often uninformed policies of the Occupation authorities. Yoshida wrote personally to MacArthur pointing out Matsumoto's connection with the Tojo government, and alleged that he had been a member of an ultranationalistic organisation which had been included in the purges under which SCAP had dismissed thousands of Japanese. 'In fairness' Yoshida wrote, 'Matsumoto should join them.' He was subsequently excluded from public service. The campaign for reinstatement included trade unions, political parties, overseas dignitaries and two-thirds of the Diet membership. But when in 1950, a Japanese appeal board recommended the depurging of 10,901 people, Yoshida added his recommendation to all except Matsumoto. After two and a half years, even Yoshida gave in, and Matsumoto was allowed back into public life, 'to great rejoicing'.[27]

Not surprisingly Matsumoto and the *burakumin* organisations became very anti-American, and anti-capitalist. This was exacerbated by the fact that a lot of *burakumin* land was requisitioned after 1945 to build American air bases as part of the defence strategy which, as we will see, became such an inflammatory issue. In defence, if such can be mounted of the Americans, it should be pointed out that it could not be expected that they would be aware

27 It was John Osborne, writing in 'Life' magazine, Vol. 29, No. 22, 1950 in an article 'My dear General' who exposed the matter. Quoted in De Vos and Wagatsuma, *Japan's Invisible Race*, pp. 70–1.

of the social dimensions of such actions.[28] In 1955 the National Committee for *Buraku* Liberation became the *Buraku* Liberation League, and its political programme now began to include specific anti-capitalist rhetoric. Although as a result of a split with the Japanese Communist Party in 1965, a splinter group called the National *Buraku* Liberation Movement Federation was set up, the League remains the most powerful representational organisation.

But these were heady and turbulent days, and much of the reaction to deeply ingrained tradition was extremely worrying to those Japanese who had held power, and despite SCAP's efforts, continued to do so. There were two broad reasons why they were able to keep Japanese society, in all respects, culturally and economically from fundamental change. There was firstly American concern about communist success in China and Korea, which in eight short years led from a determination to deny the re-creation of Japanese military forces to the establishment of such forces. There was also yet another manifestation of the skill of the Japanese in combating the west. Roughly, they acceded to American demands, sometimes after great pressure, knowing that eventually the occupying powers would leave, and they could undo those innovations of which they disapproved. This was the most signal characteristic of Japanese political behaviour during the post-war period.

Social conservatism was much less obvious, and in any case was not of such interest as the fundamental changes associated with, say, land reform or the creation of democratic government. And so the position of the *burakumin* changed little, and continues to change little. In the flurry of the aftermath of the war, Buddhist authorities did something to encourage better treatment, whilst the unions offered no support. In observing this however, it should be noted that Japanese unions are notably conservative, and have rarely taken a broad view of, or stand on, social issues. There is indeed a rival to the *Burakumin* Liberation League called the Integration Association, which eschews confrontation and believes in improvement through what might be called peaceful means.

The policy of confrontation was one which the *Buraku* Liberation League continued from pre-war days. Despite the turmoil of change in post-war Japan there were still plenty of occasions for militant action, and some of these became *causes célèbres*. There was a novel written in 1951 by a Kyoto health inspector which drew a picture of *burakumin* life as 'hell on earth', which paradoxically led to money

28 De Vos and Wagatsuma, *Japan's Invisible Race*, p. 80.

being spent on improvements. In 1957, after the Occupation there was uproar over the case of an American soldier's shooting of a *burakumin* woman.[29] To prove that there was much that still had to be changed, in 1961, there was a Grand March of Liberation from Fukuoka to Tokyo, sent off by Matsumoto.

The outcome of the post-war years is that the *burakumin* people today are in a position which would be recognisable to their ancestors. There are, naturally, some improvements, for example in the lessening of violent and offensive treatment, but there have been such improvements in all the lower strata of Japanese society. But *burakumin* continue to face the same difficulties as members of other groups in Japanese society, such as the Koreans, and in other societies.

Running throughout the history of relationships between the two groups is a corpus of mythological belief about the nature of the *burakumin*. Some of these beliefs are still adhered to, and some are universal features of inter-group hostility. These include the widespread notion that the outgroup smell differently, or that their smell is offensive. It is also believed that they are physically different; that they suffer from hereditary physical weakness or stigma; that they are physically repellent. In *The Broken Commandment* a group of *burakumin* slaughterhousemen are described as such, which caused a good deal of criticism to be directed towards the author. Such generalisations include some which are bizarre; that the males had no testicles, or that people had four fingers on each hand. The word *yotsu*, which is a term of abuse directed at *burakumin* means four, but as well as four-fingered, it alleges that they are four-legged like animals. In *The Broken Commandment*, when suspicion mounts that the hero is outcaste, behind his back a colleague raises four fingers. This perception was given 'official' validation in the famous Ministry of Justice document, mentioned earlier saying that they were 'almost resembling animals'. When the Japanese die, they are often given posthumous Buddhist names. Some temples gave dead *burakumin* the names of 'male beast' and 'female beast'.[30] Describing people as animals is always offensive, but in traditional Japanese culture where animals are categorised as especially unclean, it is particularly offensive.

As well as physical demarcation, based on fantasy, *burakumin* are regarded as possessed of undesirable behavioural characteristics. It

29 Ibid., pp. 78–82, details a number of such incidents.
30 Hane, *Peasants, Rebels and Outcastes*, p. 149, quoting Hiroshima *Buraku* Kaiho Kenkyujyo *Hiroshima-Ken Hi-sabetsuburaku no Rekishi* (Tokyo, 1975).

is believed, for example, that they display aggression towards each other, towards their children, and towards outsiders. Unlike many generalisations made about groups, it is conceded that in some cases this may be true. It is also claimed that *burakumin* engage in criminal behaviour. Again, it is to be expected that a deprived group would figure in reported crime. Crime, especially organised crime, is an accepted means of success amongst groups who are blocked from advancement through legitimate channels. Prostitution is a similar alternative for women, although not attended by the same approved status as activity in male organised crime. These are global generalisations, and it should be made clear that there are no official figures which show that *burakumin* are over-represented in criminal statistics. And there are other supposed behavioural features of which the majority group disapprove. These include the eating of food which the larger community despises. *Burakumin* have always eaten meat, an 'aberrant' act as we have seen, but when in the Meiji Era meat eating became acceptable, there were still limits. Thus *burakumin* predilection for offal,[31] notably tripe is regarded as degenerate. But this perception too has to be dealt with as a prejudice. It perhaps leaves out of account the fact that before meat-eating became usual after the Restoration, 'ordinary' Japanese ate selected meat, but that afterwards when meat was acceptable, poorer people were reduced to eating offal. This merely reinforces the fact that styles of eating are linked to status. It is also claimed that their standards of dress, and use of language leave a lot to be desired.

Like all groups which are the victims of discrimination, the *burakumin* sometimes share perceptions held by the larger community. The traditional, and lowly work in which they engage, is seen by them as a mark of their low status. 'Because' one remarked 'I am a shoemaker, everyone would know of my *buraku* origin'.[32] One survey noted that they agree that they are inferior in speech, and that they recognise as a 'moral flaw their propensity to coarse, crude, even violent behaviour', and also 'their stealing and reputation for acts provoking fear in others'.[33]

This account concludes with some observations about the present position of the *burakumin*. This is important because it illustrates the

31 Wagatsuma Hiroshi and De Vos, G., 'The Outcaste Tradition in Modern Japan: A Problem in Social Self Identity' in Dore, R.P. (ed.), *Aspects of Social Change in Modern Japan* (Princeton, 1967), p. 380.

32 Ibid., p. 353.

33 Ibid., p. 357 quoting Yamamoto Noboru, *Sabetsu ishiki to shinriteki kincho* (no date), p. 53.

enormous power of historical forces on modern Japanese society. Broadly speaking, their present position suggests parallels with such groups in many societies. It is also the case that the historic discrimination to which they have been subjected, and from which the nature and quality of their lives springs, is still in evidence. So the approximately two to three million *burakumin* living in some 6,000 *buraku*, or communities, are amongst the poorest people in Japan. This can be seen in the quality of housing, and health. In respect of the latter a 1982 survey in Osaka, which has a large *burakumin* community, 'showed that 24 per cent of *burakumin* are classified as suffering from ill health compared to 12 per cent nationally. *Burakumin* in particular were found to suffer from diseases connected with physical labour, diet or general housing and physical circumstances.'[34]

Like other such groups it has been pointed out that it is claimed that they are over-represented in criminal statistics. This is always a complicated matter, and cannot be explained, as the larger community tends to do, as due to evil or degenerate nature. It is no doubt the case that deviant behaviour arises in a depressed community for economic reasons, and that it is not inhibited by that 'respect' for the law which seems to be so important to the majority group. It has to be emphasised though that in the case of the *burakumin*, there is no firm evidence of any such connection.[35] Further, there is the matter of police behaviour, since it is a commonplace that the police tend to target such groups, in part because their behaviour is visible, and in part because the police share commonly held attitudes. Nor is it surprising that the *burakumin* have little respect for state agencies in general. There have been claims that wealthy members of the community claim benefit, and generally manipulate the welfare system. Familiar to British ears is the allegation that they interfere with the electricity meters.[36] If this is true, it would echo a common offence amongst the British poor.

At the root of their continuing low status is the question of employment. To begin with their rates of unemployment are high. In 1980 official figures showed that while average unemployment in Japan ran at 2.2 per cent, in *buraku* communities it was very much higher, in one prefecture as high as 50 per cent.[37] When they can

34 *Buraku* Liberation News, No. 10, July 1982, quoted in Minority Rights Group, *Japan's Minorities*, p. 8.
35 Professor Hirasawa, in a private comment, wished the difference between allegation and fact to be firmly stated.
36 De Vos and Wagatsuma, *Japan's Invisible Race*, p. 270.
37 Minority Rights Group, *Japan's Minorities*, p. 9.

get work, it is variously traditional, unskilled, and not as well paid as most jobs. They do not of course have a monopoly of low grade work, but they dominate it. Many organisations, including Japanese international companies refuse to appoint them at all, never mind to good positions.

The government has continued to demonstrate commitment, goaded in part by the determined monitoring of discrimination, and the publicising of it. The *Buraku* Liberation League has become a sophisticated organisation with an effective communications system, which includes an English language newspaper. As a result there have been both statements of principle and practical attempts by governments to improve the situation. Initiatives often by local authorities include the building of modern accommodation, and the development of welfare facilities. But such efforts are variable, and the total effect hardly transforming. The official policy, for some years, has been *dowa*, which means integration. It has a fairly long history, and its central pillar has always been education. In 1938 the Education Minister encouraged educational institutions to work towards abolishing discrimination, and *dowa* began to appear in organisational titles. In 1942 compulsory lectures on the subject were introduced into teacher training colleges.[38] Much of this was motivated by the need to maintain Japanese unity in the face of what was becoming a disastrous war. The *dowa* concept was especially encouraged, in the adversity of the day, to diminish the hostility displayed by the 'ordinary' soldiery against their *buraku* 'comrades'.

In more recent times there has been established a *Dowa* Policy Council. In 1965 it produced a Report on 'Basic Measure Relating to the *Dowa* Problem'. Noting that in the past, and even at present, the *burakumin* are identified by names which, even if unoffensive, intrinsically mark them out, the Report goes on to make an important admission of failure, and an important statement of intent. Because of its unequivocation it is worth quoting in full:

> In short, *buraku* discrimination in modern society means the violation of civil rights and liberties. These civil rights and liberties include the freedom to choose one's occupation, the right to be guaranteed equal opportunity in education, the freedom of choosing and changing residence, and freedom in marriage. Discrimination against the *Dowa* district residents indicates that these rights and liberties are not fully guaranteed to them in reality. Among such civil rights and liberties, the lack of a full guarantee of the freedom of choice of occupation – namely, equal employment opportunity – constitutes an

38 De Vos and Wagatsuma, *Japan's Invisible Race* (1966), p. 102.

especially serious problem. History shows that a prime factor in barring the path leading to the rise of social standing and emancipation was that the *Dowa* district residents were isolated from the productive process of principal industries in each period of history, and compelled to engage in miscellaneous menial jobs regarded as debased occupations. Moreover, this argument holds to the present day. Therefore, the fundamental requirement in the effort to settle the *Dowa* problem is to fully guarantee equal opportunity in employment and education to *Dowa* district residents, to bring the surplus population stagnating in the *Dowa* districts into the productive process of principal modern industries, and thereby to enhance the stability of their livelihood as well as their social position.

As a consequence a law on Special Measures for *Dowa* was passed. It was an attempt to 'enrich *Dowa* education in schools'. This law, which was to be in force for ten years, was subsequently extended. This included experimentation in pilot schools, and subsidies to encourage what are called *dowa* families to keep children at school.[39] In schools, as in other areas, *burakumin* children are over-represented in truancy, drop-out rates, and under-achievement.

Reflection upon the persisting, historic opposition to improvements in the status of *burakumin* leads to an expectation that there would be resentment. And so there was. The target was an inflammatory one – school textbooks. In Japan textbooks have been under government control since 1903, except during the Occupation, when SCAP banned such supervision. When the Occupation ceased, supervision was restored and now all school textbooks must be approved. This has led to some legendary social and legal arguments, famously what should appear as the account of the 'rape' of Nanjing in 1937. Part of the *dowa* education programme involves making all children aware of discrimination. It is to be expected that the values which the *burakumin* wish to see in *dowa* texts will be radical, novel, and for many, unacceptable. And so it proved to be. A series of texts were variously described by opponents as revolutionary, dangerous and communist. But the attempt to use such books to educate children has met with some success. Not least because of the support given by the Japan Teachers' Union. This remarkable organisation, which has since 1945 resisted every attempt to give absolute control over education to central government, supported the *burakumin* texts. Teachers pointed out that the children enjoyed them.

39 Miura Seiichiro *et al.*, *Lifelong Learning in Japan: An Introduction* (Tokyo, 1992), pp. 54–5.

It is often difficult for members of minority groups to leave those groups even if they wish. This is especially true if there is clear physical demarcation. But in the case of the *burakumin* there is no such demarcation. For this reason alone it might be expected therefore that some would wish to gain entry to mainstream society, an action which is described as 'passing'. Of course, there have always been some, since the 1871 Act, who have done so. But it is a process that is attended by great difficulty, because of the institutionalised barriers. The core of these is the perpetuation of segregated residence. Indeed, the only certain way to know if a person is from a *buraku* community is to know the address. This, in Japan, is easy to discover since government maintains a family register, *koseki*, upon which all family trees are recorded. This means that big companies who do not wish to employ such groups can identify their background, as can parents who wish to check on the origin of a prospective spouse. There is in Japan a flourishing area of work for private detectives, who do nothing else.

Aware of this crucial means of maintaining prejudice, the authorities try to deny access to those registers to people who have no real reason for inspecting them. Predictably, there is a black market in copies of these, and this means that they are readily available. Some kinds of occupation can be an indicator, and the occasional clue can sometimes be gleaned from names. This belief is expressed in *The Broken Commandment*, where it is explained that in the Meiji Era, commoners were allowed to take a second name. In the novel the belief is stated that the people of whole *eta* villages, for registration purposes took on the name of the village. In this way they distinguished themselves, at least in the district. Location continues to be identifiable, and leads to difficulty not only in getting work, but to problems when 'marrying out'. Some of the legendary and tragic stories in *burakumin* history concern people who want to marry, or have married, across the line. Different surveys at different times produce different statistics about marrying-out. In 1967 one estimate was 10 per cent, and another about 50 per cent.[40] Family pressure in Japan is intense, and many of the estimated 'thirty *burakumin* suicides a year directly related to anti-*burakumin* discrimination'[41] can probably be associated with despair associated with marrying-out.

Not all *burakumin* want to 'pass', and for some good, deep-rooted

40 Hane, *Peasants, Rebels and Outcastes*, p. 149 and Minority Rights Group, *Japan's Minorities*, p. 9.
41 Minority Rights Group, *Japan's Minorities*, p. 9.

reasons. It takes considerable psychological and emotional strength to leave a community, which, even if deprived, is familiar, where people have evolved a *modus vivendi,* and where there is a normative order which is understood. Such factors encourage immobility, especially where the option is uncertainty, hostility, and the permanent need to lie about origins, a process which is handed on to offspring, and indeed descendants. There is another disincentive, which concerns the changing self-perception of the *burakumin.* The point has been made that negative stereotypes are often adopted by the victims. But since the establishment of organisations such as the *Burakumin* Liberation League, there is evidence of a new acceptance with pride, of being a member of the community. The refusal of the *Burakumin* Liberation League to tolerate indignity, and active resistance to it, has created something akin to pride, or at least a challenge to classification as inferior. The parallels with the attitude of the Koreans are striking.

One expression of this new social dimension is the links which have been developed with other groups and other movements world-wide. There is, for example an 'International Movement Against All Forms of Discrimination and Racism'. The Movement participates in UN Human Rights Activities, carries out investigations, holds conferences, and publishes material, all of which is designed to show common denomination between minorities throughout the world, and to put collective pressure on governments and institutions to redress grievances. Japan is very active. The Headquarters is in the Matsumoto Jiichiro Memorial Hall in Tokyo. At the General Assembly in 1992, elections were held which resulted in the President of the *Burakumin* Liberation League becoming Honorary President, and the five Japanese being elected as Directors included the Secretary-General of the *Burakumin* Liberation League and the Chief Director of the Ainu Association of Hokkaido. A sixth election was of a Korean living in Japan.[42]

The overall assessment of the position of *burakumin* in present-day Japan seems to be that, not surprisingly the worst excesses of their traditional treatment have been removed. There have been, and continue to be, modest attempts on the part of authorities to facilitate improvements, although these are sporadic and uneven. It is generally agreed that discrimination is common, and that the status of their communities is depressed. A consideration of the position leads to the conclusion that the weight of history is heavy,

42 Newsletter, IMADR, Tokyo, February 1993.

and that there is a long way to go. Consideration of minorities, or of ordinary people is of as little concern to the powerful today as it was in the Meiji Era. Then, as now, the powerful addressed what was for them the only important question: how to retain their power.

CHAPTER FIVE

'All Citizens are Soldiers'

Overleaf ▶
Triumph in Shanghai, 1937

'All Citizens are Soldiers'

This statement was made as part of a speech by one of the most powerful men in modern Japanese history, finally to be honoured as Field Marshal Prince Yamagata Aritomo. The occasion was the inaugural ceremony of the Imperial Military Reserve Association in November 1910.[1] The phrase embraces all that the military, notably the army, believed that they had achieved, and served notice that what had been achieved would never need to be changed, since Japanese society was, if not perfect, near perfect. The shape of the society Yamagata was observing had arisen from a determination, from the beginning of the Restoration, that the only way in which Japan could become stable and strong would be by cleaving to military values, ancient and new, real and imagined. By 1910, just before the death of Meiji, the military were able to point to the success of the wars against China and Russia, and the annexation of Korea, as evidence of the speed with which the military, by practical and spiritual means, had made Japan a world power. But at all times the military made two things clear. One was that they would tolerate no interference with their conviction of what was best for Japan. The other was that the ideals of the previous fifty years were constantly endangered by laziness, neglect and subversion.

In political history, one of the interesting questions is how the military manage to subvert democratic institutions and take control. This is not the dominating question in Japan. The Japanese had a traditional social structure which was, as we have seen, based upon militarism. At the time of the Restoration, this militarism, far from being eroded, was reinforced with vigour by new and fresh younger men who were steeped in its traditions. Their object was not to seize

1 Smethurst, Richard J., *A Social Basis for Pre-War Japanese Militarism* (Berkeley, California, 1974), p. 2 quoting *Teikoku zaigo gunjinkai samjunenshi* (Tokyo, 1994).

power, but to ensure that militarism and its attendant myths, retained it. This they were able to do until 1945 through constant reiteration of those myths, by circumventing even the elementary organs of broad government, by naked repression, and by using the authority of the emperor. To understand how they managed this, it is important to remember that the stunning industrial advance of Japan had little or nothing to do with political 'advance' as understood in the west. Japan remained an Asian country ruled by an oligarchy, jealous of its alleged unique qualities, determined to become a world power. All of their efforts were conditional upon acceptance of western skills, and rejection of western values, except, if it can be called a value, of the wish to build an empire. Nor, at least until 1945, did the Japanese fully understand the nature and power of the west, especially the army which, unlike the navy, believed that Japan, being inherently superior, could win everything. This thinking led to the devastation of the Pacific War. This chapter is concerned with the reasons for the power of the military, and especially how it was that the great political movements of the late nineteenth century and early twentieth were kept at bay.

To understand this power it is necessary to return to the pre-Restoration turbulence, and the place in it of the Choshu clan. Because they had opposed Tokugawa Ieyasu, the landholding of the clan had been reduced. But by the middle of the nineteenth century they were growing in strength, partly because their estates were in the very far west of Japan and so a long way from Edo, and partly because they had a fairly advanced education system much influenced by ideas from the west. The clan's historical hostility to the Tokugawa shogunate encouraged their early subscription to the slogan 'revere the emperor, expel the barbarians'. Their support for the emperor was demonstrated in practice by the fight with foreign warships which has already been described. Later events leading to the acceptance of the need to 'open up', found the Choshu clan supporting the new Emperor Meiji. This was despite the humiliation of their bombardment. Yet they not only accepted this, but they learned that the old order could not join in modern battle. The Choshu decided to form a new force which would defend their territory. The core of the force was *samurai*, but an innovation which was in a short time to transform the national army was the recruitment of commoners. As well as this very radical composition, this new force is notable in the history of the military because of its recognition of the superior strength and tactics of the foreigners, and its open determination to learn from them.² One of the soldiers in this new Choshu force was Yamagata Aritomo, and he is both such a powerful example of the new order in Japan, and such a cardinal figure in its development that some account must be given of his early career.

He was born in Hagi, the chief town of the Choshu domain in 1838, into the family of a low-ranking *samurai*, like so many who became the backbone of the Meiji government. He was an enthusiastic participant in the 'revere the emperor, expel the barbarians' faction, and was especially active in the crushing of the last pockets of resistance to imperial rule in northern Japan and Hokkaido. Nevertheless he exemplifies the Japanese capacity for change since it was not long after he wrote this verse in 1863, that he negotiated easily with the west:

Even if I should
die in the water
I will spit
on the ugly barbarians.³

Upon the Restoration, he was appointed assistant vice-minister of military affairs in 1870, but only after he had previously declined such an appointment, because of the inchoate nature of military organisation which was centred upon the domains. When he was sure of the eventual establishment of a national army, he accepted. Together with a Satsuma clansman – notice the careful balance – he was amongst the first of the new Japanese to spend time abroad after the Restoration.⁴ From this point his influence grew, and he remained one of the most powerful men in Japan until his death in 1922. Although his influence can be traced on the civil administration, especially his steady resistance to the attempts to move to democratic government, his involvement in the creation of prefectural government and the formation of a national police force, he is most notable as the person who created the modern Japanese army, integrated it into Japanese society, made it the most powerful force in that society, and suffered no erosion of that power. He was the quintessence of everything the Japanese imperial army represented. His supporters and critics agree on his devotion to his emperor, his organisational brilliance, and his judgement, best seen

2 Ibid. Chapter II gives a more detailed account of the new army.

3 Hackett, Roger F., *Yamagata Aritomo in the Rise of Modern Japan, 1838–1922* (Harvard, 1971) quoting *Yamagata den, 1*, 299 (Tokyo, 1933), p. 24.

4 For a more detailed account of this remarkable man, see Hackett, ibid.

in the restraint he encouraged when some of his more volatile colleagues, or the people generally, wanted precipitate action.[5]

Within a very short time after Yamagata took his post in government, the nucleus of a national army was set up around an imperial guard which was to become, as imperial guards always have, the elite formation of the army. This meant weakening the forces of the domains, a process which was an important step towards their abolition which was a cornerstone of the creation or re-creation of imperial authority. Yamagata's next act, the most important in his political life, was the support and structure he gave to universal conscription to the armed forces which, in 1872, were separated into army and navy. Like so many of the initiatives in the early Meiji Era, it was suggested by contemplation and experience of the west. There, many countries had a conscription system, and the idea of introducing it to Japan is generally attributed to Omura Masujiro, a predecessor of Yamagata's in the military department, who was a member of the Choshu clan. He was one of the earliest to take western military technology seriously, and before the Restoration he was a teacher of military affairs both for the *shogun* and in the Choshu domain. After distinguished service in the civil wars, he became vice-minister in the Meiji government and he prepared a blueprint for an imperial army which would be conscripted. This radical proposal was the principal cause of his assassination in 1869. Japanese indebtedness to his creation of the army was commemorated by the erection of a huge statue in Yasukuni shrine, commemorating the war dead, in Tokyo.

Some three years after Omura's murder, an Imperial Rescript appeared which added to the arguments for a national, conscripted army. This claimed that in previous ages 'there was no distinction between soldiers and farmers', and went on to say that it was important to maintain 'the nation's security by establishing a system of universal military service'. This reference to history was designed to remove what everyone knew was a major objection to the proposal, which was the traditional monopoly of the *samurai* to carry arms. The *samurai* were further demeaned in a notice by the Council of State which said that they 'wear two swords' but are 'indolent and arrogant' and are 'no longer the *samurai* of former times' ... 'all are now equal in the empire'.[6]

One of the most remarkable features of the leaders of Meiji Japan was their ability to reject certain areas of tradition and to consider,

5 Ibid., Chapter 2.
6 Ibid., pp. 65–66 quoting *Yamagata den, 11* (Tokyo, 1933).

free of a remarkable degree of prejudice, the best course of action. Their overwhelming characteristic was their pragmatism. Yamagata's attitude to conscription illustrates this well. He was himself a *samurai* with fervent belief in all that Japanese tradition stood for. Yet he was prepared to undermine the privileges of his group in the certain knowledge that they would revile, or as in the case of Omura and others, even kill him. This determination to press ahead in what he believed to be in the best interests of his country may have been based upon his survey of western armies, a belief that the *samurai* were indeed decadent and incapable of forming an army of the kind he so admired in the west, or a variety of other reasons. One very important reason was the outcome of hard experience. Both in his field experience in the 'model' Choshu army, and in the war against the Satsuma, he had observed the fighting quality of the lower classes. This was a quality which was commended even by his adversary Saigo, whose life turned upon a belief in the alleged supremacy of the martial skills of the *samurai*. The verdict must be that his determination and his success was a turning point in the evolution of modern Japan.

Each of the milestones to conscription bears his mark, as did the ameliorative measures to counter the considerable objections. As early as 1871 it had been suggested to the *samurai*, by the government, that they should abolish those historic personal distinctions which marked them out, notably the carrying of swords. In 1873 the Conscription Act was passed. It ordered three years in the full time army and four in the reserve. In addition, all men aged between seventeen and forty had to register as available in the event of an invasion. The development of such a professional military made the spectacle of people carrying swords not only redundant, but absurd and, in the light of the structured potential animosity of the situation, extremely dangerous. In 1875 Yamagata supported abolition of the right to wear swords, and in 1876 the government issued an order to this effect. There was, as could be expected, uproar, especially since the order was followed by the abolition of the hereditary payments to what by now were no longer called the *samurai*, but the *shizoku* – the former *samurai*.

The latter now rallied around the Satsuma leader Saigo Takamori who, it will be remembered, was so angry at the rejection of his proposal to invade Korea that he had returned home. From there in 1877 his doomed rebellion took place, but the relevance of this frequently mentioned episode to this discussion is twofold. Firstly, that Yamagata was the commander of the government forces, and in a war which was finely balanced, he added to his credibility by winning. Secondly the Satsuma, the great rival to the Choshu, were now discredited for having rebelled, whatever the cause might be, against the emperor. So Yamagata was able to place members of his clan in key positions, and thus achieve ascendancy over the army. In particular he was able to increase his power over the Imperial Guard. Saigo had been the commander of this unit until his return to Satsuma. When he defected, many of his clansmen left with him, and although this could have been a serious destabilising factor, this was avoided by dint of judicious appointment of Choshu officers. In 1874 Yamagata again personally led a force to suppress another uprising in another of the great domains, Hizen. This too was a government victory. By getting control over the army, he was on the way to controlling the country *through* the army. This was a major step towards military domination, provided he could persuade the people of the need for conscription. Remarkably perhaps from a modern western perspective, this was to be more difficult than might be supposed.

Notably because of the Pacific War, one of the stereotypical views of Japan is of a nation dominated by military values. However, it is a view which must be modified when the opposition to conscription is considered. The fact is that the military had to work hard, over a long period, to create a milieu in which they would be acknowledged as the paramount authority. It is certainly the case that Japan's rulers, personified in the *samurai*, had a military code. But the bulk of the Japanese people in the last part of the nineteenth century were farmer peasants, and had the same attitudes, born of the same experience, as the same groups everywhere. The *samurai* were their oppressors. The peasant view would be that these people were parasites to whom food had to be given, ostensibly because they were protectors against what became in the Tokugawa era an increasingly mythical enemy. The *samurai* had power of life or death over people, and the Council of State in its reflection on their degeneracy, noted their exercise of the privilege: 'in extreme cases (they) irresponsibly murder innocent people with impunity'.[7]

To the reluctance to die for authority must be added the principal objection of peasants to military service, which is the removal of an able-bodied man from the crucial and difficult task of growing food. Not only is a family deprived, but in Japan where the village was a very cooperative and close-knit unit, the prospect of

7 Ibid., p. 65.

losing all the men between the ages of twenty and twenty-three was bound to provoke opposition. The ferocity of the opposition paradoxically is a measure of the boldness of the measure. The ways in which the opposition was dealt with, are a model of the manipulative skills which were to be a hallmark of Japanese government.

The opposition to the policy of turning Japan into one huge barracks took several forms. The first was civil disturbance, which was not unusual in such brittle times. As Hackett points out, although the exact or major cause of such disturbances is difficult to pinpoint, it is likely that 'opposition to conscription was the primary cause of at least fifteen major peasant uprisings'.[8] But the peasants also employed more peaceful tactics to avoid military service, which while being similar to those used at all times, latterly in Britain in the First World War, or America in the Vietnam war, were not imitative. They were a *spontaneous* response to an intolerable situation born of rural guile: for example they would arrange for the disappearance of the potential recruit by dispatching him to other parts of the country, notably the unsettled area of Hokkaido.[9] Or they would arrange for a younger son to be adopted by someone who was childless, thus making him an heir, one of the categories of exemption. This is an interesting permutation of the modern Chinese practice which, coping with the limitation to one child, sends subsequent children to childless people.

Such refusal to subscribe to the designs of the Meiji oligarchs was handled by the latter with a mixture of force and deviousness, reinforced by the success of international war. Force was applied by the new professional soldiers and police upon disturbances which were ill organised, and devoid of a central political principle. The more subtle means centred around the matter of exemptions. Again, a universal dispute in the adoption of a conscription system arises because of exemption, and again modern examples are the treatment of people in the First World War, and the war in Vietnam. In Meiji Japan those exempted included, naturally, people such as the physically disabled. But the Conscription Act also included those who were household heads and heirs, which was a loophole exploited by the peasants as we have seen. More generally, and controversially, certain professionals were excluded; teachers and students of some schools, and amongst others anyone who could pay two hundred and seventy yen. As in all conscription laws,

8 Ibid., p. 68 quoting Matsushita Yoshio, *Chohei seitei shi* (Tokyo, 1943).
9 Ibid., p. 67.

exemptions favoured the wealthy and their families, because of professional status, and of course the possession of two hundred and seventy yen. The fact that the former oppressive class which had boasted of, and depended upon martial skills was so favoured, added to the fury of the peasantry. But as he generally did, Yamagata reviewed the problem coolly, and in 1883 the conscription laws limited the range of exemptions, by the abolition of the two hundred and seventy yen clause. But the same laws increased the total period of service to twelve years, it having been increased from seven to ten in 1879. In 1889 the system of exemptions was abolished altogether. There was however further amelioration because of the fact that until 1937 'only 12 to 16 per cent of Japanese twenty-year-olds and only 25 to 35 per cent of those who passed the physical examination ''went to the barracks'' '.[10]

There was much more reluctance on the part of the *shizoku* to settle into the new society, since they had lost so much. The Saigo rebellion is the most famous expression of their discontent, but they were never far away from political crises, especially in foreign relations. There had been such a crisis in 1871, because a number of sailors from the Ryukyu islands were murdered by Formosans. China which was in dispute with Japan over the question of the sovereignty of the islands, would not agree a settlement, and so a demand grew in Japan for a punitive force to be sent to Formosa. The pressure was such that in 1874 a mixed force of the regular army and, inevitably, Satsuma *shizoku* invaded Formosa. The upshot was that China paid an indemnity, and *de facto*, Japan assumed sovereignty over the Ryukyus.

Yamagata opposed the attack because his army was ill prepared. He also hardly welcomed the prospect of giving free rein to the *shizoku*, who were undisciplined and dangerous, and remained a threat to his vision of a strong national army. It was events such as this which led to direct action, such as the abolition of sword-carrying already described. With the required support from allies in the government, Yamagata set out to militarise Japanese society. To this end, until the end of the century, there was increasing activity intended to induce a belief in the essential place of the military; the especial indoctrination of the forces; restrictions on the freedom, especially the political freedom of the latter; and the reduction of civilian control.

The process began with the issue of a handbook in 1872 which

10 Smethurst, *A Social Basis for Pre-War Japanese Militarism*, p. 6.

made clear the duties of servicemen. These revolved around one, which was carrying out the wishes of the emperor and making 'loyalty to the emperor their guiding principle'.[11] But the *shizoku* were still not prepared to accept blindly the orders of the new government, and in 1878 the Imperial Guard, in which their influence was strong, mutinied. They were put down, and fifty-three soldiers were executed. This caused the government in the same month to issue very strict instructions to prevent soldiers engaging in political activity. This 'Admonition' reminded servicemen of the need to be loyal and obedient, and was followed up in a more precise instruction in a set of regulations two years later, in 1880. This forbade membership of political associations, or attendance at political meetings, not only to the active military, but to reservists, the police, teachers and students. To ensure compliance in 1881 the formidable military police, the *kempei-tai* was formed. The considerable authority of this body was much enhanced in the period leading up to and including the Pacific war. When the war-time outrages were analysed and punished after that war, the *kempei-tai* was revealed to have been heavily involved.

All the instructions and warnings issued to the new Japanese forces culminated in the proclamation of the Imperial Rescript to Soldiers and Sailors in 1882. A 'Rescript' in imperial China was the outcome of a process in which the emperor would send an edict to an officer who would make a report on it, upon receipt of which the emperor would add notes called Rescripts. Revised copies were made and the process was thus complete.[12] In Japan a Rescript was an imperial statement carrying absolute authority. The declaration of war and surrender in the Pacific War were both announced through Rescripts.

The 1882 Rescript was not only promoted by the still unsettled behaviour of the troops, but was also intended as an antidote to civilian unrest, especially the 1881 crisis surrounding demands for a Constitution. The burdens of loyalty and obedience which had been defined in the earlier notices, were now put more strongly and their content expanded. Its tone, that of the sanctity of the emperor as head of the forces, was an indication of the intent of the military both to emphasise the emperor as deity, and an underlining of the direct, unhindered relationship between him and his forces. A few

11 Hackett, *Yamagata Aritomo in the Rise of Modern Japan*, quoting Matsuhita Yoshio, *Chohei seitei shi* (Tokyo, 1943).

12 Peyrefitte, Alain, *The Collision of Two Civilisations: The British Expedition to China in 1792–4* (London, 1993), p. 267.

weeks before the Rescript appeared, in another strategy to reduce or ideally eliminate civilian influence, Yamagata had advised Meiji that in military affairs the emperor was commander-in-chief, and actions taken by him in that area did not need the authority of the prime minister.[13]

This action illustrates well the strategy of the military in their clear goal of maintaining authority against increasing civilian and popular demand for a reduction of that authority. This was both to make civilian organisation to that end difficult, and at the same time to create governmental structures which would enable independent action by the military, without any reference to civilian members of the government. An example of the first is the severity of the Peace Preservation Law of 1887, which was discussed in a previous chapter. But there were other measures, such as a press law in 1875, which curbed the freedom of newspapers; indeed press censorship was a feature of Japanese government's restriction until 1945. The overall objection was to meetings and to 'demands', since the military, like their counterparts at other times and in other places, were convinced not only that they had the knowledge to rule Japan, but that they had a sacred duty to use it.

The creation of structures was skilfully done, and in the long term very effective. The beginning of this process came in the 1870s when once again the various options for the development of the army were considered, and as had been the case previously, the two most favoured models were those of France and Germany. A Choshu protégé of Yamagata, Katsura Taro who was to be prime minister three times, returned from an inspection of both with the recommendation that the German model should be used.[14] France had just fallen to the Germans and so was hardly a good example. Yamagata had always preferred the German system, and so the French model used hitherto now began to change. There then followed the establishment of a General Staff Headquarters, and its first chief was Yamagata. The significance of this was that this made the army independent not only of civilian control, but also of the army minister who, as a member of the government might have been subject to civilian objections and pressure. The Chief of the General Staff was solely responsible for advising the emperor on important military matters. The navy also set up the same arrangement, although their model as a navy was the British navy.

The position was consolidated in the 1889 Constitution. There, as

13 Hackett, *Yamagata Aritomo in the Rise of Modern Japan*, p. 86.
14 Ibid., pp. 82–3.

we saw earlier, the emperor was put in supreme command of the forces. This meant that not only the chiefs of staff of army and navy, but ministers of each might have direct access to the emperor. Neither, according to Smethurst 'ever used this constitutional prerogative to circumvent the prime minister', but the threat to do so was bound to influence decisions.[15] The change which was to give both the army and the navy that power until 1945 was an imperial ordinance which was passed in 1900. This ruled that the army minister could only be appointed from amongst the generals and lieutenant generals who were on active service, and in the same way the navy minister had to be selected from the admirals and vice-admirals who were similarly on active service.

What this meant was that if one or both of the arms of the service disapproved of the proposed action of the government, the relevant minister would resign, and this resulted in the fall of the cabinet. It could not be re-formed until an appropriate minister would agree to serve, and this the armed services could refuse to arrange until the government's position was acceptable. This clever move was to dominate Japanese political life. From time to time, fortunately for the Japanese, there was at least disagreement between the two services, with the navy, as a rule, trying to restrain the excesses of the army. Such differences could not of course compensate for the distortion in the balance of power which had been introduced.

The ambitions of the military leaders went beyond ensuring dominance through structures, and beyond ensuring that Japan had forces which could control disturbance, internal or external. Their mission was altogether more all-embracing. It was to create a national ethos which would be infused with 'traditional' values. Control of the governmental apparatus was only one essential stage in the creation of a milieu, as was the indoctrination of young men through military service. But it was realised, by very single-minded and clever men, that the expectation that young people can change things is one of the greatest of misplaced hopes. The cultural change they wished to occasion needed a conversion of other groups, especially women. To this end they established patriotic organisations. Although this happened towards the end of the Meiji Era, and continued until 1945, it is appropriate to discuss it at this point since it is part of the theme of the military take-over of Japan.

The point has been made that the conscription exemptions

15 Smethurst, Richard J., 'Militarism' in *Kodansha Encyclopedia.*

system meant that only the poorest had to serve. The consequence was that the army was not held in the esteem which Yamagata wished. It followed that the values which he sought to raise were not being promoted by the right people. The answer was to do what was common in the west; to reinforce relationships between civilians and military. To the military, the blurring of distinctions between the two was essential. General Tanaka Giichi made this clear in an address in 1915: 'The outcome of future wars will not be determined by the strongest army but by the strongest populace.' The latter, he went on to say 'is one which has physical strength and spiritual health, one which is richly imbued with loyalty and patriotism, and one which respects cooperation, rules and discipline'.[16] As part of the reduction of exemptions, it was arranged that an officer system be set up, in which volunteers from the landlord class would serve one year with the colours, and would then be commissioned. This formal reinforcement of a feudal relationship appealed to the local lords, and was a success. It was also consonant with the indigenous martial societies of the day.[17]

As Smethurst points out:

> Military leaders established a judicious balance between local hamlet and village custom and national goals and interests in order to make their organisations an integral part of rural Japan and to popularise military, national, and nationalistic practices and values.[18]

Yamagata was made a prince in 1907. After that his posts were formal but appeared decorative. His power remained paramount until his death in 1922. His successors who naturally shared his beliefs, continued his campaign. One of the most energetic of these was Tanaka Giichi, who was to be a central figure in the political life of Japan. Once again his career illustrates the mood of times. He was born into a low-grade *samurai* family in Choshu in 1864, became an officer in the army, served with distinction in the war against Russia, and as part of that experience concluded that the reason for Russia's defeat lay in national disunity, most disastrously expressed in the divisions between the army and the people, and the officers and the soldiers. As a staff officer in Tokyo, one of his jobs was to develop means to improve communications between the army and civilian society. His excellence in this was such that 'it is difficult to

16 Smethurst, *A Social Basis for Pre-War Japanese Militarism*, p. 25 quoting *Tanaka Giichi denki* (Tokyo, 1960).

17 Ibid., pp. 7–8 quoting Sasaki Ryujii, *Nihon gunkokokushugi no shakaiteki kiban, no keisei* (Tokyo, 1963).

18 Ibid., p. 50.

downgrade the role ... (he) played in building the organs of civilian indoctrination in military values'.[19]

Ways of carrying out such indoctrination had been under discussion for some time in the early twentieth century. Yamagata and other Choshu leaders approved of the idea, and discussed it, but it was Tanaka who set up a network to complete their goal. There were already in existence ex-service organisations, and these were an obvious target. The intention was to control them, and to include in them people who had not seen active service. The way in which this was done is a model of the subtle manipulation which is a hallmark of Japanese political behaviour. The local organisations were to be independent, but supervised by the army ministry, with local 'support' being given by regional military commanders. The critical nature of the Japanese community was recognised by allowing villages to choose their leaders. This recognition of the importance of collusion with the strength of village life is an echo of Omura's blueprint for a national army, which proposed that officers should be elected by their men. In 1910 the situation was formalised with the inauguration of the Imperial Military Reserve Association.

Over the course of the next few years this became an important national network, but it was still, by definition, limited. As far as males were concerned, it excluded those who were under conscription age, and those who were medically unfit for service. Tanaka's next step in 1915, was the establishment of a National Youth Association which would coordinate the existing youth groups, and as well as maintaining the traditional community work carried out by such groups, would give authority to the ethical education which was the reason for governmental interest. One of the exhortations was to cooperate with authority, but this was only to give an imprimatur to established community behaviour. But now was the period of Taisho democracy, when suspicion of the military was at its height, and such encroachment upon civilian life had to be handled with care. The military made sure that their influence, nationally and locally, was exerted informally rather than attracting attention by being structured. The army was never quite satisfied with the looseness of the arrangement, and in 1926, the army minister Ugaki established youth training centres, and posted officers to schools as instructors. The latter idea, as a response to demands for disarmament, was very clever. If there is a need to mobilise and expand the number of soldiers, the problem is likely to

19 Ibid., p. 14.

be a shortage of well trained and experienced officers. Such people in thousands of schools became not only agents of propaganda, but were the nucleus of a shadow army which could quickly be mobilised. Indeed, the policy created a need to recruit more officers. The new centres provided education for those who had finished compulsory schooling, and were now at work. The curriculum was dominated by military training carried out substantially by ex-servicemen, and subject to inspection by senior serving officers. In 1935 these centres were merged with the technical schools which had been set up at the end of the nineteenth century. This increased the numbers of young men subject to military training, and exposed young women to the military ethos.

It was inevitable, even in a male-dominated society like Japan, that women would have to be taken into account if a given set of social values were to be instilled. There had existed from 1901 a Patriotic Women's Association which helped in the war effort when need arose. But in 1932 a much more broadly based organisation was established, the Greater Japan National Defence Women's Association. This quickly came under the control of the army, and the organisation embraced a huge membership which concerned itself with civilian as well as military matters.

A very important boost to the morale of the army came in the shape of the victories over China and Russia which have been discussed. Emperor Meiji moved to Hiroshima in western Japan where he ostensibly commanded the forces, sharing to an uncertain extent their deprivation and discomfort. Not only did the Japanese win, but the behaviour of the victors towards the vanquished attracted widespread approval in the west. This behaviour was an expression of another aspect of Japan's importation of western ideas. In early 1873, in the course of his mission Iwakura visited the Red Cross in Geneva,[20] and in 1886 Japan became a full member of the organisation. Between the Chinese and the Russian wars, in 1899, the Hague Peace Conference drew up a code for dealing with prisoners of war 'in particular the idea that they should be treated in a manner analogous to that of the troops of the Detaining Power'. The treatment of Chinese prisoners was punctuated by brutality, although many who were sick and wounded were cared for in Japanese hospitals. In the Russian campaigns, the many thousands of casualties after the battle for Port Arthur in January 1905 were

20 Checkland, Olive, *Humanitarianism and the Emperor's Japan 1877–1977* (London, 1994), pp. 5–8.

cared for and went home to Russia.[21] The behaviour of the navy was especially commendable, and is exemplified by the visits made by Togo personally to the senior Russian commanders in hospital. Such behaviour was in vivid contrast to the behaviour of the Japanese forces forty years later. In those forty years the military had persuaded the ordinary people to accept the need for conscription, and had subdued the dangerous dissatisfaction of the former *samurai*. They had 'arranged' structures which meant that they had considerable control over government, and most of all when they were called upon to fight, they won. The empire had expanded and an historic emotive goal had been achieved with the annexation of Korea in 1910. This success promised that the western powers would now treat them as equal. Much later, in 1925, the confidence of the army and its contempt for politicians was summed up by General Ugaki Kazushige in a persisting view of its excellence. Like so many pronouncements by Japanese politicians, especially soldiers, it is simple, clear and logical: provided only that his initial premise is acceptable to a degree which will not cause a critic to disagree because of its simplicity:

> Party politics is like a three-cornered battle and interrupts the flow of events. Only one party can hold power at any time. Thus, the work of leading our seventy million fellow citizens under the throne as a truly unified and cooperating nation in both war and peace, however you think about it, has been assigned to the army. The navy has but limited contact with the populace. Only the army, which touches 200,000 active soldiers, 3,000,000 reserve association members, 500,000 to 600,000 middle school students, and 800,000 youths, has the qualifications to accomplish this task.[22]

It was a conviction which was not shaken until the atomic bombing in 1945, and in the case of many soldiers, not even then.

Meanwhile, in the first decade of the century, the military were confident of their position supported by an emperor who was now approaching a state of infallibility. Then, in 1912 it was announced that Emperor Meiji was ill, and in the summer he died a little short of his sixtieth birthday. Predictably the nation was deeply shocked, and further confused by the consequent behaviour of General Nogi, the army commander against Russia. He apparently killed his wife, with her agreement, and then killed himself in the classic fashion by slitting his abdomen and trying to cut off his head. Several reasons

21 Ibid., pp. 46–7.
22 Smethurst, *A Social Basis for Pre-War Japanese Militarism*, preface, quoting *Ugaki Kazushige nikki I* (Tokyo, 1968–71).

are commonly offered for these actions. The obvious one is that he did it to be able to serve his lord, Meiji in the after life – the custom called *junshi*. Another, rather more unlikely, is that he wished to atone for the guilt he felt because of the huge number of casualties in the Russian war, including his two sons. Yet another is that his suicide was a protest against the degeneration, as he saw it, of Japanese life, and the failure to maintain the levels of loyalty and sense of duty without which Japan would disintegrate. In fact, he left a document indicating this.

The shock and grief felt by the nation was compounded by the character of the new emperor who would, in any event, have found it difficult to succeed such a paragon. Yoshihito had the crippling disadvantages of being both physically unwell, and mentally unstable, which may have been the result of meningitis when he was a baby. It was normal in the imperial family for an emperor to be the son of a concubine, as it had been in the Tokugawa family, but Yoshihito was the last. In the early 1920s the concubine system was abolished. His early life marked a departure from tradition, since he was educated publicly and in the process was much exposed to western teaching.

However, by the time he became emperor, now in his early thirties, his conduct was giving cause for concern. Although he was a heavy drinker and sexually promiscuous, this was acceptable imperial behaviour, and was a hallmark of the social style of the revered Meiji. Concern about his son arose from his bizarre posturing dressed as his hero, the German kaiser, his violence, sometimes in public, and his increasingly manic behaviour. Although he had periods of lucidity, as time went on it became clear that he would have to be taken out of public life. The last straw came with the famous occasion when addressing the Diet. He rolled up his speech, and using it like a telescope, giggled at the delegates. In 1921 his son Hirohito became regent, and in 1926 Emperor Yoshihito died. The name chosen for his era had been Taisho, which means Great Righteousness. As far as imperial style and behaviour were concerned, it had been something of a disaster. But the period, in the political life of Japan is very important since it saw the beginning of attempts to assimilate western democratic traditions, and the continuing, and ultimately successful, determination of the military to prevent them. The Japanese call the period, from about 1905 to 1932 when party government was abolished, the Taisho Democracy.

The end of the Meiji era presented another challenge to the

oligarchy, and this was no less than a plan to assassinate Meiji himself. Commonly known as the High Treason Incident of 1910, it seems to have been the work of anarchists, notably a young worker Miyashita Takichi, in whose accommodation materials were found which the police believed could be used to make bombs. In a very short time the authorities had arrested a well known group of anarchists and left wingers, and became convinced that there was indeed a plot. Two of these were Kotoku Shusui, and a remarkable woman Kanno Sugako. Both had been imprisoned for political activity and Kotoku, although he was very prominent and a fervent anarchist may not have been involved in, or at least disapproved of, the plan. Yet, there is evidence that he helped Miyashita to get materials and facilitated his learning how to make them.

When the court heard the case twenty-five men and Kanno were charged with the offence of 'inflicting harm' against a member of the imperial family. Although the evidence against most was slight, all were found guilty and twenty-four were sentenced to death, two to imprisonment. Twelve of these had their death sentences commuted. Twelve were executed including the conspirators mentioned above. One of those who has always been a focus of interest is Kanno, because she was a woman, and on that account alone behaved in ways which the Japanese of the time regarded as reprehensible and inexplicable. She never once expressed regret for what she had done, but only for the failure of the attempt:

> Emperor Mutshito (Meiji) ... seems to be popular with the people and is a good individual. Although I feel sorry for him personally, he is, as emperor, the chief person responsible for the exploitation of the people economically ... A person in such a position, I concluded, must be killed ... I have no regrets ... I shall die without whimpering.

After a final plea to the judge on behalf of some of the codefendants, who were innocent, she went to her execution with dignity. This was the woman whom one newspaper described as the 'personification of vanity'.[23]

The impact of the case was, as may be expected, considerable. The proposal to assassinate the revered Meiji shocked ordinary Japanese, but there was also a good deal of damage done to the growth of radical politics. Not only did it become increasingly

23 Hane Mikiso (ed.), *Reflections on the Way to the Gallows* (California, 1988), pp. 56–7 quoting Hosoda, *Meiji no Gunzo* (Tokyo, 1969), Itoya Sumio, *Kanno Suga* (Tokyo, 1970), Nagabaka Michiko, *Honoho no Onna* (Tokyo, 1981).

dangerous to be associated with left-wing parties, but these were in tatters as the membership went into hiding, gave up activity, committed suicide, or went abroad. To the oligarchy it added to their certainty that political freedom posed great danger. Although this was a stunning event – one wonders what might have happened if it had succeeded – it could not halt the movement towards political democracy, and the establishment of institutions to achieve this.

There were many reasons for progress, however slow. The first was the result of the education which had been put in place as a priority of early Meiji reform. The Japanese were moving to that pre-eminence in literacy in Asia which they still retain, and one effective consequence was that they were able to read the newspapers. Nor were all of the latter mindless supporters of the existing order. There was nothing equivocal in the editorial in the *Osaka Ashahi* of 27 September 1912, at the very moment of change: 'To measure the politics of Taisho by that of Meiji is the ideology of those who are captive of the Meiji period ... until today the people have been deceived and we have walked the road of military politics.'

The newspaper went on to state that far from wanting a reassertion of ethics, the hope was expressed that the new era would 'expel the reactionary and conservative indolence which have cast a pall over the people'.[24] Later, especially because of the mobility of people during the First World War, and the excitement caused by the Russian revolution, newspapers continued to inform the public, including articles on socialism and communism.[25] One of the problems which historians have with the Taisho period is the relative credit which should be given to the many elements which created a more questioning attitude in Japanese society. Education and popular literature are certainly two of the most vital.

One of the increasingly common forms of political agitation during the Taisho and early Showa eras was the mass demonstration. There had been civil disturbances during the Meiji Era, especially as we have seen, by farmers. Nor was the motive behind a demonstration always clear, as is demonstrated by the Hibiya Incendiary Incident of 1905. This was a major destructive episode which had as its ostensible cause public dissatisfaction with the

24 Harootunian, Harry D., 'Introduction: A sense of ending and the problem of Taisho', in *Japan in Crisis: Essays on Taisho Democracy*, Silberman, Bernard S. and Harootunian, Harry D. (eds) (Princeton, 1974), p. 9.
25 Waswo, Ann, 'The origins of tenant unrest' in Silberman and Harootunian, *Japan in Crisis*.

terms of the Treaty of Portsmouth, which concluded the Russo-Japanese war. A 'Joint Council of Fellow Activists on the Peace Question' was formed, comprising a wide range of organisations and interests and in defiance of a government ban, a meeting was held at Hibiya Park in Tokyo, followed by a march to the imperial palace. The army was called out, martial law was declared, but considerable damage was done to property, with many hundreds of casualties. The debate which is still carried on is whether this was simply a nationalistic outburst, or whether it was an early example of political activism which characterised the Taisho Era.[26] Some historians in support of the latter view underline the proposition that Taisho democracy should not be seen as narrowly contemporaneous with the era, but had earlier roots, and of course included a part of the Showa era.

Other riots and demonstrations punctuate the period. In 1908 left wingers and anarchists paraded in Tokyo, in an event called the Red Flag Incident, which was followed by heavy repression by the government. The latter regarded this as an outrage following another act of disloyalty by one of the most famous of the Japanese socialists, Katayama Sen. For during the Russo-Japanese war, he went to the International Congress of Socialists and shook hands with a Russian. There was more violence in 1912 after a crisis caused by public resentment over military interference in the government. The prime minister of the day was Saionji Kinmochi, a prince of the Fujiwara family, members of which had been the closest advisers, friends, wives and concubines to the emperors for almost 1,300 years. It was a member of the Fujiwara family, Prince Konoe Fuminaro who was prime minister in 1937 when the war with China began, and who committed suicide in 1945 rather than face trial.

The crisis arose because Saionji refused to support army demands for a substantial increase in its budget. The minister of war, General Uehara exercised his right to resign and with added piquancy informed the emperor and not the prime minister. The army, following the tactic outlined earlier, refused to nominate a successor, and so the government had to resign. The new prime minister was General Katsura, who, although he had held the position twice before, was deeply unpopular. This, together with the blatant manipulation by the *genro* to secure his appointment outraged the Diet, the newspapers and the public. After a verbal assault on Katsura in the Diet, there were riots in several cities in which people

26 See Okamoto Shumpei, 'Hibiya Incendiary Incident' in *Kodansha Encyclopedia*.

were killed. Katsura resigned, but his successor in 1913 was no more pleasing to an increasingly vigilant community.

He was Admiral Yamamoto Gonnohyoe, not to be confused with the admiral of the same name who organised the attack on Pearl Harbour in 1941. He made an important contribution to Japan's development, for example in the naval tactics which were so important during the Sino-Japanese war. Yamamoto also, perhaps oddly, changed the rule about service ministries having to be headed by serving officers. It is not clear why he did so, but it could have been an acknowledgement of growing social and political resentment. In any event nothing changed, since the custom prevailed, serving officers continued to be ministers, and in 1936 the rule was reinstated.

Yamamoto's government fell after just over a year because of a bribery scandal involving naval officers and companies in Britain and Germany. Several officers and businessmen were fined and imprisoned, but Yamamoto himself seems not to have been involved, and was to become prime minister again in 1923. There were high expectations of the next prime minister in 1914, who was that Okuma who had years before lost a leg in an assassination attempt. In the meantime he had founded Waseda University, which is one of the most prestigious in Japan. In 1914 he was seventy-six, and not surprisingly he had lost some of his determination to resist the *genro*. Nevertheless, he managed the country for two and a half years which is, in the history of Japanese government a very long time indeed, especially since the latter part included the first years of the First World War.

As well as the crude use of soldiers and police to curb demonstrations, the oligarchy issued formidable documents to legitimise their actions. Already by the end of the nineteenth century the process of industrialisation had created a workforce which was beginning to understand the power they could wield if they were organised. The oligarchy recognised this too, and enacted the Public Order and Police Law of 1900. Its provisions included restrictions on the rights to organise, to strike, and to free speech. It also forbade women to join political associations. In part because of the Hibiya Incendiary Incident, in part because of the Red Flag Incident, and mainly because of a perceived deterioration in public behaviour, in 1908 the Boshin Imperial Rescript was issued. The prime minister of the day was the same General Katsura who has been mentioned above, and he was very cooperative in this exhortation to remember Japanese values, to cooperate rather than cause division, and to eschew rich living. This last, deriving from deeply religious values is commonly found in Japanese appeals to cleanse society. This particular Rescript is only slightly less important than the 1890 Rescript on Education, the cornerstone of Japanese faith until the end of the Pacific War.

The several governments of Japan, like all governments, realised that behind public disturbances lay not only grievances about standards of living, but political ideas which had an intellectual base. The issue they had to address always poses a problem for autocrats which is how to control how people think, and what they think about. This is why, as we shall see in a later chapter, the issue of education is so very important in Japanese history. At this stage one example will be given, that of *kokogaku*, meaning 'national learning'. This is a complicated term, 'defined as the philological study of Japanese classical literature and ancient writings with the aim of identifying peculiarly Japanese cultural elements or examples of a typical Japanese mentality'.[27]

Kokogaku had always been a powerful intellectual force in Japan from the seventeenth century, when, it may be noted the stability which the Tokugawa shogunate brought enabled such intellectualism to develop. Although concerned with classical literature, it was infused with Shintoism and often sought a Japanese identity which was spiritual and unique. In the years after Meiji, the debate about the meaning and importance of the cultural nature and influence of *kokogaku* deteriorated into an insistence that it justified the ideology of *kokutai* – 'national polity'. The scholar Yamado Yoshio is notable for his exploration and support of the policy. But he is not unusual, either in time or place since scholars and academics are often the first to answer to the appeal for intellectual justification for social order.

The coming of the First World War did not have the traumatic effect on Japan that it had in Europe. Japan entered the war on the British side, fulfilling her treaty obligation to do so. No troops were sent to Europe, and Japan's sole contribution was to accompany merchant ships. But the concentration of the west on the war gave Japan a marvellous opportunity for adventurism in east Asia. Before the end of 1914 Japan occupied most of the islands in the western Pacific which had been German colonies, and most important the Chinese province of Shandong, and the German leased port of Tsingtao. This was a large, rich and strategically important part of

27 For a detailed discussion, see Koyasu Nokubini, 'kokogaku' in *Kodansha Encyclopedia.*

north Asia. Much encouraged, in 1915 Japan issued the notorious 'twenty-one demands' to China. These demands were grouped into five categories and notably ordered that Japan be allowed to build a railway straight through a strategically vital area of north China, to have effective control of Manchuria, and to be the sole lender to China. Furthermore, there were to be no more concessions to western powers, all areas of Chinese government were to be overseen by Japanese advisers, and half of all Chinese war material had to be bought from Japan.

The effect would have been to turn China into a Japanese colony, and neither China nor the west, especially the Americans, were prepared to agree. Nevertheless, because of the war, substantial concessions were made, including the occupation of Shandong, and certain rights in Manchuria and Inner Mongolia. But the general view is that the issuing of these demands was a grievous mistake. It displayed political ineptitude, aroused considerable anti-Japanese feeling in China, and helped the deterioration in relationships with America.

Before the war ended, Japan was to engage in a further piece of adventurism, and this time it was one which was unpopular in Japan. The Russian revolution could not be ignored by the Japanese, since they had been historic enemies. The prospect of a Bolshevik government in Siberia was very worrying, and with the support of the west the Siberian expedition was mounted. The western powers were particularly concerned about large numbers of prisoners of war, many from the German-led forces, and Czechs who if they could be released would fight for the anti-German armies. The situation turned out to be chaotic, which is natural enough during a revolution, and the years until the Bolsheviks were firmly in control were marked by massacres and brutality on every side. It was not until 1922 that the last Japanese troops left Siberia. The episode had achieved nothing, and the army lost a good deal of credibility, which was expressed by manifest civilian distaste for soldiers to the point when the latter were apprehensive about wearing their uniforms in public.

Apart from adding to their empire, the war brought considerable economic advantage to Japan. As was to be the case in the Korean war of the 1950s, there was a great demand for materials, which Japan could produce since her involvement in both conflicts was slight. Business flourished, at the pinnacle of which were the increasingly powerful *zaibatsu*, and Japan became a creditor nation. Not everyone shared in this prosperity however, and wages did not keep pace with the inevitable inflation which accompanies growth. Before discussing the consequential political and social effects, we will round off the Japanese experience of the war with their reaction to the peace treaty.

The conference to settle the world after the tumult of war met at Versailles in January 1919. The issues were formidable, but for Japan were few. She wished to be counted as one of the 'big five', and this was agreed. The next ambition was the retention of the land seized during the war. This was more difficult, but by threatening to leave the conference, and by exposing the secret support given by Britain and France in 1917 to the annexation of Shandong, the United States in particular was forced to agree. It proved to be a high price, since Congress dissatisfaction with the government was partly responsible for the American refusal to ratify the peace treaty, and ultimate rejection of the League of Nations.[28] But the most inflammatory issue was one on which Japan could not have her way. It was an issue which had been simmering for some time and it was to be the cause of profound resentment. It was racial discrimination.

The problem went back to the end of the nineteenth century, when Asians began to go to the United States to build the railways. When this work was finished, demands from white workers led to legislation which ordered the Chinese to leave, which most did. Before the turn of the century some Japanese had migrated to the United States, and to Hawaii, and when the latter became part of the Union in 1900, many thousands of Japanese moved from Hawaii to California. Their presence provoked resentment from white workers and from farmers, leading to organised and institutional demand, for example from the American Federation of Labour, for discriminatory legislation. The outcome was an ordinance in San Francisco in 1906 which ordered segregated schooling because Japanese children were 'vicious, immoral, of an age and maturity too advanced for safe association with the younger American children'.[29] The Japanese everywhere were outraged, as was President Roosevelt, who appealed to Congress to restrain the racist momentum. But the United States with its large black population was deeply racist, and recognising this political fact, the only thing Roosevelt could do was to reach an informal understanding with the Japanese that they should restrict emigration to the west.

These events took place at about the time of the Portsmouth Treaty, when the Japanese were furious at the failure of the

28 Storry, Richard, A History of Modern Japan (London, 1960), p. 162.
29 Murakami Hyoe, Japan: The Years of Trial 1919–52 (Tokyo, 1982), p. 19.

Americans to support their demands for a sizeable indemnity against the Russians. In 1913 the Californian state legislation proposed that the Japanese should no longer own land – many were farmers – and that there should be restrictions on their right to rent. Once again the President – this time Wilson – tried unsuccessfully to intervene. America had other preoccupations during the war, and in any case Japan was an ally. But after the war, a further bill was proposed which would forbid the Japanese to rent land at all, and in 1921 the United States Supreme Court ruled that the Japanese could not qualify for citizenship.[30] In 1924 an Immigration Act was passed which effectively ended Japanese immigration.

It was the indignation felt by the Japanese because of such action that made them determine to pursue the insertion in the League of Nations Covenant of a clause rejecting racial discrimination. Although the Americans and British had some sympathy with this proposal, the British Commonwealth ministers were generally hostile. Specifically, the Australian Prime Minister Hughes was determined that no such clause should be accepted. Australia's record of racism, and ill-treatment of indigenous people, was at least as bad as that of the United States. A number of Japanese were already in northern Australia in sugar cane plantations and pearling, but the newly formed Australian Commonwealth prohibited all Asian entry in 1901. Hughes' near hysterical determination to reject the proposal caused even South Africa's Prime Minister Botha to tell Makino the principal Japanese delegate: 'Strictly between ourselves, I think he is mad'.[31]

Mad as Botha may have judged him, Hughes had his way, and the proposal was rejected. Many people believed the decision to be both unfair and unwise, including Europeans as expressed for example in the French press. When the final draft of the Covenant of the League was presented, many sympathised with the view of Makino when he said:

> If it is to be a principle of the League of Nations that certain peoples are not to be given just and equal treatment this will strike those people as odd, and in the future will undermine their faith in the very principles of justice and equality that are supposed to regulate relations between member nations.[32]

The issue went further than the treatment of the Japanese in the

---

30 Hoyt, Edwin P., *Hirohito: The Emperor and the Man* (New York, 1992), p. 46.
31 Murakami, *Japan*, p. 20.
32 Ibid., p. 22.

United States, or the obduracy of the man called by Storry, 'the vinegary little Mr Hughes'.[33] Not only the Japanese but also the Chinese were very resentful of their being regarded as second class, and worthy only to be ruled and exploited by westerners. It was an intolerable and dangerous situation which Yamagata recognised when he explained his 'premonitions of a bitter conflict between white and coloured peoples in the future'. It was not something he welcomed since he was against 'the question of a league of coloured peoples'.[34] Despite China's subjugation to Japanese imperial ambition, there were those in China who were angry about western attitudes, and rejoiced in Japanese success against the Russians, and their eradication of extraterritoriality. On the way to the Versailles conference Prince Konoe, one day to be Japanese prime minister, visited China. There he met Sun Yat-sen, the father of the Chinese revolution. Much of their conversation was about Japanese success and the way in which it inspired the nationalist movements throughout Asia.[35] The next thirty years were to witness the challenging and destruction of European supremacy in Asia and Africa, despite hostile relationships between individual and groups of nations. It was a challenge which Japan was to use to justify the invasion of other countries, in the event not in the cause of pan-Asian idealism, but for continuing colonialist exploitation. But a very important development which was a result of imperial ambitions was the attitude of the Japanese towards other Asian countries. As they came into contact and conflict with these, there was to develop an increasing tradition of mutual contempt, the effects of which still plague Japan's foreign relations. Nowhere is this clearer than in the case of Korea.

33 Storry, *A History of Modern Japan*, p. 162.
34 Hackett, *Yamagata Aritomo in the Rise of Modern Japan*, p. 274.
35 Murakami, *Japan*, pp. 15–16.

CHAPTER SIX

Unfriendly Neighbours:
The Peoples of Japan and Korea

Overleaf ▶
Hideyoshi: Japanese hero; Korean villain

Unfriendly Neighbours:
The Peoples of Japan and Korea

There is a seemingly implacable enmity between the Japanese and the Koreans which is based upon sound and long Korean experience of their treatment by the Japanese. It remains an important feature of Japanese political and social life, because of the proximity of the countries and their need for mutual accord because of their membership of the economic 'Pacific rim', and because some 676,000 Koreans live in Japan today. During the period 1905 to 1945, Japan achieved its historic ambition to colonise Korea, and since this is the period under discussion, it is appropriate to analyse this pivotal relationship in some detail.

The prospects for international accord, or for a breakdown of the hostility between the two groups in Japan are not good. In large part this is because their infelicitous relationship has a long history which goes back to the fourth century, and contemplation of that history gives little cause for optimism. It is claimed that a feature of the legendary Empress Jingu of that period is the 'indisputable historical fact (of) Japanese aggression against the states on the Korean peninsula in the late fourth century'. Such is the depth of such memories, on the part of both, that this connection, between Jingu and Korea, was introduced in Japanese school texts as justification for the annexation of Korea in 1910.[1]

An early obligation to Korea for much of what came to be regarded as Japanese culture was rewarded by the belligerence of the sixteenth century *daimyo* Hideyoshi Toyotomi. For hundreds of years before, much of the culture, religion and scholarship of China and even India had been introduced through Korean links. Hideyoshi was to plant the first modern seeds of hatred. He is best known

1 Aoki Michiko Y., 'Empress Jingu: The Shamaness Ruler' in Mulhern, Chieko Irie, *Heroic with Grace: Legendary Women of Japan* (Armonk, New York), 1991, pp. 29, 36.

127

for the fact that he brought Japan's interminable civil wars to an end, and created a base upon which the Tokugawa *shoguns* were to build the stability which was to be the signal characteristic of their two hundred and fifty year reign. After his death in 1598, he was declared a divinity of the first rank by the emperor, and his biographer concludes that he was 'the most remarkable man in pre-modern Japanese history'.[2] That is a commonly accepted Japanese view.

Koreans regard him rather differently. For them his behaviour in Korea justifies a special place in the demonology of Korean tradition. He organised a massive invasion and occupation of Korea. The scale of the Japanese invasion was impressive: 158,700 soldiers, with a reserve of 100,000, together with a navy of 9,200 sailors began the attack in 1592. During the seven year occupation, Koreans were made slaves, both at home and in Japan. Highly specialist artisans and scholars were also forcibly removed, making a significant impact, to the detriment of Korea and the benefit of Japan. Libraries were looted, and the country was denuded of its best livestock. Perhaps the most outrageous behaviour, especially bearing in mind the legendary Japanese respect for imperial tradition, was the plundering of the royal Yi tombs. Small wonder that Koreans regard Hideyoshi more 'as a plunderer of Korea than as a unifier of Japan'.[3]

But Hideyoshi, like Japanese invaders who came after him, suffered an excess of ambition, and no proper perception of the strength of the opposition. For his intention was to conquer China, and quickly, an aim which proved impossible then, and was to continue to be impossible when the Japanese tried again some three hundred and fifty years later. The Koreans began to fight back and engaged in a scorched earth policy, which proved to be an important factor in the gradual demoralisation of the invading force. Eventually, although his claims and demands remained charged with his characteristic arrogance, they began to be modified. The invasion had been criticised by noblemen in Japan, and it was unpopular with footsoldiers who were not attracted by the possibility of death when they could have been on their farms. We have seen that the glory of dying for country and emperor is a relatively new tradition in Japan.

When Hideyoshi died in 1598, his successor, Tokugawa Iesayu,

2 Berry, Mary Elizabeth, *Hideyoshi* (Harvard, 1989), p. 1.

3 De Vos, George and Lee, Changsoo, *Koreans in Japan: Ethnic Conflict and Accommodation* (California, 1981), p. 17.

founder of the great dynasty which bears his name abandoned the invasion, and contact between the two countries was slight until the Meiji Restoration. One of the first sources of conflict with which the new Meiji regime had to deal was the resurrection of the idea that Korea should be subjugated. As we have seen it was to lead to an insurrection which marshalled the last resistance by adherents to the classical *samurai* tradition and demonstrated that, at least in its classical form, it was a tradition which was no match for a modern army, even the modest, very new emerging army of Japan.

Very soon after the Restoration, an oligarchy had established itself which was dominated by four clans, the two most important of which were the Choshu and Satsuma. The history of late nineteenth-century Japan was dominated by individuals from these clans and the rivalry between them. An early important issue concerned imperial expansion, notably to assume sovereignty over Korea. A mission was sent to try to insist that it engaged in relations with Japan. At the time Korea was trying to cope with aggression from Russia, and the historic insistence from China that she was the latter's vassal. Furthermore Korea, like her Asian neighbours, was in political turmoil over western demands which traditionalists wished to resist. Korea rejected the Japanese overture, which led to a faction led by Saigo Takamori, a Satsuma noble, demanding that Korea should be invaded and punished. His reasoning seems to have derived from the offhand attitude of the Koreans, the need for Japan to have access to the spoils which Korea offered, and a determination – always very important in Japanese thinking – to establish an empire on western lines. There was also the social problem of larger numbers of disgruntled degraded *samurai* who needed an opportunity for dignified employment: just the people to conquer Korea. The attitudes of key Japanese figures of the early Meiji Era to Japan was however more varied than that of the Saigo faction. These included those who saw the problem as an opportunity for expansion, and those who wanted to help Korea in the seemingly inevitable need to modernise. There were 'progressive' Koreans who were made welcome in Japan by, for example Fuku-zawa Yukichi, a famous reformer whose work will be discussed several times in this book.[4]

In 1873 the emperor ordered an end to pressure to invade, Saigo resigned and went home to establish a school for martial arts. In 1876, the *samurai* class was abolished. In the next year, 1877, he led

4 Mitchell, Richard H., *The Korean Minority in Japan* (Berkeley, California, 1967), pp. 7ff.

a rebellion against the government he had helped to establish. The rebellion, which involved some 15,000 Satsuma warriors, against about 40,000 government troops lasted about nine months with some 30,000 casualties. When he lost, Saigo was executed, at his request, by a colleague. This was the end of a tradition, but as is typical of the period, the Japanese were, and are, ambivalent about whether or not he was a hero. Most people probably believe he was, since his faith lay in patriotism, chauvinism and asserting the best in Japanese tradition, against the immorality and cowardice of those misguiding the emperor. He is a singularly Japanese figure, in a tradition which found its more recent expression in the suicide of people who wished to die with Emperor Hirohito, and the dramatic self-destruction of the writer Mishima Yukio in 1970, despairing of Japanese degeneracy, after a dramatic public attempt to rouse a spirit of nationalism in the armed forces.[5] Imperial opposition to Saigo and an invasion was not, even in the short term, to save Korea. Most cynically, the judgement may be that the hesitation was based only on expediency and a cool assessment that the time was not right.

Such threats from Japan were not new to Korea: nor were they now from the west. As early as 1831, western predatory powers had been exploring the possibilities. In that year a British merchant ship was in Korean waters, and this was followed by French, German and Russian interest and activity. In 1866 an American merchant vessel the *General Sherman* went aground, and after the crew behaved in a barbaric fashion, they were massacred by the locals. Subsequently there was a battle with an American retaliatory force. Around 1866, the constant anxiety about the corrosive cultural activity of the Roman Catholic Church, shared by Japan incidentally, led to the killing of some 8,000 Catholics, including a number of French priests, which was provoked in part by the refusal of France to help to offset Russian ambition. The response of the Koreans to such events was to declare a policy of isolation in 1871. The regent, the father of the Korean king, was encouraged by initial success, and as a boost to his people, he put up stones, which became famous, throughout the country, on which were inscribed: 'Western barbarians invade our land. If we do not fight we must appease them. To urge appeasement is to betray the nation.'

This was a brave, but futile gesture, which displayed a forgivable ignorance of the power and cynicism of the west at the time.

5 For an account of this remarkable individual see Nathan, John, *Mishima: A Biography* (Tokyo, 1974).

Pressure was maintained and after a treaty with the United States in 1882, similar treaties were signed with other western powers. One consequence was that in 1881 and 1882, delegations from Korea went to Japan, whose speed of development was astonishing the world, and the United States to learn, as Japan had done a short time before, of the source of western power. The effect of such visits had the inevitable effect of eroding the long-felt wish for isolation.

The Japanese meanwhile had appeared, physically, ostensibly carrying out marine work off the Korean coast. In 1875 the Japanese ship *Unyo* was fired upon, and Japan retaliated with the dispatch of a fleet of warships, a demand for apologies, and an insistence on treaties. Inevitably, the cause of Korean independence was dented, and Japanese ambition enhanced. The Treaty of Kanghwa which followed in 1876 recognised Korea as independent – of China that is – but included the opening of a legation in Seoul, trading concessions in Pusan, whilst there followed in 1883 the opening of the ports of Wonson and Inchow. Such demands were irresistible because Japan's imperial core had increased significantly. After a force had been sent to Formosa in 1874 where a number of Ryukyu islanders had allegedly been ill-treated, both Formosa and the Ryukyus were taken over by Japan. The Kanghwa treaty was both a step forward in expansion, and a redress of the 'humiliation' believed by Saigo to have been inflicted by Korea. The halting steps to reform by Korea were to move too little and too late.

The other nations threatening Japan for supremacy over Korea were possessed of critical disadvantages. Russia had few allies, and Britain in particular was conscious of, and apprehensive about Russian ambitions in Asia, including north-east Asia. China's empire was crumbling because of the unpopular Manchu Qing dynasty, and because of western and nationalist ambition. Indeed, at this time, the Chinese 'empire' was something of a fiction. Although the western powers notoriously were exploiting China, they had also expressed unease about the remarkable growth of Japan. But the Japanese were increasing in strength and confidence, occasionally judged well and when their chance came in 1893, they were able to take it.

In that year there was another civil disturbance in Korea. During the previous fifteen years there had been many reformist and reactionary battles between the King, Kojong, generally being 'progressive' and the opposition led by Queen Min, supported by the Chinese. The parallels with China at the time are noticeable since in that country emperors *tended* to want to accommodate new trends, only to be outdone by the formidable Dowager Empress Cixi. It was a rivalry which was to lead to the end of their respective dynasties. The lone survival of the Japanese throne is a case study in the pragmatism which, despite upheaval, is the central feature of Japan's political behaviour during the same period. The rebellion of 1893, which set in motion a group of anti-western and anti-Japanese Koreans called Tonghak. This was a religious sect – the term means 'Eastern Learning' which had been established about 1860. What was special about it was that the Chinese sent troops to try to subdue it. It was against corruption, privilege, injustice and 'Western Learning', by which was meant Roman Catholicism. It also proclaimed 'Reject Japan and repel the foreigners'. Japan, recognising themselves as the main enemy, pronounced this as unacceptable, and also sent troops.

After the Tonghak were put down, events followed quickly. In July the royal palace was invaded and the Japanese forced the king to expel the Chinese. Also in July the Japanese navy sank a Chinese troopship. Within seven months the Japanese controlled the sea lanes between China and Korea and the Kwantung peninsula, significantly Port Arthur at its point, and the whole of Korea. In this process, as Hoyt points out, there can be seen the first example of a Japanese practice which continued up to Pearl Harbor in 1941: they did not declare war until the first strike had been made.[6] Such issues were international. But at a social level the assessment by the Japanese of the people for whom supposedly they were fighting, only served to increase animosity. A Japanese sergeant's recorded views are commonplace: 'Though we belong to the same East Asian race, the only thing in common is our yellow faces. Not a single custom or habit is the same ... Their character is very mild but they are lazy and have no spirit for progress.' The same man pronounced himself appalled at the 'filth and disorder' of Korea: 'I have never heard of, nor seen, in Japan anything like the hopelessness and depression to be found here.'[7]

The outcome was the Treaty of Shimonoseki in 1895. Under this Treaty Japan received enormous reparation from China, and demanded and got huge concessions, such as an entry point for trade on the Shandong peninsula, and vast tracks of territory such as Formosa. For the purpose of this analysis, it is especially important to note that it was now that China finally gave up any claim to

6 Hoyt, Edwin P., *Japan's War: The Great Pacific Conflict* (London, 1986), p. 35.

7 Lone, Stewart, *Japan's First Modern War: Army and Society in the Conflict with China, 1894–95* (London, 1993), pp. 59–61.

sovereignty over Korea, and the way forward for Japan seemed clear.

But the western powers, reflecting on this, began to take very seriously the speed of Japanese advance. As a consequence, there occurred 'The Triple Intervention' by Russia, Germany and France. Of these Russia had the heaviest interest, especially about the potential Japanese power in the Kwantung peninsula, which included Port Arthur, an area of Manchuria central to the Russian goal of a warm-water port. The outcome was a threat from Russia, a realistic but humiliating acceptance by Japan which gave up the claim to the peninsula, and a surge of anti-western feeling in Japan. This accumulating feeling of resentment for the west is an important key to the understanding of Japanese behaviour in the succeeding fifty years.

Because of this blow to Japanese prestige, there was a resurrection of hope in Korea that this newly evidenced Russian strength could contain Japanese ambitions. There was, in any case, a strong nationalist feeling in Korea which displayed itself in the activities of organisations such as 'The Independence Club', which had as its goal the elimination of foreign influence. But Japan continued its pressure. In 1895 the Japanese murdered the Korean Queen Min, who had always supported China. This astonishing act, it is usually agreed, was known about by a Japanese government minister, Miura Goro, of the Choshu clan. It is not forgotten by Koreans that the perpetrators of this crime suffered no punishment, which added to the hatred. In 1896 the Korean king fled to the Russian legation, an act which consequentially gave Russia important concessions. In the same year Japan made what turned out to be a last offer to Russia. It was to divide Korea. The Russians rejected it.

Russia was pleased. By 1898, the tip of the Kwantung peninsula had been leased from China, and all important links with the trans-Siberian railway established. For Russia disaster came with the expression of British disapproval of Russian ambition with the signing of a British–Japanese alliance in 1902. Its contents agreed that Japan had a special interest in Korea. Despite Japanese attempts to negotiate with Russia in the years 1902–04, the Russians were resolute. It was a resolution which was based upon a profound ignorance of the strength and skill of the Japanese forces. These had been carefully developed and trained, and supplied with first-class equipment such as warships by the British. By 1903, all was ready and one of the two legendary commanders of the subsequent war, Admiral Togo Heihachiro of the Satsuma clan, and British-trained, attacked the Russian fleet in Port Arthur. There was a simultaneous attack on warships in Chemulpo in Korea. Typically, war was not declared until after these events. Togo went on to engage the Russian Baltic Fleet in one of the greatest sea battles of all time, in the Tsushima Straits.

Meanwhile in land battles in Manchuria, another Japanese legend, General Nogi Maresuke, albeit with heavy losses, beat the Russian forces. Not only Japan, but Britain also, was delighted. Emperor Meiji was made a Knight of the Garter, Togo and Nogi, together with War Minister Oyama, were made members of the Order of Merit, a most distinguished British award, limited to 27 members. The dutiful Nogi was regarded as a great warrior, and in that tradition accepted the loss of his two sons in the war. To add to his dignity in Japanese tradition, when Emperor Meiji died in 1912, Nogi killed his wife and committed *seppuku* to continue to follow his emperor. This was a *samurai* custom called *junshi*, which in fact was banned in 1662.

The victory was swift and complete, and both countries were anxious for peace. Theodore Roosevelt, then President of the United States, offered his services as peacemaker, and at a meeting in Portsmouth, New Hampshire in 1905, Japan got considerable advantages. These included exclusive rights in Korea, the Kwantung peninsula, important sections of railway, and the southern half of Sakhalin island. Yet sections of the Japanese public rioted over what they believed to be the inadequacy of these provisions. In particular they were angry because the United States would not support the paying of indemnity. But Korea's fate was sealed. In 1905 Korea was made a protectorate of Japan. In that year it was said that:

> It would be very hard to find a Korean child who does not drink in, almost with his mother's milk, a feeling of dislike against the Japanese. On the other hand, the Japanese seem to have imbibed as strong a feeling towards the Koreans.[8]

In the next two years the process, already in place of the Japanisation of Korea, continued. All that was now needed was a pretext. There were many, but one was irresistible. In October 1909 Prince Ito Hirobumi, resident-general, was assassinated on a visit to Harbin in Manchuria. The Japanese blamed a Korean, An Chung-gun, quite correctly according to historians of Korea.[9] The result was that the

8 Mitchell, *The Korean Minority in Japan*, pp. 12–13, quoting *The Korea Review*, 1905, p. 161.

9 For example, Lee, K i- baik, *A New History of Korea* (Ilchokak, Seoul, 1984), p. 310.

Japanese moved into key positions in Korea, and martial law was declared. Korea was now to enter a forty-year period of colonisation which, for brutality, in any league of modern imperial degradation rates as an entrant for the lamentable ascription of serious contender.

Although Korea had announced its neutrality in 1904, this flippancy was ignored by the Japanese. They forced Korea to agree to a classic Japanese document; the essence was later to be used in several Asian countries. It ostensibly guaranteed Korean independence. It even guaranteed the personal safety of the Korean emperor, but to ensure this, Japanese forces were to be allowed to police key positions, and to take over key installations. After the Treaty of Portsmouth, Korea, under The Protectorate Treaty of 1905, deteriorated further. The country was no longer to engage in foreign relations, and effectively every aspect of life came under the autocratic Japanese resident-general. This turning point was given some kind of legitimacy by a number of Koreans who were, and still are, regarded as some of the worst traitors in a country which was to experience exceptional degrees of treachery. Notably, these were Song Pyong-jun, and Yi Yong-gu.

By 1910, the Japanese were ready, and General Terauchi Masatake arrived. This powerful Choshu clansman was, in that year, the first chairman of the Imperial Military Reserve Association: an unpromising prospect for Korea. With the help of no less a person than the Korean prime minister, Yi Wan-yong, the annexation treaty was drawn up. Terauchi took over all police powers, of course with Japanese officers, all 'subversive' organisations were suppressed and their leaders imprisoned, and Korean newspapers closed. Japanese rhetoric historically has been both powerful and remarkable. All of what followed, which can be seen as the essence of Japanese foreign policy up to 1945, was described in the treaty as promoting 'the common wealth of the two nations', and assuring 'permanent peace' in Asia.

Terauchi as governor-general, was in a position which could only be held by high-ranking Japanese Officers, and repression began in earnest. Tens of thousands of people were arbitrarily arrested and tortured, all political activity was banned, and all adverse comment in newspapers led to closure. Naturally, to deflect such international criticism as there was, there was a Korean 'Central Council' on which Koreans sat, but which had no power whatsoever. Crude violence was a necessary preliminary to the real purpose, which was to use Korea for Japanese purposes. The list of assets and the degenerate behaviour in securing them, might have formed a salutary warning to what was to follow in the Japanese occupation of the rest of Asia.

There was first the vital question of land. This is always important to colonising powers, none more so than Japan with an expanding, increasingly prosperous population living in a country large tracts of which were uninhabitable. A number of Japanese companies were set up, of which the most infamous was The Oriental Development Company, which by 1930 held 269,000 acres. In the same year, the Japanese government held 40 per cent of the total land area of Korea.[10] This is merely an illustration, since the same applied to minerals, especially gold, forests and fishing. Hugely profitable monopolies were given to specially formed Japanese companies. Transport, communication and finance, in fact every form of business, including the business of everyday living, was taken over for Japanese advantage and profit. Of especially disastrous effect was the immigration of Japanese settlers, since this led to the ending of traditional Korean landownership, and, throughout the period, an exploitive tax system, for example in rice payment, led to serious deprivation. Even without the studied and effective invasion by the Japanese, Korea would have been in difficulty. There was still discord over modernisation, emerging industries were under-financed, the fishing fleets were traditional and therefore not very effective, and communications were poor. But the final curb on development was a law of 1911 which gave the Japanese administrator total control over business matters.

Despite internal dissent, and the activities of collaborators, there was considerable resistance to the Japanese throughout the occupation. Early in the century when Japan's intentions became clear, there were violent demonstrations which increased in ferocity at the times of vital treaties, such as 1905 and 1910, and when the emperor was forced to abdicate in 1907. In 1907, the Japanese decided to demobilise the Korean army, but such of the army as was left fought the Japanese army. However, the main resistance came from the 'Righteous Armies', which were joined by the remnants of the regular army. As the repression by the Japanese soared, these guerrillas moved to neighbouring territories. Between 1907 and

10 Ibid., p. 319. For a detailed account of Japan's colonial policy in Japan, see Mitchell, *The Korean Minority in Japan*, and Weiner, Michael, *Race and Migration in Imperial Japan* (London, 1994).

1910 there were 2,810 clashes with Japanese forces, and nearly 18,000 guerrillas had been killed.[11]

The Korean government tried, as best it could before total annexation, to solicit help from abroad, including, famously, the emperor's sending of a delegation to a Peace Conference in 1907, which was, equally famously, denied a place. Far from causing the Japanese to hesitate because of international concern, it was the episode which dethroned the emperor. A real problem in the organisation of resistance of any sort was the apprehension felt by upper classes, based on lack of experience, in trying to trust the mass of the population. Indeed, this is the only semblance of an excuse for the disloyal behaviour of the prime minister in 1907, since he, like others, believed he could deal with and rely on the Japanese more than he could his own people.

The resistance of the Koreans to the harsh regime being imposed upon them was reasonably contained until 1919. This was a very important year in Korean history, since this was the year of the March First Movement. By this time there had been a considerable exodus of Koreans overseas, and several varieties of resistance came into being. There were those who continued armed attacks from neighbouring territories, and others who relied on building links with countries who might help, such as a group in Shanghai. Similarly, as early as 1909, in Hawaii the Korean National Association was formed by one of the best known, though controversial Korean political figures, Syngman Rhee. Unfortunately, the experience of such groups, some seeing new Bolshevism as a solution, others putting faith in capitalism, established the political stances which still divide Korea. In addition within Korea, there was still a resistance movement which was fuelled by religious and educational activity.

All of this resistance came to a point of physical expression by the instability consequential upon the end of the First World War. Koreans were especially excited by the fact that old empires were being dismantled. The Korean group in Shanghai tried again to solicit the help of a Peace Conference, this time the great one in Paris. Of great significance was the declaration of Korean independence by Korean students in Tokyo in February 1919. The activity of women in this insurrection should be especially noted. The proposed funeral rites for former Emperor Kojong in March were agreed as a focus for a Declaration of Independence, especially

11 Ibid., p. 317.

since there was some suspicion that he had been murdered. The Declaration was issued on 1 March 1919. The leaders were arrested at once, but there were widespread demonstrations all over Korea. These were planned as peaceful, but the central demand – that Korea be given independence – was clearly unacceptable. The violence of the Japanese reaction was predictable, when it is remembered that this was a military occupation, in contrast to the European colonial practice which was to rule with 'a cadre of civilian officials supported by a minimal military presence'.[12] Even though the Japanese were surprised, they quickly recovered and engaged in the killing and injuring of many thousands, and the destruction of much property, often attended by great cruelty. Internationally, Japan reaped its reward as an ally of the victors in the war, and Korea received no support. This despite the Korean casualties, set by the Japanese at some 600 dead, 1,400 injured, with some 27,000 injured. Korean figures, for a rather longer period after 1 March list nearly 8,000 killed, and almost 46,000 injured.[13]

Japan was, nevertheless shaken by these events, and determined to make changes. These were not though changes of policy, but changes in the allegations about policy. Despite the power of the military, the 'liberal' voices which have been raised throughout recent Japanese history could be heard. These were people who pronounced that the destruction of Korean identity had failed, that the Koreans should be freed especially since, in the 'spirit of democracy ... to try to assimilate the Koreans in these circumstances would be as futile as an attempt at extinguishing a furious fire with an antiquated hand-pump' and the Japanese sympathy for Korea was further evident by student support for trying to understand both the Chinese and Korean ambitions.[14] The term used for the new regime, the 'Enlightened Administration' was a foretaste of the duplicity which was to follow. The principal features of the regime were to be the possible appointment of a civilian as governor-general, which never happened; the police system, which was especially brutal would be changed, which in practice led to an increase in police numbers and power; the education system was to be improved, which it never was; and control of the press would be

12 Weiner, *Race and Migration in Imperial Japan*, p. 39.

13 Mitchell, *The Korean Minority in Japan*, p. 21, quoting Lee, *The Korean Nationalist Movement, 1905–1945*.

14 Ibid., pp. 22–3, quoting Clarence N. Weems, *The Korean Reform and Independence Movement*, and Sakuzo Yoshino, 'Liberalism in Japan' in Kawakami, K.K. (ed.), *What Japan Thinks*.

eased, but the severe restrictions remained in place. The upshot was increasing Korean militancy.

The fact is that not only did the colonial regime remain harsh, life for the Koreans deteriorated. A variety of things had gone wrong for the Japanese outside Korea at about that time. There were food shortages in Japan which had caused riots in the country. The peace settlement, in giving the former German colony of Shandong to Japan, had provoked violent opposition in China which Japan regarded as insolence. More effrontery, not to say bitterness was felt by the restrictions introduced on Japanese immigration, notably into America. An especially traumatic event which added to the edifice of hatred was the great Tokyo earthquake of 1923, and its ensuing mayhem.

On 1 September of that year the region in which Tokyo and Yokohama stand underwent a huge earthquake. The nature and scale of the disaster have often been described, and can be imagined. Eighty per cent of Tokyo was destroyed in the fires and explosions which followed, and Yokohama was almost totally devastated. The earth did not settle, and the fires continued for three days. The death toll was estimated at about 100,000. The potential for disorder in such chaos was enormous, and had to be controlled. In particular the authorities wished to avoid a repetition of the Rice Riots of 1918 which had posed such a threat to the authorities. The way in which it was controlled was by the instigation of rumours that the Koreans, even though they could not be held responsible for the earthquake, were taking advantage of the situation by looting, lighting fires, poisoning wells, raping and killing.

It was a deflection which the media and the authorities exploited to the full. A Tokyo daily newspaper, on 2 September carried a story that the government had ordered the killing of Koreans, and that 'Koreans and Socialists were planning a rebellious and treacherous plot. We urge the citizens to cooperate with the military and the police to guard against Koreans'.[15] The government ordered martial law, and the Army was mobilised. It was believed that there was to be an invasion from Korea. As a precaution all Koreans were to be killed, and vigilante groups were set up. These latter, the *jikeidan* accounted for the deaths of some 2,000 Koreans. There were about 80,000 in the whole of Japan at the time.[16] Whatever doubts may exist about Koreans committing crime, there can be no doubt about what followed. The evidence of atrocities is well documented and

15 De Vos and Lee, *Koreans in Japan*, pp. 22–3.
16 Mitchell, *The Korean Minority in Japan*, p. 38.

based upon statements not only of Koreans and vigilantes, but of Japanese soldiers, one of whom reported how after a particularly savage assault: 'Our cavalry was excited with this bloody ceremony and started the main Korean hunting that evening'.[17] Eventually the government decided to intervene in the slaughter, but maintained the fiction that Koreans had been the chief instigators of disorder. Their specific policy was to encourage the belief that this disorder had not involved all Koreans, but the public verdict must be, in part for overseas consumption, that Koreans and Japanese extremists were to be held responsible.[18]

The upshot of such events was calamity for Korea. Rice and other foodstuffs were compulsorily exported to Japan, with the result that Koreans had to make do with third-rate food, or even, in bad times, tree bark. As Lee points out[19] even by Japanese calculation, of almost three million farm families in 1924, about 45 per cent were unable to grow enough both to placate alien demand, and to have enough to eat. Korea was also a dumping ground for highly priced market goods. The country also became attractive for Japanese investment, not least because of the quasi slave state of the labour force. The great Japanese industrial *zaibatsu* such as Mitsubishi, Mitsui and Yasuda moved in. Yet the colonial regime became more tyrannical as Japan began its next phase of expansion, first in Manchuria in 1931, then China in 1937, with the climax coming with the attack on Pearl Harbor in 1941, and America's entry into the war. Japan found it needed enormous resources of materials for war, and Korea, for one, could provide them.

This had a shattering effect on Korea. But Japan also needed human beings, and the effect on Korean society was traumatic. Koreans were shipped to Japan to work in mines, in factories and as support for front line troops, for example as guards in prisoner of war camps. A particularly inflammatory issue was of the forced enslavement of Korean women to provide sexual services for the Japanese forces, and we will return to this as an example of the misery into which the Korean people were put, but also as one explanation for the endless mutual hatred of the two peoples in Japan at the present time. The scale of the movement to Japan can be gauged by the fact that in 1945 there were more than two million

17 De Vos and Lee, *Koreans in Japan*, p. 24, quoting Kan Dok-sang and Kum Byong-dong (eds), *Kanto Earthquake and the Koreans* – 'the authoritative compilation of reports and documents'.

18 Weiner, *Race and Migration in Imperial Japan*, pp. 82–3. Weiner sets out a detailed analysis of these events.

19 Lee, K i- baik, *A New History of Korea*, p. 357.

Koreans in Japan, mostly taken forcibly.[20] A specific example of the impact, and the contribution by Koreans however enforced, is the fact that by 1945, 43 per cent of the mining labour force in Hokkaido were Koreans.[21] Those few who had gone voluntarily occasionally were successful in business. But in the main they were a depressed group, unskilled and living in ghettos and stereotyped by the Japanese as 'rebellious Koreans'. In the 1920s the Korean-organised 'Mutual Friendship Society', tolerated by the Japanese, was replaced by a government-controlled 'Concordia Society' with concomitant claims about integration. All Koreans had to join and had to carry identity cards.

Even under such pressure, Korean resistance continued. Within the country cultural attempts to maintain national identity could not be suppressed, there was industrial action by people conscripted to work in factories, and a 'Wind and Lightning Society' planned to assassinate Crown Prince Hirohito on his wedding day. The approximately 8,000 Korean students in Japan in 1937[22] continued to support the several political movements, but these were prone to spending more energy on fighting each other than they were the Japanese. In China in about 1932, there were six Korean armies, one division of which was commanded by a woman, Yi Hong-gwang. One obvious result of this was that by 1945 there were many experienced Korean soldiers, which after the Japanese defeat did little to bring peace to Korea. For the vacuum which was left in 1945 was extremely volatile.

One might have supposed that with the beginning of the Pacific War, Japan would have tried to maintain such equilibrium as there was in Korea. Instead it announced a new policy with the motto 'Japan and Korea are one entity'. This was a prelude to a hopeless attempt at assimilation. The Korean language was banned in print, both newspapers and books, and in speech in schools and home. Similarly the study of Korean history was forbidden, worship at Shinto shrines was made compulsory and most absurd of all, Koreans had to take Japanese names – but not those of emperors or other important Japanese.

This final indignity is of much more interest than as a simple piece of repression. Discouraging or even forbidding the use of indigenous language has been, and remains, a popular means of cultural imperialism. Examples are legion, from Wales and Den-

20 De Vos and Lee, *Koreans in Japan*, p. 58.
21 Ibid., p. 53.
22 Ibid., p. 42.

mark in the nineteenth century to the attempt to suppress Kurdish in the twentieth. But what is of political interest is why Japan should undertake such an inflammatory step when it must have seemed clear that there was no point. One of the reasons may have been the remoteness of the rulers of Japan from the real world. It was a remoteness which was compounded by a conviction that they were superior. It may be, in addition, that it was a last attempt to assert authority over an inferior people in advance of the certainty that that authority was crumbling. Whatever the reasoning, if reasoning there was, about 84 per cent of Koreans were sufficiently frightened, or clever enough, to take Japanese names.

The heritage of the colonial period is bitter and two case studies will serve to illustrate some of its worst aspects. These are the involvement of Koreans in criminal activity in Japan, and the matter of the sex slaves, 'comfort women', used by the Japanese forces in the Pacific War. One of the singular alleged and mysterious features of Japanese society is the low crime rate. It is a criminological commonplace that the amount of crime which is reported is likely to represent only a proportion, in the case of certain offences a very small proportion, of actual crime. There are many reasons for this, notably the reluctance of victims to report to the police. In the case of Japan the reasons for the low crime rate have been attributed to a variety of factors. These range from the closeness of the police to the community, especially through the highly visible police boxes – *koban* – to, inevitably, the discipline with which the Japanese are generally credited.

Yet there is crime in Japan, and it broadly has two segments. The first of these is the operation of the remarkable *yakuza*, who are powerful gangs of professionals controlling gambling, vice, and other lucrative business. The second is the more familiar lumpen-proletariat of criminals, mostly thieves, and mostly young. The reason for discussion about crime here is that, allegedly, historically and at present, Koreans are involved. It is a classic case study about minorities. It is a view which is deeply ingrained in the attitudes of Japanese police, politicians and society at large. It is also central to the understanding of the relationship between the groups. It is based upon some evidence, some prejudice, and lack of under-standing of the nature of deviant behaviour. Because of this lack of understanding, the political 'non conformity' of Koreans in Japan is lumped together with criminal behaviour, and both are seen as a threat to social stability. In addition, in Japan as elsewhere, people whose social milieu comprises discrimination, unemployment and poverty are very likely to appear in criminal statistics. There is also the phenomenon of 'scapegoating', which is the universal habit of focusing all responsibility for trouble upon minorities. Indeed, it would be remarkable if such minorities did not cause trouble.

After the takeover of Korea, it was not long before Koreans began to migrate to Japan. As the latter continued to prosper, conditions for the former deteriorated. At the end of the First World War, Korean migration increased rapidly. In 1923 the Korean population stood at 80,000,[23] which rose to nearly two million in 1938, and after 1945 decreased again to the present day total of about 676,000, of whom 75 per cent were born in Japan.

Their situation in Japan was typical of migrants everywhere from colonial dependencies to the imperial centre. They were unskilled, exploited and consigned to ghettos where conditions were bad. They were the object of vilification and distrust, in part for the very good reason that they depressed the level of wages, thus incurring the wrath of poor Japanese. Thus, substantial numbers of Koreans in Japan recognised their position, and like such social groups everywhere, had little interest in aiding the stability and development of a state which despised them. Korean animosity expressed itself in familiar ways. On the part of young people, straightforward criminal activity, on the part of adults by political action which has tended to be regarded in Japan *as* criminal, or rarely by joining the *yakuza*.

Korean involvement in the *yakuza*, apart from generalised allegations, centres upon a man whose Japanese name is Hisayuki Machii.[24] He rose to prominence during the Occupation during which Koreans supposed, naturally enough, that their status, and the attitude of the Japanese would change. In a later section the turmoil of the period, especially its disappointments for Koreans will be discussed. The opportunity it provided for Hisayuki was to engage in black market activities, and later to form 'a largely Korean band of Yakuza' called *Tosei-Kai* (Voice of the East). This group not only controlled rackets, notably in the Ginza, the entertainment district of Tokyo, but also was involved in the political violence which attended the attempt to set up democracy after the Pacific War. Predictably, the Japanese press emphasised the Korean involvement in the *yakuza*, one newspaper, for example, noted that this gang was 'one of the most feared and strongest underworld

23 Ibid., p. 36.
24 Dubro, A. and Kaplan, David E., *Yakuza: The Explosive Account of Japan's Criminal Underworld* (Tokyo, 1987).

organisations'.[25] The only observation to be made is that this illustrates a commonplace of ghetto experience which is that wealth and power can be achieved by alternative illegal means, if legitimate ladders are blocked. What is interesting about his career is that it illustrates, in some important respects, the position of the Korean community during the Occupation and since.

But much of the cause of the problem lay, and continues to lie, in the racism which seems immanent in all people, and which commentators, Japanese and non-Japanese, claim is especially deep in Japanese tradition. In the recent history of relationships, as we have seen this was especially fuelled by the March First Movement in 1919 in Korea. This high point in Korean resistance both made the Japanese nervous of the manifest 'instability' of the Koreans, and also legitimised police oppression. Further evidence of the need for apprehension and vigilance was provided by Korean terrorist activity, which is always seen as valid by the oppressed, but is a source of wonder for the oppressors, who expect gratitude for their condescension in trying to help inferior people. The 1919 rising coincided with increasing emigration, and together with the aftermath of the earthquake illustrated Japanese excess, added significantly to Korean hatred and provides a classic case of scapegoating, exemplifying the difficulty of distinguishing between crime, subversion and politics.

The folk memory of Hideyoshi, the brutalising of the Koreans in the Japanese Empire, the bitter memories of the great Tokyo earthquake mean that the colossal animosity between the two peoples is deeply ingrained. The Pacific War when the treatment of the Koreans, both in Korea and Japan reached a nadir, exacerbated the position – if such exacerbation were possible – and left one heritage which is singularly emotive and illustrative. It is one that makes Koreans feel especially bitter. This is the matter of what are called 'comfort women'. These were sex slaves imprisoned for the use of the Japanese forces. They included women from many of the Japanese occupied territories, but the majority were Koreans.

The initial official Japanese response to the revelation that this practice existed was to deny that it had happened. But in recent years widespread publicity, admission by Japanese ex-servicemen, and evidence from 'comfort women' made such a position untenable. It has been common to see on television ex-soldiers describe the abuse of Korean women sometimes with regret but often, it

25 Ibid., p. 240.

must be said, in an alarmingly matter of fact way. At the same time there have been television presentations in which Korean victims have described to Japanese women's groups, what happened to them. These accounts have, not surprisingly, been charged with a lot of emotion, both on the part of the speakers and the listeners.

Faced with such evidence in July 1992, the Japanese government investigated the charges, and produced a report which was in the words of the *Mainichi Daily News*[26] 'ambiguous'. At that point it seems to have been admitted that the events were not fictional, but were complicated. There were two complications. The first is that it was 'the lower end' of the Imperial Army which engaged in such practices, and secondly, in any case, there was insufficient evidence of coercion. To accept such conclusions would necessitate a belief in the behaviour of armies and of women which would fly in the face of experience.

To suggest that only 'the lower end' engaged in sexual activity is convenient because officers would be absolved. To give such blanket absolution to any officers would require an abnormal faith in human nature, but to give it to officers of the Imperial Army, when their brutality is so well documented, is excessive. With the explosive issue of war-time behaviour, especially that of the Imperial Army still remaining an inflammatory matter in Japan, the saving of the honour of the officer class is vital. But it might, at least infer, that even if they did not take part, these abuses were carried out without the knowledge of the officers. This is not only unlikely, but given the nature of the regimental life, leaving aside that the women had to be medically examined, transported as the unit moved, and died, must be dismissed out of hand. With regard to the suggestion that they were voluntary camp followers, it is the case that people have always offered sexual services to soldiers but this truth must be qualified in this case. In the first place camp followers are usually local, attaching themselves to armies as they appear, or at most pursuing them over short distances. These however were transported many thousands of miles, in documented cases based on first-hand evidence, from Korea to Manchuria, Nanjing and Singapore. Secondly there were thousands of women 'recruited', and this reduces the likelihood that they were volunteers.

The response of the South Korean government to this prevarication was to mount its own investigation in 1992, and 103 women gave evidence. The pattern described was common. In 1939 whole

26 5 March 1993.

families who refused to take Japanese names were rounded up, and the women enslaved. These women were, typically, sterilised, sent all over Asia, while some were shot trying to escape, or committed suicide. They were forced to have sex with about twenty soldiers a day, and refusal would lead to beating, as did speaking Korean. They were regularly tested for venereal disease, and returned to 'duty' when they were cured.

When this report was sent to the Japanese government, its officials interviewed not only Korean women, but women from China, Taiwan, the Netherlands and the Philippines. The outcome, as reported in the press, was an apology to the women, and a promise to report what the women said to the Chief Cabinet Secretary.[27] The problem for the Japanese government is, ostensibly, compensation. For a diminished and diminishing group of elderly women, this is hardly a crippling expense. The real difficulty is that to concede would mean admitting the brutality of the Imperial Army, and whilst individuals are prepared to do so, the government, especially the Liberal Democratic Party, which has mostly ruled post-war Japan is unwilling to do so, both because it means attacking national integrity, and because it realises the political dangers of doing so, even after fifty years. The Koreans, arguably, have identified, and isolated, the 'real' question. The money may not be a problem, although to be fair, compensation questions are notoriously complex. The first democratically elected civilian President of South Korea, asked by Japanese journalists what Japan could do to compensate, said 'It is not your money we want. It is the truth we want to make clear. Only then will the problem be solved.'[28]

The two million Koreans who were in Japan when the Americans began their occupation no doubt shared the high expectations of their compatriots at home. There were a lot who left Japan, sometimes to return illegally because of conditions in Korea. The Japanese contempt for Koreans was unchanged in defeat. They were accused of involvement in civil unrest, by amongst others Prime Minister Yoshida who wrote about 'the activities of the Japan Communist Party, who abetted labour strikes, incited riots of Koreans, and created all manners of disturbances throughout the country.'[29] Police surveillance increased, and the government resis-

27 *Mainichi Daily News*, 20 March 1993.

28 Buruma, Ian, *The Wages of Guilt: Memories of War in Germany and Japan* (London, 1994), p. 297.

29 Morita Akio, Reingold, E.M. and Shimomura, M., *Made in Japan: Akio Morita and Sony* (London, 1987), p. 134.

ted Korean demands for their own schools. In 1949 this led to widespread protests and in Hyogo Prefecture 30,000 Koreans were arrested.[30] During an anti-crime campaign, a Korean emblem was used as a background in a poster, and generally the stereotypes were perpetuated.[31] The Korean community set up a variety of organisations to forward their interests, but like the Korean movements in exile in the colonial period, these reflected the political and other divisions in Korea. There continues to be discrimination, notably in employment, education and housing. Although the majority were born in Japan, their status remains that of aliens. Perhaps the most poignant and lasting symbol of animosity has been the refusal of the Japanese government to allow monuments to be erected to the 20,000 Koreans killed at Hiroshima and 2,000 killed at Nagasaki ostensibly because there is no room.[32] It is scarcely any wonder that one summary is that 'No two people on earth liked each other less.'[33]

30 De Vos and Lee, *Koreans in Japan*, pp. 165–6.
31 Ibid., p. 75.
32 Hane Mikiso, *Modern Japan: An Historical Survey* (Colorado, 1986), p. 401.
33 Olson, Lawrence, *Japan in Post-War Asia* (London, 1970), p. 102.

CHAPTER SEVEN

*Japanese Tradition
and the Curbing of 'Dangerous Thoughts'*

Overleaf ▶
Businessmen giving alms to a monk

Japanese Tradition
and the Curbing of 'Dangerous Thoughts'

By comparison with the instability which had wrecked European empires in the First World War, Japan remained stable. The war brought territorial advantage to Japan, thus ostensibly strengthening the power of military and nationalistic aggression, but in the eyes of militarists national affairs seemed to be in disorder. They had to cope with the hostility of the people to the Siberian adventure, which it seemed might eradicate the pride and pleasure felt by those at home with the victories in the Chinese and Russian wars. More seriously, and a much longer-term threat to the unity of the empire, were resurrected civil unrest, the continuing burgeoning interest in politics, and the creation of parties to channel that interest.

The famous example of unrest at the end of the First World War were the rice riots of 1918. Disruption easily occurs if a staple crop proves to be prohibitively expensive, and thus unavailable, and can be disastrous, as is exemplified in the several potato famines in Ireland in the nineteenth century. The protest began in the summer of 1918 because of the price of rice, and a well founded suspicion that manipulation and hoarding had created a monopoly or cartel. By August, humble petitions turned to violence and looting in most of Japan, with police stations – an interesting and familiar revolutionary target – being destroyed, together with industrial sabotage and arson. The army to the number of some 92,000, a huge force, were called in to help the hard pressed police, and at the end of the punitive process, of 25,000 arrested, and about 8,000 charged, 6,000 were convicted and punished with fines or death.[1] Even the oligarchy were unnerved, and by processes which, as always in govern-

1 See entry under 'Rice riots of 1918' by Radin, Robert B. in *Kodansha Encyclopedia*.

ment are difficult to discern, the Prime Minister Terauchi, the general of Korean notoriety, resigned and in his place came Hara Takashi, who has the historical distinction of being the first prime minister in Japan to head a majority party in the lower house of the Diet. It seemed to some that Taisho democracy had moved a stage forward.

The significance of the rice riots continues to be debated. It has been argued that they were simply an expression of anger at the cost of living. If this is to be agreed, it requires a remarkable communication system, outside of political organisation, to validate it. Alternatively they have been seen as a 'popular' explosion consonant with the mood to create a democratic Japan. Again, they were seen as an insidious or beneficial influence (depending upon viewpoint) which derived from the intellectual ferment which study and contemplation of the west continued to excite. There does though seem to be a substantial degree of agreement that Hara's rise to the premiership owed a lot to popular, oligarchic and even imperial concerns, of which the riots were an expression.

To understand the dismay of the oligarchy at such behaviour one would have to be a member of that oligarchy in 1918, suffused with the interminable conviction that what is right is right, and to feel that the Japanese people were not worthy, were degenerating, and in need of correction. Before the authorities could address themselves to these problems, they had to submit to further attack, which came in 1919 with a number of challenges, two of the most significant of which were the establishment of the Japan Federation of Labour, and a demonstration by the Universal Manhood Suffrage Movement, an increasingly urgent group, but one which had its origins in late Meiji times. Further agitation in 1920 led in 1925 to what was in some ways the triumph of Taisho democracy, universal male suffrage. It was moreover productive of an electorate which, at least initially, had some sort of a choice.

But the issue of suffrage was not the sole, or even the most important cause, of civil unrest. Japan was undergoing the inexorable processes of dysfunction set in train by urbanisation and industrialisation. Rural Japan has sometimes been assumed always to have been stable, but poverty there, as in other rural countries, was never far away. Nor did the causes of that poverty differ much from those in other countries. At the heart of it were heavy rents, which could amount to half a rice crop. While it is difficult to prove that there is a relationship between rents and civil disturbance, it has to be accepted that it was a major contributing factor.[2] But there were others, such as the expanding opportunities for factory work in the war, which created something of a shortage on the land, a situation which was however to be reversed in the depression of the 1920s. Waswo adds other factors such as the broader experience gained through military service, and the possibility that education may have been having an effect. Waswo also draws attention to the changing relationship of landlord and tenants. Traditionally this was interdependent, and expressed as landlords being 'the host plants of the land; tenants, like ivy, coil round them and are protected from the weather'.[3] But phenomena such as absenteeism amongst landlords, and investment by the latter in industry rather than land, began in the 1920s in particular, to loosen such relationships.

Japanese employers had to deal with increasingly complex questions in the field of industrial relations. As industrialisation expanded, employers carried over classical cultural values. Central in these was a belief that the company was rather like a family, with a caring head who knew what was best, and who would look after the employees. The latter, certain that they would be looked after, would respond by a display of 'filial piety'. During the 1920s, at least for a core of workers there was security of tenure, a bonus system, and other characteristics of Japanese employment practice which remain substantially unchanged. There also developed the much under-reported feature, even in modern times, of the presence of 'temporary' workers, who paid the price for the security of others, and the smooth operation of the company. For these, as Totten points out 'formed the ballast to be discharged when the work force had to be reduced'.[4] There were industrial disputes, which ranged from 293 a year before 1926, to 397 in 1928, with the length of individual disputes increasing.[5] Totten uses as a case study the biggest strike up to 1927–29, which took place in the Noda soy sauce company. Not only does his account chronicle the hindrances to effective action, such as systematic strike-breaking tactics, but it reminds us that the paterfamilias method of management did not extend to the elimination of the squalor in which workers lived and

2 Waswo, Ann, 'The Origins of Tenant Unrest', in Silberman, Bernard S. and Harootunian, Harry D. (eds), *Japan in Crisis: Essays on Taisho Democracy* (Princeton, 1974) goes into detail about such questions.

3 Ibid., p. 389 quoting Amano Fuji, *Noson shakai mondai: jinushi to kosakunin* (Tokyo, 1920).

4 Totten, George O., 'Japanese industrial relations at the crossroads: The Great Noda Strike of 1927–1928', in Silberman and Harootunian, *Japan in Crisis*, p. 400.

5 Ibid., pp. 406–7.

worked. Not all were as bad, or as anti union as Noda. In 1919 a minority of businessmen, with critical government support, formed the Harmonisation Society, which was agreeable to unionisation, and to the implications about collective bargaining and the consequent implications.[6]

Political parties proliferated, as they had at the beginning of the century. Although there was an array of parties and alignments, there was little difference between them. Their power rested upon a very small electorate, qualification for which depended upon wealth. They believed in the imperial system, were suspicious of western ideas, and disagreed only on issues such as taxation to pay for military expenditure, which directly affected their pockets. By the early 1920s, after a series of metamorphoses the two most prominent of these were the Constitutional Association, whose main antecedent had been a party founded by General Katsura, one of Yamagata's faction, and the Friends of Constitutional Government, which also reflected interests of powerful groups notably bureaucrats. It was this latter party which forged another link in the democratic chain by forming the first party cabinet in 1918 under the leadership of Hara Takashi. This event is substantially attributed to the fear inspired by the violence of the rice riots, and the government's mishandling of it.

Hara was not only the first Japanese to lead a party cabinet, but he is regarded as the first commoner prime minister. This meant that he was not the holder of a title, although he was in fact born into a *samurai* family. He had been a newspaper editor, a civil servant, a member of the Diet, a diplomat and a minister. The new prime minister was a firm believer in political parties as the only way in which bureaucrats, and the military, could loosen their grip on the nations' affairs. During his career he paid special attention to strengthening party organisation in the prefectures. This was a considerable ambition, involving opposing extremely powerful people, and the verdict is that he was successful. Just how successful can perhaps be measured by the fact that in November 1921, he was stabbed to death on the platform of Tokyo station by a young man variously regarded as a fanatic, or an ultra-nationalist. The ostensible reason for the murder was that in taking over the post of minister of the navy while the minister was at the Washington naval conference, Hara had besmirched the Constitution. Strangely, there was some popular support for the assassin. Hara's career as

6 Ibid., p. 399.

prime minister had disappointed many people because of his conservatism, especially his failure to support universal male suffrage, which was a natural ambition at the time.

There were some radical political parties in the Taisho Era. We saw earlier how quickly they were banned in the early part of the century. The successful revolution in Russia interested some Japanese, notably intellectuals, and in July 1922 the Japan Communist Party was founded. It foundered over the course of the next ten years for predictable reasons. There was the determination of the authorities, legitimated by powerful ordinances, to prevent the growth of a party which wished to establish a workers' state, a stage in which was to be the abolition of the imperial institution. Next, although intellectuals found in Marxism a fascinating solution to all kinds of problems, such as the authoritarianism and poverty of Japan, it was far removed from the real world of workers and farmers. Nor was there any serious communication between intellectuals and workers and farmers, both of which groups had difficulty in subscribing to the idea of moderate unionism, never mind revolution. The final reason for the failure of the Communist Party was one which has often afflicted revolutionary groups. These tend, after a time to engage in fratricidal debate, exacerbated by the defining of activities and people as opportunist, so that all the energy and skill of activities is drained into ideological squabbling, which not only achieves nothing, but leaves the lower classes totally bewildered. The contrast with the right-wing parties in Japan is notable. Although the right wing had its differences and quarrels, somehow they seemed in the Taisho Era, as today, to be able to subordinate enough of their policies to negotiate some collaborative agreement which would keep them in power.

Radical ideas, cultural or political, had an especially difficult time in Japan in the early twentieth century. The problem arose because of the classical Japanese belief that the basic social unit is the group, not the individual. This is what was exploited and consolidated by the various Meiji Rescripts, reminding the people that personal subordination is the greatest of social values. Such a belief is exactly the opposite to that in the western intellectual tradition, which can only exist in a society which allows discord, at least of ideas. The history of authoritarian regimes in this century in Europe is notable for insistence upon uniformity and loyalty, the cost of which is intellectual submission. Such states require that the population as individuals abrogate their right to decide for themselves, and support that demand with force. The peculiarity in Japanese society was that this was a demand which was consonant with a central tradition. Therefore when an intellectual, reflecting on how the country might be changed for the better, advanced a proposal, the reaction as time went on was swift and strident.

A famous example whose career demonstrates a hesitant acceptance, at first, of intellectual challenge to the dogma enshrined in the Meiji Constitution was Inobe Tatsukichi. He was a professor of law in Tokyo University from about 1902, and advanced the idea that the emperor was only one, albeit the highest, of the 'organs' of the state. People in academic and official life were intrigued, some agreed, some disagreed, but it became a main debate for some thirty years. Despite the demonstration of his eminence by his appointment to the House of Peers in 1932, his opposition to right-wing encirclement of civil liberties at last led to his downfall, in the increasingly vocal nationalist mood. In 1935 he was the victim of a sustained harangue in the Diet and some of his books were banned. He was told that unless he resigned he would be charged with offences against the state. He had to resign under the volume of threats. He was also seriously injured in an attack by an extremist. It has been suggested that the subject of Minobe's theory, Hirohito, was deeply interested in the professor's fate. He is supposed to have said to his Grand Chamberlain: 'Many people are criticising Minobe these days, but there is nothing disloyal about him. Is there anyone of his stature these days? It is sad indeed, that such a fine scholar should be treated in this manner.'[7]

The nature and morality of individuality was constantly debated as Japan experimented with democracy, but it was a debate which went to the heart of Japanese tradition, and was fraught with danger.

Debates about the nature of democracy, civil disturbance – notably the rice riots – and such left-wing activity as there was, met firm opposition from the authorities. They saw danger everywhere, and no-one was safe, not even the imperial family. In December 1923 a young man tried to shoot Crown Prince Hirohito on his way to open the Diet, but missed. The would-be assassin was probably an extreme right-winger, motivated by disapproval of the recent visit by the prince to the west. It has never been clear who, if it was organised, was behind the attempt. It was in the same year that the great Kanto earthquake occurred, destroying Tokyo and Yokohama, an event discussed in the chapter on Koreans, whose treatment as a consequence is one of the most wretched in their history. The

7 Kawahara Toshiaki, *Hirohito and His Times: A Japanese Perspective* (Tokyo, 1990), p. 67.

earthquake was, of course, nobody's fault, but it did seriously upset what the authorities wished for, social peace. In 1925 a Peace Preservation Law was passed, significantly in the year in which all Japanese males over the age of twenty-five were given the vote. One specific reason why the Peace Preservation measure was enacted was that it seemed likely that the broadening of suffrage to include poor as well as rich increased the likelihood of 'deviant' political behaviour.

Since 1911 the operational arm established to control 'deviance' had been the Special Higher Police. It will be remembered that under the Law of 1900, political groups and meetings were strictly controlled. After 1918 the activities of this unit sometimes known as the 'peace' police, but more commonly as the 'thought' police, were much expanded. The 1925 Law further increased their powers, and the unit increased in size and developed specialist branches. In the face of agitation, real and potential, because of the Depression which affected Japan as much as it did other countries, the police tightened their grip even more. At the same time the activities of teachers were more strictly controlled since then, as always, they were regarded as obvious channels for 'dangerous thoughts'.

In 1928 too, the first elections since universal suffrage were held, and this led to a resurgence of left-wing, notably communist, political activity. The ministry of justice established a 'thought section' to plan an offensive against left-wing organisations, but the target was much wider, including almost any body or individual who might harbour 'dangerous thoughts', a term which was to become a hallmark of the next twenty years. The planning led to what is called the March 15th Incident, since on that day in 1928 thousands of thought police raided political, trade union and newspaper offices, as well as private homes. Arrests continued throughout 1928, and these totalled some 3,500. Several organisations of farmers, young people and unionists were proscribed, ostensibly because they were 'dangerous'. In 1928 the Peace Preservation Law was strengthened, notably by raising the maximum penalty from ten years' imprisonment to death. Such provisions were regarded by the Diet as excessive, and it refused to pass them. The amended Law was therefore put into place by an imperial ordinance.

The March 15th Incident had been especially directed at communists, and in 1929 the operation continued, to what the authorities rightly assumed was a successful conclusion. The April 16th Incident of that year was the rounding up of about 700 alleged communists, many of whom were imprisoned, including key party leaders. The two Incidents together effected the demise of the communist party in Japan until the end of the Pacific War, although a remnant remained underground until about 1935. The government had also to cope with anarchists. The latter continued to publish devastating criticism of government and military policies. The army for example was regularly described as a 'collection of idiots playing at war'. That the anarchists were not dismissed as a lunatic, harmless fringe, can be seen from the fact that when military manoeuvres took place, they were arrested.[8] All these repressive measures took place under the government of Tanaka Giichi. An interesting indication of the location of real power at the end of the period of Taisho democracy is the fact that the Choshu were still in control of the army, and of the government; General Tanaka was, by birth, Choshu.

As Japan became more belligerent in the 1930s and engaged in total war in the 1940s, the work of the thought police became more and more thorough. Spy systems were set up which encouraged the populace to report on each other and agents were posted to other countries, including European and American cities. By 1941, some 65,000 people had been arrested by them.[9] Despite the number of arrests, only relatively few were prosecuted, and the thought police seem not to have accrued a universal reputation for brutality. It has been suggested that they were more anxious to make people orthodox, in part, through persuasion, than to murder them. The military police, the *kempei-tai*, which was an entirely separate organis- ation, were much harsher and much more feared in Japan. Yet the view has been expressed that their activities should be put into perspective by comparison with apparently parallel police forces. Nor, the argument continues, were the Japanese thought police in the same league as the several murderous secret police forces of Hitler, Stalin or Mao.

Nevertheless, they played a central role in the crushing of articulate opposition to the Japanese right-wing government, thus reducing debate to a point where the Japanese people were deprived of the opportunity to consider alternative forms of govern- ment. The ruthless, even if not brutal silencing of not only violent action, but 'dangerous thoughts' was an important aid to the progress of the military towards their constant determination to

8 Crump, John, 'Anarchist opposition to Japanese militarism 1926–1937' in *Japan Forum*, Vol. 4, No. 1, April 1992 (Oxford), p. 77.

9 For discussion, see entry under 'Special Higher Police' in *Kodansha Encyclopedia* and Richard Deacon, *A History of the Japanese Secret Service* (London, 1982), Chapter 15.

return to the Meiji system where the military were in control, untrammelled by alien political ideas. To be expected in this context was press control and indeed censorship was total.

By the end of the 1920s, the period called Taisho democracy was coming to an end. Its significance in the evolution of modern Japan is a matter of debate. There were, manifestly, political developments which justify if not the term democracy, then an awareness of what it meant, and some steps towards it. Two notable examples are the establishment of the first cabinet government under Hara, and universal male suffrage. In respect of the latter the speed with which it was introduced from the initiation of any vote at all – some forty years – compares favourably with some western countries which took several hundred years to graduate from restricted suffrage to universal, albeit confined to males. The Taisho period also witnessed the discussion of political ideas, even about the emperor's position, although amongst intellectuals of a liberal persuasion there was little or no advocacy of a republican cause. That was very much confined to tiny numbers of anarchists and other extremists. But scholars and writers did examine one of the central tensions to which reference has been made, which is the concept of individuality. Harootunian is one writer who emphasises the critical and central nature of the outcome:

> If Taisho culture possessed any meaning distinct from Meiji civilisation, it is to be found in the development and triumph of that conception of private interest and atomised individuality which is at the heart of the liberal political and social creed. In short, it is to be found in the transformation of the distinctively political into the social.[10]

And although the causes were not always political, the street demonstration seemed to be some sort of an indication that people were prepared to challenge authority, which is always a symptom of social maturity.

In such respects the period can be considered significant in the development of Japan. But, as we have begun to see, for complex reasons the initiative faltered. Divisions between liberal and the many varieties of left-wing theorists and activists was just one element in a situation where a united 'government', in the broadest sense, was able to contain, repress and eventually extinguish the turbulence of those years. Historians not only debate the sig-

---

10 Harootunian, H.D., 'Introduction: A sense of an ending and the problem of Taisho' in Silberman and Harootunian, *Japan in Crisis*, p. 14.

nificance of this 'democracy', but also argue about whether or not it was an aberrant episode between the authoritarian regimes of Meiji and the military in the 1930s and early 1940s, or whether the latter constituted a pause in the continuing movement towards reform which culminated in the constitution set up after the Pacific War. Or indeed whether there can be found in each, characteristics of Japanese ethical and social values, and historical experience. If so the conclusion may be that the whole period of recent Japanese history, especially the transition from Taisho to military rule is smooth and in some ways unremarkable. After all, it may be argued, the military and their allies never did lose control during the Taisho period.

It is impossible to be sure as to when 'democracy' ended. But without doubt, an important milestone in the process, if not the last, occurred in 1932, since it was in May of that year that the Prime Minister Inukai Tsuyoshi was assassinated. He was not the first Japanese prime minister to be murdered, as we have seen, but his death was of particular historical significance. To understand why it is necessary to go back to some of the international repercussions of the First World War.

In 1921, under pressure from the United States, the British declined to renew the Anglo-Japanese alliance. Grave doubts were expressed at the time and later by the British, and the Japanese were shocked. In the process of looking for new allies they turned eventually to Germany. Winston Churchill in later years expressed a commonly held opinion that the breaking of the alliance created: 'a profound impression in Japan and was viewed as the spurning of an Asiatic power by the Western world. Many links were surrendered which might afterwards have proved of decisive value to peace.'[11]

In 1921 in an attempt to maintain friendly relations, Crown Prince Hirohito went on an official visit to Europe, with especial attention being paid to Britain. The visit was warmly welcomed, and was acclaimed as a great success. Like his grandfather, the prince was made a Knight of the Garter, and their commemorative plaques are in St George's Chapel, Windsor Castle, alongside the most eminent in British history. But the diplomatic damage had been done.

The American success in splitting the erstwhile allies, and at least in theory moving closer to Britain, was reflected in the results of a conference which were to provide justification for violence against

11 Deacon, *History of the Japanese Secret Service*, p. 124 quoting Winston Churchill, *The Second World War*, Vol. i.

political figures in Japan. The Americans initiated a conference to reduce international armaments, which was held in Washington in 1921, the first of five in which Japan took part. There were two major areas of discussion. The first was the need to ensure peace in the Pacific. To this end America was given permission to install defences in the Philippines, Guam and Wake Island, and Japan in its home islands. These defences though were 'limited', and the Japanese public could hardly be accused of being unreasonable when they complained that in practice this meant that America was being allowed to expand in the Pacific while, even in defence of the home islands, Japan had to reduce its ability to defend itself. The second decision concerned capital, that is very large, warships. Once again the Japanese lost in a formula which allowed a ratio of American five, Britain five, Japan three. The negotiation by the west was much helped by the fact that they had broken the Japanese codes, and thus could decipher diplomatic traffic.

The last humiliation came with the London Naval Conference of 1930. This conference established the ratio of lesser warships, and once again Japan lost out, despite strong resistance from the Japanese naval establishment. The nationalists regarded this as the last straw, especially since, despite naval opposition, Prime Minister Hamaguchi Osachi defended the arrangement. Some saw in this civilian interference with military prerogative, the same accusation which had been levelled against Hara. Like the latter, Hamaguchi was attacked on Tokyo railway station in November 1930. Although not killed at once by the gunshot, he died just under a year later. The attempt was made by a man called Sagoya, who was imprisoned, but amazingly was in the news again as late as 1956 when as leader of something called the National Defence Corps, he organised a bizarre mock funeral for the then prime minister at a Tokyo station.[12]

Also in 1930, there came into being one of a number of ultra-nationalistic secret societies, called the Cherry Blossom Society. It was founded by Lieutenant-Colonel Hashimoto Kingoro, who is a case study of the new breed of military officers who were to be so powerful in the 1930s. He had some experience of other countries, and particularly admired Kemal Ataturk, who in his modernisation of Turkey had shown that strong leadership could drastically change a society.[13] He was a middle-grade officer, and membership of the

12 Butow, Robert J.C., *Tojo and the Coming of the War* (Princeton), 1961, p. 49.
13 Murakami Hyoe, *Japan: The Years of Trial, 1919–52* (Tokyo, 1982), p. 39.

society was only open to those of his rank or below. This illustrates the growing feeling among younger officers that the most senior ranks were too staid, and too inactive, to go to the roots of what they believed were the problems of Japan. In many of the events which were to follow can be found the influence of, or active participation by, this officer. One of his more belligerent acts, when he was commander of a regiment of artillery in China in 1937, was to fire on a British ship, HMS *Ladybird*. Reflecting on this, Admiral Yamamoto Isoroko, remarked: 'I'm always expecting someone to put a bullet through Hashimoto, but it never seems to happen.'[14] Nobody did, and Hashimoto, despite being put on the reserve on several occasions for his revolutionary and precipitate behaviour, continued his active career as soldier, plotter and even politician: in 1944 he was elected to the Diet. Yamamoto's 'bullet' came in the form of Hashimoto's conviction in the post-war trials, when he was sentenced to life imprisonment. Lucky as ever, he was released in 1955, but died two years later aged sixty-seven.

Soon after its formation the Cherry Blossom Society was involved in two plots to overthrow the government. In March 1931, with the aim of establishing a military government led by General Ugaki Kasushige, the minister of war, the first attempt was made. The plan was to attack the prime minister's residence, the headquarters of the political parties, and surround the Diet. The plot failed because the organisation of it was ill prepared, and because Ugaki, whose role in it is debatable, became lukewarm. Undeterred, Hashimoto continued to plot, and the authorities, having heard of a new attempted coup tried to dissuade him. Araki Sadao, a lieutenant-general, was the arbitrator, which had a bizarre aspect since, without his knowledge, the plotters planned to make him head of a military government. Araki failed, and the ringleaders were put into custody. No actual damage was done in the 'October Incident', but it underlined the worrying character of the younger officers, especially their growing disrespect for their seniors. Murakami, for example, recounts how, having learned of the plan, Major General Tatekawa 'had a two hour long, heated discussion' with Hashimoto.[15] Not only is it very remarkable that a senior officer in the Japanese army should have a 'heated discussion' with his junior, but also that it was to no avail.

In these several attempts to topple the government, the military

14 Agawa Hiroyuki, *The Reluctant Admiral: Yamamoto and the Imperial Navy* (Tokyo, 1979), pp. 134–5.
15 Murakami, *Japan: The Years of Trial*, p. 40.

revolutionaries allied themselves with sympathetic civilians who held equally extreme views. A noteworthy civilian equivalent to Hashimoto was Dr Okawa Shumei, an employee of the Japanese-owned South Manchurian Railway company. He was a member of the Black Dragon Society, and worked with Hashimoto in the several 'incidents'. He held several university posts, and was an effective and popular propagandist for Japanese ultra-nationalism, and the cleansing of Japanese culture from pernicious western influences. His lectures were popular with the army, and he formally lectured at the military academy. His book 'Japan and the way of the Japanese' was a best seller. Eventually he too appeared before the judges in Tokyo at the end of the war. But to the astonishment of the court his behaviour was extremely odd. He started undoing his clothes – the accounts vary – and either smacked or tried to smack General Tojo, upon which he was rushed from the room. He then spent some months receiving psychiatric treatment, but he never stood trial. His 'insanity' some believed to be feigned, and certainly his recovery was very quick, and for a psychotic illness remarkably complete. Within two years he was engaged in substantial writing and publishing. For a variety of reasons, the recalcitrant organisers of these failed coups were either never punished, or given derisory sentences. This was partly because those who could have initiated punishment were often in sympathy with their aims, and whether they were or not, most of the military were very nervous of standing up to these extremists who cared for nothing, and respected nobody.

There is general agreement amongst historians trying to fathom the most difficult question of Emperor Hirohito's involvement in his country's affairs, that he was concerned about the direction in which the country was moving. He was especially worried about the behaviour of junior officers and was anxious to identify a prime minister who could somehow control the military. Discussion resulted in the appointment of Inukai at the end of 1931. Despite the failures of March and October, there was no diminution of revolutionary ambition. Another civilian, Nissho, set up a Brotherhood of Blood whose members were from fishing and farming families, to assassinate key political and business leaders. They succeeded in killing a former finance minister and a top Mitsui businessman before they were all arrested. They were thus deprived of the opportunity, as they intended, to kill the prime minister. This was achieved by a group of young naval officers and army cadets, who burst into his house on 15 May 1932 and shot him. This was such a significant event that there have been many accounts which try to reconstruct the details as to exactly who was in the house, and what precisely happened. The agreed facts are that Inukai remained calm, suggested they take their boots off since they were on his *tatami* floor, and there was initial hesitation by the assassins. The fact that really matters is that he was dead by the end of the day. The allies of the conspirators simultaneously attacked installations in Tokyo, but the attempt at revolution failed.

At the death of Inukai it became clear that the political and social milieu in Japan had changed drastically. A central difference was in the nature of the military. Until the First World War the commissioned ranks of both the army and the navy were drawn from pre-Meiji ruling groups, with key positions being occupied by Choshu and Satsuma respectively. This narrow base was broadened with the expansion of military experience, the encouragement to young men from all backgrounds to become regular officers, and the realisation that this offered an opportunity for social advancement, advancement which was consonant with the greatest of ambitions which was to serve the emperor. Such young men were predominantly from relatively humble backgrounds, with large numbers coming from the countryside. They were deeply traditional, and had a vision of a Japan which somehow would have moral and social codes which would honour its past, and shape its future. Many were disappointed. By 1929 Japan, like the rest of the world, was in deep economic depression.

In the cities there were wage cuts and massive unemployment, while in the countryside the plummeting of the price of silk because of the collapse of demand in the United States was ruinous. It was the production of silk which kept many farmers marginally in credit. The fall in the price of rice, compounded by a failure of the crop in the north in 1932, created such devastation that farmers had to resort to the ancient practice of selling their daughters into prostitution. When soldiers went home to the countryside they saw the misery in which their families and neighbours lived. They did not blame the depression, but the politicians and industrialists. The former seemed to be corrupt, and indeed the period was full of corruption scandals. Big business, especially the *zaibatsu*, seemed to be prosperous, but it was a prosperity which stopped at their boundaries, and was in marked contrast to the wretchedness of their home areas. The contempt with which soldiers regarded businessmen had a long history. In the war against China in 1894, the troops in the field were chronically cheated by the home suppliers of food and drink, so much so that the latter were publicly warned that

'Japanese troops after defeating the Chinese would return home for revenge on the merchants who put profit before patriotism.'[16]

The impatience of those who took part in, or encouraged, the 'incidents' did not spring only from a wish, born of itself, to establish a military government. It was a result, they might say, of the deterioration which was evident. Oddly perhaps since the word 'fascist' is sometimes applied to them, these Japanese radicals made demands which seemed to be very similar to those of the left. At the time of Inukai's murder they distributed leaflets which provide a useful summary of their dissatisfactions, which is therefore worth quoting at length.

> Look at politics, foreign policy, the economy, education, ideas, military matters – where is the true imperial Japan to be seen? The political parties, blinded by their own interests, conspire with the *zaibatsu* to squeeze sweat and blood out of the common people, while the bureaucrat defends them and oppresses the people; our foreign policy is spineless, our education decadent, our military corrupt, our ideas are perverted, our working class and farmers suffer in direst distress, and vain speeches are made all the while! Japan is on the verge of dying in a cesspool of depravity. Fellow citizens, to arms! In the name of the emperor, slay the evil courtiers! Kill the enemies of the people – the parties and the *zaibatsu*! Wipe out the privileged classes! Farmers, workers, people of our country! Defend your Japanese fatherland! Built a healthier new Japan! To reconstruct, first destroy! Demolish the present abominable system totally![17]

Kanno Sugako and her fellow conspirators in the 1910 plan to kill the emperor, would have agreed with very nearly all of it.

Whether these were minority opinions can be gauged by public attitudes to the trial and punishment of those who plotted and murdered. It has been pointed out earlier that the punishments were light; no death sentences, and much commutation and remission. This was not simply the courts, out of sympathy for the offenders, taking mild action, although there was certainly sympathy in some powerful quarters. Lieutenant-General Araki for one opined: 'What they did, they did in the genuine belief that it would be for the good of the empire . . . I cannot hold back my tears.'[18] The sentences were a reflection of popular support for their acts. The Brotherhood of Blood conspirators were not executed as had been

16 Lone, Stewart, *Japan's First Modern War: Army and Society in the Conflict with China 1894–95* (London, 1994), pp. 74–5.
17 Murakami, *Japan: The Years of Trial*, pp. 47–8.
18 Ibid., p. 48.

expected, but received prison sentences, admittedly long ones, but at least they could be shortened later. The 'May 15' trials were surrounded by extravagant support from the public. Many thousands of petitions were received, and a number of men sent pieces of their fingers, with an offer to be executed in the place of the defendants if they were condemned. There was no danger. The sentences were to imprisonment, including Okawa who had apparently planned it all, having been acquitted in the Blood Brotherhood trials. The exercise of appeal, amnesty and remission ensured the early release of all. The military were dispersed to other units, some to the Kwantung army at the southern tip of Manchuria. The reasoning probably was that they would be as far away from Tokyo as possible, but this move seems to have ignored the critical fact that the Kwantung army was in a state of constant near-mutiny.

Civil administration then lost its last frail grip. In 1932 the two major, and only legal parties combined to form one party, with the quaint name of the Socialist Masses Party. The final blow was struck when the army refused to nominate a minister of war, in a government at the head of which was to be a party leader. Thus did the manipulation by Yamagata so long before, bear its final fruit. The emperor was powerless, even though he made clear to Prince Saionji, the last of Meiji's *genro*, that he wanted to hear the nomination of someone who would uphold the Constitution, would be incorruptible, would amongst other things seek for peace in foreign affairs, and would restore discipline in the armed forces.[19] The intention was honourable, but such desiderata were anathema to the army in particular. The inevitable compromise was the appointment of a respected, if somewhat over-relaxed elderly admiral, Saito Makoto. Civilian government had gone, the prime minister was a figurehead, and power was now in the hands of a familiar figure, Minister of War Araki Sadao.

The emperor in his list of qualifications he looked for in his prime minister, referred to harmony in international relations. Already by 1932, this was a forlorn hope. As civilian control was gradually eroded, the army began to be split into two factions. The first of these was the 'Imperial Way' faction, led by two generals, Araki and Mazaki. As the name suggests these were officers, mostly junior, who were devoted to the emperor, and believed in violence to cleanse what they believed to be a decadent society. They also advocated war with the USSR, partly because of the historical enmity

19 Kawahara Toshiaki, *Hirohito and His Times*, p. 64.

between the two countries, and partly because that enmity was now exacerbated because of the army's hatred of communism. It was also known as the 'strike north' faction, for obvious reasons. And although the rivalry between the army and the navy was constant, the faction had its naval supporters known as the fleet faction.

The rival group was known as the 'Control' or 'strike south' faction. This group, supported by elements in the Naval Air Force, also believed in 'traditional values', but its main divergence from its rival was a commitment to move south, after the consolidation of Japanese rule in Manchuria, to attack China. The several ways of reforming the state were subsumed under the slogan the Showa Restoration. What this reflected was a belief that the authority of the emperor had been undermined by politicians and businessmen, in the same way as the *shoguns* had appropriated imperial power. Simply, there was a need to return that authority to the emperor. As far as can be judged, Hirohito's position seems to have been that he had no sympathy with their cause. Their precise aim is set out in the manifesto of a body called 'soldiers of the gods'. This proclaimed that they 'are ready with celestial swords to accomplish the restoration of Showa as their life mission for the glory of the empire', and went on to propose the annihilation of the usual groups, business leaders, political leaders and even 'the villains of the Imperial entourage and their watchdogs'. Before they could engage in their work, intended to begin on 11 July 1933, the police arrested the members. Once again, the trials which followed were infused with sympathy for their motives, and all the charges were dismissed for the astonishing reason that 'the plot had been discovered before any damage had been done'.[20]

Despite the turmoil in the army, Japan had begun its policy of imperial expansion, and at its centre were those units which were stationed in Manchuria. They were based on the Kwantung peninsula, and it was by the name Kwantung army that the units were known, and it is as such that they appear in historical accounts. Firm involvement with Manchuria began after the Russo-Japanese war, when Japan took the peninsula from Russia and renamed it the Kwantung Leased Territory. They also took over the railway from Port Arthur to Changchun which the Russians had built. Not only was the peninsula of great strategic significance, but it was commercially wealthy, since Manchuria was agriculturally rich, and possessed of enormous natural deposits. The area attracted Japanese

20 Butow, *Tojo*, pp. 58–9.

and Chinese, and the result was some social instability which together with a sustained suspicion of Russia, led to the posting of Japanese soldiers to maintain order. During the First World War Japan extended the lease, and as Japanese influence increased, dominated by the army, the size of the latter increased. By 1919, the Kwantung army was firmly established, and after the Siberian expedition, still maintained its hold. They were, obviously, a long way from Tokyo and in addition contained especially radical officers. The Kwantung army was to be critical in the chain of events in the 1930s.

For some time in Manchuria there had been economic competition between the Japanese and the Chinese. There were other causes for Japanese concern, such as the encouragement by the Chinese government to ethnic 'han' Chinese to move into Manchuria, in a policy which continues to affect the provincial areas of China which were dominated by racial minorities to this day. The Chinese were commanded by Marshal Chang Hseuh-liang, whose father had been murdered by officers of the Kwantung army, who were of course never punished, even though the prime minister had to resign in 1929. Chang's behaviour made the army resolve to occupy the city of Mukden and other towns. The government in Tokyo heard of this, reported the matter to the emperor, who called for the minister of war and ordered him to stop these developments. In a famous episode the minister gave a general a letter to deliver to the commander of the Kwantung army ordering him not to take any action against the Chinese. The messenger took his time in travelling to Manchuria, and upon his arrival began an evening's entertainment without having delivered the letter. At the very time when he was enjoying himself, in September 1931, the Manchurian 'incident' began.

The facts are straightforward, although the officers responsible, and the chain of command in the event have always been obscure and argued over. There is general agreement that two colonels in the Kwantung army, Ishihara and Itagaki, directed most of the events, but the role of senior staff, such as the general commanding the army, Honjo Shigeru, has never been clear. In September 1932 in an audience with the emperor Honjo claimed that neither he nor the Kwantung army had conducted 'any plot whatsoever'.[21] It may have been that he knew what was going on, but did not intervene for a variety of reasons; that he approved, or that he was frightened.

21 Coox, Alvin D., *Nomonhan: Japan against Russia 1939* (Stanford, California, 1985), p. 55.

Whatever the truth may have been, the officers of the Kwantung army were not penalised, but, on the contrary rewarded. In the case of the three key people mentioned above, Itagaki eventually became a general, Ishiwara a lieutenant-general, and Honjo senior imperial aide-de-camp.[22]

The Manchurian, or as it is sometimes called, the Mukden incident began on 18 September 1931. There was an explosion on the railway line just outside Mukden, and a group of Japanese soldiers who went to investigate reported that they had been fired upon. This was followed by an attack on the Chinese barracks, an assault on Mukden, and a request for more troops from Korea. Attempts by Japanese civilian authorities to restrain the army were firmly put down, on one famous occasion an official being threatened by an officer with a drawn sword. The Japanese alleged they had uncovered a Chinese plot, and claims were made about secret documents purporting to blame the Japanese. The truth emerged at the end of the Pacific War, when a number of Kwantung officers who had been involved at first hand admitted that the Japanese were to blame, having set the explosives and opened the rifle fire.[23]

The Japanese officer who gave the orders on that day was Itagaki, since Honjo was in Port Arthur. He returned to his base on the next day, and General Tatekawa, the same man who had failed to deliver the message ordering restraint, tried again. He attempted to persuade Honjo not to advance north, but the latter submitted to pressure from the more junior officers. Mukden was occupied, the town of Changchun was attacked, and Kirin was taken. The next target was Harbin where resident Japanese and Koreans had asked for 'protection'. Tokyo refused permission, saying instead that their nationals would have to leave. Meanwhile the officer commanding the army in Korea having asked for permission to cross the border, received no reply. He nevertheless did so, and presented Tokyo with a *fait accompli*. In October Chinchow was bombed. The Chinese Marshal Chang had established his headquarters in this city, and Ishihara's order to bomb it, with resulting civilian casualties, added to the mounting disapproval in the west over Japan's behaviour, since to many in the west such action was government policy. It was incomprehensible that an army could wage war on its own initiative. In the north the army continued to advance.

The attitude of Tokyo was a mixture of despair, frustration and embarrassment in its foreign relations. There was also support for

22 Ibid., p. 56.
23 Ibid., pp. 31–2.

the actions in Manchuria with the hawkish general Araki, minister in the Inukai government, sending substantial reinforcements in 1931 and 1932. The Kwantung propaganda machine was impressive, not only delivering fabricated versions and distortions to the government, but also ensuring press support, and ultimately public enthusiasm. The Japanese government though were unable to control events. Faced with the seizure of Kirin, for instance, they had to agree, with the proviso that the Japanese military should be withdrawn as soon as possible. In the same way, they were unable to deny permission for the Korean army to cross into Manchuria, and when it did, merely acknowledged the fact. Even the emperor was appalled at this episode, and told General Kanaya so.[24] The movement of troops overseas required imperial authority, and this act was therefore a grave offence.[25] In general, Coox points out, the emperor only knew as much as the public. In fact the information he received was so doctored that he sent messages of support, and issued a Rescript of appreciation in January 1932.[26] This raises again the question of Hirohito's responsibility for the aggression of the imperial forces, since others would ascribe much more awareness on his part of, and enthusiasm for, the behaviour of the Kwantung army.

The one hope they had was the policy they advocated of 'localisation' or containment.[27] Nor could anyone stop the next stages which were the occupation of Chinchow, with the concomitant eviction of the Chinese forces, and their eventual retreat behind the Great Wall, the occupation of Harbin and Tsitsihar, and the diversionary Shanghai incident. Such behaviour was justified by Ishihara who pointed out that orders from the army high command in Tokyo were 'not really imperial orders'. This meant that the army chief of staff in Tokyo had to ask the emperor for orders, thus losing direct command over the armies in the field.[28]

The Shanghai incident of early 1932 was a ruse by Kwantung officers including Itagaki, to deflect attention from their take-over of Manchuria. A Major Tanaka, who was stationed in Shanghai was persuaded without a lot of difficulty, to create trouble in Shanghai. He did so by arranging riots and arson, which led to the predicted call for protection from the Japanese community. Fighting started

24 Ibid., p. 39.
25 Murakami, *Japan: The Years of Trial*, p. 34.
26 Coox, *Nomonhan*, p. 57.
27 Murakami, *Japan: The Years of Trial*, p. 34.
28 Coox, *Nomonhan*, p. 41.

in late January between Chinese communist and nationalist forces, and the Japanese navy. The latter who were outnumbered were reinforced by the army. This was, incidentally, another cause of disagreement between the army and the navy, since the latter strongly disapproved of the provocation and Tanaka's part in it. The Kwantung militants, increasingly out of control, and increasingly disdainful of the effects of their actions achieved little. The assault on Shanghai united the various Chinese military factions, exacerbated Chinese dislike of the Japanese, and increased western concern. To take offensive action in Manchuria was one thing, but Shanghai was replete with western interest.

The Kwantung army remained unconcerned. Within a short time they had gained control over the whole of Manchuria, had driven out Chang's troops, and reached an agreement with the very popular General Ma Chan-shan, 'the ablest Chinese chieftain in Manchuria' who had been one of their principal opponents.[29] They also began to move towards Inner Mongolia, allegedly to counter Russian threats in Outer Mongolia. By now, in the latter part of 1931, the League of Nations was beginning to disapprove strongly of Japanese policy, and it established a commission of inquiry, chaired by the Earl of Lytton. In February 1932 the Lytton commission arrived in Tokyo, to learn the startling news that a new state existed in Manchuria, with a chief executive who was to become emperor.

The ground had been prepared in late 1931 by an approach to the last of the Qing dynasty emperors of China, Xuan Tong. He had been deposed when he was six in 1912, and now was identified as a credible, and of course malleable head of state for a new state to be called Machukuo-Manchuland. He was now known as Henry Pu Yi. The Qing dynasty was Manchurian, one of the reasons why it faced incessant opposition in China, and no doubt this was a factor in the choice. The Japanese moved him to Port Arthur in November, and in the next few months they began to establish organs of government and administration, nominally controlled by local people. In February 1932 a conference announced the establishment of the new state, which would be a republic at first, with its capital in Changchun.

Pu Yi was now concerned, since there was talk of a republic of Manchuria *and* Mongolia. Furthermore he was to be president in the first instance. The Kwantung officers proclaimed that they wished only for 'an era of happy coexistence and mutual prosperity

29 Coox, *Nomonhan*, pp. 41–2.

for the population of 30 millions inhabiting Manchuria and Mongolia'.[30] Tokyo was alarmed, and its attempts to intervene led to threats by Kwantung officers to secede and set up an independent state. As usual, by dint of coercion, ambiguous discussion and weakness, Tokyo gave in. Pu Yi became regent, and he was enthroned as emperor on 1 March 1934, the culmination of a remarkable attempt to create an impressive façade, behind which lay powerlessness. In March the world was invited to recognise the new state, even before the Lytton commission arrived in Manchuria. They spent six weeks there and completed their report in September 1932.

Some members of the commission were not entirely unsympathetic to the behaviour of the Japanese, and saw parallels with the illicit behaviour of their own countries.[31] Pu Yi approved for selfish reasons. But although such sympathies led to some modification of the condemnation of Japanese behaviour, the belief of Lytton was that they were unjustified, and the central recommendation was that Manchuria should be taken out of Japanese control. On 24 February 1933, the debate on the commission's report was completed, and Japan was the only country which voted against it. The Japanese had a number of objections, including the fact that although they had emphasised the dangers posed by communism and the USSR, these had not figured sufficiently prominently in the report. The real problem, in the stated view of the Japanese, was that the report was a rehearsal of all the old prejudices of the west against the east. The Japanese ambassador Matsuoka Yosuke in a speech to that effect to the assembly said: 'The administration of Manchuria by the League of Nations will be but another name for the continuation of the aggression of the major powers that has gone on in China since the nineteenth century.'[32]

Matsuoka led the delegation which included, of all people, Colonel Ishihara who had given the orders which had led to this. On 27 March 1933, Japan announced its resignation from the League of Nations, and moved further towards isolation.

An attempt to draw a parallel with the west was made in 1932, when Japan announced its intention to promulgate a Monroe Doctrine in Asia. This took its name after the United States president James Monroe, who in 1823 established the principle that there would be no toleration of influence or interference by outside

30 Ibid., p. 47.
31 Ibid., pp. 50–1.
32 Murakami, *Japan: The Years of Trial*, pp. 54–5.

powers in the Americas. Japan's determination to emulate this was stated by a privy councillor, Kaneko Kentaro in a speech to army officers in August 1932.[33] The fairness of the comparison with the historical action by the United States was referred to by Matsuoka in Geneva, when he asked if the United States would be prepared to tolerate interference in the Panama Canal. The Japanese press, and hence the public, welcomed this cornerstone of foreign policy, offering as it did a rationale for imperial expansion.

However much the Manchurian adventure may have pleased people at home, the next piece of army misbehaviour reminded everyone how undisciplined the military had become. In 1936 the 'February 26th Incident' was the beginning of a military mutiny and rebellion in Tokyo itself. The mutiny had, as some of its several causes, those of earlier extremist disturbances. The leaders were junior officers, still disgruntled by the suffering of their country-men, and still believing that corruption, political ineptitude and lack of courage were the reasons. It was also an expression of the simmering anger in the military between the imperial way and the control factions. At army headquarters the adherents of the former were supported by General Araki, so often a powerful influence on the direction the army took, and General Mazaki, both of whom held key positions. Both left headquarters, Araki in 1934, Mazaki in 1935, and their influences began to decline. In August 1935, a Lieutenant-Colonel Aizawa Saburo, sympathetic to the young offi-cers, murdered General Nagata who was, they believed, responsible for Mazaki's transfer, and for the undermining of their cause. Aizawa's account of the episode and its aftermath leaves the observer bewildered at the state of mind of those officers who perpetrated such acts. He stated that:

> After stabbing his Excellency I went to the office of General Yahaoka. Yahaoka was greatly concerned because my left hand was bleeding badly. He bound up my wrist with his handkerchief and asked what I intended to do. I replied that I had to do some shopping at the Army Club and would then leave for my new post in Taiwan.[34]

The murderer's court martial was an opportunity for the airing of the political views of his supporters, and in the face of potentially escalating violence, the army first division was ordered out of Tokyo to Manchukuo. Again, it must have been assumed that they could

33 Hoyt, Edwin P., *Japan's War: The Great Pacific Conflict* (London, 1986), p. 108.
34 Harris, Sheldon H., *Factories of Death: Japanese Biological Warfare 1932–45 and the American Cover-Up* (London, 1995), p. 45.

do less damage there; a very debatable premise when the behaviour of the Kwantung army is considered.

On 26 February 1936, realising that it was now or never, some 1,500 troops led by junior officers captured central Tokyo, and attacked the homes of important public figures. Two former prime ministers, Saito and Takahashi, now lord keeper of the privy seal and finance minister respectively were killed, as was Mazaki's successor at army headquarters, General Watanabe. The Grand Chamberlain Suzuki was badly wounded, but pleading by his wife saved him. Makino, a former lord keeper escaped, as did Prime Minister Okada when the assassins killed his brother-in-law by mistake. They also murdered five police officers. They then demanded that army minister Kawashima should set up a new cabinet to carry out their policies. He issued a statement supporting their aims, which reflected the government's apprehension that there could be a civil war, and the perennial fact that such violent behaviour had its supporters in the high ranks of the army. The rebels claimed that they had taken their action as subjects of, and out of loyalty to, the emperor. This accorded with the historic view that if affairs were awry, this was not the fault of the emperor, but of his bad advisers, such as the people they had killed.

Hirohito, in an unusual and incontrovertible action, made clear that he disapproved of what had happened. He defined this as a mutiny, and commanded that it be put down. After martial law had been declared on 27 February, the emperor issued an imperial order that the dissidents should be brought to heel. He refused to deal with them directly, and for the rebels most serious of all, would not accept their offer to commit suicide if ordered to do so. On 29 February, the authorities started a campaign to persuade the private soldiers to give in. This was successful, and the mutiny ended. The emperor's intervention had been critical for two reasons. The first was that it clearly demonstrated that he disapproved of the action, allegedly taken in his name. The second was that it inhibited any tendency of senior officers to join the mutineers.

There were those in the high ranks of the army who had disapproved of the mutiny before the imperial intervention, but the ancient rivalry between the army and the navy, already achieving a momentum which no longer depended on clan loyalties, added to the opposition, but not before people in the navy considered their position. There was first of all the fact that some of those murdered by the terrorists, Suzuki, Okada and Saito were all veterans of the Japanese navy. The navy, of course, had its share of 'young officers', both in terms of age and of ideology. These arrived in the office of Yamamoto, later to be the mastermind of the attack on Pearl Harbor, and said that the army, that is the mutineers, should not be allowed to monopolise this initiative. Yamamoto sent them away.[35] Another group in the navy believed that the navy should put the army down. There is some evidence that Yamamoto had sympathy with this, and certainly the actions of the navy supported the anti-army tactic. Senior officers in the imperial navy were well aware that the rivalry between the services did not reach down into the junior commissioned ranks, in which there was a common interest which has already been described. Nevertheless the superior discipline of the navy caused warships to be deployed in Tokyo bay. A stabilising person in the navy was Inoue Shigeyoshi, an experienced seaman who was well aware of army attitudes, and the need for the navy to balance them. He recognised that a navy, faced with an army with large numbers of land-based foot soldiers, had to make provision against violent army action. As chief of staff in Yokosuka, an important naval base near Yokohama, he tried to forbid sinister meetings of radical young officers, which, not surprisingly in the mood of the times, made some contemptuous of him. But, more practically, he arranged for the training of naval land forces who could defend the ministry in Tokyo, and for a light cruiser always to be ready for action in Tokyo bay.[36] How much of the navy's attitude to what was happening was based upon principle is of interest, but in the sequence it was the split between army factions, and navy and army antagonism which shaped events.

The mutineers, after two committed suicide including the leader, faced trial. This was conducted in secret, and thirteen or some say nineteen were executed.[37] Others were sentenced to imprisonment, but most of the private soldiers were not prosecuted. The end of martial law was proclaimed on 18 July 1936. This did not bring peace between the factions. The outcome of typically complicated Japanese factionalism, which has always appeared to be incidental to the best interests of Japan, and focusing instead upon designs remote from those interests, was the seemingly inevitable victory of the army. One of the oddities of the 'incident' was that the army proposed the astonishingly acceptable idea that the reason for the

35 Agawa, *The Reluctant Admiral*, p. 96.
36 Ibid., p. 100.
37 Storry, Richard, *A History of Modern Japan* (London, 1960), p. 199, says thirteen, or depending on how you interpret his text fifteen, including Kitta Ikki an important right wing theorist; and the officer who killed Nagata. Shillony, Ben-Ami, *Kodansha Encyclopedia* under 'February 26th Incident' counts nineteen, including Kitta Ikki.

incident was that the military needed more resources. The Hirota cabinet of early 1936 supported the army. So, instead of the army being finally brought into line: 'The February 26th Incident was thus an important landmark in the ascent of the military to a position of dominant political power in Japan in the late 1930s.'[38]

As Shillony goes on to point out, this brutal episode served as an inspiration for books and films which rejoiced in the 'spirit' of the mutineers.

The increasingly strong grip of the army compounded two events which led to the further isolation of Japan. The first was her withdrawal from the London naval conference in 1935, and the second was the signing of an anti-Comintern pact with Germany in 1936. Nor did the appointment of Prince Konoe as prime minister in 1937 control military ambitions. Although distinguished and popular, he failed his first test, a failure which set the course for the Pacific War. One month after he took over there was an exchange of fire at the Marco Polo bridge near Beijing, between Chinese and Japanese troops. The latter were entitled to be in the region under a post-Boxer rebellion agreement of 1901. A few days later a local cease fire was agreed. Japanese officers in China, supported by the unlikely figure of Ishihara, tried to make this conclusive but the Army Minister Sugiyama Hajime and his supporters in the control faction were determined that China should be taught a lesson, especially when, in the same month as the Marco Polo incident, Chinese troops at Tungchow killed their Japanese officers and a large number of civilian Japanese and Koreans. Sugiyama was confident, and in a famous statement to the emperor, boasted that the China incident could be finished within a month. Others, including Ishihara, understood the skill both of Chiang Kai-shek and the rival communists: 'As long as China holds sovereignty over a single acre, Chiang's government will find popular support for protracted resistance.'[39]

The campaign began well for Japan. In a series of battles in the north Beijing was captured, and there was jubilation in Japan. The truth was though, that the Chinese fought well, and engaged in tactical withdrawal and re-formation of their army. In August 1937 heavy fighting began in Shanghai, and it took the Japanese three months to capture the city. The League of Nations condemned Japan, peace negotiations failed abysmally, and the optimists in Japan put their faith in a belief that the capture of the then capital

38 Shillony, ibid.
39 Murakami, *Japan: The Years of Trial*, p. 70.

Nanjing would result in Chinese collapse. The Japanese advance on Nanjing was victorious after more heavy fighting, and was followed by what has been called the Rape or Massacre. In one of the most brutal episodes of the twentieth century, hundreds of thousands of people were raped, tortured and murdered. The impact at the time was considerable, especially since it happened before the world observed the later German excesses. The Japanese authorities immediately tried to suppress the facts, which were documented in considerable detail by foreigners in the city. Even today, as with German excesses, there is a 'revisionist' denial in Japan which defines the Nanjing massacre as fiction.

The massacre led to condemnation which was compounded by the bombing of an American ship, the *Panay,* and the shelling of HMS *Ladybird* by troops under the command of Hashimoto King-oro, that same Hashimoto of the Cherry Blossom Society. Despite apologies and demonstrations of regret by the Japanese government, since the actions were completely unauthorised, the United States' anger was almost translated into action. In the event the worst that happened was a further deterioration in the relationship between the two countries.

Meanwhile the fall of Nanjing did not lead to the expected end to hostilities. Prime Minister Konoe, chronically uncertain, was one of many who were certain of one thing; that there was no foreseeable end to the China 'problem'. Some, even high-ranking officers such as Lieutenant-General Tada, second in command of the army general staff, advocated a peace offer sufficiently restrained to be acceptable to the Chinese. This did not meet with agreement and in one of the misjudgements which punctuate modern Japanese history, in January 1938 Konoe announced that Japan would no longer recognise the nationalist Chinese government, but would negotiate with its successor, when that successor emerged. Despite this there continued to be failed efforts to end the conflict, including dealing with an important defected nationalist Wang Ching-wei who was eventually nominated as the official Chinese leader by Japan. The Japanese continued to gain ground, including Hankow and Canton, and soon effectively controlled the cities. Still Chiang Kai-shek would not surrender, and the Japanese were to be drained by a conflict which they could not win, and from which they could not disengage. The war was only brought to an end in 1945.

Meanwhile, the Japanese army in Manchuria engaged Soviet forces on two occasions. The first was in July 1938 over a hill called Changkufeng on the borders of Korea, Manchuria and Siberia.

Faced with Russian occupation of the area, the Japanese tried to dislodge them, but failed. The Japanese local forces then wanted to mount a full-scale attack, but for once the army high command in Tokyo forbade it, and after negotiation conceded Soviet ownership. A much more serious 'incident' occurred in 1939 at Nomonhan, on the border between Manchukuo and Outer Mongolia. This was a disaster for the Japanese who were crushed by the Russians, notably because of the mechanised armour the latter deployed. The realisation of Russian strength did much to cool the ardour of those who wished to attack the USSR.

The lesson drawn from these two affairs was that the Russians were not to be trifled with, especially since they had superior weaponry. This experience was an important factor in the lessening of the demand for striking north, and the consequent strengthening of interest in southern Asia. There were still elements in the army who believed that Japan could engage in all-out war with both China and the USSR, and aware of the danger which such persistent and unrealistic militarism presented, Hirohito again seems to have acted as a constraint. He informed the chief of the general staff, and the war minister that the behaviour of the army had been 'abominable'. Henceforth 'you may not move one soldier without my command.'[40] Significantly this order, given before Nomonhan, did not prevent that bloody conflict.

Prime Minister Konoe made one last attempt before his resignation in 1939, to achieve some kind of stability. In 1938 he proposed a new structure which would comprise a total union of China, Japan and Manchukuo. Apparently inspired by a well known philosopher Miki Kiyoshi,[41] who advocated a unified Asia which would learn from western mistakes, Japan sought to promote what was to become the Greater East Asia Co-Prosperity Sphere. Not only did Chiang Kai-shek dislike this idea, but the west was bound to identify it as a threat to its interests. Gradually the idea of a 'sphere' began to include south Asia, since the 'new order' would need materials from there. Opposition to such ideas were ridiculed, and a speech by one especially articulate member of the Diet, Saito Takeo, led both to the expunging of his speech and his expulsion from the House.[42] Gradually the Japanese theorists, notably in the navy, came to

40 Storry, *A History of Modern Japan*, p. 206.

41 For a detailed account of the development of the idea see Crowley, James B., 'A New Asian Order: Some Notes on Pre-War Japanese Nationalism' in Silberman and Harootunian, *Japan in Crisis*.

42 Ibid., pp. 282–3.

regard the United States as the main obstacle to Japanese 'needs' in south Asia, especially since the European colonial powers' grip was weakened by war. The United States, for its part, responded with a statement that 'any change in the Dutch East Indies, except by peaceful means, would be prejudicial to the cause of stability, peace and security ... in the entire Pacific Area'.[43]

A good deal of time was now spent in the guessing of events, and developing a policy to cope with them. The Japanese watched the United States, and tried to prepare either for American intervention in the European war, or abstention from it. The debates were confused, with a mixture of a wish to negotiate with the Netherlands to gain access to their colonies, the desirability or otherwise of going to war, and a statement in December 1940 to the effect that 'the Greater East Asia Co-Prosperity Sphere now comprises the south seas region ... to counter their (the United States' and Britain's) economic strangulation of Japan'.[44] As time went on, Japan became more and more convinced that she was the victim of western, especially American, encirclement. This was articulated in terms of western imperialism, colonialism and racism, and the belief was widespread in Japan that she had no option but to go to war for survival. Many American historians in particular find this view unacceptable, and are fixated on a belief that the behaviour of the Japanese, before and during the Pacific War, was unjustified and reprehensible.[45] Whatever the reasons may have been, one truth seems to be that Japan was now on an unalterable path to world war.

How true is it that the calamity which was to follow was the result of the behaviour and influence of the military? It is certainly the case that they were beyond the control of the civil government in the 1930s, and that sections of the army could not be disciplined by their own superiors. There have been many suggestions as to how an army in a nation dominated by a culture of discipline and obedience could so deteriorate. One is that the dignity exemplified by Admiral Togo in 1905, began to disappear as the dominance of the clan system gave way to an officer class from a nondescript rural tradition. Persuaded that the emperor was the only source of authority, the belief grew that all that was wrong was because of advice given to him by evil people, and that to protect him, such

43 Ibid., p. 286.
44 Ibid., p. 290.
45 This is the starting point of much American writing. Just two examples are Bergamini, David, *Japan's Imperial Conspiracy* (London, 1971) and Hoyt, *Japan's War*.

people had to be eliminated. This belief in which they had been nurtured, justified everything, and quickly led to a blurring of the distinction between war and murder, a distinction which characterises a disciplined army. The infamous 'young officers' would have been perplexed by a statement made by Inoue when he was commander of a battleship, and which, because it illustrates the change in the code of behaviour in the officer class, is worth quoting in full. It is also a profound commentary on the difference between discipline and anarchy in armed forces, in this case, the Japanese:

> The reason why military men are allowed to carry swords in peacetime and why we are proud to be seen so accoutred is that we are charged by the nation to use these weapons, should the occasion arise, in safeguarding the country. However, to determine whether the 'occasion' has arisen or not is the job of the nation itself. In other words, it is only when the nation has decided on war and the supreme command has given the go-ahead that a military man is permitted to kill the enemy and destroy his possessions. When a military man takes advantage of the weapons he has always to hand in order to kill others unlawfully, of his own will and without word from the supreme command, his role is transformed immediately from an honourable one to that of the worst kind of criminal, and the sacred weapons are degraded into vile instruments of murder.[46]

There seems to be a parallel between what was happening in Japan in the 1930s and events in Germany, since the latter too seemed to be controlled by the military. The differences are important, since Japan had always been ruled, in effect, by the military, whereas Germany may have been influenced by military values, but in fact even under Hitler, was under civilian control. Even the premise that the military controlled Japan has been disputed. Smethurst, for example, claims that 'the army and navy were never able to dominate Japanese society totally', going on to point out that at several critical points in politics and the economy, non-military forces were victorious.[47] It could be argued that this view underestimates the influence of the military. But it could equally well be the case that, as in Nazi Germany, the military were just one of a number of factions, in an uneasy balance, which battled for influence, but no one of which was strong enough to seize total power. The certainty is though that by 1940 Japan was isolated, could hardly expect help from such allies as she had and that,

46 Agawa, *The Reluctant Admiral*, p. 99.
47 Smethurst, Richard, 'Militarism' in *Kodansha Encyclopedia*.

rightly or wrongly, the military were the rogues. The country remained convinced of the justice of its cause, and a belief in the superiority of the 'spirit' blinded many decision-makers to the danger which would follow, if some accommodation with the west, notably the United States could not be achieved. The prospects were grim, and the next steps were to be the most disastrous of all; the persistence of the faith that China could be conquered, and the attack on Pearl Harbor.

CHAPTER EIGHT

'The Wish of the Dead Child'. Women in Japan: A Wish Denied?[1]

1 It was the arrival of her stillborn child in 1922 which caused the writer Takamura Itsue to reflect on the position of women, and to study women's history. Watanaba Kinko, 'The Wedlock Deadlock' in *Look Japan*, September 1992, pp. 44–5.

Overleaf ▶
Half naked women and men cutting coal, 1915

'The Wish of the Dead Child'.
Women in Japan: A Wish Denied?

Throughout this history there has been reference to the role of women in modern Japan. Sometimes this has been dramatic as in the case of Kanno Sugako. But from the Restoration, and especially during the period of Taisho Democracy, their struggles for equal rights became an important part of the configuration. This chapter considers the place of women in some detail. Much is made of the fact in writing on the history of women in Japan, that a very long time ago women were not alleged to be as notoriously inferior to men as they later became. One piece of evidence which is marshalled as a symbol of the fact is that the legendary progenitor of the imperial family, Amaterasu Omikami was a goddess. More tangible evidence is adduced from the fact that in the upper classes, before the triumph of the shogunate in the twelfth century, family residence was matrilocal, which is to say that when marriage took place the man went to live with his wife. Or, more correctly, his several wives who all lived in their own households, since Japanese society seems to have been polygynous. Polygyny and matrilocality commonly go together. For a very traditional society polygyny has a number of advantages. Such societies generally contain more women than men, and for a number of reasons including strict division of labour, a woman needs a husband. A matrilocal pattern means that a woman has her own household, which is a distinct advantage.

But matrilocal patterns do not indicate female equality, much less dominance. Nor does the fact that during the seventh and eighth centuries there were six women emperors, or that during the Tokugawa shogunate but when emperors were powerless there were a further two. One would have to know a good deal more about how they came to occupy the position, and the real extent of the power that they exercised. A final example of feminine influence which is quoted is the role of shaman in which women feature 'to mediate between humanity and divine forces'.[2] This spiritual quality is often associated with temporal power. In the prehistory of Japan, a good deal of archaeological evidence has been marshalled to support the existence of matriarchal groups led by female chieftains who had religious, spiritual and military authority.[3] A strong case has been made out for the creation – for such it seems to be – of the Empress Jingu, based upon 'strong vestiges of matriarchal society'.[4] She appears in the first Japanese histories, the 'Record of Ancient Matters', 710 AD, and the 'Chronicle of Japan' 720 AD, and supposedly lived from 200 to 269 AD. There is evidence to support the existence of strong female figures, but the Jingu legend is regarded as an amalgam of the characteristics of many:

> Not only does she embody certain real life female leaders in particular, but also testifies to the sincere respect and the honoured place commanded by Japanese women in general in ancient times, despite the active effort of the male-chauvinistic Neo-Confucian scholars in the feudal Tokugawa period to ignore historical evidence and discredit women's social contributions in the past.[5]

There are more historical cases of women leaders. Masako, the wife of the first Kamakura *shogun* Minamoto Yoritomo is an illustrative, even if exceptional example:

> During her husband's lifetime she wielded immense influence and after his death she virtually ruled the empire. This seems to be the only recorded instance in the history of Japan when the supreme power was wielded by a woman who was neither Empress nor Empress-dowager.[6]

And officially, in government-approved textbooks in Japan today, history begins with Himiko or Pimiko. She is recorded in Chinese chronicles as living in western Japan, and sending tribute to the Chinese emperor in 238/9 AD.

Again, it is common in many societies for women to be regarded as having magical, religious, and sometimes evil 'gifts', but this says

2 Oguri Junko and Andrew, Nancy, 'Women in Japanese Religion', *Kodansha Encyclopedia*.

3 Aoki Michiko, Y., 'Empress Jingu: the Shamaness Ruler' in Mulhern, Chieko Irie *Heroic with Grace: Legendary Women of Japan* (Armonk, New York, 1991), p. 34.

4 Ibid., p. 34.

5 Ibid., p. 36.

6 Ratti, Oscar and Westbrook, Adèle, *Secrets of the Samurai* (Vermont, 1973), p. 16 quoting Mere, Gerald, 'Japanese Women, Ancient and Modern' in *Transactions and Proceedings of the Japan Society*, Vols 18–19 (London, 1920–22).

little about the distribution of power between male and female. The fact that shamanism was banned in 1873, but possibly ineffectively, was probably not so much because it was a source of power for women, but because its manifestly primitive nature was incompatible with the vision of a modern Japan. Nevertheless, whether or not such traditions as that of powerful women rulers are accepted, or even if in the early history of Japan there was a relationship of equals, it has not been present for a considerable period.

Perhaps better evidence for the position of women, at least in the upper reaches of society, can be seen in the fact that from the middle of the seventh century they were barred from service as government officers, under laws which were already a reflection of the influence of Confucianism.[7] The latter, together with Buddhism, were to be important agents in the institutionalised repression of women. As we shall go on to see, Confucianism made a very special contribution. But Buddhism, from earliest times affected the position and role of women. It has consisted of so many sects that it is impossible to make a definitive statement, but a fair judgement is that it has ranged from being ambivalent to being hostile to women, with its promulgation of texts pointing out that women are flawed, and cannot be saved unless reincarnated as men. As time went on and new varieties of Buddhism appeared, some sects were more accepting of women. It is fair to say that by the Kamakura period (1185–1333) there were Buddhists who pronounced salvation as available for both sexes.[8] From about the thirteenth century there were Buddhist nuns, and in the succeeding years some of these came from the most prestigious families including those of the emperor and *shogun*. The Meiji government refused to allow such eminent women to become nuns, although other female members of society continued, and continue, to enter religious orders.

From about the thirteenth century power struggles proliferated in Japan, and there was a descent into anarchy which was not to end until the rise of the Tokugawa shogunate. The turmoil seems to have changed the position of women. There was, at the highest levels, the finish of the flowering of a native Japanese female literary tradition, of which the eleventh-century *The Tale of Genji* by Murasaki Shikibu is one of the most famous examples. But as such traditions died others changed, notably to the disadvantage of women. Thus, one of the earliest moves to the patriarchy which was

7 Andrew, Nancy, 'Women in Japan, History of' in *Kodansha Encyclopedia*.
8 Hane Mikiso (ed.), *Reflections on the Way to the Gallows: Rebel Women in Pre-War Japan* (California, 1988), p. 4.

to be the cornerstone of the cultures of the Edo and Meiji Eras was the shift from a position where women had property rights, to one where they had none.

Another way in which the sexes were increasingly differentiated in the period of instability was through language. There had been references to gender differences in language in texts going back before the eleventh century, but especially during the period from the mid-fourteenth to the mid-sixteenth century a distinguishable women's language emerged. Japanese is a complex language with many variables used in social relationships. Naturally, these are learned, but the use of certain forms and vocabulary by women make their language distinctive to a degree where it has a special name – *nyobo kotoba*. Jorden, in her discussion of this phenomenon, points out that 'gentleness' is its characteristic, and it is best described as comprising 'feminine oriented features'. This language is used by men in certain circumstances, and there is 'sexually neutral' language which women use.[9] Jorden draws attention to another feature of discussion about these language differences which is that more attention is paid to feminine language in writing on Japanese, than there is to masculine. The implication, she suggests, is that the male language is seen as normal, and the female as 'deviant'. The implication of superiority and inferiority is inescapable. Despite such common denomination though, the existence and retention in present-day society of such a very unavoidable, constant reminder of gender difference, is of the greatest significance as a statement of the depth of that difference.

The victory of the Tokugawas led not only to stability, but to rigidity in the social structure. Especially in the *samurai* class the subordination of women continued, with the enforcement of primogeniture and the abolition of property rights for women. Although it was no more disadvantageous to women than to men, the arranged marriage became normal. This was a practice which had grown up during the civil wars, where political alliances were important. They continued to be regarded as vital if the new peace was to hold. The governmental control over the upper classes was such that all proposed marriages had to be reported and approved by officials. The custom was adopted, in different degrees, by people living in the towns, but in rural Japan, where some 80 per cent of the population lived, the choice of marriage partners was probably less formal. Certainly the difficult lives of country people made the

9 For a detailed discussion see Eleanor H. Jorden, 'Feminine Language' and 'Masculine Language' in *Kodansha Encyclopedia.*

formality of upper class life irrelevant. All members of the family worked hard, and together, and there is evidence that women in the rural areas not only shared authority, but had considerable influence over what went on in the home.[10]

The accepted authority for the consolidation of male authority was a work entitled *Onna Daigaku* – (*Great learning for women*) published in 1716. This was firmly rooted in Confucian belief, and its authorship is generally attributed to Kaibara Ekiken, who was a well known writer on education at the time, although at least one authority, Katagiri Kazuo, regards the attribution of the book to Kaibara as 'mistaken'.[11] This book was, for a very long time, one of the most influential in the definition of the role of women. Nor are the values it advocates without relevance to modern Japan. A woman had three duties: to her parents, to her husband, and to her sons. She was expected to be completely obedient, industrious and silent. Failure in any of these, or if she were barren, unfaithful, jealous or ill, would be cause for divorce. Her relationship with her husband was akin to his with his lord. But the author was not optimistic, because five maladies 'indocility, discontent, slander, jealousy and silliness ... infest seven or eight out of every ten women, and it is from these that arises the inferiority of women to men. Such is the stupidity of her character that it is incumbent on her, in every particular, to distrust herself and to obey her husband.'[12]

Although the ideology expressed in the *Onna Daigaku* was so pervasive, it did not go unchallenged. The influence of the *kokugaku* school which has already been mentioned, did something to counter it, since in its emphasis on things Japanese, it contained a strong vein of anti-Confucianism, and anti-Buddhism. Notably, scholars of the *kokugaku* school rejected the Confucian implication that Japanese traditional literature had a bad influence on women. Nor were Confucian strictures on women acceptable to Japanese intellectuals. Two of the most important of these in the period after the Restoration were Mori Arinori and Fukuzawa Yukichi. The former was the first Minister of Education in the Meiji government, with a few radical ideas based on his western experience. He deplored the way in which Japanese women were treated, especially the custom of concubinage. In an influential and radical journal

10 See Hane, *Reflections on the Way to the Gallows*, pp. 6–7 and Pharr, Susan J., 'Women in Japan, History of' in *Kodansha Encyclopedia.*
11 Katagiri Kazuo, 'Kaibara Ekiken (1630–1714)' in *Kodansha Encyclopedia.*
12 Hane, *Reflections on the Way to the Gallows*, p. 6, quoting Chamberlain, Basil, *Things Japanese* (London, 1939).

'Meiroku Zasshi', he wrote 'jus   between husband and wife are not in the least practised u   national customs. In truth, the husband is entirely the master of the slave, and wife is no different from a chattel.'[13] This journal was the organ of an intellectual and radical club called Meirokusha, established in 1873, with Fukuzawa as one of its founders. Because of government pressure, the journal ceased in 1876. Fukuzawa in his magisterial work *Encouragement of Learning* wanted a reassessment of family relationships, in which the key relationships would be between husband and wife since this 'is the great foundation of human relations'. This relationship 'emerged before that of parents and children or brothers and sisters', and furthermore women should have the same rights as men, including the same education.[14]

These were powerful, but rare voices. As we shall go on to see, whatever the Restoration government set out to do, it did not include changing the place of women in society. Nowhere is this clearer than in the question of concubinage and prostitution. The former was a standard feature of Japanese family life, and was related to the more formalised polygyny. Emperor Showa (Hiro-hito) has the distinction of not only being the first emperor for several generations not to have been born of a concubine, but he was the first not to have had any concubines officially. Far from addressing the question of concubinage, the Meiji government in a law of 1870 made the practice legal, and until 1882 concubines were included in the family register.[15]

Prostitution is a much more complicated issue, since even if a society wishes to suppress it, it is impossible to do so. The major issue surrounding prostitution is whether or not governments should legalise, condone or outlaw it. If it is made illegal, a principle is at least established which is that women are not going to be exploited officially. One of the problems faced by those who pressed for making prostitution illegal, is the fact that it had been legal and under government control from the twelfth century. Tokugawa Ieyasu, as part of his authoritarian policy, was determined to control, but not of course to abolish, prostitution. The growth of towns and the grinding poverty in many rural areas, established a pattern of prostitution which channelled poor girls into a well

13 Ibid., p. 8, quoting Braisted, William (tr.), 'Meiroku Zasshi' (*Journal of Japanese Enlightenment*) (Tokyo, 1976).
14 Ibid., p. 7, quoting *Fukuzawa Yukichi Senshu* (*Selected Works of Fukuzawa Yukichi*) (Tokyo, 1951–52).
15 Ibid., pp. 9–10.

organised trade. It was very often the case that such girls were sold by their families to brothel owners, both in Japan and overseas, as if they were volunteers. There was a considerable trade at the end of the nineteenth century, and the beginning of the twentieth, in Japanese women for the brothels of Asia. One estimate is that in 1910, there were over 22,000 Japanese prostitutes working abroad.[16] Those who found themselves in foreign countries were euphemistically termed 'stowaways' in the Meiji press.[17] The problem was exacerbated in the Meiji Era because of the outlawing of two ancient practices, abortion and infanticide. The tension which was present in the rural family lay in the fact that a woman had to bear enough children to work the farm, but not so many as to be unsupportable. This balance was made more precarious by the high mortality rate, and when there were too many children, then they would be killed or abandoned, the former practice persisting well into the Meiji Era, despite it being made a capital offence. Hane reports an interview with one old woman who had killed some of her children.

> To keep the children we already had, the others had to be sent back. Even now, rocks mark the spots where the babies were buried under the floor of the house. Every night I sleep right above where they're buried. Of course, I feel love and compassion for the babies I sent back. I know that I will go to hell when I die. I have a feeling the babies are there, too. When I die I want to go to hell so that I can protect them as best I can.[18]

Surplus children would be abandoned in the hope that someone would pick them up, for whatever purpose. The making of abortion and infanticide into capital offences arose from a studied policy of expanding the population, as part of the process of change. It followed that birth-control was frowned upon, and since the policy took no account of women's wishes, it is not surprising that as part of the post-1918 interest in democracy, birth-control became an important part of the women's movement. The pioneer American family planner Margaret Sanger was allowed, very grudgingly, to visit Japan in 1922 and 1936. On her first visit which was only managed by subterfuge, such as taking out a visa to visit China when she was refused a visa to go to Japan, and ingratiating herself with important Japanese officials on the voyage, she was allowed to land. She managed to carry out what was a furtive, but high profile series of

---

16 Hane Mikiso, *Peasants, Rebels and Outcastes: The Underside of Modern Japan* (New York, 1982), p. 219, quoting Yamamuro, Gundei, *Shakai Kakusei-ron* (Tokyo, 1977).

17 Ibid., p. 207.

18 Ibid., p. 82, quoting Shimonaka, *Nihon Zankoku Monagatari* (Tokyo, 1972).

lectures and discussions, and the publicity was enormous. Kato Shidzue, who was herself a pioneer of birth-control and other radical causes, summed up her visit: 'Not since Commodore Perry had forced Japan to open its doors to foreign commerce, in 1852, had an American created such a sensation.'[19]

But as time went on the government became more and more determined to prevent birth-control. Thus a pioneering Japanese gynaecologist, Ota Tenrei, developed an intra-uterine device in 1930, and introduced it to a learned society in 1932, but its manufacture and sale were quickly banned.[20] As the insatiable demand for fighting men increased in the 1930s, the official slogan became 'bear children, swell the population'. In 1952 and 1954 Margaret Sanger returned to Tokyo, on the second occasion to attend the triumphant foundation ceremony of the Family Planning Federation of Japan. She also addressed the Health and Welfare Committee of the House of Councillors.

The Meiji government introduced legislation which put some limits on prostitution. The first Act was in 1872, and was a consequence of a very famous international incident. A Peruvian ship the *Maria Luz* docked in Yokohama. While she was there two Chinese coolies escaped, and complained about their treatment. The British minister intervened, and the outcome was the appointment of a Japanese judge to investigate. The Peruvian captain was declared guilty of illegal imprisonment, with the court ruling that the contract which caused the enshipment of the coolies was illegal for a number of reasons, which included the allegation that it allowed the coolies to be transferred to another party, which smacked of slavery. This ruling, together with widespread desertion resulted in the loss of the Chinese, and the inability of the captain to sail his ship. The case attracted international dispute, and eventually in 1875 the Tsar having been asked to arbitrate, supported Japan. The pleasure of the recognition of Japan as a respectable international legal equal, was tarnished by a Peruvian defence that Japan condoned slavery in the form of selling women to brothels. Henceforth such trade was forbidden, but not of course brothel-keeping itself.[21]

19 Kato Shidzue, *A Fight for Women's Happiness: Pioneering the Family Planning Movement in Japan* (Tokyo, 1984), p. 52.

20 Wagatsuma Takashi, 'Family Planning' in *Kodansha Encyclopedia*, p. 247. For a detailed and personal account of the fight for the right to birth control, see Kato Shidzue, *Fight for Women's Happiness*.

21 Hane, *Peasants, Rebels and Outcastes*, p. 208, quoting Okada Akio *et al.*, *Nihon no rekishi* (Tokyo, 1959–60). See also entry under 'Maria Luz', no author, in *Kodansha Encyclopedia*.

A second restriction was made by the courts in 1900 when prostitution by girls under eighteen was outlawed. In the same year the government licensed brothels, in part to keep disease in check. The expanding empire needed more and more able bodied men and it was felt that sexual promiscuity was having a deleterious effect. The authorities may well have been right. In 1920 '22 per cent of men reporting for military service had venereal disease'[22] which was attributed to the scale of prostitution. Also in 1920 the government tried to stop the shipping of Japanese women overseas. But officially approved prostitution, despite all the efforts of reformers, notably Christians, remained in place until 1945 and beyond.

The making illegal of infanticide and abortion for reasons of social engineering was symptomatic of the increasing depression of the status of women. This started at the very top of society with the barring of female emperors in their own right. As part of the 1889 Constitution, Article II ruled that 'the imperial throne shall be succeeded to by imperial male descendants, according to the provisions of the imperial house laws'. For more humble women, in 1898 a civil code of marriage consolidated the power of the heads of households when it ruled that it was they who had to agree to a marriage, not the participants.[23] More specific to women were restrictions on their right to engage in property transactions, the requirement that they needed their husband's permission to take up legal action, and the demand that they be sexually faithful. As we have seen the next few years were to bring legal restrictions on female political activity. When it came to the establishment of education, the advocacy of people like Fukuzawa Yukichi of equal education for the sexes found some support. Before the transforming Education Act of 1872, the department of education had recommended that girls should receive the same education as boys.[24] No less a person than Emperor Meiji himself supported women's education. As part of the Iwakura mission of 1871, which has been discussed, five girls were sent to be educated in America. It was this which led him to remark:

> We lack superior institutions for high female culture. Our women should not be ignorant of those great principles on which the happiness of daily life frequently depends. How important the education of mothers, on whom future generations almost wholly rely

22 Takenaka Kazuro, 'Prostitution' in *Kodansha Encyclopedia*.
23 Hane, *Reflections on the Way to the Gallows*, p. 9.
24 Ibid., p. 11.

Only introduced legislation when army was affected

for the early cultivation of those intellectual tastes which an enlightened system of training is designed to develop.[25]

The reality was different, since in 1876 for example, 46 per cent of the eligible boys were at school, but only 16 per cent of the girls. In 1879 boys and girls beyond the elementary school age were separated, and in 1899 the ministry made a famous definitive statement about the purpose of female education which was to make them into 'wise mothers and good wives'. Ministry intentions were reinforced in a 'morals' textbook of 1900:

> Girls must be gentle and graceful in all things. In their conduct and manner of speech, they must not be harsh. While remaining gentle, however, they must have inner strength in order not to be easily swayed by others. Loquacity and jealousy are defects common among women, so care must be taken to guard against these faults. When a girl marries she must serve her husband and his parents faithfully, guide and educate her children, be kind to her servants, be frugal in all things, and work for the family's prosperity. Once she marries, she must look upon her husband's home as her own, rise early in the morning, go to bed late, and devote all her thoughts to household affairs. She must assist her husband, and whatever misfortune befalls the family she must not abandon it.[26]

Such beliefs were not confined to government officials or men. As is still the case in the developing world as well as the west to some degree, many parents, even mothers, see little purpose in educating daughters. In rural Japan there was another important barrier to female attendance which was the need for labour at home. Japanese rural poverty during Tokugawa and Meiji times has been well documented.[27] It is a grim story of people who could never be sure of having enough food, and trying to lessen their abject poverty by disposing of children in the ways which have been described. The growth of industrial activity enabled rural people to solve the problem of surplus children in a new and rather more humane way. This was by sending them to work in the new factories. Women were especially in demand, amongst other reasons because they were paid less.

25 Furuki Yoshiko, *The White Plum: a Biography of Ume Tsuda, Pioneer in the Higher Education of Japanese Women* (New York, 1991), p. 5. She makes reference to William Elliot Griffis, *Verbeck of Japan: A Citizen of No Country: a Lifestory of Foundation Work* (Edinburgh, London, 1901).

26 Hane, *Reflections on the Way to the Gallows*, p. 12 quoting Kaigo Tokiomi (ed.), *Comprehensive Collection of Japanese Textbooks: The Modern Age*. 27 volumes (Tokyo, 1961–67).

27 See, for example, Hane, *Peasants, Rebels and Outcastes, passim.*

One of the most important products was textiles, which had a firmly based tradition, and buoyant overseas demand. The rate of expansion was such that in 1893 silk formed 42 per cent of Japanese exports, and by 1909 34 per cent of the world's raw silk was produced in Japan.[28] Young women and girls were indentured to work in the factories for long hours, and of course low pay. It should be remembered though that conditions of work were hardly better in the west. It was during this period that certain traditions in employment were established which are still present in Japan. There is firstly the accommodation which was, and is, for unmarried men and women, in dormitories. This was, and continues to be, necessary because many of the workers came from areas far removed from the factory. An additional factor for young women is that their parents expect them to be sheltered and protected, which the patriarchal nature of the Japanese company is well able to ensure. Even today the conditions for women are much stricter than they are for men.[29] The second pattern is that women in such factories were paid less, could be part time, had no job security and were expected to leave upon marriage. They could then be replaced with younger people who would earn less. A measure of employer satisfaction can be judged from the fact that in the last decade of the nineteenth century, women in the textile industry outnumbered men.[30]

An especially vile workplace for women were the coalmines. In 1915 Kato Shidzue, a well known radical, went with her husband to a mine in Western Japan where he was to work. She went underground and wrote an account of the fourteen-hour day worked both by men and women. She recounted how the latter worked 'all but naked', sometimes carrying babies, sometimes pregnant. They gave birth underground because they could not afford to stop work until absolutely necessary. And as soon as possible they began work again.[31]

Although town life was hard in Meiji Japan, it was nevertheless better than in the countryside, where the overwhelming number of people lived. Many of these started with a serious problem if they owned land. After the Restoration it was possible to own land, and the peasants increasingly did so. The disadvantage lay in the change in the system of taxation, since now the landowners had to pay tax in

28 Ibid., p. 173.
29 See Lo Jeannie, *Office Ladies, Factory Women: Life and Work at a Japanese Company* (Armonk, New York, 1990), *passim.*
30 Lebra, Joyce C., 'Women in Japan, History of' in *Kodansha Encyclopedia.*
31 Kato Shidzue, *Fight for Women's Happiness*, pp. 29ff.

cash, instead of by a percentage of the crop, and if the crop was poor, since the tax was no longer related to it, the farmer had to pay a cash amount which could be crippling.[32] It was because of such hardship that rural people sent their daughters to factories; but the daughters were prepared to go where they would at least have more to eat, even if the conditions under which they lived and worked were dismal. During the late Meiji and Taisho Eras, the increasing prosperity of the cities, and the continuing dejection of country life did not go unnoticed. City dwellers regarded country people with contempt, one observing in the 1920s:

> There is no one as miserable as a peasant, especially the impoverished peasants of northern Japan ... they are black as their dirt walls and lead grubby, joyless lives that can be compared to those of insects that crawl along the ground and stay alive by licking the dirt ... they show no feelings, no energy, no strength.[33]

Such contempt was reciprocated by rural people. A proclamation of the Agriculturalist's Self-Rule Society in 1925 reflected this:

> The cities are living off the sweat of the farmers. They pilfer and live on what the peasants have produced with their sweat and blood. While the cities and city dwellers prosper ... the peasants who labour to support and keep them alive are on the verge of starvation and death.

One of the organisers of the society, Shibuya Teisuke, was not content with merely reflecting on their plight. He demanded that war should be declared 'on modern industrial commercialism' in places like Tokyo, 'a murderous machine'.[34] One of the manifestations of this widening division was the expression of resentment by the 'young officers' in the military who were well placed to see the gap in living standards.

The rural people who had moved to urban areas to work, especially the females, because of their cultural background were pliable, and generally put up with whatever the employers did. There were however successful protests in 1886 in a silk factory against an attempt to depress wages, and another strike in a cotton plant in 1889 for a pay rise, which was not successful. There were in fact substantial numbers of strikes in the last years of the Meiji Era,

32 Hane, *Peasants, Rebels and Outcastes*, pp. 16ff.
33 See Hane, ibid., pp. 34–6 for much more of this diatribe, quoting Usui Yoshimo (ed.), *Collection of the Soil and Home Villages* (Tokyo, 1976).
34 Ibid., p. 36, quoting Shibuya Teisuke, *Nomin Aishi* (Tokyo, 1970).

many of which involved women workers.[35] Gradually the treatment of females at work began to concern even some employers, and in 1911 a Factory Act was passed, which ostensibly would improve their conditions.

The importance of the Act probably lies in its very existence, rather than in its effect. Attempts to introduce legislation had been stopped by vested interests for some thirty years. Under it women were not allowed to work for more than twelve hours a day with a one hour rest, night work was restricted, and the Act introduced a variety of health and safety regulations, including minimum conditions in dormitories and bathhouses. The Act, which came into force in 1916 suffered from one serious flaw: it applied only to organisations with a minimum of fifteen workers, thus excluding large numbers. It is largely for this reason that the usual judgement of the Act is that it was half-hearted, and its ineffectiveness is shown by the continuing publication of books describing the persisting wretchedness of factory life for women. A survey in twenty-eight of the forty-seven prefectures in 1910 showed that only about 40 per cent of female textile workers eventually returned home, and of those that did, about 16 per cent were seriously ill, many with tuberculosis, an especially prevalent disease.[36]

Such industrial action as there was in Meiji Japan was part of a determination of women, albeit a minority, that in the much vaunted social revolution in which they were living, consideration should be given to their place in the new society. For this reason women were involved in the organisation called the Freedom and People's Rights Movement which took shape in the 1870s. The origins of the movement lay in the split between those who wished to invade Korea, and those who did not. We have seen how the consequent civil war saw the death of the chief advocate, Saigo, but others, from the Hizen and Tosa clans, who supported him, had to consider ways in which they could maintain an influence on events. There was loose talk of popular representation, although in fact its leaders were ex-*samurai* with all the expectations of limited rule by their group. Despite the inevitable splits and quarrels, the society and its offshoots propagated the ideas of western democracy, especially focusing upon the cause of a national assembly. In 1880 a national meeting of almost 97,000 people indicated that the move-

35 Ibid., pp. 193–5.

36 Brinton, Mary C., *Women and the Economic Miracle: Gender and Work in Post-War Japan* (California, 1993), p. 113, quoting Ishihara Osamu, *Factory Girls and Tuberculosis* (Tokyo, 1914?1913).

ment was now beginning to attract commoners.[37] The influence of the movement on Japanese political development is a matter of debate, as are the reasons for its demise. Perhaps the two most important reasons are the expert methods of repression used by the government, and the promulgation of the 1889 Constitution, the achievement of which had been one of its aims.

Although women were, naturally enough, attracted to movements whose policies seemed to offer hope, it soon became clear that the men who controlled the movements were not, despite their polemics, so much interested in 'freedom', as in engaging in a male, elitist, struggle for control. There were some examples of remarkable women who challenged such assumption of superiority. Tanaka describes the case of Kusunose Kita who in 1878 in the clan homeland of the Tosa on Shikoku island, and an area which was very active in the Freedom and People's Rights movement, challenged the prefectural authorities. Her complaint was that as head of the household she had to pay taxes, but she was not allowed to vote. In the same year the prefectural governors confirmed the invalidity of voting by women with her qualifications. But in 1880 one Tosa town granted local suffrage to both males and females who qualified, and further allowed them to stand in local elections. Both provisions were overturned by the central government's rules on local government in 1884.[38] Meiji and Taisho history contains several examples of such outstanding courage.

Faced with the implacable resistance of men to their political ambitions, women became involved in other forms of protest. Some joined socialist or anarchist organisations. Some of these, such as the anarchist involved in the plot to assassinate Meiji, Kanno Sugako, have already been discussed. But women joined a variety of organisations some of which had broader goals than purely political, much less violent, change. One of these was the Bluestocking Society which was founded in 1911. This was an organisation designed to interest the new, emerging groups of professional and artistic women who had managed to overcome social hurdles, and take part in the new occupations which came in the wake of Japanese transformation. It began mainly as a vehicle for women's writing, and upon its inception published a journal 'Bluestocking'

37 Soviak, Eugene, 'Freedom and People's Rights Movement' in *Kodansha Encyclopedia*.

38 Hane, *Reflections on the Way to the Gallows*, pp. 16–17 quoting Tanaka Sumiko, *Thought and Behaviour in Women's Liberation, Pre-War Years* (Tokyo, 1975), pp. 29–30, 52.

which was to become famous in the history of female literary output in Japan, an output which had been present and active for a thousand years. Naturally the work which was published was much concerned with women's issues. It was also to be expected that such an organisation, with a high profile publication outlet, would attract women with very advanced, unusual, or as the police no doubt supposed, 'dangerous thoughts'. The writing, although sometimes controversial was probably tolerated, but the views and the behaviour of some of the members was not. There was a scandal about a lesbian painter, Otake Kokichi, whose forced resignation only served to heighten the society's advocacy of women's rights.[39] Another woman, unacceptable because of her views was Ito Noe who took over the editorship when it took a radical turn in 1915. She was critical not only of the old order, but of socialists who were, in her view, insufficiently belligerent. In her late twenties she was murdered by the police. The journal and the parent society were closed in 1916, partly because the issues dealt with, like abortion and prostitution, began to alienate the membership.[40] And, as always, government agencies both pressured the organisation and articulated public concern.

The hopes and aspirations of those Japanese who wished for change were raised by the appointment of the first cabinet government, and the crisis of the rice riots both in 1918. Women too were spurred to action. In 1920 a New Women's Association was founded, which was reformist in tone, and was especially concerned with women's political rights. One of its leaders was Hiratsuka Raicho, who had been a leader in the founding of the 'Bluestocking', but had had to hand it over to Ito because she was in financial trouble, and because she was not happy with the increasingly radical tone of the journal. The New Women's Association only survived for two years, again because of repression and ideological differences, but it achieved one considerable success: the law against women attending meetings was repealed.[41] This took the form of an amendment to the Public Order and Police Law in 1922.

Just before the repeal there was established the Japanese Socialist Federation, and because the restriction on political activity by women was still in place, women could not join. Both men and women of left-wing persuasion had been inflamed by the rice riots,

39 Neuss, Margret, 'Seitosha' in *Kodansha Encyclopedia*.
40 See Hane *Reflections on the Way to the Gallows*, pp. 20ff., for an account of the journal.
41 Lebra, Joyce C., 'Women in Japan, History of' in *Kodansha Encyclopedia*.

and constant police repression and harassment, but they had a new source of inspiration in the Russian Bolshevik revolution. Because of the restriction, women set up their own organisation in 1921 called the Red Wave Society. Membership was small, but their exhortation to action was dramatic. They made the 1921 May Day march a target for a demonstration of their principles. In their manifesto for the parade they proclaimed:

> May Day is the day for the proletarians, for us workers who are oppressed. For centuries and centuries, women and workers have endured together a history of oppression and ignorance. But the dawn is approaching. The morning gong that was struck in Russia signals the first step in the victory that will minute by minute banish the darkness of capitalism from the face of the earth. Sisters, listen to the power of women that is embodied in the sound of the gong. Let us exert the utmost of our strength and, together with our brothers, strike the gong that will signal the liberation of the proletarians of Japan. Women who are awake, join the May Day march! ... The capitalist society turns us into slaves at home and oppresses us as wage slaves outside the home. It turns many of our sisters into prostitutes. Its imperialistic ambitions rob us of our beloved fathers, children, sweethearts and brothers and turn them into cannon fodder. It forces them and proletarians of other countries to brutally kill each other. The Sekirankai (Red Wave Society) declares all-out war on this cruel shameless society.[42]

The march took place and the police broke up the meeting, and arrested several of the women including Hashiura Haruko, whose photograph under arrest created a sensation because of her dignity and elegance. The movement did not continue for long, and it was dissolved in 1925.

Meanwhile the specific issue of suffrage continued to be pressed, especially as it became increasingly likely after 1918 that men would get the vote. A noteworthy organisation was the Women's Suffrage League. This was established in 1924 by Ichikawa Fusae who had been exposed to women's movements in the United States since she had been active in the by now defunct New Women's Association. In some ways it was the specific nature of their objective, suffrage, which gave the league a very difficult task. It should be remembered that most Japanese women were deeply traditional, and could not understand the purpose behind the agitation. As in women's suffrage groups in other countries, there was opposition from

42 Hane, *Reflections on the Way to the Gallows*, pp. 126–7 quoting Esashi Akiko, *Women Wake Up!* (Tokyo, 1980).

women who were traditionalists, or at the other extreme, criticised the league for not being radical enough, or for not concerning itself with broader issues affecting women. Although the league canvassed the Diet, its cause was much weakened by the chronic non-conservative divisions to which reference has been made. The conservative groups, both political and cultural, recognised that once female suffrage had been granted, the whole edifice of gender discrimination would be seriously undermined. The achievement of universal male suffrage in 1925 was, in a sense, discouragement, since this seemed to mark the limits of reform.

With remarkable persistence the league continued its campaign, despite the fact that there was no diminution of the opposition. However, as the military tightened its grip, and 'triumphs' like the conquest of Manchuria dominated public life, it became increasingly difficult to maintain any momentum. In 1930, very briefly under the cabinet of the doomed Hamaguchi, there was a glimmer of hope when a bill for female civil rights passed through the lower house of the Diet. Fervent campaigning by opponents prevented its passage through the House of Peers. As Japan's perception of itself developed into a nation which was persecuted, but had to strive to save itself and Asia, traditional values overcame the pressure for reform. Tradition, and women's place in that tradition had served Japan well, and anyone who doubted it was tainted by disloyalty. The Women's Suffrage League, after some sixteen years of struggle had failed, and was dissolved in autumn 1940.

The success of the Japanese authorities in suppressing dissent, does not lessen recognition of the bravery of the group of women leaders in the late nineteenth and early twentieth century who suffered and died for the cause of women's liberation, in all its manifestations. Several have been mentioned, but two more examples will perhaps serve to highlight some of the qualities of all of them. The first is Takamura Itsue who was born in 1894, the child of a frustrated father who, failing in his ambition to become a government official, became a teacher. Takamura began to train as a teacher, but did not finish. She also failed to become a reporter, worked briefly in a factory, and then took a teaching post. She married and had a child which was stillborn, an event which turned her interest to the history of Japanese women, which was, she believed 'the wish of the dead child'. Eventually her husband recognised her talent and gave her total support, even though her main attack was on the institution of marriage. She published a magazine called 'Women's Battlefront', which was a vehicle for her view that the battle was 'to completely destroy male-oriented culture', and she deplored women who 'joined with men in toppling, piercing and reviling themselves'. Her especial importance lies in her contribution to an assessment of the history of women in Japan with a six volume study, and a dictionary of Japanese women. In this she helped to redress the gender balance in history, which was an important intellectual act.[43]

The second woman who represents much of what these remarkable Japanese women stood for was Tanno Setsu. She was born in 1902. Her father was a miner, and she became a nurse in the Hitachi company, where the treatment of labour activists so appalled her that she went to Tokyo in 1921, and joined the Red Wave Movement. She and her husband helped to establish the radical Japan Labour Union Council in 1924, and they organised strikes in several companies. After joining the Communist Party in 1926, she became the first head of the women's section. She was one of the many activists arrested in the March 15th Incident of 1928, and eventually released because of ill health. Meanwhile her husband had died in Formosa, either by his own hand or murdered by the police. On her release from prison she continued her subversive activities, for which she was gaoled for six years in 1932. Despite everything she survived the Pacific War, after which she became involved in the less radical improvement of health care. Takamura and Tanno chose different paths to the same end – greater freedom and the ending of tyranny.[44]

Apart from tiny pockets of resistance to the war-time government, women's radicalism, likes its male counterpart, was subordinated to the national mood, first of triumph, then of anxiety as the tide began to turn. There came into existence two major women's organisations which supported the government and the war effort. The first was the National Defence Women's Association, and the second the Patriotic Women's Association. The first was founded in 1932 after the Manchurian incident and in 1934 came under military control. By 1941 there were 10 million members who made it their business to bid farewell to servicemen, to console bereaved families and generally to support the war effort. The Patriotic Women's Association was an older organisation. It was founded in 1901 with the same objectives and there developed rivalry between

43 These details are taken from an article by Watanabe Kinko, 'The Wedlock Deadlock' in *Look Japan*, September 1992, p. 44.

44 'Tanno Setsu' (no author) in *Kodansha Encyclopedia*. See also Hane, *Reflections on the Way to the Gallows*, pp. 175ff.

the two. In 1942 these were merged, together with a smaller organisation to become the Great Japan Women's Association. Women who were unmarried had to work in industry and commerce, whilst those who were married worked at home, especially in the rural areas. Part of the latter policy was due to the need for large families, heralded by the ban on contraception. There was to be no change until 1945. That change, when it did come, was to put in place everything for which earlier women had worked, been imprisoned, and died.

The new Constitution of 1947 revolutionised the position of women in Japan. Two central Articles were numbers 14 and 15.

14. All of the people are equal under the law and there shall be no discrimination in political, economic or social relations because of race, creed, sex, social status or family origin.
15. The people shall have the inalienable right to choose their public officials and to discuss them.

These Articles were the consolidation of a debate and action which had taken place earlier. It seems that Japanese women, and women officers in the occupation forces, began discussion of women's rights as early as late 1945, just a few months after the war ended. A bill was set out in December 1945 which gave women over the age of twenty the right to vote for members of the lower house, and those over twenty-five eligibility to stand in national elections.[45] Considering how repressed women had been, and how demoralised people were in defeat, the results of this enfranchisement were dramatic. In the first 'new' election in 1946, seventy-nine women stood and, a remarkable thirty-nine were elected.[46] This leap into political maturity was to be maintained, since Japanese women are determined to exercise their right to vote. Today, of the population under fifty years of age in Japan, women outnumber men in voting.

A new Labour Standards Law in 1947 included protection for women workers. Not only was this long overdue, but the move was given added urgency by the high numbers of women workers. These had always been substantial but their participation in the workforce was even more necessary because of the need for reconstruction and because of the enormous male casualties during almost ten years of war. The law contained Articles about equal pay, maximum hours of work and limits on overtime, and banned overnight work, with a few exceptions, and underground and dangerous work. Under the law

45 Molony, Kathleen, 'Women's Suffrage' in *Kodansha Encyclopedia.*
46 Ibid.

women are entitled to childbirth leave, time at work to feed children, and in some cases of heavy work, paid time off during menstruation. Present-day judgement on the 1947 law, widely and rightly regarded as very advanced at the time, is that it has brought some disadvantages. Much labour legislation affecting women in industrial countries in the nineteenth and twentieth centuries has been designed to protect them from physical strain and abuse. The universal prevention of women working in underground mining is an example. This was the intention in the 1947 law, but it is regarded by some modern Japanese women as restricting the opportunities for women, provoking employers to argue that, for example, they cannot develop a career pattern for women if they cannot work for the same length of time as men. This is an issue which predictably has divided women, with professionals wanting changes in the legislation which so effectively hampers their prospects, and those lower in the hierarchy identifying the law as an important safeguard.[47] And it is an issue which as we shall go on to see still dominates discussion about women at work. There is also the fact that a crucial part of provision has not been implemented – equal pay. The Labour Standards Law is a case study of the tension in trying to equalise treatment and opportunity, and the claimed needs for special provision for women.

The new Constitution also went to an important root cause of the structural inferior status of women:

> Article 24. Marriage shall be based only on the mutual consent of both sexes and it shall be maintained through mutual cooperation with the equal rights of husband and wife as a basis. With regard to choice of spouse, property rights, inheritance, choice of domicile, divorce and other matters pertaining to marriage and the family, laws shall be enacted from the standpoint of individual dignity and the essential equality of the sexes.

Much of this article has been translated into practice. Key elements of the traditional civil code have disappeared. Thus, for example, either party can proceed to divorce for the same reasons. At the age of consent – eighteen for men, sixteen for women – people can marry without parental permission, and in the matter of registration of names, a woman can do so in her own right.

There were two famous historical matters in the history of women's campaigning which were not directly addressed in the new

---

47 Hargadine, Eileen, 'Women Workers, Protective Legislation for', in *Kodansha Encyclopedia.*

Constitution, but which the latter through its statements of principles, and its stress on women's choice and removal of abuse,
enabled the campaign to continue. These were birth-control and
prostitution. With regard to the former, it will be remembered that
before and during the war there were stern laws against it. After
1945, as in other countries, there was a dramatic increase in the
birth-rate, at a time when Japan was in a parlous state. To counter
this, abortion was widely used, and in 1948 a Eugenic and Maternal
Protection Law was passed which legalised the practice, and also
allowed sterilisation. There were a number of reasons for this. A
familiar one was to minimise the dangerous practice of illegal
abortions. Another was to prevent births which were the result of
the rapes of Japanese women during the retreat from the colonies,
or contact with the occupying forces, a very important consideration
in racially conscious Japan.[48]

At the present time there are family-planning agencies, although
the adequacy of provision is sometimes questioned. Even so the
entire society has adjusted to restriction in family size. It is especially
significant that in the last forty years, the size of rural families has
decreased to a par with urban levels. Some forms of contraceptive
devices are easily available, especially the condom, the commonest
form, with the notable exception of the contraceptive pill. The
Japanese medical profession opposed its introduction, in advance it
should be noted of the concern in recent years about ill effects.
They did so because of its effectiveness in preventing pregnancies,
which would reduce the need for abortions which are common and
profitable. When opinions began to be expressed about the safety of
the pill, these ill effects were held up as justification for banning it.
A new objection is that its use could increase the danger of Aids.
The profits to doctors specialising in abortion are high. It is
estimated that almost three-quarters of a million women have
abortions each year, and that about one third of all married women
have had at least one abortion.[49] Visitors to Japanese temples will
notice rows of small stone statues, often dressed. Some represent
aborted children, and bear witness to the centrality of abortion in
the lives of Japanese women, and their feelings of guilt.

The other campaign, against prostitution, while it can never be
successful nevertheless has established an important principle,
which is that although it persists, it does so without government
approval, and in some forms attracts legal sanctions. As soon as the

48 Wagatsuma Takashi, 'Family Planning' in *Kodansha Encyclopedia*.
49 Ibid.

Occupation began, there was, as might be expected, a considerable upsurge in prostitution. This was encouraged by the Home Ministry who recruited prostitutes for the Occupation forces even before the latter arrived.[50] Very soon after the Occupation, authorities stated that the system of licensing brothels should stop. The reaction was unenthusiastic and a network of prostitution continued. In 1952 women campaigners from a wide range of organisations successfully pressed the government to act, and the latter, probably conscious of the voting power wielded by women, against great opposition passed a Prostitution Prevention Law in 1956, which is similar to laws in other advanced countries. It is recognised that the act of prostitution cannot be stopped, but public nuisance and the exploitation of women can be detected and punished. For young women, there is a system of counselling as an alternative to punishment. As in other countries, quasi-brothels exist. The best known used to be called 'Turkish baths', until it was agreed that the term was offensive, and now they are known as 'soaphouses'. In bars and clubs, one pre-war situation has been reversed. The export of Japanese women to Asia for prostitution has been replaced by Asian women being imported to Japan, to act as what are euphemistically called hostesses.

The legal changes in the position of women after 1945, while they may have altered relationships within marriage did not undermine the institution itself, nor did the traditional method of choosing a partner disappear. The expectation is that people will marry, girls in their early twenties, men in their late twenties. By this time it is assumed, both will be in a financial position to do so, not least to engage in the prodigiously expensive business of the ceremony itself. The social pressures to conform to this pattern, as in all aspects of modern life, are difficult to resist. Lo in the late 1980s records how the young factory women she lived with talked incessantly about boyfriends and the possibilities of marriage.[51] If people are not married by thirty, not only are they regarded as deviant, but their attraction is diminished. The common description of unmarried women in their late twenties is 'stale Christmas cake', indicating that they are less attractive as time goes on.

At that point the traditional machinery is often used. This is to use a go-between or arranger to identify a potential partner. After a meeting, the relationship may develop to a point where marriage is agreed. Entire families are involved in the exploratory meetings,

50 Takanaka Kazuro, 'Prostitution' in *Kodansha Encyclopedia*. See also Sawanobori Toshio, 'Prostitution Prevention Law' in *Kodansha Encyclopedia*.
51 Lo J., *Office Ladies, Factory Women, passim.*

which is an historical pattern where the union was of families, and the couple a symbol of that union. The use of go-betweens is by no means confined to older people. Meeting people of the opposite sex in sufficient privacy to develop the intimacy which leads to marriage in the west is difficult, and although young women especially entertain ideas of romantic love, go-betweens are widely used. The difference between the traditional and the modern customs lies in the fact that the ultimate choice is made by the candidate, not by the family. When marriage does take place, the women almost invariably gives up work, at least for some time.

The next social expectation is that a newly married couple will have children; in most families there are two. The wife is entirely responsible for the bringing-up of the children – hence the expectation that she will give up work – and this is attended to with great devotion. It involves ensuring that educational chances are maximised, and that the total environment for children is perfect. She does this within the context of her absolute control of the household. Her husband will work a day the length of which is legendary, especially if he is a white collar worker, a 'salaryman', with the result that it is not feasible for him to take any active part in the management of the household. His wife makes sure that everything runs smoothly so that he can devote his energy to work. Nor is there a widespread demand for change in this division of labour. Lo records how:

> One twenty-four year salaryman said 'it's bad enough to have a wife who neglects her housework and husband by pursuing a career, but a mother who dashes her child's hopes of entering Tokyo or Keio University or any other institution of higher learning (and in effect destroying his chances for a successful future) is unthinkable.'[52]

The nature of married life in modern Japan, precluding as it does much opportunity for contact between man and wife, creates an accepted pattern in which both have separate lives. The only time the family can be together is on Sunday or one of the public holidays. Otherwise, when the children go to school, a woman will socialise with friends or family, or attend classes or meetings. Rather as in the traditional western-European working classes, the closest and most confidential relationships are between women. This is not to suggest that there is no warmth between man and wife, only that this seemingly unchangeable pattern, of necessity, creates distance.

There is perennial discussion in Japan about 'filial piety' which

52 Ibid., p. 10.

not only has submission to authority as its linchpin, but also regard and care for older people. This is central to the classical extended family, and where it has not survived because of the exigencies of modern life, there is still a duty to care for the elderly. Since the Japanese are amongst the longest-living people in the world, and since there are high expectations of families to care for them it is not surprising that the extended family, or perhaps more correctly the extended family which does not share the same domicile, is still an integral part of Japanese society. This can be seen from figures which show that in 1955 45.3 per cent of all households were nuclear, and although this figure rose to 59.6 per cent by 1991,[53] this means that a substantial number of Japanese still live in extended households. With regard to the role of women these figures are important because the woman is the person with total responsibility for the household.

This is an added responsibility for women caused by what has been called the 'greying' of Japan. In 1970 people over 65 comprised more than 7 per cent of the population. At present the figure is nearer 12 per cent.[54] In 1989 the life expectancy for women was eighty-two and for men seventy-six.[55] Not only does this phenomenon create a problem for society at large, since fewer and fewer people relatively have to look after old people, but the tradition that the family looks after its old people, even if they live in separate houses is still firmly part of the expectation in the Japanese family. And by 'the family' is meant the women.

Such family duties raise questions about the commonest debate concerning the role of women in Japan; their attitudes and position in the workforce. There can be no doubt about the importance of that position. Although for most of the Pacific War, women were not engaged in jobs for the war effort in the ways which were common in the west, soon after 1945 their numbers increased. This was due to the considerable loss of men in the war, and because of the rapid growth of the Japanese economy in the 1950s and since. At the same time, the movement from agriculture to industrialisation has meant that fewer women are employed on the land, and more in the towns. Another important pattern is that whereas before the Pacific War most Japanese women at work were single, today the group contains many married women: 'Since 1955 the percentage of married women in the female labour force has almost tripled, rising to 64.9

53 Kodansha International, *Japan: Profile of a Nation* (Tokyo, 1994), p. 151.
54 Itakura Kimie, 'The Greying of Japan' in *Look Japan*, February 1990, p. 4.
55 Kodansha International, *Japan: Profile of a Nation*, p. 148.

per cent in 1990.'[56] Women form some 40 per cent of the total workforce, of whom some 70 per cent are married.[57] The considerable representation of women in the workforce, especially married women, whose entry is sometimes regarded as a symbol of emancipation, has to be circumscribed by some facts which are proving almost impossible to change.

The first is the kind of work carried out by women. This is overwhelmingly clerical, production and service. In the very important area of self-employment, people carrying out 'piece work' from home are mainly women.[58] In the professions, numbers are small; for example 'fewer than 1 per cent of female civil servants occupy managerial posts',[59] and only 8 per cent of managers are women compared with 17 per cent in West Germany.[60] At the root of this is the same discrimination against women which is found in many countries. This comprises an almost inseparable mixture of rational and irrational. Men understand that if there were to be true equality of opportunity, there would be a serious reduction in male chances both of getting work and of being promoted. It is not difficult to find irrational responses, as to a complaint in the mid-1970s. Fukao Tokiko records that a complaint by a women's group that all newscasters were men was met by a justification that 'if women read the news, viewers might lost confidence in it'.[61]

Not only are most women employed in low-status jobs, but in 1989, about one quarter of those employed were part time.[62] These are paid low salaries, and have no more job security than women had in the Meiji and Taisho textile factories. There can therefore be no career structure of the kind which many Japanese men expect as a matter of course. And even if these women worked full time, they would meet another piece of structured discrimination, since they would not receive as much pay as men: 'Wages in Japan are typically reported as monthly rates, and the female/male ratio in 1987 was 57.6, substantially lower than in any other industrial country.'[63]

It is a process which begins early, since most young women who go to universities do not go to the prestigious four-year institutions,

56 Ibid., p. 149.
57 Fukao Tokiko, 'A Man's Place ...' in *Look Japan*, August 1989, p. 3.
58 Brinton, *Women and the Economic Miracle*, p. 4.
59 Kodansha International, *Japan: Profile of a Nation*, p. 149.
60 Brinton, *Women and the Economic Miracle*, p. 7.
61 Fukao Tokiko, 'A Man's Place', p. 3.
62 Ibid.
63 Brinton, *Women and the Economic Miracle*, p. 8 quoting Ministry of Labour, Japan, 'Status of Women Workers' (Tokyo, 1988).

but instead attend the two-year junior colleges. Since employment is closely related to the eminence of the educational institution attended, it is clear that there is a barrier even for the best educated women. Even those who do go to four-year universities only rarely benefit: 'The industries that female junior college and four-year university graduates enter are surprisingly similar'.[64] Logically this is not what you would expect in a system where four-year attendance accrues explicit advantage in employment.

In all of these exceptional discriminatory practices, the trouble, if trouble it is, lies in the expectation of Japanese society of the nature of the family and the roles of male and female in it. It is expected that people will marry, and especially in the case of women, 'concern' begins to set in if they are not married by the late twenties. Recent surveys show that less than a quarter of women are single by the age of twenty-seven.[65] The pressures to conform are overwhelming. The social pressure, educational discrimination, the wish to be 'normal', and the working tradition all make statements such as this perfectly rational:

> The director of Brother personnel stated in a recent discussion with the directors of other industries on the changing roles of women that 'women will leave the company to fulfil their roles as housewives and mothers. That is why it is difficult to give them equal treatment'.[66]

This is an especial argument used to deny women equal training opportunities, which in Japanese companies are regarded as an expensive investment only to be made in permanent, therefore male, employees. The logic of all of this is that women have created this discrimination by their own actions. For the very determined woman who achieves a position which could be filled by a man, there are still discriminatory practices to be faced. It is she, for example, who will be required to handle telephone calls at night, or early in the morning when men are out socialising or have not arrived for work.[67] There are other ways of pursuing a career. There are women in the Japanese Diet, including Doi Takako, the first female leader of a major party, in this case the Japanese Socialist Party, in 1986. Some rejecting tradition will stay single and enter professions even though they are conscious that their marriageability will plummet. Others will work for foreign companies where the

64 Ibid., p. 145.
65 Ibid., p. 97.
66 Lo, *Office Ladies, Factory Women*, p. 71.
67 As an example, see Rubinstein, Catherine, 'High Finance – High Flyers' in *Insight Japan*, February 1993, Vol. 1, No 3, p. 44.

Japanese tradition has no place. Some have been involved in divorce, although the proportion at 1.25 per thousand in 1988 is small compared with other advanced countries. The claim is often made that the rate is increasing. However there has been a decrease from a peak of 1.51 in 1983. Comparative figures in 1986 are 4.8 in the United States, 2.3 in Sweden, 2.0 in France, and in Japan in that year 1.4:[68] by 1993 the figure had risen slightly to 1.5 per thousand.[69]

Apart from these individual alternatives, there has always been organised pressure to eliminate discrimination. This goes back, as we have seen, to the Meiji Era. In more recent times, as the feminist movement has developed across the world, Japanese women have tried to improve their position. Thus, there are organisations such as the Japan Women's Council which includes amongst its objectives world peace, 'full liberation for women', and saving the environment. The National Women's Education Centre is especially interested in education to such ends, advocating 'men's increased participation in home life', and 'an individual identity for women'.[70] But there have been attempts to change the position of women, notably at work, by recourse to the law. These rare cases were brought as long ago as the late 1960s, using as a basis for an action the Labour Standards Law of 1947, which required equal pay for equal work. This was problematic, but at least there was the law. Other forms of discrimination demanded an appeal to Article 14 of the Constitution which states that 'all of the people are equal under the law'. This proved to be a minefield in a legal system which eschews confrontation and seeks compromise. Employers, aware that movement towards equality would bring in its train questions about tenure, part-time work and other cornerstones of Japanese employment practice and would mean complete reconstruction, were in no mood to compromise. On the contrary, employers had constantly complained that the 1947 law was too protective, especially since it adversely affected the work of smaller firms.

Because of a need for more labour in the mid-1960s, the government eventually took action to revise the 1947 law and out of this came the Working Women's Welfare Law of 1972. This did not forward the cause of equality, but instead tried to help women to arrive at some compromise between family and work. Employers for their part were to help with 'welfare' by understanding childcare

68 Foreign Press Centre (ed.), *Facts and Figures of Japan* (Tokyo, 1989), p. 16.
69 National Women's Education Centre Newsletter (Tokyo, May 1994).
70 Foreign Press Centre (ed.), *Facts and Figures of Japan* (Tokyo, 1995).

needs. The result was an enormous increase in the number of part-time women workers, with the traditional role of the mother unscathed.[71] The next event was the signing by Japan of the United Nations Convention on the Elimination of All Forms of Discrimination against Women. This carried a requirement that by 1985 there would be legislation to provide equal opportunity in employment to men and women. Japan faced a king-sized problem. In 1981 it was revealed that many companies discriminated in recruitment, wages, job placement, training, promotion and retirement. Amongst other things, 83 per cent had positions from which women were barred, and 43 per cent would not promote women. And these were official figures.[72] For several years there had been intense discussion, including by official bodies, as to what should be done. The battle lines were predictable. On the one side the employers, that 'protection' should be minimal, and that management should be obliged rather than compelled not to discriminate. Women and unions, together with the majority of the 'experienced' people who are always appointed to such committees in Japan, wanted instead protection and compulsion. The law which was passed in 1985 has a long title: 'The Law Concerning Promotion of Equal Opportunity and Treatment Between Men and Women in Employment and Other Welfare Measures For Women Workers'.[73] It is usually called the Equal Employment Opportunity Law.

Its provisions fall short of what the more radical advocates wanted. Discrimination is prohibited in some areas, such as fringe benefits, but employers are variously 'encouraged' or should 'endeavour' to treat women equally in key areas such as recruitment, job allocation and promotion. Under the new law the hours of overtime were doubled, certain categories could now work at night, but maternity leave was increased. The law is a classic piece of Japanese legislation, in that it has incited considerable argument about meanings, and its absence of coercion means that complaint is difficult, while there is the maintenance of the main tradition in the Japanese legal system which is compromise. It is also typical in that the proponents of the status quo, the employers, won. The legislation and the debates leading up to it also demonstrate a universal problem about framing gender equality laws, which is the

71 For a detailed discussion see Lam, Alice C.L., *Women and Japanese Management: Discrimination and Reform* (London, 1992), especially Part II.

72 Ibid., p. 14, quoting Ministry of Labour, Japan, *Survey on Employment and Management of Women Workers* (Tokyo, 1981).

73 Ibid., p. 101.

deep-rooted conflict in the employment of women between protection and equality of opportunity. What is certain is that the law has sufficient flexibility for employers to continue to discriminate.

The most recent law which especially should affect women, but includes men is a Law to Improve Management of Part-Time Workers, enacted in 1993. This draws attention to the lengthening of the periods of time which part-timers work, and the broadening of the practice in the employment field. The 'anxieties' of such workers should be addressed by the improvement of welfare, training, fringe benefits and better management. They should have contracts and representation. The Minister of Labour is enjoined to provide guidance, to call for reports, and to set up 'support' centres. In April 1994, the first of these had been established. It is too early to comment on this initiative.

There can be no doubt that the position of women in Japan has improved over the last fifty years. Their standard of living is amongst the highest in the world. This naturally applies equally to men. Women take a variety of views about whether or not their place in society needs changing. It is recognised, especially by older women with independent children that there are, at least in their opinion, great advantages in being free of the stress which accompanies working life in Japan, and which is currently of such concern. They have free time, the opportunity to socialise, to engage in education and to pursue expensive hobbies. This freedom is sometimes advanced as evidence that they are free from their former quasi-imprisonment in the home. Further, that they are setting an example of a better lifestyle to men.[74]

More politically active feminists would not agree. They point out, as women have done for generations, that inequality is the norm in education and in employment: that the former continues to stereotype through textbooks, and conditions through practices like putting all the boys' names before the girls on school registers: that childcare leave, although theoretically for both husbands and wives, is invariably taken by the wife. Such activists are relatively few, but they represent an important historical tradition in the evolution of Japanese society. They commonly claim that a lot has to be changed, and that there is a long way to go. It is difficult to disagree.

---

74 See, for example, 'Women making Choices: New Priorities for Living and Working' in *Japan Pictorial*, Vol. 16, No. 4, pp. 2ff.

CHAPTER NINE

The Pacific War
– 'hakko ichiu'[1]

---

1 Hoyt, Edwin P., *Japan's War: The Great Pacific Conflict* (London, 1986). On p. 2 he describes the policy of *hakko ichiu* as 'all eight corners of the world under one imperial roof'.

Overleaf ▶
Surrender in Singapore, 15 February 1942

The Pacific War
– 'hakko ichiu'

By the late 1930s the Japanese army, and probably a majority of the Japanese people, subject as they were to carefully processed information, felt that Japan was now a world-class power. The record, since the Restoration, had been of unqualified military success, and increasing imperial expansion. Such evidence proved the uniqueness of the Japanese people, and justified the exhortations to which they were constantly subjected, which were crystallised in the all-pervading 1890 education Rescript. The disastrous collapse of the 1935 London conference on naval agreement was simply further proof that Japan could not be dictated to. The fact that their behaviour in Manchuria, and now China proper was condemned by most countries, only served to sharpen this self-portrait of being strong and right. The shrewdest of the Japanese leaders however knew that there were two serious issues to be faced. The first was that the war in China, or 'the China Incident' as it was and is known, was not going well. The second was that world opinion, notably dominated by the United States, was not going to tolerate their increasing interference in the balance of power for very much longer.

One of the early and major disappointments in China came with the fall of Nanjing, then the capital, in 1937. The Japanese had hoped that with that victory it might have been possible to arrange a truce. The government was divided into those who wished to negotiate peace with the nationalist government, and those who wanted to carry on fighting. The view of the latter, led by Prime Minister Konoe, was that negotiations should be broken off with Chiang Kai-shek, and that a more malleable regime should be encouraged. Their opponents, led somewhat remarkably by an army officer, Major-General Ishihara, knew enough about the situation in China to realise that any further fighting would mean disaster for

217

Japan. This was the same Ishiwara who had been involved in the Manchurian incident. Now though he was unusual amongst the generals because he foresaw what would happen if the Chinese adventure were pursued. He also comprehended the scale of Chinese determination which his colleagues, with a pathological contempt for the Chinese, failed to see. As noted, Ishihara warned that: 'As long as China holds sovereignty over a single acre, Chiang's government will find popular support.'[2]

In this he proved more realistic than the war minister Sugiyama, who had told the emperor that once war was started, China could be beaten in a month. Senior naval officers, generally forces for restraint, had been against the activity in north China. Admiral Yonai, the navy minister was an opponent of the events after the Marco Polo bridge incident, as was Admiral Yamamoto Isoroku.[3] Those who wanted to break with Chiang and carry on won the day, and in the process involved Japan in a calamity. The nationalists moved to Chungking, deep inside China, and joined with their enemies the communists in common cause. The Japanese carried on their campaign, taking important cities like Hankow and Canton. But by the end of 1938 it was clear that the 'Incident' was incapable of resolution. Over one and a half million Japanese troops were engaged, able only to maintain a few positions, while the nationalists and communists regrouped, and retrained ready for operations which would drive the Japanese out in 1945.

Meanwhile foreign governments did little, for very good reason. Events in Europe, notably Franco's success in Spain, but most particularly Hitler's behaviour in Europe, were the major concerns of governments. The United States was in the grip of isolationist policies, which exacerbated the American perception of the place of Japan as a minor power. The League of Nations passed resolutions about sanctions against Japan, and the attitude of western powers was hardened by the increasing control exerted by Japan in north Asia, and the news of atrocities. One important positive act by the United States was the giving of financial help to the Chinese nationalists.

In Japan there was constant and passionate discussion about alliances; about who were friends and who enemies. In 1936 Japan and Germany had joined in an anti-Comintern pact, and in 1937 Italy joined them. Germany hoped that this could develop into a military group, which would not only oppose Russia, but could be

2 Murakami Hyoe, *Japan: The Years of Trial 1919–52* (Tokyo, 1983), p. 70.
3 Hoyt, *Japan's War*, p. 146.

mobilised against America, Britain and France. This provoked lengthy debate. At this stage the imperial navy did not consider itself a match for the western fleets, and there was the constant worry about Russia, an enemy of very long standing. By the middle of 1940, when Konoe, having been out of office for eighteen months, returned to be prime minister again, the situation was explosive, and western Europe was in turmoil. For the Japanese this was a golden opportunity to move into the colonies of the British, French and Dutch, since none of these, with the possible exception of the British, could defend their empires. Even the imperial navy was excited by the possibility of access to the rich natural resources there, notably oil for their warships.

When Konoe formed his new cabinet he brought into it two of the most belligerent public figures in Japan. The first was General Tojo Hideki as army minister. He had established an impressive reputation in Manchuria. There, he had brought some discipline and order to the unruly Kwantung army, and in other posts impressed enough people to be a rarity at the time – a government official who commanded some respect. During the Pacific War he became the principal hate figure in the west, and his capture, trial, and execution afterwards was a cause of great rejoicing. The other appointment was that of Matsuoka Yosuke as foreign minister. When still a child he went to the United States, had experience of racism there and at the 'college at the University of Oregon ... apparently fine tuned his hatred of things American'.[4] He had held senior posts in the South Manchuria railway company and in the diplomatic service and it was he who led the Japanese delegation out of the League of Nations in 1933 in protest against the Lytton commission. Matsuoka was enthusiastic about the Japanese, German, Italian tripartite pact, signed in September 1940, and about a concomitant non-aggression agreement with the USSR. He spent time there and in Germany in March and April 1941 cementing relationships, and Stalin saw him off personally from Moscow station. It was in Moscow in April that Matsuoka signed the non-aggression pact with the USSR.

But by September 1940, these agreements, which were a threat to countries under attack from Germany were compounded by another Japanese move. In that month they invaded Indo-China. The ostensible reason for this was that the Japanese needed the airfields in that country to launch attacks against the Chinese, and

4 Ibid., p. 191.

they also needed to block supplies to Chiang. Clearly the French were not able to stop them, and so the first major step since the invasion of China was taken. This led to a further deterioration in relations with the west. Britain reopened the Burma road into China, which had been closed for several months under pressure from Japan, and its reopening meant that Chiang Kai-shek could now be supplied with necessities for his campaign. The United States response was to put in place an embargo on iron and steel imports to Japan.

Now the Japanese government and military had to reconsider their priorities. Their two experiences against the USSR at Chankufeng in 1938 and Nomonhan in 1939 had given them experience of Russian power, and had given added strength to the strike south faction. But the USSR's agreement with Japan had removed any threat from that quarter. The European colonial powers were in disarray, and the major area of speculation was now about the intentions of the United States, a country which the Japanese, for reasons set out in earlier chapters neither liked nor trusted. Opinion in Japan was now divided in two. The first faction wished to face the issue that war against the United States would be inevitable, if Japan continued in its determination to establish an empire in Asia, with a resultant hegemony in the Pacific. This group understood that such domination would not be tolerated by the Americans. The second view was that accommodation should be sought with the Americans, variously because war was not inevitable, or that Japan would lose. Matsuoka was one of those who objected to negotiations with the United States, especially when he discovered, after his triumphant trip to Berlin and Moscow in 1941, that negotiations had been going on for several months without his knowledge.[5] He was, after all, foreign minister.

These negotiations were, oddly, initiated by two American clergymen. While in Japan they met influential senior army officers, and on their return to the United States gained access to President Roosevelt. He was sufficiently interested to tell his Secretary of State, Cordell Hull, an important figure in the events of the time, to encourage the move. Out of further discussion there emerged a document called the 'Japan–US Draft Understanding'.[6] Although it was welcomed by key figures on the Japanese side such as the Japanese ambassador in Washington, Nomura, and Prime Minister

5 Murakami, *Japan: The Years of Trial*, p. 80.
6 For more detail see ibid., p. 80ff.

Konoe himself, much fired by Nomura's optimism, the proposals would have been quite unacceptable to the Japanese leadership. One example was the condition that Japan should withdraw all its armies from China, if the latter recognised Manchukuo. Matsuoka's proposed amendments provoked the United States into further demands, such as a condition that Japan should leave the Tripartite Alliance. The inevitable collapse of the discussion was hastened by Germany's invasion of Russia, which caused Japan, once again, to consider its alignments.

One option, which came from Matsuoka, was that Japan should attack Russia. The resurrection of this idea was opposed by every-body of consequence, in favour of continuing to move south. Konoe then engaged in a familiar Japanese device. He resigned, was reappointed, and when forming his new cabinet excluded Mat-suoka. Before this happened the latter did everything to press his case, especially when Germany, having realised what they had taken on in Russia, demanded that Japan move against Siberia. The total situation was reviewed at a very important Imperial Conference on 2 July 1941.[7] A variety of views were expressed, ranging from that of General Sugiyama, chief of staff, who spoke of the need 'to stamp out the intrigues of Great Britain and the United States'[8] by a war which he had favoured, to encouragement from the spokesman for the imperial throne that the USSR should be attacked. The action which was to emerge was the complete occupation of Indo-China, a tactic which was designed to enable a launch into the two great prizes of Malaya and the Dutch East Indies. It was a tactic which was to commit Japan irrevocably to world war.

The United States, having gained intelligence of the plan, made clear that a move into southern Indo-China would mean the end of talks. It would also mean the freezing of Japanese assets, a course supported by Britain and Holland. The occupation in the event provoked an even sterner response: the United States banned oil exports to Japan. This was the greatest threat to Japan yet, since other suppliers did the same. The navy was thoroughly alarmed, since they knew well that they only had enough oil to operate the fleet for between one and two years.[9] The shortage of fuel would not only mean the ending of imperialist ambition, but the crippling of Japanese industry. The choice now was clear. The Japanese could either stop their advance and negotiate again for peace, which

7 For further discussion see Hoyt, *Japan's War*, pp. 203ff.
8 Ibid.
9 Murakami, *Japan: The Years of Trial*, p. 85.

would almost certainly mean giving up territory, or could engage in war with the United States and her allies.

There was certainly a peace 'party', at the head of which was the emperor himself. There is overwhelming evidence for his distrust of the army, because of their ill discipline, and their recklessness. Konoe for his part believed that a personal meeting of the heads of state might avert war, a view shared by the navy, but not by Tojo and the army. Roosevelt was sympathetic, but his advisers were not. The idea was discussed, but was dropped. By early September, although key figures in the imperial navy still encouraged negotiation, they were much more concerned about the navy's preparedness in the increasingly likely event of war. That depended on oil, the supply of which needed an attack on the Dutch East Indies without delay.

This consideration is what motivated Admiral Nagano, the naval chief of staff, to make a speech at the crucial meeting of government and military leaders on 3 September 1941, in which he said that there would eventually have to be an end to diplomacy, and then there should be quick engagement of the enemy. It would in any case be a long war, but initial advantage would lie with the Japanese.[10] Sugiyama wanted the expansion plan in south Asia to be pursued, and then the USSR could be attacked. When, shortly after the conference, the emperor asked Sugiyama and Nagano for an estimate of how long conquest of all of south-east Asia would take, the reply was five months. This led to the infamous exchange when the emperor asked Sugiyama how long a war against the United States would last, to be told three months. Hirohito reminded him that in 1937 Sugiyama had predicted that the China incident would be finished in a month, and that was four years ago. The general pleaded that China was huge, to which the emperor replied that vast as it was, the Pacific Ocean was bigger.

At the Imperial Conference on 6 September, all the familiar arguments were rehearsed, and the future was mapped. There would be preparation for war within the next months, but diplomacy would still be tried. Konoe then tried to persuade some of his senior colleagues to moderate their views. Tojo was adamant. He insisted that the time was now very near for movement. The always rather depressive Konoe finally gave up. He resigned, and through the usual procedures, Tojo was appointed as prime minister. The reasons from the Japanese point of view were sound. He was very loyal to the emperor and if the latter commanded him to continue

10 This important speech can be seen in full in Hoyt, *Japan's War*, pp. 211–12.

negotiations, Tojo would do so, which in the event he did. He also still commanded the respect of the army, which would be in mutinous mood if any concessions were made. The Americans regarded the appointment as a clear indication of the deterioration in the position, and made fresh and harder conditions, such as the withdrawal of all the forces in China, which were impossible to accept.

As early as the end of 1940, Admiral Yamamoto, convinced that the 'idiots' in the army would lead Japan to war against the United States, had begun to plan a campaign to strike the American fleet in Pearl Harbor in Hawaii. Where the idea originated is not clear, but one authority[11] describes the existence of such a plan drawn up by a Lieutenant-Commander Kusaka, which, with the references to the United States deleted, was widely known amongst senior officers. This was in 1927–28, and its novelty lay in the appreciation of how aircraft would affect future warfare. Paradoxically, at about the same time a remarkable American officer, William Mitchell, was court-martialled for criticising superiors who refused to accept his firm conviction of the priority of airpower. Mitchell's writing on the subject was known to the Japanese, and almost certainly to Yamamoto who spent time in the United States.[12] Mitchell further outraged people by predicting that the next war would be against Japan. After the war, and after his death, he was promoted and decorated.

Yamamoto did not approve of war with the Americans, apart from anything else because he did not believe they could be beaten. Unlike many senior officers, especially in the army, he had a lot of experience of the west. He had served for four years in the United States, had been a delegate to two naval disarmament conferences, and he understood the power that Japan would meet. His view was unequivocal, and often expressed as in this memorandum:

> A war between Japan and the United States would be a major calamity for the world, and for Japan it would mean, after several years of war already, acquiring yet another powerful enemy – an extremely perilous matter for the nation … Japan and America should seek every means to avoid a direct clash and Japan should under no circumstances conclude an alliance with Germany.[13]

Many Japanese who went to the United States after 1945 for

11 Agawa Hiroyuki, *The Reluctant Admiral: Yamamoto and the Imperial Navy* (Tokyo, 1979), pp. 193ff.
12 Ibid., pp. 186–7.
13 Ibid.

training would have agreed. They were usually astonished that the Japanese government could ever have contemplated taking on a country with such resources. Because of these views, Yamamoto's friends, anxious for his safety advised him to go to sea. Upon the conclusion of his period as naval vice-minister, he did so. In 1939 he boarded the flagship *Nagato* as Commander-in-Chief of the Combined Fleet and the First Fleet, and began to prepare for war.

Leaving aside army opinion, there were sections of the navy who disapproved of his views. There were, for example, the persistent 'young officers' who had been so prominent in the earlier attempts to destabilise the country. Above all, there were those senior officers who thought he was quite misguided about the role of aircraft. As the latter improved technically, Yamamoto's interest in them grew; he even learned to fly. He became convinced that the mighty battleships of the recent past were vulnerable to air attack, and were therefore an anachronism. What especially angered some of his colleagues was his opposition to the building, then in progress, of two massive warships, the *Yamato* and the *Musashi*. These ships were to be revolutionary in design, and would carry huge eighteen inch guns. Yamamoto had no demonstrable precedent for his doubt, but in the event both were sunk by American aircraft. These criticisms of conventional naval warfare annoyed and worried traditionalists. But his plan for Pearl Harbor convinced some that he was unbalanced. The operational plans of the navy at the time were based on war games which, broadly, presumed a Japanese invasion of the Philippines, the American fleet sailing to their aid, and a sea battle which the Japanese would win. The plan was static, out of date, and assumed too much. Yet the Japanese military authorities found it difficult to be adaptable or to change. It was this tradition of rigidity which was to be an important factor in their losing the war, and in not admitting this was the case before such appalling loss of life had occurred.

The plan that Yamamoto proposed is well known. It was based on the belief that the Americans had to suffer a surprise crippling blow, from which it would take a long time to recover. This would give Japan a chance of victory. It would be done by attacking the American fleet in Pearl Harbor with aircraft which would be taken to the target area by aircraft-carriers. Destroyers would protect the aircraft-carriers and the attack would be supported by submarines. The fleet would take a northern route where, in winter there was little shipping. Everything depended on surprise, and it might have been said, good luck. Much of the opposition, including that expressed by his fleet officers, was justified. There was a consider-able risk that they would be discovered, for example. Some of the fears were no doubt based upon their apprehension about what they were attempting. It took a long time, much persuasion, and a few threats to resign before Yamamoto finally achieved his goal. In October 1941 the Naval General Staff gave approval. In mid-November the task force began to sail for the Kuriles, where they were to assemble. On 2 December the famous message to proceed was dispatched: 'Climb Mount Niitaka'. Finally, on 3 December, the emperor, giving Yamamoto his orders said 'the whole fate of our nation will depend on the outcome'.[14] Yamamoto was determined to do his best, but right until the end he expressed his reservations. He found his 'present position extremely odd – obliged to make up my mind to and pursue unswervingly a course that is precisely the opposite of my personal views'.[15]

The attack on Pearl Harbor on Sunday, 7 December 1941 is one of the most discussed topics in recent history.[16] The events are well known. The Japanese fleet was not detected, it manoeuvred into position, and aircraft and submarines launched their attack. Battle-ships were sunk, aircraft and airfields destroyed. But almost at once, the plan went awry. It emerged that the American aircraft-carriers were at sea. Not only did this mean that these most vital of ships had not been destroyed, but that they now represented a danger to the Japanese fleet. Next, when Commander Fuchida, the leader of the attack, returned to the fleet commander Admiral Nagumo to report on the damage, in classic fashion he told Nagumo what the latter wanted to hear; that the American fleet would be out of action for six months. The question for the Japanese was what should now be done.

It was at this point that one of the decisions which affect the course of wars was made. Fuchida recommended that another attack should be made, so that vital installations should be destroyed. The pilots and aircraft were ready, and the expectation was that the plan would be executed. Nagumo ordered instead that the fleet should sail for Japan. There has been considerable analysis of this remarkable decision, and the consensus is that there were three elements in it. The first was that Nagumo was never happy

14 Ibid., p. 246.
15 Ibid., p. 231.
16 One of many detailed accounts can be seen in Prange, Gordon W., Goldstein, Donald M. and Dillon, Katherine V., *Pearl Harbor: the Verdict of History* (New York and London, 1986).

commanding aircraft-carriers, having had experience almost entirely of battleships. This nervousness was compounded by the fact that the American carriers could, being at sea and their whereabouts unknown, attack his fleet. He did not know how many there were, or where they were. Lastly, he had been opposed to the attack all along, and felt enough risks had been taken. Yamamoto, in his flagship in Japanese waters, was devastated. His subordinates suggested he order Nagumo to resume the attack, but he refused. He seems not to have believed that Nagumo had the ability or will to pursue his advantage. He did however instruct Nagumo to attack Midway Island, an important American base, on the way home. This Nagumo failed to do. He came home in triumph, to public jubilation which he felt would protect him from an angry Yamamoto. The latter realised immediately that his plan for a sudden and complete disablement of the American Pacific fleet had failed. On 8 December 1941, in an Imperial Rescript, Hirohito declared war, and around the same time the Japanese advanced further into south-east Asia.

To the American fascination with these events should be added their obsession with the questions as to why they were unprepared, and why they were surprised. It is only possible to consider some of the main answers which emerge from the welter of discussion. There is firstly the deep-rooted policy of isolationism in an America horrified by the events of the First World War, and disappointed with its outcome. This led to a conviction that Americans need not be involved in quarrels not of their making, and not to their advantage. Prange describes the consequences:

> The isolationist lawmakers had fought to the last ditch against lend-lease and repeal of the Neutrality Act. Nye had opposed special naval appropriations tooth and nail. 'We do have an adequate national defense' he proclaimed in 1938. 'Anyone lying awake at night worrying about an attack on the United States is wasting a lot of energy that might be expended in more useful ways.'[17]

Linked to this was an over-confidence in American 'might', which was fed by an isolationism which encouraged ignorance of what was happening in the world. It caused over-confidence in the ability of the armed services, and left unchallenged such claims as that by Secretary of the Navy Frank B. Knox that the 'navy is superior to any' and had 'at this time no superior in the world'. This appeared in the

17 Prange, *Pearl Harbor*, p. 17.

New York Times on the morning of 7 December 1941.[18] Naturally, there were people who challenged such expressions of invincibility, but general confidence was boosted by the fact that the idea of the United States being menaced by Japan was almost laughable. Their distaste for Japanese immigrants which was translated, as we have seen, into discrimination against them, also led them to suppose that it was possible to generalise from these about the Japanese nation. A common enough view in the west was expressed *officially* by the British Permanent Under-Secretary of State for Foreign Affairs, Cadogan, when he told the British ambassador in Washington to pass on to the Americans 'our information about the machinations of these beastly little monkeys'.[19]

Perhaps the circumstance which most puzzles historians is that for years before Pearl Harbor the Americans had been able to break the Japanese diplomatic codes, and so there should have been no surprise. The code watchers knew that around the fateful weekend the Japanese Embassy was expecting some very important messages. For a complexity of reasons there was delay in their transmission and translation with the well known consequence that the attack took place before war was declared. This is supposed variously to be because, as was usual the Japanese deliberately opened hostilities before the declaration, or in part because it was a weekend, or organisations were incompetent and disorganised, or information which clearly indicated that a Japanese attack was imminent, was deliberately withheld.

This hardened into a conspiracy theory, and those who subscribe to it are called revisionist.[20] Much of their venom, for so it must be called was, and is, directed at Roosevelt. It is claimed that he was either stupid or malicious. And the most serious allegation is that he plotted to allow the Japanese attack, and thus give him the opportunity to enter the war to support his friend Winston Churchill, who also, it is claimed, knew about the attack in advance. Perhaps, the argument runs, the President expected the American fleet to repel the Japanese, but this, like so much of this revisionist theory, begs colossal questions. In this case, if he wanted an American victory, would he not have alerted the navy so that they could have been prepared?[21] The argument rages, but the sober facts are firstly that the Americans were humiliated by the Japanese, and they found it

18 Ibid., p. 200.
19 Ibid., p. 71.
20 Ibid., Chapter 3 discusses the revisionist versions.
21 Ibid., p. 43.

difficult to believe that this had happened because of American weakness and Japanese superiority. Next, the damage to the fleet was not irreparable, since the repair facilities and other installations were intact, and much of the damaged shipping was quickly recovered. Above all, the aircraft-carriers were ready for action. What probably surprised the Japanese, and which was good for the allied war effort, was the anger felt by the Americans, and their determination for revenge.

As far as the Japanese were concerned, the exhilarating outcome was that a great victory had been won. Furthermore, and simultaneously, the long-awaited invasion of south-east Asia was begun. The first essential step was the attack and capture of Malaya and Singapore. The latter was important because of its strategic position, which was precisely why it had been identified by Thomas Raffles in the early nineteenth century. Especially in the decades leading up to the Japanese attack, it had been developed into a powerful commercial fortress by the British. It was also, and this was of great significance, a symbol of British imperial power, and its invincibility. Consciousness of that invincibility had led the British administration to believe that its judgement was impeccable. Thus, in the planning of the defences of Singapore, it was assumed that it was impossible to attack the island from the rear. The danger would come from the sea, and so it was that the heavy guns which were to defend one of the empire's bastions pointed outwards, and were of no use in a land-based attack.

There were many reasons for the staggering speed of the Japanese advance. The first was their bases in newly acquired Indo-China which, together with the acquiescence of the Siamese in allowing them to use their territory, gave them short lines of supply and communication. On 8 December, the day after Pearl Harbor, the Japanese went into Siam, and the latter was soon to be accorded membership of the Greater East Asia Co-Prosperity Sphere. Siam was never roundly condemned for this, and the role of Siam in the history of the period is often assumed to have been neutral. The next advantage the Japanese had was in the quality of their commander-in-chief, General Yamashita Tomoyuki. He was an officer of considerable experience and reputation, much influenced by a period he had spent with the German army, not long before he took command of the Malayan invasion force. He was involved in the military political tensions of the day, and had been associated with the February 26th Incident. His loyalty was to the Imperial Way faction, whereas General Tojo was a member of the

Control Faction. The inevitable result was that having made their commitments, they were irreconcilable, and possessed of mutual distrust. Such deep-seated divisions in military society were to contribute to the lessening of Japan's strength.

The Commonwealth and imperial forces who had to defend Malaya, on the other hand, had few advantages. Although there were large numbers of these, they were mostly inexperienced, undertrained and ill-equipped. For example the 'British maps were large scale but mostly dated from about 1915, and did not show the recent development of estates'.[22] The quality of the leadership, especially that of General Percival has become a central theme in historical accounts of the defeat.[23] The morale of many of the defenders was very low, and reached new depths when the Royal Navy suffered a very serious blow. On 2 December 1941 two ships, the battleship *Prince of Wales*, and the battle cruiser *Repulse* arrived to help in the defence of Singapore. Because the supporting aircraft-carrier which was supposed to join them had run ashore in the West Indies, these prestigious ships and the destroyers accompanying them had no air cover. Nevertheless, on 8 December they sailed north to try to engage the Japanese where they were landing troops. But in another display of the accuracy of Yamamoto's prediction about air power, the two huge ships were sunk on 10 December, after an hour of bombardment. Yamamoto himself directed the battle from his flagship in Japanese waters. Churchill reflected general opinion when he said: 'In all the war I never received a more direct shock ... As I turned over and twisted in bed the full horror of the news sank in upon me ... Japan was supreme and we everywhere were weak and naked.'[24]

Throughout the next two months the Japanese moved quickly down through Malaya, and on 15 February Singapore fell, and the British surrendered. Yamashita had 'gained the greatest triumph of any general in the history of the Japanese army'.[25]

To Winston Churchill, when he learned of this, the news was a staggering blow; Singapore having no landward defences 'no more entered into my mind than that of a battleship being launched without a bottom'.[26] There was a famous precedent, about which any senior officers concerned with the design of defence should

22 Swinson, Arthur, *Defeat in Malaya: The Fall of Singapore* (London, 1969), p. 75.
23 Ibid.
24 Ibid., p. 62.
25 Ibid., p. 149.
26 Ibid., p. 105.

have known. In the First World War T.E. Lawrence was able to capture the port of Aqaba from the land, because the Turks too believed such an attack was impossible, and their guns were on fixed mountings facing the sea. Such symbolic incompetence helped the Japanese in the ultimate stage of their Malayan campaign.

After the initial success in Malaya, Hong Kong was attacked and taken on Christmas Day 1941. Earlier in the month the tiny American force defending Guam was overwhelmed. Wake Island, another important American position, proved more resistant. The Americans were still recovering from Pearl Harbor when the first bombs were dropped by Japanese aircraft on 8 December from the Marshall Islands, which had fortuitously been handed over as a mandated territory after the First World War. The United States navy provided some relief but it had suffered a serious blow because Admiral Kimmel, one of its best commanders, had been made a scapegoat for Pearl Harbor. The Japanese took Wake on 22 December.

The seemingly endless conquests continued in a series of key victories. In March 1942 the Japanese were in Rangoon, the Dutch East Indies and the Philippines. In Java the Dutch defence seems to have been as weak as that of the British in Malaya, and the local people offered very little resistance. In the Philippines the fighting was harder. After an initial devastating Japanese air attack launched from Formosa on 8 December, the American air force was effectively wiped out. The American and Filipino forces retreated to Bataan and the fortress of Corredigor. It took the Japanese until early April to complete the conquest. MacArthur had already left on 10 March for Australia to prepare for counter-attack: not that Australia was beyond the ambitions of the Japanese. In February 1942 Australians were made aware of that when Darwin was attacked, and eight ships were sunk. Darwin was attacked again in March, as were the other northern towns of Derby and Broome.

The speed of the advance, and the increasing distance of their forces from the home islands, caused the Japanese to consider their position and their priorities. They did so in March 1942 at a time when they had access to all the raw materials they needed, when American and British naval vessels had all but been eliminated from the area, and Japanese control had been extended to the borders of India and New Guinea. The navy advocated the capture of Hawaii and Australia, but for practical reasons alone this was judged to be impossible.[27] The real 'problem' remained China. The planners,

27 Hoyt, *Japan's War*, pp. 204ff.

though not those with field experience in China, seemed unable to comprehend the scale of the task in China, an inability which was to be a major contribution to Japan's eventual defeat. The whole adventure had degenerated into a stalemate reminiscent of the trenches of the First World War, with no prospect of victory. Yet the group planned the next stage of the war in China. It was also planned that the next targets would be New Caledonia, Fiji, Samoa, New Guinea and the Aleutian Islands.[28] The navy would go for Midway, which was, as it turned out, a fateful decision.

Japanese achievements were remarkable. The reasons for their success in the first four months of the Pacific war have often been discussed, but in broad outline rarely disputed. There is always something of a mythology about the 'fighting quality' of races, regiments or units, but in the case of the Japanese at that time there is no doubt that the quality of the individuals in battle was extremely good. They were highly motivated, convinced as they were of their supremacy and the justice of their cause. They were well trained, and many of them, and their officers, brought battle experience to this new conflict. They were physically harder, and were more able than their adversaries to cope with relative deprivation, and the extremely difficult climate. All of this applied equally to their generals, especially two of the most important Yamashita and Homma Masaharu, the latter of whom took the Philippines. The British imperial forces, the Americans and the Dutch were disadvantaged in almost equal measure. The troops were often ill trained, inexperienced, and were sometimes put into battle, of necessity, before they were properly acclimatised. There were, of course, occasions when great courage was shown by individuals and groups, for example in the last defence of Bataan in the Philippines. The historical consensus is that the troops were not well served by key senior officers. Some of these grievously underestimated the skill and determination of the Japanese. While realising, for example, the size of the Japanese air forces, some believed that the pilots could not fly the planes properly. Even MacArthur has been criticised for his response to the Japanese threat. He was, it has been alleged, overly optimistic;[29] he did not prepare wisely when the threat was known, nor did he respond properly when the threat became reality. The defences were weak in the Philippines, and Japanese intelligence knew that,

28 Ibid., p. 261.
29 Mayer, S.L. *The Biography of General of the Army, Douglas MacArthur* (Greenwich, Connecticut, 1984), pp. 34ff.

and he mishandled his air resources, which were destroyed immediately.[30]

An extremely important factor in Japanese success, at least at first, was the image they presented of Asians who had come to throw out white imperialists. Colonial regimes which were so resented by Asians, and which were by 1940 provoking hard political opposition, were not only about economic exploitation, but what is today called racism. This was as deeply ingrained in the colonial Europeans, as it was in the Japanese. The common European attitude was summarised in a remark by a 'certain British high official' who said: 'if the *Prince of Wales* could be sunk by the yellow Japanese, I'd rather have let the Germans have her'.[31] This is the common attitude which caused the response to an address to some 45,000 Indian troops by a Japanese officer when Singapore fell. He told them about the Indian National Army – called by the British the Indian Renegade Army – and how they could be released to fight for Indian independence. 'The Indian troops leapt to their feet and tossed their hats into the air amid a tumult of hurrahs.'[32] In the Dutch East Indies a Dutch army of 100,000 surrendered to a Japanese army of 25,000, and most locals deserted. Achmad Sukarno was released from prison. One of the leaders of the independence movement, he was appointed to the 'Supreme Military Advisory Body'.[33] The idea of 'Greater East Asia', although a fiction, was based upon racial common denomination, at least by the very optimistic. There were ritual displays, such as the Conference of Greater East Asia which took place in Tokyo in November 1943, and which was attended by the pro-Japanese leaders of most of the conquered territories, and representatives of 'free India'.

The political advantage of having such indigenous support did not influence the behaviour of the Japanese army towards civilians or prisoners of war, especially the Chinese. The savagery of that army had already been noted by an appalled world in China, and early indications in the Malayan campaign were that it would continue. The fall of Hong Kong on Christmas Day 1941 was attended by great brutality. Wounded prisoners were butchered and burned on funeral pyres, and there was mass rape of nurses. At the collapse of the last resistance in the Philippines, some 76,000 Americans and Filipinos were forced marched on what was to

30 Ibid., p. 39.
31 Murakami, *Japan: The Years of Trial*, p. 103.
32 Ibid., pp. 104–5.
33 Ibid., pp. 108–9.

become one of the most vivid testaments to brutality in the war. On the Bataan march some 7,000 prisoners died, or were murdered when they became too weak. A notoriously cruel Lieutenant-Colonel Tsuji Masanobu established the mood by shooting a prisoner dead, remarking 'this is the way to treat bastards like this'.[34] A factor in this, which does not amount to an excuse, is that this would have been the first time ordinary Japanese had met Americans. Not only had the latter discriminated against Japanese Americans earlier in the century, but the soldiers would have been aware of the treatment of the Japanese Americans since the outbreak of war. This ranged from physical assault by citizens to a famous Executive Order 9066 of February 1942 restricting movement, and the eventual confinement of some 120,000 people in internment camps.[35] Cruel behaviour by the Japanese was usual, and the building of the Burma railway has become a legend because of the especial suffering of the prisoners of war.

The reasons for such cruelty, which the world has found impossible to forgive or forget, are the object of much speculation, as is the question of where responsibility lay. Some believed that cruelty is something inherent in the Japanese personality. Such a sweeping theory would have to explain the difference between the behaviour of the victorious Japanese in 1905 and 1942. Some apologists point to the lack of total subscription to the Geneva Convention, but this could be a legal defence, not an explanation of behaviour. The truth may well lie in the culture of the imperial forces. The junior ranks were brutalised by more senior ranks, with the famous slapping being a normal part of daily intercourse. In short the treatment experienced by soldiers and sailors was so inhuman, and their dignity so disregarded, that they passed cruelty on to helpless people. And always this was compounded by their hatred of other races, especially the Chinese, and their disgust at fighting men who surrendered.

We shall go on to see that after the war, many of those who originated, perpetrated, or even condoned brutality were called to account. A Japanese Foreign Minister said then that he tried to persuade senior officers to 'ensure correct treatment' and they agreed. But the middle-ranking officers and the other ranks took little notice of orders.[36] This, it may be noted was a constant, and

34 Ibid., pp. 110–11.
35 More details about the treatment of ethnic Japanese can be found in Murakami, ibid., pp. 115–16.
36 Storry, Richard, *A History of Modern Japan* (London, 1960), pp. 217–18.

contradictory phenomenon in the Japanese military. Some of the most senior officers tried to enforce discipline, including the eminent Yamashita and Homma. The former strongly objected to the behaviour of one of his major-generals, Nishimura Takuro of the Imperial Guards Division, who was not only blatantly disobedient in battle, but encouraged the rape of civilians, and the murder of wounded prisoners. It took a long time for Yamashita to have Nishimura sent home in disgrace, and to ensure that the Imperial Guards were not honoured with an Imperial Rescript. Homma was similarly outraged, notably at the behaviour of his troops on the Bataan March, and the way in which many senior Filipino officials were executed at the whim of Tsuji. Neither Yamashita nor Homma won. The former, still seen as a rival to Tojo, and despite his success in Malaya was sent to a command on the Siberian border. Homma was, amongst other alleged defects, accused of not being hard enough on the Filipinos, sent home, and taken off the active list. This was not the end of their somewhat unjust deserts. Both were executed after the war, in what is agreed was a vindictive act by a MacArthur determined to be revenged for his humiliation.

Even though the Japanese were so dramatically successful in the early stages of the war, it became clear after about eighteen months, even to realists in Japan, that Yamamoto had been right: if the war was not concluded in a very short time, Japan would not win. The reasons for the reversal, gradual at first and then inexorable, were partly to do with military tradition, more generally with a continuing refusal to face facts. The army 'factions' of the 1930s still persisted, with serious effects on military capability. It was this which deprived the Japanese army of two of its best leaders, Yamashita and Homma. Not only was the army subject to irreparable divisions, but the by now ancient animosity between army and navy was still in place. It is difficult to imagine that not very many years before the war, Yamamoto had gone back to sea at the behest of his friends, because he might have been murdered. Thus would have been lost one of the most skilful commanders in imperial naval history. But perhaps a startling symbol of the disastrous lack of cooperation concerns submarines.

It would seem to be beyond dispute that submarines should be regarded as the responsibility of navies, and the imperial navy did indeed have a respectable fleet. Yet the army, not to be left out, built twenty-six transport submarines of its own, even though the navy had such vessels. Furthermore the army declined the navy's offer of help in design and construction, the whole enterprise being described by one expert historian on submarines as an 'extraordinary episode'.[37] The question of submarines raises another general weakness which was to diminish the chances of total victory. This was the inflexibility of the services. Homma for example was advised by his field commanders to cut off the American retreat to Bataan, but his orders from Tokyo were to conquer Manila.[38] There could be no question of disobeying these orders because of ground assessment. In respect of the submarine fleet the problems faced in using them were substantial. There was the vastness of the area they had to patrol; there was the need to transport men and equipment to areas where the United States was regaining dominance. To make room, torpedoes and guns were removed, and in consequence so was fighting capacity. In the same way they were used to transport oil to Japan. Their crippling inflexibility though lay in the very strict rules about who they might attack. In general they were only allowed to engage warships, and so invaluable, and vulnerable merchant ships were allowed to pass unscathed. If submarine commanders, like other officers at the front, had been encouraged to use initiative, very much more damage might have been done. But that would have been very much against a central tenet of Japanese social behaviour.

The Japanese also gradually alienated their new Asian allies, undermining their potential cooperation by indiscriminate brutality. The stories of the treatment of the Chinese which had worldwide circulation, had in some cases caused important leaders, such as Nehru, to wonder about the meaning of co-prosperity. Nevertheless the idea of a cooperative Asia, freed from colonialism was an idea which the more reasonable Japanese believed in, as did people like Sukarno and Chandra Bose, the leader of the Indian National Army. More usual was the view of General Terauchi, an important officer in south-east Asia, who reflected deep-seated racist feeling when he made it clear that he despised Bose's army. In any case he shared the view of his father, the terrifying first Governor General of Korea, that colonial independence was not to be contemplated.[39] As well as Japanese misbehaviour in China, there was also the rather glaring absence of independence in Korea to be explained. The truth was that despite the idealism of the theory, the Greater East Asia Co-Prosperity Sphere was a fiction which was useful in solving the

37 Miller, David, *Submarines of the World: A Technical Directory of the Major Submarines from 1888 to the Present Day* (London, 1991), p. 100.
38 Murakami, *Japan: The Years of Trial*, p. 107.
39 Storry, *History of Modern Japan*, p. 219.

pressing problems of Japan. The one lasting outcome, which was not of much help to Japan as relationships deteriorated, was that after the war the restoration of colonial rule for good, was unthinkable.

Three other elements contributed to the reversal of Japanese fortunes. The first was the speed of recovery of the allied forces. In March 1942 at the planning meeting in Tokyo to which reference has been made, the navy advised Tojo that the United States Navy would not be in a position to fight until December 1943.[40] Like all such estimates, it did not take sufficient account of the resources available to the Americans, nor of their determination to win. Japanese judgement at the time was based on the ease with which they had beaten the westerners, and on the conviction that the Japanese soldier was driven by a conviction and a spirit which made him unbeatable. Secondly, there was the indomitable China. Draining Japan of men and resources, with the factional Chinese armies united in common cause, the conflict was no nearer resolution than it had been in 1937, five years before. It was a situation which was to be crippling, and one which is sometimes underacknowledged in assessments of why Japan was defeated. Finally there was the already unmanageable size of the Japanese empire in the middle of a major war. In mid-1942, outside of the home islands, this comprised Korea, Manchuria and other parts of China, Formosa, Indo-China, the Philippines, Malaya, the Dutch East Indies and many islands in the south Pacific. These had to be defended not only against a powerful external enemy, but also against an increasingly hostile local population.

And still, in the first months of 1942, the outcome was uncertain. There was an optimistic mood in Japan, carefully nurtured by the government and newspapers and radio, although realists were worried. Amongst the allied powers, and especially the Americans, morale was low, and depression increased with the seemingly invincibility of the Japanese. There was good reason for that dejection. Admiral Nagumo, who had commanded the Pearl Harbor attack, had attacked Darwin in northern Australia in February, sinking and damaging seventeen ships. This was followed by further bombing attacks on towns in Australia. In April and May the Japanese were building up their forces on Rabaul in New Britain, and initial landing in Papua New Guinea had been accompanied by the bombing of Port Moresby, the capital. In May they moved to

40 Hoyt, *Japan's War*, p. 261.

build bases in Tulagi and Guadalcanal in the Solomon Islands. Also in April Ceylon was attacked, and merchant vessels and warships sunk, including a British aircraft-carrier. But the picture given to the Japanese public, as is always given to publics in wartime, did not include the negative aspects of events.

The first indication that the Japanese were going to meet resistance occurred within days of Pearl Harbor. On 11 December, a Japanese invasion force intent on occupying the crucial United States base on Wake Island, was turned back by American shore defences. Japanese reinforcements took the island eleven days later, but the first failure was the first Japanese reversal of the war. The failure to reinforce and hold Wake is generally regarded as a major strategic blunder,[41] and another blow to American morale. Wake was also to be a focus which caused independently minded Japanese to reflect on the future. In early March within a few months of its capture, Wake was attacked by American ships. It was 'the first American offensive action of the Pacific War'.[42] Still American morale was low, but it was to be raised by one of the boldest strokes of the war, and which angered but rattled Japan. This was the first bombing of the Japanese home islands of the war – the Doolittle raid on 18 April 1942 – named after the pilot who led the attack.

It was President Roosevelt himself who asked his military to plan a bombing raid on Japan.[43] A scheme was drawn up, and on 1 April 1942 an aircraft-carrier with sixteen bombers left California, and joined forces with ships from Pearl Harbor. Although their approach was observed by Japanese intelligence, the Japanese were not able to intercept them. All their aircraft-carriers were engaged elsewhere, and this occasion demonstrated how even the might of the imperial forces was overextended. On 18 April the aircraft bombed Tokyo and most made the safety of nationalist China. Of those aircrew who did not, and were captured by the Japanese, three were executed and five imprisoned. The Chinese who tried to help survivors were killed by the Japanese. The latter were not so much shocked by the damage, which was not great, as by the event itself. Yamamoto, realistic as always, wrote before the attack:

> A lot of people are feeling relieved, or saying they're 'grateful to Admiral Yamamoto' because there hasn't been a single air raid. They're very wrong: the fact that the enemy hasn't come is no thanks

41 Prange, Gordon W. *et al.*, *Miracle at Midway* (New York, 1983), pp. 5ff.
42 Hoyt, *Japan's War*, p. 262.
43 Ibid., p. 271.

to Admiral Yamamoto, but to the enemy himself. So if they want to express gratitude to somebody, I wish they'd express it to America.[44]

Bombs were dropped on Tokyo and neighbouring cities, but also the western cities of Nagoya and Kobe. The Japanese version, whilst assuring the people that 'the Imperial Household was absolutely safe',[45] tried to minimise the incident, and claimed, totally wrongly, that nine American aircraft had been shot down. Yamamoto, perhaps the best barometer of the truth in Japan, was depressed: 'some measure of his commitment to the offensive drained away, never to be quite restored'.[46]

May 1942 proved to be the indubitable turning-point. On 4 May, when the Japanese had only been there for some twenty-four hours, Tulagi was attacked by American forces. Several Japanese warships were sunk, and a number of seaplanes destroyed. This was, as Hoyt points out 'the first time since the war began the imperial forces had been frustrated in an attempt to seize territory'.[47] Also in early May the Japanese navy was seriously challenged in the battle of the Coral Sea. In the course of this battle several important ships on both sides were sunk or badly damaged, in this first sea battle dominated by aircraft-carriers.[48] Americans and Japanese claimed victory; in the words of one Japanese report 'a great victory indeed'. The historical judgement ranges from 'the Japanese had the edge'[49] to 'in fact it was a draw'.[50] It was also a setback, for the Japanese lost many of their experienced pilots,[51] as indeed they had in their earlier attacks on Colombo and Trincomalee. The Japanese commander, Vice-Admiral Inouye, was much criticised by his superiors, including Yamamoto, for breaking off the engagement too soon, when he had the advantage, and then disregarding orders to pursue the Americans. But he was even more hesitant. He decided not to carry out the planned landing by sea on Port Moresby. Whatever the outcome of the battle of the Coral Sea, there is no doubt that this represented a halting of Japanese ambition. Inouye ordered his fleet to sail north, firstly to invade Nauru, but after the sinking of the Japanese fleet flagship, and reported sightings of American aircraft-carriers, this too was cancelled and Inouye returned to Truk.

44 Agawa, *The Reluctant Admiral*, p. 298.
45 Prange *et al.*, *Miracle at Midway*, p. 25.
46 Ibid., p. 26.
47 Hoyt, *Japan's War*, p. 281.
48 Murakami, *Japan: The Years of Trial*, p. 117.
49 Prange *et al.*, *Miracle at Midway*, p. 44.
50 Hoyt, *Japan's War*, p. 283.
51 Prange *et al.*, *Miracle at Midway*, p. 48.

The battle of Midway was much more decisive. At the end of May 1942, a large Japanese fleet began to move against Midway which, because of its position between Japan and Hawaii, was of critical significance. The fleet was commanded by Yamamoto personally: 'In all, three hundred and fifty warships, one thousand airplanes and over one hundred thousand men were mobilised for this operation. It was the greatest attack force ever seen in world naval history.'[52]

Before this there had been considerable discussion amongst Japanese commanders, in which proposals to move on and occupy Hawaii immediately after the capture of Midway were examined and rejected, and ways in which Australia could be isolated were considered. As far as Midway was concerned the main force would be supported by a diversionary move towards the Aleutian Islands, and again assuming victory, the navy would then send ships south to support the isolation of Australia. The attack on Midway began in earnest on 3 June and the battle lasted until 6 June, when the decimated Japanese fleet turned for home. Naturally in a battle on such a scale even the American victors suffered heavy losses, but the Japanese casualties were such that they would never recover. Once again, in a war in which control of the air held the key for victory they had lost more aeroplanes and many experienced pilots. It had been the first defeat in Japanese naval history, and it had taken place near the anniversary date, 27 May, of Togo's victory at Tsushima.

There has been a good deal of debate about the reasons for this Japanese disaster and American triumph. Some of the consensual points are, firstly that the Japanese were over-confident, with one consequence being their inadequate training. Japanese and American commentators at the time, and since, highlight this factor. The preparatory war games, Agawa points out were conducted so badly that, in the words of the officer who led the air attack on Pearl Harbor, Fuchida Mitsuo, they were 'enough to disgust even the most hardened flying officers among us'.[53] Prange comments on 'these erratic shipshod exercises' and quotes one of the most famous of the Japanese officers, Genda Minoru's observation that 'we did not have ample time to train our fliers'.[54] Prange also reflects that the commonest Japanese explanation for the defeat was the 'victory disease', a feeling of invincibility.[55] There was too the

52 Murakami, *Japan: The Years of Trial*, pp. 116–17.
53 Agawa, *The Reluctant Admiral*, p. 303.
54 Prange *et al.*, *Miracle at Midway*, p. 49.
55 Ibid., p. 370.

personality element. Fuchida had had an operation just before and was not fit to fly; Nagumo was as cautious as ever, and broke radio silence with disastrous results; and the Americans had a commander, Nimitz, who would not let go of his belief that Midway was the Japanese target.

But perhaps the most important single advantage the Americans possessed was their ultimate certain knowledge that the attack would indeed be directed at Midway. They were able to discover this because of a famous, though still remarkable intelligence breakthrough. Admiral Chester Nimitz, now in command of the US Pacific Fleet, was an experienced and well regarded officer. One of Nimitz's virtues was that he was 'a thinking leader, a real intellectual',[56] who understood the value of intelligence information. Thus he gave credence to Commander Joseph Rochefort, perhaps the best known of a team which broke the Japanese naval codes, a process which though difficult was made easier by the recovery of intelligence material from Japanese warships which had been sunk.[57] In the Japanese signal traffic which was intercepted, there was frequent reference to a target 'AF'. To try to discover what it was Rochefort suggested a simple, brilliant stratagem. It was to send a message from Midway, which would be easily intercepted, saying that Midway was short of water. Within hours the Japanese had advised their forces that 'AF' was short of water.[58] This vital piece of information led to the decisive action which was to turn events in the Pacific War.

In the southern Pacific, MacArthur had arrived in Australia on 17 March. He left behind a legacy of some bitterness both about his handling of the defences of the Philippines, and about his evacuation.[59] Whether criticism of him was justified – he always denied it – in his new appointment as commander of allied forces in the southwest Pacific, he was in as difficult a position as it was possible to imagine. The Japanese continued their advance, the forces in Australia were slight, and there would be little reinforcement from the United States because the priority was Europe. The Australians were so worried, that they were discussing withdrawing from the north of Australia, leaving it open to Japanese invasion. He tried to tackle all these problems. He pointed out that the Japanese did not have the resources to mount a serious invasion of Australia,

56 Ibid., p. 20.
57 Murakami, *Japan: The Years of Trial*, p. 117.
58 Prange *et al.*, *Miracle at Midway*, pp. 45–6.
59 Mayer, *Douglas MacArthur*, pp. 48ff.

although in late May and early June 1942 midget submarines did some damage in Sydney Harbour. MacArthur therefore rejected an evacuation to the south. He pressed Washington for reinforcements, and began to plan the next stage to recovery.

Initially, the point of conflict was New Guinea, especially Port Moresby. The Japanese still had forces on the northern coast, but the planned seaborne invasion had been postponed after the battle of the Coral Sea. But the intention was still to take Port Moresby, now by land from the north. MacArthur's response was to identify the need for an airfield on the island. His forces would then take Buna, which involved crossing the difficult Owen Stanley mountains. In the same month, July 1942, Japanese forces landed near Buna. The subsequent battle for New Guinea was to indicate how brutal the fighting in the Pacific would be. The Japanese would not surrender, and their casualties were extremely high: about 20,000 soldiers landed on New Guinea and some 13,000 were killed. The allies lost many fewer in action but thousands suffered with disease. Eventually, in January 1943 the allies were in control, although total control would take some time.

At about the same time as New Guinea was being fought over, the danger presented by Guadalcanal in the Solomon Islands became clear. Here, a new Japanese airstrip would enable them to attack Australia with relative ease. In early August 1942 the Americans landed on Guadalcanal, to meet a Japanese force the size of which made no allowance for the numbers of the allied opposition. The battle escalated at sea, on land, and in the air, with the Japanese only belatedly realising how serious the Americans were. In February 1943, the Japanese gave in. The losses on both sides had been heavy,[60] but Guadalcanal became a symbol. To the Americans it is a symbol of determination and bravery, and further evidence that the Japanese could be beaten. To the Japanese it was a defeat which wounded imperial pride, but also forced people to face the truth: Japan was going to lose the war.

By the beginning of 1943, the Japanese government realised the seriousness of its position and had to reconsider. They looked at several ideas which ranged from the consequences of victory in New Guinea, to a renewed drive in China, to an invasion of India. The unlikelihood of any of these became increasingly clear as 1943 went on. Nevertheless as late as 1944 the Japanese tried to maintain their offensive in Burma, notably hoping to take the airfields in Assam

---

60 For detailed figures see Murakami, *Japan: The Years of Trial*, p. 131.

which were used to supply the Chinese. But in some of the hardest fighting of the war, under the notable leadership of General Slim, British and allied forces slowly drove the Japanese back. A signal victory was the battle of Kohima Imphal 'the greatest and one of the longest of the Pacific War'.[61] A major calamity occurred on 18 April when Yamamoto flew from Rabaul to visit front-line troops. The Americans intercepted messages, knew the codes, and a decision was made by Roosevelt personally, to shoot him down.[62] This was done and Yamamoto was killed. On the Aleutian island of Attu, American invaders attacked the Japanese garrison, and the latter, almost to a man, fought to the death. The Japanese promptly evacuated their garrison on the neighbouring island of Kiska. During these months the situation with regard to shipping became critical, provoking a major dispute between those who advocated continuous replacement of heavy shipping losses for war purposes and those who believed ships should be used to transport materials to Japan.

By the autumn of 1943, the allies were moving steadily north, a movement which was enabled by MacArthur's device of 'island hopping'. This meant that instead of taking the next target in logical fashion, islands would be passed over, and their defenders left to starve. Attempts by the Japanese to relieve these garrisons were, in effect, unsuccessful. So were the high profile meetings of the Greater East Asia Co-Prosperity Sphere, such as the one held in Tokyo in November 1943, in which in exchange for independence, the various countries were persuaded to mobilise wholeheartedly in support of Japan. The attacks on the important Japanese airbase on Rabaul were intense, and again Japanese counter-attacks were frustrated by pre-emptive strike by superior forces. In November too a major allied offensive was made on an important staging post, the Gilbert Islands.

In January 1944 the United States assaulted the Marshall Islands, and in the next month began an attack on Truk. This was regarded as an equivalent of Pearl Harbor,[63] and the destruction of the base was in equal measure a crippling blow for the Japanese, and healthy retribution for the Americans. In February the Marshall Islands fell. In April, the allies landed on a deserted Truk. Japan was gradually being forced back to the islands near the homeland, and this was demonstrated by the definition of Saipan as the point at which the

61 Storry, *History of Modern Japan*, p. 223.
62 Hoyt, *Japan's War*, p. 324.
63 Murakami, *Japan: The Years of Trial*, p. 141.

invaders must be stopped. Meanwhile, every attempt by the Japanese to move ships or equipment, or indeed to reorganise its strategy suffered at the hands of an increasingly sophisticated American submarine force. The latter had even entered Tokyo bay.

The Japanese could expect no help, nor indeed had they ever received any, from their axis allies. By 1944, it was clear that Germany would be defeated. Nor was there much consolation to be gained from events in mainland Asia. The attempt to support the ever fantastic ambitions of Bose, the leader of the Indian National Army, was wrecked by allied airpower. A huge Japanese army was bogged down and died in Burma. In an attempt to contain the chaos, Tojo accrued new positions of authority in a manner unprecedented even in the capricious history of the imperial military. On 6 June 6th a fleet nearly twice the size of the Japanese force at Midway began an operation which a month later would capture Saipan, designated by the Japanese as a symbol of their country's determination to halt the allied advance. Tojo had agreed with the designation, and for the last time the powerful in Japan considered his position. The upshot was that Konoe headed a group, which by dint of manipulation based upon wide experience, forced Tojo to resign. The two men asked to replace him, again a reflection of inter-service rivalry, were a general, and an admiral. General Koiso and Admiral Yonai agreed to try to form a cabinet, but they were inexperienced, and not of the calibre to direct the affairs of the nation at such a critical point.

The Japanese and the Americans had both been racing to develop a long range bomber, and the Americans won with the B29, numbers of which were sent to China in the spring of 1944. On 13 June they raided the southern Japanese island of Kyushu, and although that particular raid did little damage, it was a foretaste of what was to come, since through the agency of the B29, Japan would be flattened. The next blow was to be much more serious. As an outcome of a discussion involving President Roosevelt, and at the insistence of MacArthur, in October a major invasion was begun on the Philippines. In October 1994, there took place the final major naval battle of the war in Leyte gulf. Japanese losses, including the giant 64,000 ton battleship *Musashi*, finally destroyed the imperial navy.[64] In January 1945, Manila fell. The Philippines were lost despite the recall of Yamashita, arguably the best general in the

64 Storry, *History of Modern Japan*, p. 224.

army who had been sent to Manchukuo, in spite, by Tojo. His task proved impossible, as did any defence of the Marianas Islands.

The situation was by now so desperate that Admiral Ohnishi Takejiro in the summer of 1944 floated an idea which was one of the most bizarre of the war. This was the use of *kamikaze* pilots. *Kamikaze* means divine wind and was used to describe the typhoon which destroyed Mongol ships in their thwarted attempt to invade Japan in the 13th century. The army had been considering a similar notion, which was to use aircraft as suicide bombers. There were grave doubts about this in the higher echelons, but the first volunteers were found, and in October 1944 the first *kamikaze* aeroplanes took off and damaged and sank several ships. At the same time army aircraft did the same, and these attacks became the 'backbone'[65] of Japanese attacks, causing considerable damage and a good deal of fear amongst American sailors.

The B29s – the 'B-san' the Japanese called them – began to bomb Manchuria in mid-1944, and in October there was a massive bombing raid on Formosa. On 24 November, over a hundred B29s flew to Tokyo, and in this and subsequent raids the main deterrent was ramming by Japanese fighters, stripped of their armaments. The resistance was sufficiently strong to make the Americans look for a base from which fighter aircraft could be launched to support the bombers. The place identified was Iwo Jima, and its capture caused one of the fiercest battles of the war. The Americans lost 4,500 men, and the Japanese 21,000. It was one of the battles which was used to justify the use of the atomic bomb as a means of saving life. Meanwhile the Americans had started firebombing Japan with napalm, and in March three hundred B29s bombed Tokyo, causing about 80,000 deaths, and the loss of the homes of a million people. It was, one Japanese historian observed 'the greatest recorded conflagration in the entire history of mankind'.[66] Nagoya, Osaka and Kobe were to receive the same treatment. Even Americans sympathetic to the allies' cause have observed that although the destruction was a military masterpiece, had the Japanese won the war, people like the architect of the policy, General Lemay, would have been tried and executed as war criminals.[67]

Also in March the Americans began the assault on Okinawa with bombing raids, and on 1 April they landed. The scale of the *kamikaze* operation was a serious obstacle, and a major effort had to be made

65 Murakami, *Japan: The Years of Trial*, p. 162.
66 Ibid., p. 167.
67 Hoyt, *Japan's War*, p. 67.

to attack the points from which they came. It was not until June that Okinawa fell, again after some of the most bitter fighting of the war. The Japanese seemed determined to die for their cause, and even children became part of the *kamikaze* tradition. In Japan the civilian population were organised to fight for the homeland. But the people knew that it could now only be a question of time before the homeland was invaded, and drilling with bamboo spears seemed to be the only, and most dignified way, to prepare for the assault. The political position was precarious. Prime Minister Koiso resigned, and after a good deal of pressure Admiral Suzuki Kantaro agreed to succeed him. He was the same Suzuki who had survived the 26 February coup in 1936, and was now seventy-nine. The situation he inherited included the certain collapse of Germany, and the likely refusal of the USSR to renew the neutrality pact. The possibility that the USSR might negotiate a peace settlement was unlikely, and the reality that she would declare war on Japan was being understood.

In July 1945 the allies issued a proclamation from Potsdam which was to be the last word. Japan should surrender, unconditionally. On both sides one of the important issues was that of the future of the emperor. Since he was accorded such power in the Constitution, and since westerners believed hierarchies as defined formally meant the reality, Hirohito was an object of hate, second only to Tojo. Meanwhile, Japan was being destroyed by bombing, and the allies were moving closer. The scale and persistence of the attack was unlike anything in the history of warfare, largely because it was carried out by the still novel use of aircraft. On one raid, for example, on 29 May, 500 B29s bombed Yokohama.[68] On 22 June the emperor told a meeting of his leaders that they should 'strive now to study the ways and means to conclude the war'.[69]

The end was to come with the atomic bombs. On 6 August 1945 the first was dropped on Hiroshima, but the effects were contained and rationalised by the army. Two days later, the USSR declared war on Japan. Prime Minister Suzuki who had explored the use of the USSR as an intermediary for a surrender before the latter declared war, knew that surrender was inevitable. But still key figures refused to lay down arms. That antique tradition under which the resignation of the war minister could bring down the government was still in place, and the minister of the day, General Anami would not agree to sue for peace. On 9 August, the second atomic bomb was dropped on Nagasaki. Suzuki had to face the truth that the Japanese

68 Ibid., p. 398.
69 Ibid.

high command, having been committed, found it difficult to extricate itself. Therefore, he decided to call an imperial conference, at which the emperor would give the final verdict. And so he did, in another of his incontrovertible intrusions into public affairs. 'To make things clear' he said, 'I will tell you my reasons':

> The army and the navy reported that they could mount a decisive battle on the main islands and that they had confidence in their ability to do so; here again I feel worried. What the chief of staff says is seriously at variance with the reports of my aides-de-camp. In fact almost no defences are ready. According to what I hear not all the troops have guns even. What would happen if we embarked on a decisive battle in such a state of affairs? Continue fighting and we will be plunging the entire nation into further devastation and distress. I cannot bear any longer to see my innocent subjects tormented under the cruelties of war. There are certainly conditions that can hardly be accepted: disarmament of the Imperial Forces by foreign hands for one. But we have to bear it now. I think of the spirit of those who have died for the nation's cause and I reflect on My incapacity to respond to their loyalty. My heart aches as I think of those who have faithfully fulfilled their duties and who now have to bear the disgrace. But this is the time when we must bear the unbearable to restore peace to the nation and to the world.[70]

The words 'bear the unbearable' had a special poignancy, since they had been used by Emperor Meiji in his direction to his people, when they were angered by the Triple Intervention in 1895.

Anami was left with the problem of convincing the army of the need to surrender, especially the ubiquitous young officers. After the emperor's decision, there was an agitated meeting at which there was a clear resolution to continue the fight. This was heightened by the allied response to the emperor's message, which was ambiguous about the fate of Hirohito, and when it became clear through diplomatic channels that the emperor would not be deposed, open rebellion was proposed. A group of junior officers continued to put pressure on their seniors, and on government officers, to fight on. But the emperor was adamant, and prepared to record a speech which would appeal to the people over the heads of the army, and which was to be broadcast on 15 August. When news of the existence of the recording became known, mutinous officers launched a search of the palace environs to find it. They failed to do so and in the turmoil, one of the ringleaders, Major Hatanaka, murdered the general commanding the Imperial Guards, entered

70 Ibid., pp. 404–5.

the palace and tried to persuade people to join his revolt. Others set out to kill the prime minister, but he was not in, and they burned his official and his private residences. The realisation that surrender was inevitable led to a spate of suicides. Amongst the 600 or so were Vice Admiral Ohnishi, founder of the *kamikaze* units, General Anami, and Hatanaka who shot himself in the palace precincts. At noon on 15 August as planned the emperor's speech was broadcast. In it he repeated Meiji's famous aphorism: 'We have resolved to pave the way for a grand peace for all the generations to come by enduring the unendurable and suffering what is insufferable.'[71]

The Pacific War was over, although the Russians continued to capture Japanese troops some of whom were to be imprisoned for many years. Nor is the war between Japan and Russia finished technically, because no peace treaty has been signed. The numbed and terrified Japanese now waited for their conquerors.

How had the nation got into such a position? By what means had the people been drilled into blind subservience? It was understood then, and it is still the case, that education, properly shaped, is the most powerful influence on social and political behaviour.

---

71 Storry, *History of Modern Japan*, p. 237.

CHAPTER TEN

Education:
From 'The Fundamental Character of Our Empire' to the Cornerstone of Modern Japan

Education:
From 'The Fundamental
Character of Our Empire'
to the Cornerstone of Modern Japan

Education has always been treated with great seriousness by the Japanese. They have always understood its significance as a means of ensuring power, or conversely its potential for undermining that power. It is especially the case that any account of the evolution of modern Japan must give prominence to education in that process, since education was central to the strategy of Meiji Japan in its paramount desire to modernise. We have seen the spirit of learning in the way in which the Charter Oath exhorted the search for 'knowledge' from all over the world. But in its establishment of formal educational structures, especially because it was to the west that they turned for models, the Meiji regime recognised at once the tensions which are generic in education, and set out to resolve them. The most important of these derives from the clarity of purpose which people in authority suppose is the basis of education. For them this purpose is functional, that is to train people for the demands of modern industrial work, whether in the practical skills of the nineteenth century, or the technological advances character-istic of the present day.

However, those who define education as a means of improving technical skills quickly realise that the knowledge and the questions the process brings cannot be so easily contained or controlled. The educational experience leads to inquiry not only about how practice at work can be improved, but whether the political environment is of the best, if cultural beliefs are desirable, and if the operation of the economy could be changed. It is the wish to limit such questions, asked by an increasingly educated and sophisticated population, which dominates policy in authoritarian regimes. In the pursuit of this policy, Japan is as near a perfect model as it is possible to find. And yet so much of the success of Japan, notably its place in the industrial and commercial world, is attributed to its educational system. How the Japanese authorities have handled the complexity and contradictions in education is a critical element in the recent evolution of Japanese society.

At the time of the Restoration many Japanese were receptive to the introduction of the goal of universal education because there was a tradition of learning, at least among some of the upper classes. This tradition, which owed a good deal to Chinese influence survived even the turbulence of the years before the establishment of the Tokugawa shogunate. But it was the long period of peace after 1600 which led to considerable expansion of scholarship and learning. There were a variety of schools associated with the education for the Confucian and Buddhist priesthood. By 1600 Christian missionaries had established a network of schools. Two of the most important institutions were the domainal schools and the *terakoya*. *Daimyo* typically established the former for the sons of their *samurai* followers. The Chinese classics were central to the curriculum of such schools, and some of the prominent leaders of the Restoration movement, such as Yamagata Aritomo and Mori Arinori were educated at such establishments.

The second important institutions were mainly but not exclusively commoner schools called *terakoya*. The numbers of people attending these was substantial in the nineteenth century, with attendance higher in the towns. Dore estimates that perhaps 40 per cent of boys and 10 per cent of girls attended 'for at least a part of their childhood'.[1] Not only is it of some interest that girls attended but also that women taught in them; in Edo 'one third were run by women'.[2] The notable point in respect of girls is that they were there, even though books for the girls taught mainly about child-rearing and other aspects of their roles, including entertainment skills if, for example, they were to become servants in upper-class households'.[3] At the *terakoya* children above all learned writing, but exposure to a considerable amount of literary material introduced them to a broad base of knowledge. And it was this, together with the education available in the many other institutions, which created a solid base upon which Restoration reformers could build.

A feature of education in Tokugawa Japan which has not received sufficient attention is the involvement of adults as learners. We shall go on to see that this was, and continues to be, a feature of

1 Dore, Ronald P., 'Terakoya' in *Kodansha Encyclopedia*.
2 Ibid.
3 Tsurumi, Patricia E., 'Women's Education' in *Kodansha Encyclopedia*.

provision. Such education took a number of forms, such as the simple notices, used as early as 1642 which gave out information, instruction and exhortation to good behaviour.[4] In 1717 commoners were allowed to attend lectures given for the samurai.[5] An important pioneering venture in adult education in Japan was established by Ishida Baigan, and came to be called by one of his disciples *sekimon shingaku*. Ishida was born in 1686, was self-educated, and when he was forty-five began to give public lectures in Kyoto and Osaka. He lectured to a variety of sections of society, and a novelty in his approach was that after the lectures, which could last for several hours, he would hold discussions with the audience. Furthermore, although his lectures were rooted in the great classical philosophies, he believed that great ideas should serve people, and that people should be encouraged to discover how this could be done. He even addressed, although obliquely, the divisions in Japanese society. This was taken up by his disciples who proposed something rather like a classless society. His disciples developed his ideas, and his notion of *shin* 'the substance of things', although taking several forms became an important part of educational philosophy in the early nineteenth century.[6]

The new Meiji government, in its enthusiasm for education was greatly benefited by the tradition which had been built up. Its first action was the establishment of a Ministry of Education in 1871, and its next was the issuing of an Education Act in 1872. In all of this was evidence of the views of progressive people such as Fuzukawa Yukichi. There could be seen, for example, novel views as to the importance of gender equality, even if a central reason was that girls would eventually be so influential in the bringing-up of children in the ways of the new Japan. One measurement of this policy would be the simple arithmetical one of equal numbers of boys and girls. The tone of the 1872 Act was clear. It was that education should attend to practical learning and training which would be useful. It reflected the debate in the west at the time about the importance of 'utility', and the pointlessness of classical learning, a view dismissed in the classical defence of liberalism in education, 'The Idea of a University'.[7] Like those who dismissed western classical learning in

4 Bellah, Robert, N., *Tokugawa Religion: the Values of Pre-Industrial Japan* (Glencoe, Illinois, 1957), p. 236.

5 Ibid.

6 Nakato Yoko, 'Ishida Baigan' in Thomas, J.E. and Elsey, B., *International Biography of Adult Education* (Nottingham, 1985).

7 Newman, J.H., published this magnificent defence of liberal education in 1852.

Europe, 'practical' people saw no point in the study of the great books of Chinese and Japanese tradition.

The educational model chosen was the American, with primary, middle and technical schools, a university system, and normal schools, that is teacher training colleges. The new structure was to be based upon the older institutions which have been described: for example the *terakoya* network became the backbone of the new primary system. The administrative framework however was taken from France, which meant strong central control. Even then opposition was mobilised by those who were aware of the corrupting power of a centralised education system. The main organisation of opposition was the Freedom and People's Rights Movement. There was a further Education Act in 1879 that gave some degree of decentralised control and which, incidentally, reduced the length of compulsory schooling. But the position was reversed again in an Act of 1880, by the re-establishment of strong central control.

In 1885, upon the creation of the cabinet system, the direction of education was to be dominated by the first Minister of Education, Mori Arinori.[8] Mori was a Satsuma *samurai*, born in 1847, and therefore brought up in the middle of the movement towards the Restoration. He was one of fourteen young men who were sent to Britain for education in 1865, and in 1867 he spent a year in the United States before returning to Japan. He was marked out for office in the new government because of this international experience, because he knew English, and of course because he was a Satsuma. He was duly given a post in the foreign department, and was made chairman of a committee to establish new government agencies. It was now that he first behaved in a way that summarised the Japanese confusion over awareness of the need for change, and an unwillingness to accept it. As events developed, he can be regarded as the personification of this conflict. One example was that he proposed the abolition of the wearing of swords. Because of the outrage which was provoked, including the inevitable threat to his life, he resigned, went home and worked as a teacher.

This did not last long, and at the age of twenty-three he became the first Japanese diplomat to serve in the United States. This did not last either, and he was recalled after a couple of years, because he disobeyed his government's instructions. His disobedience was difficult to ignore because of its blatancy. When the Japanese government tried

8 A biography of Mori can be found in Morikawa Terumichi 'Mori Arinori' in *Ten Great Educators of Modern Japan: A Japanese Perspective* compiled and edited by Duke, Benjamin C. (Tokyo, 1989).

to raise money in the United States to reduce the pay of ex-*samurai* by the giving of a one-off payment, Mori successfully opposed it.[9] This is another example of his ambivalence. As we have seen however he was involved in the *Meirokusha*, which attracted radical thinkers with progressive views. He deplored a number of traditional practices, such as concubinage, and in a most extravagant gesture, he advocated the replacement of Japanese by English as the national language.

This was the confusing figure who was the first Minister of Education. It was in the operation of the new system that his traditional background proved too strong for the western ideas which commonly are regarded as an influence on him. Many of these ideas would be regarded as aberrant by westerners, or consonant with Japanese tradition. He was, for instance, regarded by his enemies as a Christian sympathiser, but the influence upon him came from a weird American 'Order of the Brotherhood of New Life', one of whose beliefs was that American society and institutions were corrupt. He was drawn to those politicians who distrusted democracy, and favoured instead control by leaders. The total experience he drew from the west and its institutions was that they were defective. He wrote and talked about the need for 'morality' and 'ethical standards', but in doing so he was reiterating the classic Japanese philosophical recipe for a good society.

There was little ambivalence in his educational policy. After his appointment, he drew attention to the importance of the emperor in national life, and he made clear, that in respect of the emperor, people had duties but no rights. In a lecture in 1879 he advocated, and later introduced, physical education with military overtones into schools. He introduced a rigid hierarchy of schools, universities and colleges. The emphasis throughout was to be on control, this being relaxed somewhat in the higher strata. The system was designed to induce loyalty, stability, respect for the imperial system and acceptance of a rational and therefore unchanging form of government. This was summed up in his Normal School code of 1886:

> Pupils must be trained to cultivate the spirit of Obedience, Sympathy and Dignity. They must be filled with the spirit of loyalty and patriotism and made to realise the grandeur and obligations of loyalty and filial piety, and to be inspired with sentiments proper to our nationality.[10]

9 Ibid., p. 51.
10 Duke, Benjamin C., *Japan's Militant Teachers: A History of the Left-Wing Teachers' Movement* (Hawaii, 1973), p. 9, quoting Dairoku Kikuchi, *Japanese Education* (London, 1909).

There is no doubt that Mori made a seminal and lasting contribution to the establishment of a new education. The claim that he brought a lot of western thought and practice to bear is probably exaggerated. Enough people in Japan thought he did, since in 1889, when he was about to attend the proclamation of the new Constitution, he was stabbed and killed by a former *samurai*. His offence, allegedly, was that he moved a curtain with his cane at the Grand Imperial Shrine at Ise, thus insulting the emperor. He was forty-two and joined the list of those who, before and since, appeared as a threat to tradition and paid with their lives. As happened before and since, his murder was approved by some, and his murderer regarded with favour.

The early adventurous mood influenced the direction of educational policy in its planning and evolution. One example can be found in the place of women in education and is illustrated by the career of Tsuda Ume, who has been mentioned in the discussion on women. An early sign of novel thinking was the sending of five women, the youngest of whom was Tsuda aged six, with the Iwakura mission in 1872, to be educated in the United States. Apart from a belief that this was intrinsically a good idea, there was a very curious purpose behind it. At the time there was established the Hokkaido Development Agency which was to develop and colonise the island. The agency's assistant secretary was a man called Kuroda Kiyotaka, and it was his belief that the settlement needed well educated people. In addition, his own international experience had convinced him that these should include women, and it was on his initiative that the five were recruited.[11] Of the five, the two eldest returned to Japan after a year, one stayed for ten years, and two, including Tsuda stayed for eleven.

Having conceded an important principle of equality, the government had no idea what to do with the five. This proved especially problematic, because by the time the last two had returned, the agency which had suggested the idea had been abolished as a result of a scandal. The last three to return, in particular, were a kind of prototype of the Japanese woman who is educated abroad and feels, and is meant to feel, alienated on return. Two of the three who had spent the longest time away settled, predictably, into successful marriages. Tsuda went on to become one of the most important pioneers in Japanese educational history. For fifteen years, from

11 Yamazaki Takako, 'Tsuda Ume: 1864–1929' in Duke, *The Great Educators*, pp. 132ff. Also on Tsuda see Furuki Yoshiko, *The White Plum: A Biography of Ume Tsuda, Pioneer in the Higher Education of Japanese Women* (New York, 1991).

1885, she taught at the prestigious Peeresses' School, but always wanted to found her own establishment in which she could develop a curriculum based upon the experience she had undergone in the west. Even allowing for the transforming process at the time, this was a grand ambition. Higher education for women was slight, and such institutions as existed were in the hands of missionaries.

Tsuda returned to the United States in 1889 and studied at Bryn Mawr. On leaving in 1892 she taught both at the Peeresses' School and at the Higher Normal School for girls in Tokyo until 1900. In that year she finally set up 'Tsuda Ume's Girls' School of English', which was to become Tsuda Women's College, and now one of the most prestigious educational establishments in Japan. Nor was she unique in her determination to overcome such massive opposition to innovation. We shall see that co-education was abolished, but before that happened, a woman had qualified as a medical doctor. This remarkable person, Yoshioka Yayoi opened a medical school for women in the same year as Tsuda founded her college. In the next year, 1901, one of the most famous educational institutions in Japan was opened, Japan Women's University. Although its founder was a notable male pioneer, Naruse Jinzo,[12] it was another important step towards the creation of opportunities for women. The career of Tsuda illustrates very well the scale of the problems to be overcome in doing so.

Although the new educational system was halting and controversial, it progressed. In the 1870s some 40 per cent of boys and about 18 per cent of girls attended compulsory elementary education for three years. This period was raised to four years in 1900 and six years in 1907. Some of the impetus for these changes came from the successful wars against China and Russia which encouraged a belief in the contribution of education to the victories, and a determination to expand it, so that industrial skills could continue to be developed. By 1910, there was equality in attendance, since by that time about 98 per cent of the children of both sexes attended school. But then the purpose of education had been defined as the perpetuation of traditional values. The nature of education affected all children, but there were some aspects of it which were especially directed at girls.

The pattern which was to become increasingly authoritarian until the end of the Pacific War, was heralded with governmental statements such as the 'Outline of Learning' which was issued in

12 A biography of Naruse Jinzo: 1858–1919 by Nakajima Kuni is in Duke, *The Great Educators*.

1879, the author of which was Motoda Nagazane also called Eifu. He published another very traditional book in 1882 entitled 'Essentials for the Education of Youth', with imperial support, which was intended as a textbook for moral education. Motoda was an important force for traditional values and he was well placed to disseminate them since he was adviser, sometimes called tutor, to the emperor.[13] In these were set out all the tenets of classical religion, such as filial piety, and loyalty. At the same time in 1879, co-education after elementary level was banned. This was not to do with any moral problems which could have arisen as a consequence of the mixing of the sexes, but was designed to underline the fact that gender roles in Japanese society were different, and would continue to be so. This policy was consolidated with an official statement in 1899 that the purpose of female education was the production of 'good wives and wise mothers'. Those who reflect on inequality in Japanese society, not surprisingly, regard this phrase as one of the most pernicious in the chronicles of suppression in modern times. There was however one substantial outlet for female ambition, and this was in the Normal school or college system. Even so the numbers of institutions were much smaller for women than for men. In 1882 there were eleven as against seventy-six.

At the heart of educational policy was the Imperial Rescript on Education, proclaimed in 1890, and in place until the end of the Pacific War. The initiative for the rescript came from Prime Minister Yamagata Aritomo. He ordered the educational authorities to produce it, and several drafts were submitted, the first probably by Nakamura Masanao, but this was regarded as rather too theoretical, and an alternative was issued by an important bureaucrat called Inoue Kowashi, Mori's successor as minister of education. The final version seems to have been a result of discussion in which Motoda Nagazane had a lot of influence, discussion which very likely may have involved the emperor himself.[14] Because of its centrality, and because of the ascription to it of so much that followed, it deserves some attention. This is the text:

> Know Ye, Our Subjects:
> Our Imperial Ancestors have founded Our Empire on a basis broad and everlasting and have deeply and firmly implanted virtue; our

---

13 Tanaka Akira, 'Motoda Nagazane' in *Kodansha Encyclopedia*.
14 See 'Imperial Rescript on Education' in *Kodansha Encyclopedia* and Hackett, Roger F., *Yamagata Aritomo in the Rise of Modern Japan 1838–1922* (Harvard, 1971), pp. 107–57 and Smith, Robert J., *Japanese Society: Tradition, Self and the Social Order* (Cambridge, 1983), p. 29.

subjects ever united in loyalty and filial piety have from generation to generation illustrated the beauty thereof. This is the glory of the fundamental character of Our Empire, and herein also lies the source of Our education. Ye, Our subjects, be filial to your parents, affectionate to your brothers and sisters; as husbands and wives be harmonious, as friends true; bear yourselves in modesty and moderation; extend your benevolence to all; pursue learning and cultivate arts, and thereby develop intellectual faculties and perfect moral powers; furthermore advance public good and promote common interests; always respect the Constitution and observe the laws; should emergency arise, offer yourselves courageously to the State; and thus guard and maintain the prosperity of Our Imperial Throne coeval with heaven and earth. So shall ye not only be Our good and faithful subjects, but render illustrious the best traditions of your forefathers. The Way here set forth is indeed the teaching bequeathed by Our Imperial Ancestors, to be observed alike by Their Descendants and their subjects, infallible for all ages and true in all places. It is Our wish to lay it to heart in all reverence, in common with you, Our subjects, that we may all thus attain to the same virtue.

The objectives expressed in the text are firstly to develop personal virtue, in itself a harmless exhortation. The others are more studied, and came to be much more sinister. The most important are the encouragement of complete loyalty to the emperor, who is infallible and above the state, and the subordination of the individual to the state. The Rescript could be defended, but never is, as a necessary attempt to consolidate a feeling of being Japanese first, rather than owing loyalty to some faction or clan, which had until very recently been the actual or potential cause of social conflict. It could also be seen as a reaction to western superficial technical society devoid, as might be supposed, of the kinds of values which held Japanese society together in such a special way. In other words it would restore spirituality to an increasingly grasping society. The manifest object was to encourage that subordination to authority, at the head of which was the emperor, which would develop a pliant population which the Meiji oligarchy could govern as it wished. It was a utopian dream, because the assumption that societies do not wish to, and do not change, is contradicted by the lessons of social history.

The basic theme, that Japan is unique, was an ancient idea. It was the singularity of Japan which occupied the *kokugaku* school with its rejection of Chinese ideas, and the raising of awareness of things Japanese. And part of this was the 'fundamental character of our empire' and the place of the emperor in it. This came to be called *kokutai*, or national polity, the mystical force in the power of Japan.

One writer of the *kokugaku* school, writing towards the end of the eighteenth century, expressed this mysticism in the imperial lineage as follows:

> The goddess, having endowed her grandson Ninigi no Mikoto with the three sacred treasures, proclaimed him sovereign of Japan for ever and ever. His descendants shall continue to rule it as long as the heavens and earth endure. Being invested with this complete authority, all the gods under heaven and all mankind submitted to him, with the exception of a few wretches who were quickly subdued.
>
> To the end of time each Mikado is the goddess's son. His mind is in perfect harmony of thought and feeling with hers. He does not seek out new inventions, but rules in accordance with precedents which date from the age of the gods, and if he is ever in doubt, he has resort to divination, which reveals to him the mind of the great goddess. In this way the age of the gods and the present age are not two ages, but one, for not only the Mikado, but his Ministers and people also, act up to the tradition of the divine age.[15]

The Mito school, which originated in the early years of the Tokugawa shogunate, was also absorbed in the nature of *kokutai*, especially with the growth of western interest in Japan. They too stressed uniqueness, and the position of the emperor at the head of society. People had 'obligations' because of this. The influence of such thinking on the movement for Restoration was considerable, which is a paradox since the school originated in the Mito domain, whose *daimyo* was a Tokugawa. Fukuzawa Yukichi tried to explore the meaning of *kokutai*, and his emphasis was the separateness of the Japanese. It meant 'people of one race' and 'the creation among them of a sense of separateness from people of other countries';[16] but both Fukuzawa and Mori, ever contradictory, actively disapproved of moral education, or for that matter a social ethos which was confined to one religion, especially Confucianism.

The Rescript came as no surprise to the Japanese. It was deeply imbued with Confucian and Shinto teaching with which they were familiar. The establishment of Shintoism as the state religion was already in place. Other Rescripts, for example that of 1882 to the military, expressed the same sentiments, and the new Constitution of 1889 indicated clearly the formalising of the imperial position when it spoke of a 'lineal succession unbroken for ages eternal', and 'the right of sovereignty of the State we have inherited from our

15 Bellah, *Tokugawa Religion*, p. 101, quoting Satow, 'The Revival of Pure Shintau'. The writer was Norinaga Motoori (1730–1801).

16 Healey, Graham, 'Kokutai' in *Kodansha Encyclopedia*, p. 262.

ancestors'. Where the 1890 Rescript was to be most influential was as the cornerstone of the education system, which had provoked its creation. Through the Rescript it was intended that western 'learning' could somehow be confined to technical matters, and traditional culture could be maintained. Until 1945 it was repeated on important occasions in the schools, together with the displaying of the imperial portraits. Students, as might be expected, had to learn it by heart. It was welcomed as the basis of moral education – *shushin* – a vexed subject which will be discussed. In 1891, the year after its issue, the Ministry of Education issued an instruction to that effect.[17] This was periodically reinforced in teachers' manuals, some of which emphasised the familial relationship between emperor and people:

> The connection between the Imperial House and its subjects is thus: one forms the main house and the others form the branch house, so that from ancient times we have worshipped the founder of the Imperial House and the heavenly gods. Our relationship to this house is sincerely founded on repaying our debt of gratitude to our ancestors.[18]

From the time of the publication of the Rescript the Japanese educational system had two characteristics. The first was the continuing expansion of educational facilities. The Japanese never lost sight of the industrial and military advantages of education, and were obviously confident that they could contain the more insidious side-effects. Attendance rates at compulsory six-year school remained extremely high – 99 per cent in 1920, with an intended policy to raise the period to eight years. In 1917 the Extraordinary Council on Education was set up. Its several reports resulted in a recommendation to increase to eight-year attendance, and the expansion of the university system by designating previously sub-university institutions as universities. This did not diminish the eminence of the imperial universities, nor was it intended that it should. The system remained selective and elitist with each level intended to produce people for a suitable echelon of society. The second characteristic was that it was dominated by the ethical system enshrined in the Rescript, which made a critical contribution to the growing power of the military, and an increasing determination to stamp out dissent by appealing to that ethical system as the linchpin of society. Despite the potential and actual opposition to state and

17 Smith, *Japanese Society*, p. 29.
18 Ibid., p. 32, quoting Caiger.

government which has been discussed in earlier chapters, education was increasingly dominated by nationalism and militarism. This domination intensified with each 'crisis'; the agitation for reform in the Taisho era, events in Manchuria, the China 'Incident' and the Pacific War. All of these increased the pressure. Increasingly, overt militarism could be seen in the schools. Between 1922 and 1924 there was a reduction in the size of the armed forces, but the officers were not discharged. They were posted instead to schools, colleges and universities as instructors. In this way military training became an ordinary part of the curriculum. A further benefit was that a huge number of officers remained 'active' and experienced and this meant that the military could quickly and easily be expanded by the recruitment of other ranks.

Texts continually appeared for use in schools, like the Cardinal Principles of the National Entity of Japan (1937). This book 'presented the Japanese origin myths as historical facts and was extremely xenophobic in tone'.[19]

By judicious removal of disagreeable teachers, and the continuing presence of a massive repressive machine, the government actually succeeded in indoctrinating educational institutions. After 1945 teachers reflected on what they had done and why. Duke describes how a teacher had encouraged his pupils to volunteer for Manchuria. Seemingly, he did not understand until after the war how murderous that advice had been. Then he opined that 'Japanese education was fundamentally evil'. His conviction was so strong that he went on to become chairman of the left-wing Japan Teachers Union.[20] One of the great symbols of opposition to textbook control at the present time, and whose campaign will be discussed later is Ienaga Saburo. He reflected that:

> The schoolroom was a place of apostasy, where we had to stamp on our own principles. I am ashamed that I taught propaganda. I shall always be ashamed of it. Mind you, I wasn't a very active propagandist for the war, but I did nothing to stop it either.[21]

By the time of the defeat in 1945, not only was Japan physically ruined, but the social fabric had been destroyed. The task of rebuilding was prodigious, and MacArthur had very clear ideas about how and what should be done.

Amongst the many Japanese institutions targeted by MacArthur,

19 Healey, 'Kokutai' in *Kodansha Encyclopedia*, p. 263.
20 Duke, *Japan's Militant Teachers*, p. 193.
21 Buruma, Ian, *The Wages of Guilt* (London, 1994), p. 190.

education was primary. This was to be expected since not only was education one of the principal bulwarks of the imperial system, but it was commonly regarded as such by the allied forces. The revolution in the education system which followed was due both to his position as Supreme Commander for the Allied Powers (SCAP), and to his personality which allowed no brooking his wishes whether from other allies, who were supposed to be sharing authority, or the Japanese themselves. What happened to the educational system was paralleled by what happened in many parts of Japanese life. Prominent in his list of steps towards democracy in Japan was the liberalisation of the entire education system.

The segment of the General Headquarters of SCAP which was responsible for setting up a new education system was the Civil Information and Education Section (CIE). This was the body which advised MacArthur, and liaised with the Japanese Ministry of Education. The CIE had a radical brief, which was to eliminate from the educational system those elements which had contributed to the militarism and ultranationalism which, the occupation forces believed, had brought such calamity upon Japan. The Japanese officials, however much they displayed a cooperative aspect to the invaders, would have been remarkable indeed if they willingly torn apart a system which had been so carefully constructed over some eighty years. And so it transpired that on 18 August 1945, just ten days after the cessation of hostilities, and just over a week before MacArthur had even arrived in the country, the new education minister Maeda Tamon announced at a press conference that 'the foundation of Japanese education could not exist' without the 1890 Imperial Rescript on Education, and the 1945 Rescript on the surrender. He went on to say that 'we should defend the national polity (*kokutai*) and international peace'.[22] Perhaps the inclusion of the last two words was intended to impress the Occupation forces, who were initially unaware of the centrality of the notion of *kokutai* or its contribution to the 'spirit' they wished to destroy. The issue of the preservation of the Rescript continued to be advocated by Maeda, and by his successor Tanaka Kotaro, as late as an occasion in July 1946.[23]

But by this time CIE were beginning to understand. After some abortive discussion about the formulation of a new Rescript, it was dropped, and was effectively replaced by the Fundamental Law of

22 Nishi Toshio, *Unconditional Democracy: Education and Politics in Occupied Japan, 1945–1952* (Stanford, California, 1982), p. 147.
23 Ibid., p. 153.

Education, to which we will return. The issue of the Rescript is important, because it reveals how determined conservative Japanese were, how little the Americans knew of the cornerstones of Japanese culture (they regarded Maeda and Tanaka as liberals), and consequently the size of the task they had set themselves. Negotiations about a new education system limped on. The Americans made proposals which the Japanese did not like, but the latter soon realised the force of MacArthur. He issued an educational order in October 1945 which required a revision of the content of all educational instruction. Amongst other things the people would be informed about how their leaders, 'active collaborators', and those who 'passively acquiesced', had created such misery for Japan.[24] It was not long before SCAP tried to identify what he perceived to be guilty parties in all walks and life, and purging began.

In education, liberals, left-wingers and those, especially students, who had been long oppressed, took heart from the promise held out. There were demands for the dismissal of heads of educational institutions who acted as though nothing had been, or should be, changed. Education had been perhaps the main tool of the leaders of pre-war Japan, and as has been said, it was teachers who encouraged students to share in the deadly policy of imperial expansion. When a screening order and methods of implementing it were issued for discussion, the Ministry of Education again tried to engage in restraint, and again SCAP became more directive. As with purges in other areas of public life, a widespread organisation began work. Before it even began 115,778 members of the profession resigned. When the screening finished in April 1949, 942,459 people had been examined, and 3,151 were purged.[25] The process of dismissing unsatisfactory teachers was, however, only a part – and judging by the numbers only a small part – of American determination to transform the educational system. To this end a major problem had to be addressed; text-book control and related to it '*shushin*' (morals education) and Shinto. The issues surrounding these had dominated the operation of education ever since the Restoration. They are deeply historical, highly controversial, and chronic; chronic because despite SCAP's efforts to make changes, when the Occupation ended, the status quo was restored, and the controversy remains. Since these matters have affected the learning of every Japanese since the Restoration and continue to do so, it is worth dwelling upon them.

24 Ibid., p. 165.
25 Ibid., quoting from SCAP documentation.

Insistence upon *shushin* being compulsory in schools was part of the Meiji system. It had been introduced from the earliest days of the new education system, advocated by the ever-vigilant group who guarded against any assault on tradition. Its objectives were straightforward. It was to create those very pillars upon which the empire was to rest, loyalty, unquestioning obedience and filial piety. It came to be expressed in its ultimate form as we have seen, in the 1890 Rescript. In 1891 the ministry put out a directive which ordered that the Rescript was to be the foundation of moral education. As soon as SCAP's office had gained enough experience and knowledge, the link between the Rescript, *shushin*, and the imperial system became obvious, and morals teaching was banned. While the teaching of morals was central to educational strategy, it was only part of the bigger issue of governmental control and direction of education, the central feature of which was textbook control.

Although there had been textbook supervision soon after the establishment of the education system – from 1886 all textbooks had to be certified – it was in 1903 that the Ministry ordered that it would approve all textbooks, a process which, gradual at first, by 1943 included even normal schools. Apart from the wish for more control, the timing was due to a scandal, because of bribery. Until 1903, books were approved by the Ministry, and selections made by the prefectures. Sales were huge and companies bribed officials to select their texts. After an investigation, hundreds of officers and company employees were arrested and convicted. So big was the scale of the corruption, that the Minister of Education resigned.[26]

An example of the seriousness with which censorship was regarded by the government, and its determination that there should be orthodoxy, especially in history, can be found in a discussion about what appears to be at first sight an ancient and irrelevant episode. It concerns the attempt by Emperor Go-Daigo to reassert imperial power in the early fourteenth century. The outcome was the establishment of two courts, each recognising its own emperor, and which lasted from 1336 to 1392. Which court was legitimate became a serious intellectual debate, which was highlighted by the preamble to the Constitution of 1889 which referred to the throne as a 'lineal succession unbroken for ages eternal'. With the Emperor Meiji's restoration, and the increasing respect accorded the imperial institution, there was a manifest contradiction between the claim in the preamble and the existence of an imperial schism. The question for

26 See 'Textbook scandal of 1902–1903' (no author) in *Kodansha Encyclopedia.*

the Meiji government was how this schism should be handled in textbooks. Towards the latter part of the Meiji Era, the political row was enormous, with violent criticism in the press, demands for the government to resign, and the enforced resignation of one of the authors of the text, which offended because the schism was even mentioned.[27] There *could* only be one line of succession. In 1911 the government because of pressure from conservatives decreed that Go-Daigo's court was the correct linear descendant.[28]

Textbook supervision remained in position until 1945, when SCAP turned his attention to the books themselves. By September CIE began to look at books first in morals, then in history and geography. What appeared there caused considerable concern, and after systematic analysis a report and recommendations went to MacArthur, the essence of which was contained in the first sentence: 'All the textbooks in morals, Japanese history and geography – textbooks, it was emphasised, that had been compiled by the Ministry of Education – had proved, after the page-by-page survey "to be most pernicious".'[29]

The upshot was that in December 1945 MacArthur ordered suspension of courses in the three subjects, the destruction of appropriate texts, and the submission of proposals for future plans.[30] The difficulties generated by such orders were immense. They included, as examples, a desperate shortage of textbooks, and an almost total rewriting of history books, charged as they were with myth, ultranationalism and racism. Although drastic, SCAP believed it was necessary as part of the strategy to change Japan. MacArthur also turned his attention to Shinto, which was natural since it, the imperial institution and education were inextricably bound up. This had been institutionalised at the time of the Restoration, with the establishment of state shrines financed by the government and the emphasis on the emperor as chief priest. There was, for the purpose of unity, a reorganisation of Shinto's many branches. In December 1945 an order was issued forbidding government support of state Shinto, an order which was intended to disestablish it from being the state religion. There was also general discouragement to the practice of Shinto and its manifestations, including a ban on

27 Harootunian, Harry D., 'Introduction: A Sense of Ending and the Problem of Taiso' in Silberman, Bernard S. and Harootunian, Harry D. (eds), *Japan in Crisis: Essays on Taisho Democracy* (Princeton, 1974), p. 25.

28 Varley, H. Paul, 'Kemmu Shikimoku' in *Kodansha Encyclopedia*.

29 Nishi, *Unconditional Democracy*, p. 177.

30 For a detailed discussion, see ibid., pp. 180ff.

memorial services for the war dead.[31] Shinto was also to be discouraged in schools.

The imperial government had always had more difficulty in controlling higher education than schools. It exerted fairly rigid control over the teaching colleges, but the universities were regarded as a potential threat to social and political stability, mostly because staff were particularly aware of, and constantly exposed to, western ideas. In fact, for the most part, university staff were government supporters. This could be ensured by the judicious appointment of right-thinking people, and the removal of trouble-makers. Ito Hirobumi, the first prime minister was constantly worried about the knowledge brought in from the west which was 'useful' bringing in its train 'dangerous' ideas. He warned the emperor of such a threat in 1879, when he spoke of 'ethics declined', 'strange ideas', and 'inflammatory thoughts casually advocated'. This was the spirit behind the 1886 Ordinance of the new Tokyo Imperial University which cautioned that teaching and research were to be guided by 'the needs of the state'.[32]

This fear was, as we have seen, translated into a plethora of laws to maintain 'peace' through repression. But the occasional individual, sometimes in universities, resisted this repression throughout the imperial period. In 1906 a set of rules was issued which sought to curb academic freedom. This notice deplored the 'theories of violence and danger ... philosophies of oppression ... (and portrayal of) the barest conditions'. As Harootunian points out such fears could be, and probably were in the eyes of traditionalists, justified by the planned assassination of the emperor in 1910 which has been described. The trial and executions provoked some protest by academics and intellectuals, including the socialist poet Ishikawa Takuboku, who concluded 'Japan, it's hopeless'.[33] Two examples of brave behaviour on the part of university staff will illustrate the weight of the pressure for conformity. One, a professor Okamura was punished merely for criticising the family system and the civil code.[34] An especially important exhibition of governmental vigilance occurred in 1932, at the time when the military were in the ascendancy. Professor Takigawa again of Kyoto Imperial, lectured on crime, pointing out what was by then a commonplace in western criminology; that the causes of crime could be social, and not

31 Ibid., pp. 59–60.
32 Ibid., pp. 14–15.
33 Harootunian, *Japan in Crisis*, pp. 23–4.
34 Ibid.

entirely the fault of individual criminals. This was construed as a defence of imprisoned communists, the university president was ordered to investigate and Takigawa's books were banned. His department supported him, but the Ministry of Education replied that freedom of expression which threatened stability was against the Imperial University Ordinance. The minister suspended Takigawa, all the staff of his department resigned, as did hundreds of students, who demonstrated, and most courageously of all, the president of the university resigned.[35]

These few examples drawn from universities illustrate, again, the scale of the problem facing SCAP. They also provide some evidence for the fact that there were, in the imperial Japanese educational service, people who were sympathetic, at least to the ending of oppression. The university system, like so much, was soon examined and restricted by SCAP. An Education Mission to Japan arrived in Tokyo in March 1946 to carry on the work which SCAP had begun. The mission had twenty-five members and remained for about a month. Their brief was formidable. Amongst other things they had to construct an education system which would democratise Japan, recommend new syllabuses and teaching methods, reorganise the administration of education, and encourage links between students and community. They submitted a report at the end of their time to SCAP. It was a transforming report which caused major changes in the practice of education. It was also culturally very American and made some proposals which were bizarre. At the same time, MacArthur told the Japanese government to set up a parallel group to work with the mission.

The mission set out with two guiding beliefs, which it had imbibed from its contacts and briefings with those who had accumulated some experience in the short time since the end of the war. The first was that the educational system had been used for the transmission of specific political beliefs, and the second was that those beliefs had maintained a style of government which had brought disaster, not least upon the Japanese themselves. In their report therefore there is much talk of freedom, of democracy and of the importance of the individual. There is also, naturally, much expression of that faith, which is a hallmark of reformers of all kinds, in the inherent decency in people which can trigger change for the better. The very words used can be found in earlier statements, commonly in those of penal reformers. In the introduction to their report for example

35 Nishi, *Unconditional Democracy*, pp. 19–20.

they affirm that 'There is an unmeasured potential for freedom and for individual and social growth in every human being ... our greatest hope ... is with the children.'[36]

At the top of the educational hierarchy were the universities. But the Japanese university system, the mission members may well have been surprised to learn, was quite unlike the American. In Japan the system was very elitist with six imperial universities at the top, headed by Tokyo. It was also noted that the people who held power in Japan had generally been to one of these imperials. The solution was to establish many more universities, mainly by upgrading educational establishments, a process already begun by the Japanese. Reorganisation and upgrading led, by the middle of 1949 to the awarding of the university title to sixty-eight new universities. By 1952 there were 220 universities, as well as some 200 'junior' two-year colleges. In 1995 there were about 500 universities and 600 junior colleges.

This solution was drawn from American educational policy, which ostensibly eschews elitism, and believes in wide access to higher education. Not only is it an example of a kind of unmodified translation of alien practice, but it confused the Japanese, and annoyed those in authority who were products of the imperials. The sternest criticism which could be made of this initiative however, is that it failed to achieve its aims. As in the United States, the creation of new universities merely served to emphasise the eminence of the old. As in the case of 'Ivy League' institutions in that country, the Japanese ex-imperials continue to produce people who dominate public life at senior levels. In 1988 the backgrounds of top administrators in the Ministry of International Trade and Industry (MITI), one of the most powerful government departments, illustrates the fact. Of the twenty-one, all of whom were men incidentally, eighteen were graduates of Tokyo university, sixteen in law, one in economics and one in engineering. Of the other three, one was a law graduate from Kyoto university which is at least the next most prestigious. The last two were specialists from lesser-known universities, one an engineer and one a mining engineer.[37]

The creation of the junior colleges was somewhat dysfunctional as well, since they were soon regarded as the places to which women could go, a process which could settle their place in the hierarchy

---

36 *Report of the United States Education Mission to Japan.* Submitted to the Supreme Commander for the Allied Powers, Tokyo, 30 March 1946, p. 10.

37 Ministry of International Trade and Industry, *A Supplement to MITI Handbook: List of MITI officials* (Tokyo, 1988).

for the rest of their lives. The 1975 figures for enrolment illustrate this. In that year, of the enrolment in junior colleges, 86 per cent were women, whereas they accounted for only 21 per cent of those entering four-year universities.[38] We shall go on to see how, as recently as the 1980s, the Japanese government has tried to re-establish some elements of the old system. But as part of the determined movement to liberalism, there was established in 1946 the Japanese Association of University Professors to initiate some degree of independence from government.

The mission was, naturally, mostly concerned with schools, and one of its concerns was with the very centralised control exerted by Tokyo. To democratise education it would be essential to hand over the running of schools to local authorities, a suggestion which again was an American transplant. But this proposal which CIE tried to implement, ran into what should by now have been foreseen as insuperable obstacles. There was of course alarm in government circles, but more seriously the idea was so totally outside of Japanese experience, that it became clear that even if school boards could be established after elections had been held (another alien concept), they probably could not operate. When school boards were estab-lished, they faltered for a variety of reasons including domination by members of the left-wing teachers' union. As with so many of the educational changes introduced by SCAP, the Japanese waited patiently, and at the end of the Occupation exerted control of the local boards by abolishing elections. From 1956 members were appointed by mayors of towns, or governors of prefectures, and variously approved by prefectural boards of education, or by the minister of education.[39]

Naturally the mission was interested in the teachers, but the latter, like their officials, could not see how the role proposed for them was at all compatible with the reality. Their class sizes for example were *limited* to eighty pupils in the elementary school, and sixty in the secondary.[40] This problem was compounded by the proposal to lengthen the period of compulsory schooling. What did please teachers though was the encouragement by SCAP to form unions as part of the democratisation process. Eventually the Japan Teachers' Union, Nikkyoso[41] dominated the scene, was active in the cause of

38 Lebra, Joyce C., 'Women in Japan, History of' in *Kodansha Encyclopaedia.*

39 For a more detailed account, see Nishi, *Unconditional Democracy*, pp. 209ff and Duke, *Japan's Militant Teachers, passim.*

40 Nishi, *Unconditional Democracy*, p. 195.

41 For an account of this most important organisation in education, in the post-war period in particular, see Duke, *Japan's Militant Teachers.*

its members and the education system, but proved to be 'leftist', a reputation which still persists because it is well founded. Another welcome move was the mission's support for 'freedom in teaching at all levels': 'Central authority should not prescribe content, methods of instruction or textbooks, but should limit its activities in this area to the publication of outlines, suggestions and teaching aides.'[42] Perhaps the one change which was made as a result of the mission report which is still intact, was one of the most significant. This was the copying of the educational system of the United States. Known as the 6–3–3–4 system, it means six years in elementary school, three in the junior high, three in the senior high, and four at university. When Japanese go all the way through the system to the highest levels, this is their pathway.

A much underestimated part of the educational system in Japan is the education of adults, called by the Japanese social education.[43] The term first appeared in the popular press in the 1880s. As with schooling, the government was interested in the potential in social education for the integration of new knowledge, but as in the case of schooling found that that wish was in conflict with the pressure of tradition. By the end of the nineteenth century, in 1892, a text was published about social education by Yamana Jiro, and at the same time attempts were being made to establish a network of lectures and night schools. Some commitment by the government is indicated by the establishment in 1911 of the Popular Education Investigation Committee. Its brief was to popularise the education of adults by the preparation of teaching materials such as films, texts and exhibitions. Then in 1917 the Extraordinary Council on Education, sometimes called the Special Council for Education, and mentioned earlier in this chapter, was established. Because of its links with the cabinet it is not surprising that in its deliberations, a UNESCO report later claimed 'liberal scholars had been conspicuously excluded'. The emerging sympathetic response to democratic ideas, it appears, was due to 'a lack of patriotic education'.[44]

Something of this spirit is found in the Council's pronouncements on the education of adults, for example in its recommendation that there should be 'strict control over publications'. But many

42 *Education in Japan*, General Headquarters SCAP, Information and Education Section, Education Division (Tokyo, February 1946).

43 For a detailed account, see Thomas, J.E., *Learning Democracy in Japan: the Social Education of Japanese Adults* (London, 1985).

44 Japanese Commission for UNESCO (1960), pp. 65–6.

of its recommendations in its report of 1918, called 'On the Improvement of Popular Education' were wide-ranging and progressive. These included the need for expansion, the allocation of responsibility to a specific ministry official, the improvement of facilities, and most advanced of all, the training of adult educators.[45] The recommendations did have an effect with, for example, the appointment of a director of social education in each prefecture, and in 1924 the establishment of a social education section in the ministry.

Apart from official government provision of social education, there were attempts to arrange provision which was independent of the authoritarianism of Tokyo, and, as was happening in other countries, to give people control over the shape and content of their education. One notable example was what were called 'free' universities. The idea was so much in opposition to the subordination which was the keynote of educational purpose, so radical, and displays such strong evidence of communication with adult educators in the west, that it is worth setting out at length part of the prospectus of Ina Free University:

> Under the present educational system anyone who shows ability to learn is entitled to receive higher education by passing through the grammar school, middle school, high school, and finally to the University. This system was devised by Comenius in the seventeenth century, with the object of securing the complete development of the individual and of avoiding every possibility of stunting individual talent. Unfortunately, though the school system of every nation has taken this form originated by Comenius, the purpose underlying it has been completely overlooked, for though in theory the universities are open to all, many people in fact are debarred by a lack of funds from using the opportunity offered them, so that higher education in practice becomes the monopoly of the wealthy classes.
>
> Now, however, the people in every country are pressing for a return to the ideals of Comenius in order to secure a share in the wider life only to be obtained through higher studies, with the result that adult educational movements have sprung up in every country and have of late years made unparalleled strides. The demand has arisen for a university which can offer opportunities for study and development which are compatible with the conditions of labour with which

45 For an account of this report see: Ishido Yutaka, 'Social Education after World War II: Prospect and Retrospect' in *Education in Japan: Journal for Overseas*, Vol. V, 1970; Kaigo Tokiomi, *Japanese Education: Its Past and Present* (Series on Japanese life and culture), Vol. XI (Tokyo) 1965; Ministry of Education, *Japan's Modern Education System: A History of the First Hundred Years* (Tokyo, 1980), pp. 186–7.

workers are economically forced to comply, and it is to the Free University that all turn for a solution of the problem. It is recognised that education is not a matter of twenty or even thirty years' study, but of a lifetime. Where can life find a truer meaning than in the development of the individual by means of education over an unlimited period? We of the Free University feel that it is unnatural to offer anyone education covering only a limited period and under conditions completely divorced from everyday life and labour on the farm or in the factory, for we believe in the combination of labour and education as an essential principle. Marx has said that he could find no objection to child labour, provided education could be combined with work. We think that the Free University which offers opportunities for study to workers following their usual avocations is the ideal school, expressing the true meaning of education. The Free University is not University Extension, nor the continuation of any form of education, but the opportunity for the free and unbiased study of the whole sphere of thought. There may be differences of opinion among the professors, but as education, in the true sense of the word, cannot be propagandist, the education offered by the Free University cannot be called either capitalist or socialist. Our aim is to offer our students the necessary mental training to turn their own judgement to the solution of the problems which they are called upon to face. We strive our utmost to preserve complete liberty of thought and wish to proceed on these lines irrespective of external relationships ...[46]

Many such attempts were not very successful 'because of successive repression and theoretical immaturity.[47] As in Britain at the same time the growth of unions brought a realisation that education must be an integral part of the labour movement, and by 1926 the Japanese General Federation of Labour had an educational programme in what was described as a college, and which was directed by Suzuki Bunji. Suzuki was one of the outstanding leaders of the labour movement at the time. He was motivated by Christianity, and a genuine concern with social problems, which led to the foundation of the Yuaikai in 1912. In 1919 this organisation had over 30,000 members, and was a cross between a welfare society and a union. In 1919 this was reorganised as the Japanese General Federation of Labour which established the college. He became a member of the Diet, and a representative at the International

---

46 'Adult Education in Japan', Bulletin XXX, World Association for Adult Education (London, 1926), pp. 18–19.
47 Hirosawa Kaoru, 'Social Education before the war' in *Education in Japan: Journal for Overseas*, Vol. V, 1970, p. 5.

Labour Organisation.[48] Its syllabus was reminiscent of similar courses in Britain, with much emphasis on social science and law. Similar 'labour' schools were to be found in Osaka in 1922, and by 1926 there were over twenty in the country, the purpose of which was 'to produce a proletarian culture'.[49]

We have seen how the experimentation with democracy in the 1920s and 30s was curbed by increasing repression. The hope expressed in the policy statements of non-governmental enthusiasts, for change through adult education could not be tolerated. The Japanese government recognised that while school education was critical, adult education could be explosive. The idea of a politically sophisticated adult population has always filled authoritarian governments with fear. And so it was that, as with other expressions of democratic ambition, the government closed in, and 1923 saw an 'Imperial Rescript for the Enhancement of National Spirit' which advocated a return to traditional values. Other moves followed, including the Bureau of Thought Supervision in 1934, and after 1937 the National Spiritual Mobilisation Movement in which social education seemed to be central. These and the plethora of similar organisations were set up 'to supervise and to remodel learning and education based on ultra-nationalism'.[50] The result was that 'during the nationalist period the army group mobilised social education institutions for the war effort'.[51]

It was not long after the end of the war that a new Bureau of Social Education was created. It had a formidable task, and a fair assessment would be that it did a good deal considering the chaotic state of the country. Some of its more prominent activities were attempts to improve provision through the opening up of schools to adults, helping to prepare people for the general election of 1946, and the establishment of *kominkan* (citizen's public halls), which SCAP welcomed as 'an important step in the decentralisation of adult education'.[52] These halls were to become the backbone of an extensive education network. The bureau also established rehabilitative programmes for the millions of returning servicemen and the

48 Kurita Ken, 'Suzuki Bunji (1885–1946)' in *Kodansha Encyclopedia*.

49 'Adult Education in Japan', World Association for Adult Education, p. 20.

50 Usui Masahisa, 'The formation of the concept of social education after the Second World War in *Adult Education and Librarianship*, No. 2, 1978, Department of Social Education; Faculty of Education, University of Tokyo.

51 Anderson, R.S., *Japan: Three Epochs of Modern Education* (Washington, 1959), p. 287.

52 *Education in the new Japan*, Vol. I, Text; Vol. II, Appendix, GHQ, SCAP, CIE, Education division (Tokyo, 1948). Vol. 1, p. 335. For a detailed account of *kominkan* see Thomas, J.E., *Learning Democracy in Japan*.

Japanese settlers evicted from north Asia, 'stunned and scarred by a disastrous war'.[53]

The US mission considered the role of social education, and the comments made are sound if not radical. It should, notably, they insisted be independent and democratised. Officials of CIE worked with people in the new bureau, and in 1948 American adult education leaders went to Japan to act as consultants. Historians of social education of that time acknowledge the critical support given by the Americans,[54] especially since the latter encouraged the decentralisation of provision which was a concept variously not understood, or resisted by ministry officials. Despite this resistance, social education provision was enshrined in law, which was the foremost ambition of practitioners.

The question of the educational laws passed during the Occupation is still a subject of heated debate in Japan, with traditionalists claiming that they are suffused with alien ideas. This debate will be reviewed later. The liberal factions in Japan regard the laws as a bulwark against the constant threat, at least as they see it, of the restoration of extreme right-wing values. The central law is called the Fundamental Law of Education passed by the new Diet in March 1947. Its promulgation signalled the end, once and for all, of the 1890 Rescript. The preamble sets the tone, and marks a turning point not only for education, but for the assumptions which underline new Japanese society:

> Having established the Constitution of Japan, we have shown our resolution to contribute to the peace of the world and welfare of humanity by building a democratic and cultural state. The realisation of this ideal shall depend fundamentally on the power of education.
>
> We shall esteem individual dignity and endeavour to bring up the people who love truth and peace, while education which aims at the creation of culture general [*sic*] and rich in individuality shall be spread far and wide.

Perhaps the most important statement was that which proclaimed that 'education shall not be subject to improper control, but it shall be directly responsible to the whole people'.[55] It was this law which established the present impressive provision of social education in Japan. A law to protect it was passed in 1949, which those concerned

53 *Report of the US Education Mission to Japan*, p. 67.
54 For example, Usugawa, M., 'Kominkan – Citizens' Public Halls' in *Education in Japan: Journal for Overseas*, Vol. V, 1970, pp. 58–9.
55 The full text of the law can be found in Ministry of Education, Science and Culture, *Education in Japan: A Graphic Presentation* (Tokyo, 1982), p. 2.

with it guard very carefully against the incessant erosion of local control by Tokyo.

The considered verdict on SCAP's involvement in the re-creation of an education system in Japan must be that, considering the enormity of the situation, the achievements were remarkable. Nevertheless, there were some oddities, upon which some Japanese commentators focus, and even at the time must have seemed weird. The first of these concerned language. The Japanese written language comprises *kanji* which is based upon Chinese characters, and two sets of phonetic symbols called *hiragana* and *katakana*. The combination of these written forms makes written Japanese a complex language. An especially bizarre reform which the Americans advocated, was nothing less than changing the written language. The proposed reforms included the sole use of *katakana*, and the use of *romaji*, that is the Latin alphabet, in schools. It appears that the idea came from an American lieutenant in CIE, and was taken up by the mission. His reasoning was unearthed by Nishi in the course of research, and is in itself a model of cultural imperialism. The American points out that prohibition of *kanji* would bar 'access to pre-war propaganda', the use of *katakana* would make censorship easier, children could learn to read more quickly, and that there would be an 'increase (in) national business efficiency'.[56]

Despite warnings from Americans with rather more experience both of the Japanese and their language, the discussion continued. There seems to have been some awareness of the scale of the proposal, or perhaps false modesty, reflected in such statements as it being 'a matter which both modesty and ease would counsel us to avoid, if our sense of responsibility to the children of Japan permitted'.[57] After extraordinary discussion about the barriers to learning presented by *kanji*, the matter was dropped. But the officer whose idea it was, Robert King Hall, went on to advocate *romaji* in the schools. The Japanese Ministry, as always, handled the proposal with skill. It set up a committee which actually recommended teaching through *romaji*. This was tried, but proved not only undesirable, but impossible to implement. The final insult, which is the only word to describe it, was the denigration of calligraphy. This is a highly traditional art form, which seemed to some to be pointless. In one of the most philistine statements to emerge from

---

56 For a detailed account see Nishi, *Unconditional Democracy*, pp. 199ff.
57 *Report of the US Education Mission to Japan*, p. 33.

the debates about educational reconstruction it was said that 'writing should be emphasised as a tool, rather than an art'.[58]

Another example of cultural imperialism was SCAP's conviction about the potential of Christianity to effect change in Japan. There is no doubt that the occupying forces arrived with the certain knowledge that Shinto, the indigenous Japanese 'religion' had been an important bulwark of the imperial system. In the United States, then as always, the evangelical tradition was strong and MacArthur seems to have subscribed to it. One physical expression of it was the establishment of an International Christian University with money raised in the United States. Optimism, or self-deception, ran high even on the part of MacArthur, who noted:

> A quite spontaneous development which offers both encouragement and inspiration as a measure of the progress of this concept lies in the increasing number of Japanese people – already estimated at over two million – who, under the stimulus of religious tolerance and freedom, have moved to embrace the Christian faith as a means to fill the spiritual vacuum left in Japanese life by collapse of their past faith.[59]

These instances are very revealing about Occupation policy at its weakest. There is the imperialist culture which seems to be ineradicable, even if its existence is recognised and understood. In the case of the Americans though, this culture was seen as positively virtuous since they were convinced that there was so much in it to lead the Japanese into a new and better life. It is a conviction which depends for its strength on grievous ignorance about how society works. This is evident from the fact that key people had no understanding of a central relationship in society; that of people and language. It can be seen as well in the inability to understand the significance of cultural tenets and to dismiss these as pointless, as in the case of calligraphy. Classical imperialist behaviour appears too in the way in which some of the local people were able to identify the obsessions of the conquerors, and for a variety of reasons to exploit them. Indeed this could be described as a central strategy employed by the Japanese. This was made easier by the high profile given to those Japanese who *did* subscribe to the ideas and systems which the Americans were introducing, and by whom the latter, naturally enough, were much encouraged. A signal example is that of Hidaka Daishiro, a Ministry of Education official, who declared when the embryonic Christian university was developing that 'there is nothing

58 Nishi, *Unconditional Democracy*, p. 206.
59 Whan, V.E., *A Soldier Speaks: Public Papers and Speeches of General of the Army Douglas MacArthur* (New York, 1965), p. 183.

comparable to Christian culture that can better grow true roots and enable them to develop into never-fading blossoms of civilisation in our future peaceful Japan'. After a high level career in the ministry, he became a professor at the International Christian University.[60]

Despite such curiosities, the SCAP regime offered great promise of freedom in education in a context of a new democratic Japan. But it was short-lived. By the late 1950s communist success, notably in China, was quickly causing the United States to rearrange its priorities and policies. The right-wing totalitarianism which had been destroyed had been replaced by a bigger, more dangerous threat. The Americans in Japan came quickly to the view that by the establishment of democracy, they might be enabling the growth of communism. With regard to education, this fear can be illustrated by two events. The first of these was the behaviour of Walter Crosby Eells, a CIE adviser on higher education. Eells first attracted attention with his plans for university government. As we shall see from his later pronouncements, Eells was an official so authoritarian and right wing, that his views were not dissimilar to those of the pre-war imperial government. Thus he advocated the control of universities by prefectural government, and when that was violently opposed, suggested a board of trustees. Just how near this was to pre-war thinking can be seen from the fact that the ministry supported the idea, which alarmed the liberals in education even more. The subsequent protests, including street demonstrations, strikes and closing of nearly a hundred universities by their staffs, led to the abandonment of the plan.[61] Eells persisted, and his fervour was excited by the opposition he encountered. The essence of his position was that communism was evil, and people who subscribed to it should not be allowed to teach. This was made explicit in a notorious lecture tour he made in July 1949 when he said that communists 'cannot be allowed to be university professors in a democracy'.[62] Japanese educators, and students immediately saw that such a move would undermine the very basis of the freedom of thought and expression which was the supposed purpose of the Occupation. Eells' campaign was regarded with fear, anger, and when he was at his most absurd, such as his claim that 'even mathematics could not be true' in communist nations, with hilarity.[63]

60 Nishi, *Unconditional Democracy*, p. 175.
61 For details see the several references to Eells in Nishi, ibid., *passim*.
62 Duke, *Japan's Militant Teachers*, p. 89.
63 Nishi, *Unconditional Democracy*, p. 260.

The arrival of the second US Education Mission in August 1950, and its report after a stay of a month, was soon to show that Eells was not a member of some lunatic group, but that he represented widely-held views in the United States. Although the membership of the mission consisted of individuals who had served in the first mission, they now reflected a world where the communist danger was proved by the outbreak of the Korean War in 1950, and in which nearly 50,000 Americans were to die. Their report started off with classic statements, such as that about the education of adults which stressed that 'in all of its phases the adult education programme must continue to lay stress on democratic citizenship'. But this was now seemingly directed at specific targets: 'One of the greatest weapons against Communism in the Far East is an enlightened electorate in Japan'.[64] The inevitable outcome was a purge of left wing educators as a kind of antidote to the purge of right wingers which had been carried out such a short time before.[65] This created uproar amongst the liberal groups, and the process of volte-face in education so affected the general course of post-war development, that the political and social consequences will be dealt with in the next chapter.

64 *Report of the Second US Education Mission to Japan* (Washington, 1950).
65 See Nishi, *Unconditional Democracy*, pp. 261ff.

CHAPTER ELEVEN

Swords to Ploughshares:
Japan since 1945

Overleaf ▶
A present-day Japanese home

Swords to Ploughshares: Japan since 1945

The sixty-five-year-old MacArthur landed in Japan on 30 August 1945, and on 2 September the surrender documents were signed on board the USS *Missouri*. This happened peacefully even though *kamikaze* pilots who had been based at Atsugi dropped leaflets threatening to bomb the *Missouri*.[1] The task he faced was gigantic, since socially and economically Japan was in ruins. As we have seen from the example of education his determination was absolute, his nerve steady, and his courage beyond question. The Japanese were soon to learn that in contrast to their tradition of trying to achieve consensus before action, MacArthur was authoritarian, contemptuous of argument and certain in the face of attempts to manipulate him. He created his own authority, and used it, as one of his biographers describes:

> At his discretion he could suspend Hirohito's functions, dissolve the Diet, outlaw political parties, or disqualify any man from public office. When he decided to dismiss all legislators who had belonged to militaristic, right-wing societies, Prime Minister Kijuro Shidehara's entire cabinet threatened to quit in protest, letting the Prime Minister form a new government. The foreign minister brought MacArthur the news. The General said coldly; 'If the cabinet resigns en masse tomorrow it can only be interpreted by the Japanese people that it is unable to implement my directive. Thereafter Baron Shidehara may be acceptable to the Emperor for re-appointment as Prime Minister, but he will not be acceptable to me.' The ministers withdrew their resignations; MacArthur's order was obeyed.[2]

The physical disarmament took place with very little trouble, and

1 Mayer, S.L., *The Biography of General of the Army Douglas MacArthur* (Greenwich, Connecticut, 1984), p. 81.
2 Manchester, William, *American Caesar: Douglas MacArthur 1880–1964* (Boston, 1978), pp. 470–1.

the wish of the allies, subsequently enshrined in the new Constitution was that the Japanese would never again be armed. The matter
of punitive action against those who were perceived to be responsible for the war, and those who had committed atrocities in its
pursuit, was much more controversial. The Potsdam Declaration,
signed by Truman, Churchill and Chiang Kai-shek, had been
published on 26 July, and in it there was a resolution that: 'stern
justice shall be meted out to all war criminals, including those who
have visited cruelties upon our prisoners'.[3]

The trials took place in several countries during the period.
There were some 6,000 people tried in 'minor' trials, and of these,
920 were sentenced to death and executed. Even at the time there
was much unease expressed about the individuals chosen for
arraignment and those not chosen, as well as about the legality of
the trials themselves. Some of the allies were much obsessed with
putting Emperor Hirohito in the dock, arguing that as the head of
the nation, like Hitler he must have directed the course of events.
We now realise that the process of decision-making in Japan at the
time was a good deal more complicated than it appeared to the
west, where the perception of authority is strictly hierarchical.
MacArthur felt that the emperor *qua* emperor had to be protected,
and he identified with, and used, the imperial aura. The safety of
the emperor was assured after he met MacArthur on 27 September
at the American embassy. Hirohito described himself as 'the person
ultimately responsible for both political and military affairs in Japan
during the war'. He asked MacArthur to help his people, and put at
his disposal the wealth of the imperial family.[4] The emperor was not
put on trial, and the controversy ended only with Hirohito's death
in 1989.

Many of the obvious figures were tried in the Tokyo Trials which
lasted two and a half years from May 1946, and either executed or
imprisoned. The twenty-eight accused, except two who died, and
one found unfit to plead, were convicted. They included Tojo, who
made an unsuccessful suicide attempt, and was hanged, and at a
lower level Hashimoto, who has been mentioned several times in
this book, who was sentenced to life imprisonment, but was released
in 1955. Others, of whom former Prime Minister Konoe is the most
notable example, committed suicide before they could be tried.
This was a bizarre conclusion to his career because Konoe remained

3 The Potsdam Proclamation, p. 10 in *Education in the New Japan, Vol. 11*, pp.
6–8.
4 Murakami Hyoe, *Japan: The Years of Trial 1919–52* (Tokyo, 1983), p. 196.

a minister of state in the early years of the occupation, and was
'urged' by MacArthur 'to take the lead in constitutional reform'.[5]
Although because of a change of government in October 1945, he
was no longer a minister the emperor appointed him 'to study the
problems of constitutional reform', which he did with enthusiasm,
despite SCAP's specific instruction to the contrary. He even, in
November, presented an outline plan to the emperor.[6]

In later years there was to be much anger at the absence of certain
individuals from trial. A notable case is that of General Ishii Shiro.
He was an erudite, highly skilled and amoral doctor who was the
head of Japan's bacteriological and chemical warfare research. This
centred on 'Unit 731', south of Harbin in Manchuria. Ishii 'turned
Manchuria into one gigantic biological and chemical warfare factory'.[7] The experimentation involved was carried out on humans,
including Koreans, Mongolians, Russians and Americans. These
were guerrillas, prisoners of war, criminals or civilians picked at
random. Ishii's work was well known since he lectured and demonstrated his success, throughout Japan. He was also quickly discovered by the Americans, but he gained immunity for himself and
everyone in his organisation, in exchange for the results of his
experiments. The supposed value of these was expressed by an
American intelligence officer who, learning that bubonic plague
had been injected into American prisoners, observed that the
results 'naturally are of the highest intelligence value'.[8] Ever since,
the United States at the highest levels has maintained there was, and
is, no reliable information about the matter. It has been pointed out
that soon afterwards, in the Korean War (1950–53), the United
States was accused of using bacteriological warfare.[9]

The lives of some high-profile war criminals in the confusion of
the immediate post-war period were dramatic and bizarre. Tsuji,
who was singled out in the fighting in the Philippines for his
brutality was high on the list of those wanted. In Saigon at the end of
the war, he became a Buddhist monk, lived in China, and eventually
hid out in Japan. When the Occupation ended he re-emerged,
wrote a succession of extremely successful books based on his

5 Cornwall, Peter G., 'Japanese political reaction to constitutional revision
1945–46' in Beardsley, Richard, K. (ed.), *Studies in Japanese History and Politics* (Ann
Arbor, 1967), p. 39.

6 Ibid.

7 Harris, Sheldon H., *Factories of Death: Japanese Biological Warfare 1932–45 and the
American Cover-up* (London, 1995), p. 5.

8 Ibid., p. 189.

9 Ibid., pp. 230ff.

exploits and eventually became a member of the House of Representatives in 1952 and of the House of Councillors in 1959. He was never brought to trial.[10] To round off an odd life, he disappeared when he was travelling in Laos in 1961.

Not only have the war trials been debated because of the unfairness which caused Yamashita to die in 'legalised lynching',[11] and Ishii to go unpunished, but the opinion was expressed at the time that they should not have taken place at all. One of the judges in the Tokyo war trials was Indian Judge Radhabinod B. Pal. He recorded a vote of not guilty in *all* cases, and explained why:

> Victory, he concluded, did not confer the right to judge the defeated, and there were no legal grounds whatsoever for the trials. He did not deny the political errors committed by Japan's leaders nor their moral responsibility. But, he argued, it was dangerous for the judges to pronounce verdicts of guilty based on acceptance of fictitious stories, a hodge podge of the prosecutors' own preconceptions and testimony of extremely doubtful veracity. It was illogical that the Soviet government, which had clearly violated an international treaty, together with the representatives of the British and American governments, which had incited it to do so, should be in a position to judge Japan, which had violated no international treaty whatsoever. Moreover – he stressed – if anyone was going to be accused of the indiscriminate slaughter of civilians, then America too should be arraigned for the dropping of the atomic bomb. In short, he warned, to impose the death penalty on the defendants in what was supposed to be a court of justice would mean a step back of several centuries for human civilisation.[12]

There was also a view that the allied behaviour left a good deal to be desired. American soldiers sent Japanese skulls home as souvenirs, and an American congressman presented Roosevelt with a letter opener made from the bones of a dead Japanese.[13] The redoubtable Charles A. Lindbergh reported on such behaviour when he was at the front, together with the murder of prisoners, and the taking of parts of their bodies for souvenirs. 'The more I see of this war in the Pacific' he wrote, 'the less right I think we have to claim to be civilised.'[14]

There were Japanese too who felt that there should have been no

10 Murakami, *Japan: The Years of Trial*, pp. 232–3.
11 The term was used by two American judges in the Manila trials. Manchester, *American Caesar*, p. 487.
12 Murakami, *Japan: The Years of Trial*, p. 213.
13 Hoyt, Edwin P., *Japan's War: The Great Pacific Conflict* (London, 1986), p. 357.
14 Murakami, *Japan: The Years of Trial*, p. 137.

trials, or that nothing that the Japanese were 'alleged' to have done came near to the horrors of Hiroshima or Nagasaki. Buruma examines and discusses such attitudes, which range from denial that any atrocities, especially the Rape of Nanjing, took place, to a demand for acceptance of the view that in any war there is cruel behaviour. In any case, the argument runs, Japan should not be held solely responsible for the war since it was part of the 'flow of history'.[15] The matter of the atomic bombs represents the peak of debate about morality. A visit to the peace museums gives the impression, if not that the bombing was unprovoked, that it was excessive. Some of those of the Japanese political left consider it was done to frighten the USSR away from its supposed intention to invade Japan. On the right can be found theories that the bombing was a studied beginning of genocide, compounded by another writer who claimed that the racists behind it all were Jews.[16] Such views, although not widely subscribed to in such extreme, appear to be held to some degree, by many Japanese when they are sufficiently informed, amongst the younger generation especially, to consider such matters at all. What is sure is that the revisionists of the west have their counterparts in Japan. The latter call the events of the war, as recorded by the west, 'the Tokyo trial view of history'.

More important for the future of Japan was the action taken by SCAP to rebuild the country, and earlier chapters describing educational reform, and the role of women, illustrate how clearly the break with what he saw as the malign past was to be made. The period of the Occupation, from 1945 to 1952 was dominated by the SCAP administration which was regarded as 'a compound of apprehension, admiration, disappointment, and boredom'.[17] The supremist rule of MacArthur has, predictably, led to much discussion about his personality, and the apparent lack of resistance by the Japanese people to his dictates. Not unusually for a man of his rank, distinction, or experience, he was arrogant and certain he knew best. It was an attitude which the Japanese people knew and respected.[18] Another odder view is offered in the context of Japanese experience of natural disasters, and their resilience in dealing with them. Their passive response to MacArthur had the same source: 'General MacArthur's occupation of Japan could be regar-

---

15 Buruma, Ian, *The Wages of Guilt: Memories of War in Germany and Japan* (London 1994), p. 107.

16 Ibid., p. 98.

17 Storry, Richard, *A History of Modern Japan* (London, 1960), p. 243.

18 Ibid., p. 240.

ded as but another natural disaster: in time its effects too would pass.'[19]

Another Japanese view is that: 'their positive response can be seen as proof that an undercurrent of democratic values already existed deep within the "value concept" of the Japanese people. Such undercurrents were nurtured particularly during the period of "Taisho democracy".'[20]

It is though generally agreed that the behaviour of the emperor was a critical factor. Because of his leadership in his 'peace' broadcast, his visit to MacArthur when he personally accepted responsibility for the war, his dignity in the photograph taken on that occasion, and his January 1946 Rescript denying his divine status, he appears to have set an example of compliance which was emulated by the bulk of his people. He visited, informally, many parts of Japan, reaffirming the fact that he had come 'down from the clouds'.[21]

The 'purging' which was an early SCAP act, already mentioned in connection with education, also took place in every part of society. About 200,000 people were affected, and the Diet was reduced to forty-eight in the process.[22] This political clean-out was an important indication of intent by, and an asset to, SCAP in his major goal, which was the demolition and replacement of the Meiji Constitution. The principal Japanese suggested draft (many parties and groups submitted drafts and proposals), was too redolent of the old organ, and so MacArthur's people drafted their own, with a well placed threat that if it was rejected by the Japanese cabinet, the people would be made aware of it before the elections due in early 1946.[23] The result was a document 'completed in five days'[24] which shocked the Japanese because of its radical nature, but which was accepted for reasons ranging from approval, to the accumulated experience that resistance would be futile. A key pressure point was the hint given by the Americans that delay or disagreement would threaten the already shaky imperial position. Many countries, as was well known, were advocating the trial of Hirohito and abolition of the monarchy. The threat was real, and came from countries as diverse as Britain and the USSR.[25] Such pressure was effective, and

19 Ben-Dasan, Isaiah, *The Japanese and the Jews* (New York, 1972), p. 18.
20 Takeda Kiyoko, *The Dual-Image of the Japanese Emperor* (London, 1988), p. 151.
21 Storry, *History of Modern Japan*, p. 248.
22 Ibid., p. 250.
23 Ibid., p. 251.
24 Murakami, *Japan: The Years of Trial*, p. 202.
25 Cornwall, 'Japanese political reaction', p. 50.

SCAP's proposals with some amendments and after some debate in the Japanese Diet were accepted. In the final analysis Cornwall considers that: 'it is obvious from a study of the Diet record that the Constitution adopted in 1946 did not represent the views held by a majority of the members on many issues of fundamental importance'.[26]

The Japanese in power agree. There is still persisting, and serious controversy about the Constitution. After a preamble which contained statements that 'sovereign power resides with the people' and that 'government is a sacred trust of the people, the authority for which is derived from the people', Chapter One transformed the place of the emperor in society. The essential feature of his new role was that he now was a 'symbol of the state', 'deriving his position from the will of the people with whom resides sovereign power'. The new Constitution goes on to order that he cannot act without cabinet approval and 'the cabinet shall be responsible therefore'. Chapter Two resolved the second obsession of the Americans about the causes of the disaster which had befallen Japan, that of military power. Article Nine, which remains one of the most inflammatory issues in Japanese political life declared that 'the Japanese people forever renounce war as a sovereign right of the nation' and to that end 'land, sea, and air forces, as well as other war potential, will never be maintained'. The rest of the provisions of the Constitution were not so controversial except to the very powerful – the peerage for example was abolished – but they completely transformed the nature of the distribution of power, and social relationships. It contained all the safeguards enshrined in the western democratic tradition, including freedom of speech, freedom from torture, and freedom of workers to organise. The whole spirit of the safeguarding of civil rights was summed up in Article Thirteen in a direct quotation from the American Declaration of Independence. 'All of the people ... have a 'right to life, liberty, and the pursuit of happiness'. This remarkable document was promulgated on 3 November 1946, and made law on 3 May 1947.

Before the Constitution became law, SCAP had also caused significant political social and political changes to be made. Soon after the surrender, in October 1945, political prisoners were released, of whom the most significant in their determination to exercise political influence, were the communists. It was this determination which before very long caused MacArthur to restrain the

26 Ibid., p. 67.

burgeoning trade union movement, the existence of which, at least in theory, he saw as an integral part of the democratic process. His vision did not include strikes, and when these took place he ordered intervention by the Japanese police and the US army. In February 1947, a proposed general strike was ordered by SCAP to be cancelled. In that process the curious mutual respect of the communists and the Occupation forces, based upon a compound of ignorance and misunderstanding of motives, quickly evaporated. In 1948 MacArthur revised the Trade Union Law passed with his support in 1945, which then seriously restricted labour activism. Another bold intention had to be modified, in respect of the gigantic corporate structures already described, called *zaibatsu*. It was believed by some that the latter had been, in part, responsible for the war. Those who thought so may have been confused by the certain fact that the *zaibatsu*, like giant business in all countries at war, had provided the material with which to fight the war. In the event, SCAP's attempt to break these up failed, mainly because of the enormous complexity of the organisations. It is also the case that the destabilisation of such huge tracts of production seriously hindered the desperate need to move towards economic recovery. Policy was progressively modified, and although there was some modest success, the *zaibatsu*, except in name remained, and after the Occupation Japanese industry and commerce returned to pre war patterns, and the present giant organisations look suspiciously like old forms.

Much more successful were the policy of land reform, and the first election since the surrender. Land reform, uniquely, was supported by the Japanese themselves, and had been recognised as necessary even before the war.[27] A quarter of the population worked on the land, but one half of the land was cultivated by tenants.[28] We saw in earlier chapters the poverty of rural life, and the desperation of poor farmers, especially in bad seasons. The Japanese urban people after the surrender were even poorer than they had been in the years of deprivation towards the end of the war. Not only were the substructures of industry and transportation wrecked, but inflation was soaring. The latter providentially helped farmers because their debts disappeared, and they were able to profit from the desperation of the millions who travelled from urban areas to try to get food. It is generally agreed that during these years MacArthur personally ensured that as much food as he could get from

27 Murakami, *Japan: The Years of Trial*, pp. 202–3.
28 Ibid., p. 203.

Washington was distributed, and that this made a considerable difference. There were other actions such as the recommendation by one American officer, Brigadier Sams, made to Prime Minister Yoshida that school lunches should be provided. An assessment of the effect is given by Murakami: 'the marked improvement in the physique of young Japanese after the war was indubitably due to the milk in the school lunches first provided in January 1947 using aid materials supplied by the American Licensed Agencies for Relief in Asia'.[29]

The land reforms put 80 per cent of the land farmed by tenants into private ownership by tenants.[30] More than two million of these became landholders, when land bought by the government at very low rates were resold at equally low rates.[31] One lasting effect was that rural people became wealthy, and were no longer attracted by the radical causes espoused by their forebears. By careful cultivation of these newly prosperous citizens, conservative political parties have retained their loyalty ever since.

In April 1946 the first election in which all Japanese adults were allowed to vote took place. The leading party which emerged was the Liberal party, and the man it was assumed would lead the party was a pre-war politician and minister, Hatoyama Ichiro. At that moment however he was purged and so banned from political life, perhaps because he was judged to have cooperated with the imperial military, or perhaps as some believe, he had criticised America for using the atomic bomb, or his vocal anti-communism upset the USSR.[32] After some hesitation one of the few memorable, or indeed relatively long-serving Japanese prime ministers emerged; Yoshida Shigeru. His acceptability to the Americans sprang from the fact that he had been arrested during the later stages of the war for advocating peace. This was maintained in the initial period of his office by his ready contact with MacArthur, and his general acceptance of SCAP's reforms, even though he disapproved of most of them. As time went on, and, as we shall go on to see, the political climate changed, his suitability, the Americans considered, was made more evident by his staunchly anti-communist pose. In all Yoshida was prime minister five times, holding office for seven years between 1946 and 1954, interrupted only by a brief period in office of the socialists between April 1947 and October 1948. He was

29 Ibid., p. 208.
30 Ibid., p. 203.
31 Mayer, *Douglas MacArthur*, p. 100.
32 Murakami, *Japan: The Years of Trial*, p. 204.

prime minister at the time of the peace treaty of 1952, but in his last years: 'he seemed, in Japanese eyes, to be no more than a very obstinate, cantankerous, dictatorial old man'.[33]

Despite the momentous consequences of such reforms, as soon as early 1948 the objectives of SCAP began to change. The reasons lay outside Japan, in the emerging Cold War, the increasing certainty of communist victory in China, and the concomitant growth of fear of communism in the United States. It was a fear which reached a peak in the McCarthy witchhunts of the early 1950s, which were such a disgrace to America. The failure of the allies to agree on a peace treaty in 1947 to end the Occupation also contributed to changes in attitudes and policy. This failure meant that the considerable expense of the Occupation would have to continue to be borne by the allies, notably the Americans. Naturally, this was not a welcome prospect, and to avoid it Japan had to move towards self-sufficiency as soon as possible. This resulted in the lessening of principle in confronting problems, and more resort to exigency. As has been pointed out, one of the most notable examples is the easing of the dismantling of the *zaibatsu*.

To solve the economic problems MacArthur invited Joseph Dodge, President of the Detroit Bank, to Japan. He arrived in early 1949, and in a foretaste of western economic policies of the 1980s simplified the problem, and so simplified the answer. The Japanese economy relied heavily on outside support and that had to stop. The way it had to stop was by cutting expenditure, until the point where the books balanced. Public expenditure was cut, taxes increased, and public utilities made more, in the jargon of the 1990s, cost-effective. Despite Japanese governmental opposition, this was done, and it led *inter alia* to some incidents which created public animosity to communism and which happily subscribed to the American policy of recruiting Japan as an ally against the new 'threat'.

One of the principal victims of Dodge was also one of the biggest, Japanese National Railways. Japanese communists at the time had been criticised by both China and the USSR for not being sufficiently violent.[34] This, together with the Dodge reforms which had resulted in staff dismissals and similar savings, gave the communists the opportunity to be more belligerent. Its members did not collect fares, and in other ways broke the law. There was also a mysterious death, that of the president of JNR, who was found dead on the

33 Storry, *History of Modern Japan*, p. 255.
34 Murakami, *Japan: The Years of Trial*, p. 218.

tracks near Shimoyama station on 5 July 1949. The question which had to be answered was whether or not he had been murdered. The result was a dispute which remains, as to whether this was the case, or whether he had committed suicide because of the stress induced by the dismissal of many tens of thousands of staff. Over the years there have been many theories, about the event and about the identities of the murderers. The communists have always been favourites, but even the Americans have been accused of the crime. Then followed what became known as the Mitaka Incident. On 15 July 1949, a driverless train with the driving mechanism tied in the operating position, crashed in Mitaka station killing six people. Ten people were arrested, all of whom were union members and nine of whom were 'prominent members of the Japan Communist Party'.[35] Their arraignment was based on the evidence of a discharged railway employee called Takeuchi Keisuke. In the event, only he was found guilty and sentenced to death. Before the interminable process of appeal against the sentence could be resolved, he died in prison in 1967.

The derailing of a train in Matsukawa, in which the crew of three were killed was the most controversial of all three incidents. Twenty people, who were all, except one, communists, were charged, went through five trials, were acquitted in 1961 – a verdict upheld by the High Court in 1963 – and were awarded damages in 1970. Chalmers Johnson's view is that much confusion was introduced into the trials through the introduction of Anglo-American adversarial styles into the Japanese system. It was, he concludes, 'a muddle'.[36] It also appears to be another example of excessive American culture transfer. Although there was no firm evidence that the communist party had been involved in any of these incidents, this did not lessen public anger, or reduce the important contribution such incidents made to the support of American policy. One result, which was perhaps the most significant indicator of the change in that policy, was that in June 1950, SCAP purged communists from public office, such as Diet members and teachers, in the same way as imperial supporters had been dismissed such a short time before. This process of evening up the political balance allowed the return of those who had been purged as imperialists, a movement which had, in fact begun.

The change of direction was given further encouragement in

35 Johnson, Chalmers, 'Mitaka Incident' in *Kodansha Encyclopedia.*
36 'Matsukawa Incident' in ibid., p. 136. See also his article on the 'Shimoyama Incident'.

June 1950 when the Korean War broke out. MacArthur was given the post of commander of the United States, and later the United Nations, forces there. The effects on Japan of this very brutal conflict were deeply important, in two ways. The first was the boost it gave to Japanese economic recovery. At critical moments in the war, the United Nation forces would have been seriously disadvantaged, perhaps to the point of defeat, had it not been for the security and support Japan offered. The UN forces needed vast quantities of equipment and repair facilities, and the provision of these gave Japan an enormous fillip to its already recovering economy, for the three years the war lasted. The result was a reconstruction of the industrial infrastructure, increased wealth and experimentation with new products, notably motor vehicles.

The other effect of the Korean War was to undermine Article Nine of the brand new Constitution, that article which renounced war, and the means of making war. Very soon after the outbreak of the war, the numbers of American troops who were involved escalated sharply, and this left security in Japan somewhat vulnerable. This was why MacArthur ordered Prime Minister Yoshida to form a National Police Reserve, to consist of 75,000 people. However the instructions were worded, and whatever the description, this was recognised at once, as it subsequently proved to be, rearmament and in clear contradiction of Article Nine. The establishment of such a force was helped by the circumstance that those members of SCAP's staff who had disapproved of disarmament, had managed to protect important former officers of the imperial forces. No less a person than Major-General Willoughby had done so, and had even managed to employ some of them in US military intelligence.[37] Now that the nucleus of a new army was formed, there was recruited to it many former officers of the imperial forces. This nucleus became the Self Defence Forces, which was very soon, and remains substantial and well equipped. By 1973 it ranked seventh in the league of international military power, and has been supported by a colossal industrial base. And as with the Japanese army of the 1920s, forced to reduce its numbers, it is 'over-officered', which means that it can now, as it could then, expand rapidly. There was considerable opposition to this breach of the Constitution, and it has remained a major debate, linked with issues such as the presence of United States bases in Japan, and more recently participation in UN peace-keeping operations.

37 Livingston, J., Moore, J. and Oldfather, F. (eds), *Post-war Japan: 1945 to the Present* (New York, 1973), pp. 233ff.

The movement towards ending the Occupation entered an important stage when the powerful American Secretary of State Dulles visited Yoshida in June 1950. Defence was high on the agenda, and the solution offered by Yoshida was the siting of American bases in Japan, which was both to ease the path towards a settlement, and cause a furore in Japan. Dulles was, in fact, the architect of the peace treaty. He had a most difficult task since he wanted to counter the considerable demands from many countries for punitive action against the Japanese, and the real fears of many about their safety if, as they believed, chronic Japanese imperial ambition were resurrected. One of his tactics was to agree a network of security treaties with countries which felt vulnerable, such as Australia, New Zealand and the Philippines. Some countries, notably India and Burma refused to attend the conference, but made peace later. The communist countries, led by the USSR, were predictably demanding, especially over territorial claims – for example in respect of Sakhalin and the Kuriles, and over which 'China' should be invited. Neither was, although Japan settled with the nationalists on Taiwan in 1952. The holding of a conference at all in such an explosive atmosphere was a triumph, and the American influence on the terms of the treaty so pronounced, that for Dulles 'it was perhaps his single unqualified triumph in the field of diplomacy'.[38]

By the time the peace conference opened in San Francisco in early September 1951, an event had taken place which, while of worldwide interest, did not alter the course of the conference. For some time MacArthur's attitude to the conduct of the war in Korea had been an embarrassment to the Truman administration. The general had made clear that he wanted victory, that this meant attacking the bases in China from which Chinese troops were pouring into Korea, and that this theatre was more important than the agreed policy in the west; that troops should be built up in Europe. The broad position of the Truman administration was that the war should be contained with, if necessary, a withdrawal. The final act of disobedience arose from a directive in December 1950 by Truman, ordering that military commanders should: 'refrain from direct communication on military or foreign policy with newspapers, magazines, or other publicity media in the United States'.[39]

In March 1951 MacArthur disobeyed this order issuing a press

38 Storry, *History of Modern Japan*, p. 256.
39 Mayer, *Douglas MacArthur*, p. 140.

statement criticising the restrictions on him. He did so twice in that month, and in April he was quoted in the British press. On 9 April Truman issued an order removing MacArthur. For the Japanese as one Japanese historian wrote 'it was as if the sky had fallen'.[40] But the same commentator noted that when: 'in his report to Congress, after his return, he declared that 'the spiritual age of the Japanese people is twelve years old', the admiration the Japanese had felt for him was dispelled in a moment, and all he left behind was a bitter aftertaste'.[41]

He returned to the United States after fifty-two years in the army to a tumultuous welcome, and continuing controversy which focused upon Truman and his dismissal of a popular commander. He was succeeded as SCAP by General Matthew B. Ridgway who held the post during the short period until the Occupation ended.

Despite the outright opposition of some countries, the absence of others, and the caution of more moderate nations, the San Francisco Treaty, formally called the Treaty of Peace with Japan, was signed on 8 September 1951, and came into force on 28 April 1952. This was the day on which the Occupation officially ended. Under its terms Japan renounced its claims to Korea, Taiwan, southern Sakhalin and the Kuriles, and the former islands mandated by the League of Nations. Two positive aspects of the settlement were that Japan was freed of trade restrictions and could prepare for 'self defence'. Related to this volatile question was another agreement, made at the same time between Japan and the United States, that the latter could establish bases for external defence in Japan. The USSR refused to sign the treaty and so technically remains at war with Japan. At the present time there is little prospect of a change, since the perennial claims and counter-claims to ownership of the Kuriles are still a barrier. The then Soviet satellites Poland and Czechoslovakia also refused to sign, and walked out of the conference.

Although the Japanese, especially officially, had accepted the fact of the Occupation stoically, the historical feelings between them and the Americans, which ranged from ambivalence to hatred soon made themselves obvious. There were riots in Tokyo within weeks of independence being celebrated, without doubt fomented by the communists, who fanned the resentment that arose from the realisation of the fact that because of the agreement about Amer-

---

40 Kawahara Toshiaki, *Hirohito and his Times: A Japanese Perspective* (Tokyo, 1990), p. 175.
41 Ibid., p. 177.

ican bases, Japan would still appear to be occupied. There was especial resentment about the amount of good land, in a land-hungry country, which would have to be designated for these bases. The media mounted an openly anti-American campaign on this account, but also because of alleged misbehaviour and inevitably, the claimed moral corruption which was undermining Japanese society. All of this was sharpened in early 1954, when an American hydrogen bomb was exploded near the small island of Bikini in the Pacific. A Japanese boat was fishing in the area, and on return home, much of the catch was sold before it was realised that it was polluted, and the crew were suffering from radiation sickness. The fear and fury at the American action was universal, and was exacerbated by what Storry judges to have been the insensate handling of the matter by the Americans, locally and in Washington.[42]

The spirit of anti-Americanism continued, and as we shall go on to see, apart from formal top level government contacts, is alive in the 1990s. An especially turbulent year was 1960, because it saw discussion about a new Security Pact, the original having been agreed at the same time as the Peace Treaty. There were many unsatisfactory clauses in the Pact as far as the Japanese were concerned, but new proposals did nothing to remove the two considerable and justified Japanese objections. These were that the Americans were to continue in Japan for a minimum of ten years, and that they could use Japan as a base for wars in Asia, or indeed elsewhere. The controversy led to violence in the Diet in May, with a diminished membership ratifying the Pact, and considerable street violence. Involved in this were right-wing extremists, one of whom murdered the secretary-general of the Socialist Party at a public meeting. Perhaps the scale of the disturbances can be gauged from the fact that an arranged visit by the United States President Eisenhower was postponed. Ever since, official visits by leaders of 'controversial' countries have proved to be something of a nightmare for the Japanese police.

A review of the historical panorama since the Occupation seems to indicate that the fears, by the several vested interests, of a an extreme government of either left or right were never real, nor are they today. This can be exemplified in the first instance by the transmogrification of the classical, primary person in the Japanese hierarchy, the emperor. Hirohito showed himself to be realistic and

42 See Storry, *History of Modern Japan*, pp. 260ff for more detail.

adaptable, at least ostensibly, when caused to give a national lead in defeat. As far as can be judged, he worked to conform to the limitations of his position as set out in the new Constitution, and in many ways symbolised that flexibility which seemed to be so remarkable in Japanese behaviour in 1945. There were those in the west who never gave up their conviction about his responsibility for the Pacific War, especially the vile treatment of prisoners of war, and throughout Europe there was widespread public protest at his visit as late as in 1971. Personal support was given to this conviction by Lord Louis Mountbatten, who had received the Japanese surrender in Singapore. He ostentatiously absented himself from the elites who met Hirohito when he visited Britain in 1971. With Hirohihoto's death the question was finally buried, but not by all the living. In Japan in the 1990s his successor Akihito is not tainted, since he was only eleven years old in 1945. Further, he was brought up in an educational system which was shared by wealthy fellow countrymen. His marriage to a commoner was a break with a tradition of great importance, and was a further example, to the Japanese, of the need to change. There is little doubt that the emperor and the institution are still highly regarded by the Japanese. The explanation for this continued respect, despite the transition from god to man, is summed up by Suzuki Yoshio:

> The notion of the Japanese people towards the Imperial House transcends all laws, and their respect has nothing to do with power, but is purely moralistic and emotional. Their respect and affection towards the Emperor is not affected in the least whether he has administrative power or not.[43]

If there is a vestigial remnant of the old system, it may lie in the behaviour of the formidable Imperial Household Agency. Japanese regard the Agency as responsible for trying to seclude the emperor and his family, notably by blocking information. The mysterious illness of the present Empress Michiko in 1994, or the rumours in 1995 that the wife of the crown prince was being repressed by the guardians of imperial behaviour, are commonly ascribed to the Agency. In fact, this perception of the Japanese people has in itself a familiar echo: the imperial family is not to blame. The fault lies in the people who surround them, variously politicians, generals and bureaucrats. It is a cry which links the 'young officers' of the 1930s to young Japanese today.

The party political system in post-war Japan settled down remark-

43 Quoted by Cornwall, 'Japanese political reaction', p. 55.

ably quickly. The most important year was 1955, when a pattern in Japanese politics was established which was to last for nearly forty years. The main issues in the immediate post-war years included relationships with the United States, especially over the security arrangements, and the best way forward economically. Left-wing parties attacked those on the right who aligned firmly with the west, especially since this meant a restoration, as they feared, of Japanese military power. Extreme right-wing groups wanted to revise the Constitution which they felt had been imposed upon them, to the disadvantage of Japan. The political pattern began to crystallise in October 1955, when the left and right wings of the Japan Socialist Party reunited after a four-year split. In November the two right-wing parties also joined together to form the Liberal Democratic Party (LDP). This initiated what was to become a two-party system, called by the Japanese 'the 1955 set-up', and which was to result in government by the LDP for thirty-eight years.

There is a view[44] that the 'set-up' was not really consolidated until 1960, since it was in that year that the clear distinctions between the parties were made, and their attitudes fossilised. Before 1960 the broad right wing was committed to revising the Constitution, while the broad left sought the creation of a socialist society and economy. After 1960 both looked for causes which would appeal to a society which wanted to continue the economic recovery, already under way, and for which people had longed. The LDP was more convincing and successful, because it promised stability and the maintenance of traditional social values. There remained, as part of this, a stated intention to revise the Constitution, but the emphasis was on economic growth. This was spectacular, and since it was presided over by the LDP, the period, until well into the 1990s has been described as the 'golden age of postwar conservative politics'.[45] The socialists on the other hand advocated policies which appeared increasingly irrelevant and unacceptable. Some of these were the refusal to accept the fact of the existence of the Self Defence Forces, rejection of the security pact, and the denial of official recognition to South Korea.

The success of the LDP had in it, from the beginning the potential for electoral reverse. There was first of all the electoral system itself for the lower chamber, the House of Representatives.

44 Kitaoka Shin'ichi, 'Reinjecting competition into politics' in *Japan Echo*, Vol. XX, No. 4, Winter 1993, pp. 33–4.
45 Kishimoto Koichi, *Politics in Modern Japan: Development and Organisation* (Tokyo, 1988), p. 25.

Under this system nearly all the electoral districts return from three to five members, and it follows that to ensure re-election, the ruling party must nominate several candidates who must compete against each other. This eventually involved getting, and spending, considerable sums of money, and gaining a place in the plethora of groupings in the party machines. The way that money was acquired is familiar in politics everywhere. The politician would have to funnel requests from pressure groups to the bureaucracy, try to ensure that the outcome was feliticous, and would receive political funds in return. Then there was the existence of 'factions'. We have seen that the structuring of groups in Japanese society to which duty is owed, and from which protection is secured, is deeply rooted in Japanese social organisation, and that as modern forms of government were evolved, the system was adopted together with that of its relation, the *genro* phenomenon.

The persistence of such customs became clear very soon after the Occupation began. After the first post-war election it seemed obvious that Hatoyama Ichiro, as leader of the Liberal Party, would become prime minister. He was, however purged, which created the vacancy which led to the long rule of Yoshida. Although the latter became prime minister, Hatoyama 'was to assist him behind the scenes with party affairs . . . until such time as (Hatoyama) should be restored to political life'.[46] The functioning of latter-day *genro* is visible in the operation of the factions which have replaced the old clans. A notable case was that of Tanaka Kakuei, who, although deeply involved in the Lockheed bribery scandal, and consequently forced to relinquish his premiership, which he held from 1972 to 1974, still controlled his faction. His power was such that from 1978 to 1984, he decided who the leaders of his party, and the leaders of the nation would be. He was a 'shadow *shogun*'.[47] A new member of the Diet has to join a faction. Having done so, the member will then vote at the faction's direction, for party president and prime minister. It is naturally vital for a faction to recruit as many people as possible, and the reward for the member is an allocation of faction funds. The member will, in turn, choose a faction which is wealthy. This pattern in Japanese public and political life has been a constant theme throughout this book.

The question which occupies some commentators is whether a form of government presently being described, can be classed as

46 Murakami, *Japan: The Years of Trial*, p. 205.
47 Kishimoto, *Politics in Modern Japan*, p. 101.

'democratic'. After all, it does rather look like one party rule, and even if the opposition could persuade the electorate to give them power, it would appear that for some thirty-eight years there has been very little evidence that they would want to exercise it. In any case, over the years the emergence of a serious challenge has been much reduced by fractionising of the opposition. As early as 1960 some Japan Socialist Party members formed the Democratic Socialist Party, and in 1964 the 'Clean Government Party' was established, associated with a Buddhist sect, and usually provides the third largest membership in the Diet.[48] This breaking-up of parties has continued. The claim that Japan is not a democracy is one of many criticisms of modern Japan, made mostly by American writers, and tends to the practice collectively described by the Japanese as 'Japan bashing'. A typical example is that of Harvey who points out 'the enormous influence of money in Japanese politics and the favours-and-patronage system', the advantages a Diet member can secure for his constituency, and the giving by businessmen to politicians of 'insider' share tips.[49] If these were ever distinctions between democracy in Japan and the western countries, the most cursory reading of newspapers in the 1990s must convince even rabid 'Japan bashers' that they have disappeared.

Perhaps the firmest evidence that a democratic electoral system, however moribund it may be claimed to be, is capable of causing change, can be seen in political events in Japan in 1993. Towards the middle of the year, the LDP was beginning to lose all credibility amongst the Japanese electorate. There was an increasing recognition that there could be no attack on the malaise in Japanese government without fundamental reform. This centred upon the replacement of the multi-seat districts which have been described, and their replacement by single-seat constituencies, and proportional representation. Related to this was the question and scandal of political donations, and bribery and corruption which were not new: Japanese public life ever since Meiji has been punctuated with massive corruption. But the 1970s saw a series of especially famous scandals, of which the most spectacular was the Lockheed bribery case, which caused the downfall, but not the political demise, of Tanaka Kakuei, found guilty in 1983 of accepting bribes. Nor was this the end. In succeeding years the evidence of corruption was a feature of newspaper reporting. The Japanese were by now very

48 For details of post-war party groupings see ibid., Chapter 6.
49 Harvey, Robert, *The Undefeated: the Rise, Fall and Rise of Greater Japan* (London, 1994), pp. 382–3.

disillusioned with the erosion of standards in public life, and the seeming impossibility of removing the perpetrators. They were equally despairing about the supreme power of the bureaucrats. This was especially the case amongst the best educated people. It seemed that every political initiative was blocked, in time-honoured tradition, by people who were concealed both from public view and public accountability.

Apart from such general disillusionment, there was one specific internal change of attitude, and a shift in world affairs which were important contributors to the public mood. The first of these concerned farmers. Ever since the boost to their fortunes as a result of the chaos and shortages after 1945, they had been protected by the government. Reciprocal support by the farmers had been an important pillar in the LDP's edifice. But pressure was on, especially by the United States, to change what were regarded as disadvantageous trading terms, especially the importation of rice. Farmers began, rightly, to suspect that their shelter was about to disappear, and the loss of their support would prove disastrous.

Globally, the Cold War was over. The division between communists and capitalists since 1945, had been the framework upon which Japanese politics had hung, and now it had disappeared. There had to be new renegotiated policies towards Russia, North Korea and China, as well as the central ally, the United States. A critical element in this renegotiation would be the ageing matter of defence, which had been cocooned, and subject to ritual posing from time to time. This was just one reform, and a major one, which it became clear the LDP could not begin to discuss. Added to all the other needs, the view of many seemed to be that it was necessary for the party political structure to be the first target of reform, before anything else could be done.

The first sign that people were determined this should happen was on 18 July 1993 when the most exciting event in Japanese politics for forty years took place: the LDP lost its overall majority in the elections. Despite this they tried to block a coalition of anti-LDP members who wanted to form a government. They must have realised this was pointless, since large numbers of their members had already defected to form new groups. On 21 June a group of ten formed the new 'Harbinger' party, and two days later a further forty-four members set up the Japan Renewal party. Yet the hard-line LDP members persisted in their obstruction, for example by challenging the appointment of Doi Takako, former leader of the Japan Socialist Party, as Speaker of the lower house. Ultimately, on 5 August, prime minister and the LDP government resigned. They were replaced by a coalition of seven established and new parties, to which was added a small party which only had a few seats in the upper house. They were led by Hosokawa Morihiro, who had broken away from the LDP before it seemed wise to do so, and had led his New Japan Party to win thirty-six seats in the election of 18 July.

Hosokawa at fifty-five became the second youngest prime minister in the history of Japan. Even in Japan, where age is respected, the prospect of a younger man in office proved as welcome as it usually is in other countries weary of gerontocracy. The newspapers pronounced him as personable, courageous and determined. He had established a sound reputation as a prefectural governor. He was, for those who believed in the certain transmission of hereditary excellence, the grandson of Konoe Fumimaro, who had been prime minister at the end of the 1930s and early 1940s. In short, hopes and expectations were high. At a ceremony for the war dead in the very month in which he became prime minister, he expressed sympathy for Asian victims of the Pacific War. While the more traditional reaction to such explosive remarks as his observation that 'Japan was the aggressor in the Pacific War', was that he had 'shaken the trust of the people in their own country',[50] others were encouraged. One commentator saw in the new prime minister's remarks a glimmer of hope, a rare feeling at the time, in the fact that he had written the speech himself, thus indicating that the bureaucratic monotone would not be heard on every occasion.[51] Another wrote a short time after Hosokawa's appointment: 'There is no longer a way to stem this tide and preserve or revive the old LDP. The times demand a complete dissolution and reconstitution of the political parties, ruling and opposition alike; there can be no return to the past.'[52]

Others, manifestly those with a lot to lose, were more apprehensive. A former ambassador to the United Nations, later senior adviser to the largest consumer electronics company in Japan, after Hosokawa resigned, wrote:

> The collapse of the triangle of politics, business and the bureaucracy is greater than foreign observers might think ... Now that one dominant party has ceased to exist, business no longer knows where

50 Watanabe Michio, 'My differences with Ozawa and his coalition' in *Japan Echo*, Vol. XXI, No. 1, Spring 1994, p. 20.

51 Yamaguchi Jiro, 'Three betrayals' in 'Seven views of the Hosokawa administration': *Japan Echo*, Vol. XXI, No. 3, Autumn 1994, p. 8.

52 Iwami Takao, 'Japanese politics in an age of realignment' in *Japan Echo*, Vol. XXI, No. 1, Spring 1994, p. 11.

to go for favours and bureaucrats feel there is no power centre ...
The whole cement of Japanese society has collapsed.[53]

This remarkable analysis, which the independent observer might claim as evidence for terminal torpor in Japan, has in fact been proved wrong. For Hosokawa's period as prime minister lasted only eight months. The period was marked by only one attempt at reform, the effects of which are uncertain in 1995. In November 1993 four reform bills passed through the House of Representatives. These were tough measures, in tune with Hosokawa's commitment to basic reform. Yet these measures were to be modified because of pressure. The ramifications of Japanese politics are such that in the lower house the original measures for reform were supported, while in the upper house the Social Democratic Party's left wing, a party which was part of the coalition, voted against, as a protest about what they saw as sympathy in some groups in the coalition, for involvement by the Self Defence Forces in UN operations. The compromise which resulted damaged both the coalition and Hosokawa's reputation which depended on much firmer action against the in-built potential for corruption.

Finally, in early March 1994 the coalition government agreed on four central laws which embraced the following changes. Each district would have one representative, with a parallel system of proportional representation. Politicians and factions, who could previously have as many 'support groups' as they wished, would now be limited to one, and a ceiling would be placed on corporate contributions which had to be declared, and would remain for five years, when all contributions would be forbidden. There would be stricter enforcement of the electoral procedure laws.

There has been extensive speculation on Hosokawa's failure, and on its effects. His sternest critics probably include those who hoped for most, but the disappointment was widespread. Amongst what are described as his failures, one that is very common was his inability to control the bureaucracy, one of the crucial elements in the campaign. The same professor of politics, Yamaguchi Jiro, who reflected the hope which was gleaned from Hosokawa's comments on the war, was to write of the re-emergence, if they had ever retreated, of the bureaucracy. In respect of key policy statements about finance and adjusting the trade balance with the United States, Yamaguchi detects the priority of bureaucratic caution over political initiative.[54]

53 Quoted by Dawkins, William, 'Tokyo adjusts to tempestuous times', *Financial Times,* 27 June 1994, p. 23.
54 Yamaguchi Jiro, 'Three Betrayals', pp. 8–9.

A prominent journalist agrees: 'the bureaucrats' he wrote 'watched Hosokawa with the coolest eye'. He quotes a senior official as saying 'We never had any illusions about Mr Hosokawa'.[55] In the case of finance his proposals were met with considerable popular opposition, partly because of his remarkable mismanagement of the announcement of tax changes. He called a press conference in the early hours. Japan woke to hear the news, and this excited such opposition that he had to withdraw his plan the same day.[56]

One of the other criticisms, or more harshly betrayals, levelled by Yamaguchi is that Hosokawa 'became a pawn of the political tactics of Ozawa and Ichikawa'. These tactics, it appeared, were 'aimed to strengthen the base for regrouping into a new party ... Hosokawa destroyed the coalition governments' distinctive flavour'.[57] Ichikawa Yuichi was the general secretary of the Clean Government Party, one of the members of the coalition, but Ozawa Ichiro was altogether a much more complicated figure. It was Ozawa who planned and carried out the LDP split, but following the well established *genro* tradition, he did not seek to take public office as prime minister. Instead he used the situation to further his own aims in more oblique fashion. Naturally enough, the Japanese recognised this, and parodied the fact: 'Cartoonists depict him as a puppet master, manipulating a doll-like Mr Hosokawa on strings'.[58] Ozawa for a long time was one of the most controversial figures in Japanese politics variously because he was regarded as especially skilled, but also because he broke a political mould of such long standing, and in which there was so much investment of every kind.

The final damage was done to Hosokawa when he was accused of one of the very offences the commission of which he had resolved to smash. It was charged that he had taken money from a shipping company, which had already brought down an LDP vice-president in a famous scandal not long before. Hosokawa's resignation left the Japanese people more disillusioned than ever, and bitterly disappointed. His successor, of the Japanese Renewal Party, was Hata Tsutoma, who lasted nine days. A respected newspaper observed that his collapse on 25 April 1994 was a symbol of the new instability of what used to be one of the world's most stable political

55 Tase Yasuhiro, 'The enigma of Hosokawa Morihiro' in 'Seven views of the Hosokawa administration': *Japan Echo*, Vol. XXI, No. 3, Autumn 1994, p. 11.

56 For a detailed account see Kato Hiroshi 'Thoughts on the tax reform fiasco' in *Japan Echo*, Vol. XXI, No. 2, Summer 1994.

57 Yamaguchi Jiro, 'Three Betrayals', p. 9.

58 McCarthy, Terry, 'Puppet-master in a hall of mirrors', *The Independent*, 6 August 1993, p. 13.

systems.[59] His downfall was occasioned by Ozawa's attempts to manipulate the socialist left and right wings. The chairman of the Social Democratic Party of Japan, Murayama Tomiichi, was Hata's successor. This was enabled by a triple alliance of the LDP, his own party and the new 'Harbinger' party, and Murayama became prime minister in June 1993. This alliance is remarkable because it contains those parties who had formed the government and main opposition for nearly forty years. Equally noteworthy is the fact that Murayama became the first socialist prime minister in forty-seven years, and the second since 1945.

He is regarded by commentators notably as a decent and honest man, and a rarity in Japanese political life on that account. He is also commonly regarded as somewhat uninspiring, but someone who has made a good start nationally and internationally. The main task in early 1995 was the implementation of the proposed reforms, and the tackling of perennial problems such as taxation, and developing new relationships in a turbulent international configuration.[60] The situation remains unclear as to whether these 'reforms' will alter things. In the view of one commentator they do not amount to political reform. 'It merely marks the second stage of a restructuring process that began with the ousting of the LDP from power last summer.'[61] The usual prediction after some months, was that the Murayama government would last longer than its predecessors, as it has. It was also the expectation that the next set of elections, under the new rules, would develop a stable balance of power, probably between the 'giant' parties.[62] But the Japanese voters are apathetic, the coalition is based on convenience and collusion, and 'the nation craves strong leadership and a premier with better decision-making capability'.[63]

Many socialists, especially on the far left, had always been uneasy about coalition, especially with their historic political enemies of the LDP. Japan waited with interest to see how Murayama, who had been a loyal socialist party member since 1946 would deal with the centre-piece of the party's political ideology which, regardless of what happened in practice, created a chasm between them and the LDP. This was the issue of arms. The new prime minister's inaugural speech to

---

59 Dawkins, 'Tokyo adjusts', p. 23.

60 Bull, George, 'Murayama Tomiichi' in '*Insight Japan*', Vol. 3, No. 2, September 1994, pp. 11–12.

61 'From the editor', *Japan Echo*, Vol. XXI, No. 1, Spring 1994, p. 4.

62 Yoshikatsu Takahashi, 'State of Flux' in *Look Japan*, Vol. 40, No. 459, June 1994, p. 7.

63 Yasuhiro Tase, 'The Nikkei Weekly', 13 March 1995, p. 6.

his first Diet meeting contained the answer. In it he abandoned the policy of unarmed neutrality, and accepted the existence of the Self Defence Forces. There was an expectation by commentators that there would be a rebellion in socialist ranks. On the contrary there was broad acknowledgement that the policy about arms and security was an anachronism, and that Murayama was being realistic. A typical response came from a lower house member for Okinawa. From being a supporter of the traditional line who 'has long called for closure of the US military bases in Okinawa', he now 'basically approves continuation of the Japanese–US security treaty in light of its diplomatic importance for the party in power ... "it was a Rubicon we had to cross someday"'.[64] *The Economist* in London, in its analysis of Murayama's shattering announcements, observed that in Japan 'socialism has been finished off'.[65] All principles, on both wings of the Social Democratic Party and for that matter throughout other parties, were suspended and subordinated to the need for a stable period in a very unstable situation.

These events are indicative of the position of traditional left-wing political strength in Japan since the 1980s. The Japan Communist Party, the most orthodox of the parties of the left has never been influential in the post-Occupation years, but they had some modest success, unusual in democracies, in gaining seats. But this most pragmatic of measurements has not been encouraging. The road downhill can probably be dated to the 1976 House of Representatives election when 'the JCP suffered its first stunning electoral setback since the late 1950s: Communist representation in the lower house was cut in half from 40 to 19 (out of a total of 511)',[66] albeit there was an increase in their vote. The numbers more than doubled in 1979, and were then around 10 per cent of the vote.[67] In mid-1994 there were fifteen JCP members in the lower houses,[68] and since 1974 there have been about twelve to sixteen members in the upper house. The JCP like all communist parties is working at the problems consequent upon the ending of the USSR, and as with the socialists the central problem is discarding historical lumber. But they are still in the Diet.

64 Yoshida Reiji, 'The Japan Times Weekly International Edition' August 15–21 1994, p. 4.
65 Quoted in Bull, 'Murayama Tomiichi'.
66 Berton, Peter A., 'Japanese Euro-communists: running in place' in 'Problems of Communism' July–August 1986, p. 2.
67 Kishimoto, *Politics in Modern Japan*, gives an account of the varying fortunes of the Japanese Communist Party.
68 Yoshikatsu Takahashi, 'State of Flux', p. 5.

Another important element in the left-wing camp, and a classical ally of democratic socialism in the west, is the trade union movement. From time to time in this book the interest of the Japanese in the creation of unions has been discussed. The awareness of the potential for influence of organised labour was an early feature of the industrialisation and urbanisation of the Meiji Era, which was encouraged and influenced by events in the west in the Taisho Era, crushed in the 1930s and 1940s, and resurrected in the welter of enthusiasm in late 1945. There followed the MacArthur reversal, and the unions then settled into a collusive relationship with conservative politics and conservative moods. This pattern of compliance has been established because big companies allow in-house unions, thus destroying the classic organisational strength derived from job-based unions across the industrial spectrum. The consequent reduction in bargaining power is consolidated by active support from the company for union activity. This includes direct collection of dues from pay, and release of employees for union work to the extent of keeping jobs open. Company union membership is not extended to part-time or temporary workers, who are the most vulnerable to company pressure.

The positive side of the picture is that industrial relations are harmonious, or at least are not typified by strikes. Firms employing fewer than a hundred people are very different. There, only 1.8 per cent of such firms have unions.[69] The bedrock of socialist parties in some western countries is the union movement. In Japan, a beginning where many suffered for the right to unionise, by general agreement, has deteriorated to the ritual *shunto*. This 'spring offensive' is a curious street demonstration, and demand for a raising of wages. At its conclusion the employees accept the offer made by the employers.

The overall criticism which has been levelled against political parties and movements of the left is that they are fossilised into stances which were fashionable in 1945 at worst, and based upon bitter experience at best. That experience was of that systematic misery and terror into which the military ethos had taken Japan, and which, so some believed had been inherited, absorbed and was being promulgated by the 'conservatives', even though they did not sport military insignia. The question which the Japanese ask at present, is what the shifts in political and social attitudes and

69 Yoshimura Yosuke, 'Progressively more conservative' in *Look Japan*, Vol. 39, No. 450, September 1993, p. 8. This article is a typical commentary of the passive nature of union behaviour.

loyalties mean since the shock of the transition from the rigour of imperial Japan to the first excitement of the Occupation to the present day. Was there, and is there, any chance of a 'reverse' course, a common expression used 'to describe any manifestation of an alleged reactionary nature'? Is such a reverse inevitable, and especially insidious because, as a Professor Maruyama of Tokyo University suggested, it is gradual and the Japanese 'must be very careful not to become accustomed to it'?[70] It is impossible to distinguish deeply ingrained social attitudes and relationships, from those which arise as a consequence of opportunist political ma-noeuvring. A consideration of the present position of some of the debates raised in this book shows this. It is no doubt the case that the present position of the *burakumin*, Koreans, or women is still of sufficient concern to heighten, rather than diminish or eliminate, campaigns. Such are not popular causes; but are they susceptible to political solution? The campaigners believe so, and argue that if the supporters of the LDP persuasion were to have wished it, barriers to integration, and hindrance to access of all kinds would be removed. They point out that the 'reverse course' is all too evident, albeit as Professor Maruyama observed 'very slow'.

Just one issue around which antiquity, tradition, pride and fear quarrel is that of the Yasukuni shrine in Tokyo. This shrine honours the Japanese killed in all wars. In the 1960s, in an early attempt to restore its status, a group of LDP Diet members proposed political and financial support for it. Since 1974 prime ministers have visited the shrine 'privately', but naturally attracting enormous media attention, as did the 'deification' there of fourteen wartime people classed by the allies in 1945 as 'Class A criminals'.[71] A major step to rehabilitation was taken by Prime Minister Nakasone Yasuhiro who was in office at the time of the fortieth anniversary of the ending of the war. He honoured the shrine with an official visit on 15 August 1985. It was an act which created a furore, gave him a place as a hero in the recovery of Japanese values, displayed considerable personal courage and worried liberals. In the west where visits to war memorials by the highest authorities are routine, such response may seem excessive. But to the Japanese such an act, whether or not they disapprove, is of the utmost significance.

A key debate about institutional features of modern Japan is now, as it has been since the Restoration, education. This is because dispute about its purpose is perennial, because the Japanese value it

70 Storry, *History of Modern Japan*, p. 262.
71 Takeda Kyoko, *Dual-Image of the Japanese Emperor*, pp. 155–6.

highly and because its role in the shaping of Japanese history has never been forgotten. It provides a case study of the tensions between the old and the new, between the 'imperial' and the 'democratic' in modern Japan. A main tension which lies at the very heart of education is the curriculum, and control of that, as we have seen in earlier discussion, lies in the content of textbooks. SCAP's insistence on the ending of central control was tolerated until the ending of the Occupation, but in 1963 the government reasserted control over textbooks, despite determined opposition from the Teachers' Union. This led to a spectacular protest by a man who is now an emeritus professor of history, Ienaga Saburo. He was the author of a popular textbook which he revised in 1962, and submitted for approval. He received in reply instructions to revise certain passages. The controversy is so important in Japan, so illustrative of varying perceptions of history, and so persistent, that the following extracts from a text supporting Ienaga, need to be very carefully considered:

> Professor Ienaga described the Japanese army's brutal acts in the war, according to the actual facts, in order to convey the tragedy of these acts to young people. For example, he described Unit 731, formed in order to wage bacteriological warfare in China, in the following way: *A unit specializing in bacteriological warfare called the Unit 731 was stationed on the outskirts of Harbin and until the Soviet Union entered the war, this unit engaged in such atrocious acts as murdering several thousand Chinese and other non-Japanese by using them in bacteriological experiments.*
>
> Though the activities of this unit are a well-known fact, the Ministry of Education ordered the deletion of the entire passage on the grounds that: *No credible scholarly research exists concerning the Unit 731. It is still premature, therefore, to take up this matter in a school textbook.*
>
> In reference to the oppression of the Korean people and the anti-Japanese resistance movement there, Professor Ienaga wrote the following description: *The Sino-Japanese War began in 1894. The Japanese Army enjoyed successive victories in the fighting that continued through the following year but they were faced with repeated outbreaks of anti-Japanese resistance by the Korean people, whose land was turned into a battlefield.*
>
> The Ministry of Education ordered the deletion of the expression 'anti-Japanese resistance' on the grounds that 'it is not clear what is meant by the anti-Japanese resistance by the Korean people'. Instead, they ordered that the passage be rewritten to read 'there were numerous instances where the Korean people's cooperation could not be gained in the procurement of labour and material goods in the Korean battle arena'. This reflects the Ministry's desire to hide the truth of the Korean people's struggle from Japanese children.

The issue, predictably, concerned especially the events of the

Pacific War, and the behaviour of the Japanese imperial forces. This led to Ienaga instituting proceedings which may have finished after nearly thirty years of litigation.[72] His first lawsuit, for damages, began in 1965, and until 1993 his claims, both for damages and for the unconstitutional nature of textbook supervision were variously upheld, partly upheld and rejected. In March 1993 the Supreme Court ruled that the system was not unconstitutional. An indication of his widespread support is in the editorial of *The Japan Times* of 19 March 1993 which states:

> Yet he has performed an invaluable service in keeping before the public eye a government activity that many view as excessive inter-ference, which has angered textbook authors and publishers over the years and has led to international criticism that this country was whitewashing its wartime actions.

It was the tension underlying such controversies, concern about what was happening in schools, such as excessive competition and bullying, which led to the establishment of a National Council on Educational Reform in 1984, which produced its fourth and final report in August 1987. Its failure to achieve very much, even though it was set up by the powerful Prime Minister Nakasone, provides an excellent example of the resistance to change which arises from deeply held prejudice, a wish for consensus, and constant social and political suspicion in Japanese society. The final report, as Schoppa points out,[73] thwarted everybody, largely because of the by now familiar labyrinthine political networks which on some issues, for example the undesirability of decentralising educational administra-tion found Ministry officials and the Teachers' Union in accord, while they were in opposing camps on textbook control. Indeed the report's statement on the latter is typical of the anodyne nature of the 'recommendations':

> As regards textbook systems, there is the opinion that efforts should be made so that the free publication and free adoption of textbooks may be realised in the long run, while there is also the opinion that we should be sufficiently cautious as to the abolition of textbook author-ization and as to the shift to the free publication of textbooks.[74]

72 There is a National League for Support of the School Textbooks Screening Suit in Tokyo which published in 1993 *Truth in Textbooks, Freedom in Education and Peace for Children*, from which these extracts are taken, and reproduced, with permission, pp. 2–3.
73 Schoppa, Leonard James, *Education Reform in Japan: A Case of Immobilist Politics* (London, 1991), *passim*.
74 National Council on Educational Reforms, Government of Japan, *Fourth and Final Report on Educational Reform*, 7 August 1987, p. 51.

In its international relations, there are the same ambiguities, tendencies to caution, and concerns for Japanese dignity and pride in tradition as in the few domestic cases which have been briefly discussed. Set against the astonishing and continuing economic recovery after the war exemplified by the country becoming the first non-western member of the Organisation for Economic Cooperation and Development in 1964, there was a gargantuan task of international readjustment. The issue of Asia was most pressing since it was the Asian countries which had taken the brunt of Japanese imperial rapacity. In the years immediately after the war, perhaps understandably, the Japanese did not take much interest in Asia, but the countries which had been pillaged were not going to let their suffering be forgotten. Until the shift in American policy caused by the success of communism, large quantities of industrial equipment had been moved from Japan to China, Indonesia and the Philippines. But this stopped when allied policy changed.[75]

American hopes were that the question of reparations would be dropped, and that the issue would not be mentioned in the Peace Treaty.[76] But Asia was not prepared to agree, and the Treaty, in Article Fourteen concedes that: 'It is recognised that Japan should pay reparations to the Allied Powers for the damage and suffering caused by it during the war.' The Article goes on, however, to underline the need not to damage Japan's economy in the process. Negotiations went on for many years, and Japan 'reparated', for example by clearing harbours of wartime detritus. But although the Japanese government wanted 'influence abroad', it was 'nevertheless reluctant to accept any obligation for greater aid to the undeveloped portions of the world'.[77] Even in the 1950s Japanese business began to develop in several countries, because of credit and trade agreements and advanced Japanese skills, compared with its neighbours, and since then Japan's relationships with its neighbours, especially China and Korea, have been dominated by two things. Firstly a prospering economic relationship which has allowed the expansion and location of Japanese industry and commerce into those areas. Secondly a residual, but widespread sourness over Japanese refusal to admit, never mind apologise for, their behaviour during the war and colonisation. The Japanese have come closer to public acknowledgement in more recent years. Emperor Akihito made a statement in his visit to China in October 1992 which was moderated by argument over

75 Olson, Lawrence, *Japan in Post-War Asia* (London, 1970), p. 16.
76 Ibid.
77 Ibid., p. 73.

translation. Hosokawa's statements, mentioned earlier, were less equivocal, but a cool analysis must conclude that the Japanese attitude is still grudging. Prime Minister Murayama has proposed a programme of 'historical studies and exchanges with Asian nations' – surely promising interminable scope for dispute – but this does not include 'direct official compensation to individual war victims'. These include notoriously the 'comfort women'. The latter in the Philippines immediately 'denounced' the plan saying the 'Japan is unwilling to face the ugly facts of history'. In North Korea the comment was made of such schemes that they 'virtually rule out a probe into the truth and compensation' in respect of comfort women: 'The liquidation of Japan's past is not a matter that can be glossed over by Japan.'[78]

The truth may be in an article by Yoshihide Soeya when he writes that 'social and political "re-Asianisation"' will not come about easily. He goes on to observe that a 'new Asia' needs to be 'rid of the ghost of imperial Japan'.[79] The *official* Japanese attitude seems admirable enough. It was given in a speech by the ambassador to Britain, Fuji Hiroaki in June 1994. Quoting a speech by the Japanese prime minister in 1977, he reaffirms the rejection of any military role, the consolidation of 'the relationship of mutual confidence and trust', and equal partnership in ASEAN with positive cooperation 'in their efforts to strengthen their solidarity and resilience'. The ambassador drew attention to assistance given by Japan, and how 'Japanese private investment in the region had increased dramatically'. Against this background he 'identified harmony based on genuine reconciliation as an essential element'. The Japanese people 'were keenly aware of the suffering their country had inflicted and the government 'had expressed its deep remorse and sense of apology for what had happened'.[80]

Of equal complexity is the relationship between Japan and the United States. This important relationship which has been recounted in this book, has ranged from ambivalence to hostility. The former had, since 1945 until the collapse of the USSR, rested upon the need of the Americans for Japan as an ally. The relationship has been deeply racial, based upon rival imperialist ambitions, and exacerbated by military humiliation experienced by both sides.

78 'The Japan Times Weekly International Edition', 12–18 September 1994, pp. 1 and 6.
79 Yoshihide, Soeya, 'The "re-Asianisation" of Japan' in *Look Japan*, Vol. 40, No. 468, March 1995, p. 17.
80 'Japan', No. 572, 5 July 1994, pp. 2–3.

There is concern in Japan over the increasing influence of those aspects of American, and more generally western, life which are perceived as being detrimental to society. These include fast food, pop music and the undermining of parental authority. Since the 1980s there has been a new dimension, which is the anger over Japanese economic success because, Americans believe, of unfair practice. A common focus of attack is the Ministry of International Trade and Industry, known commonly as 'Japan Inc'.[81] This is the body which controls and regulates Japanese economic activity in the highly centralised bureaucratic fashion which would have been familiar to the Meiji bureaucracy. And it is very successful; but it is a success which engenders fury and chronic complaints.

Marvin Wolf has written of MITI as 'a national conspiracy', 'one that is becoming as potentially dangerous to world stability as the once military-political threat of the former Soviet Union'.[82] He supports such claims with cases, such as his alleged organised policy to destroy IBM computer sales. With regard to the balance of trade, there is no dispute that the Japanese government restricts imports, and that pressure to change regulations is very difficult to exert. Thus it is, as the American motor car industry gives way to Japanese imports, that 'Japan bashing' is a regular feature of newspaper articles, books and political speeches in the United States. The Japanese for their part do not submit without a protest to such attacks. One response to a particularly violent article in the 'Atlantic Monthly' of May 1989, led to a firm retort: 'if you go out into the world thinking that the strength of the United States is indisputable, you're going to be faced with a lot of problems that never get solved ... it may be a factor that the country which achieved this rapid growth is Asian'.[83]

The brittle relationship remains. The rejection in 1994 by Japan of trade targets proposed by America, left the increasing imbalance at an 'all-time high' accounting for 60 per cent of the entire US trade deficit.[84] But the United States economy was recovering and it turned its economic attention to other expanding Asian countries. This led to the notion of 'Japan passing', that is that the United States should shift its focus away from Japan. This has proved likely to be a new worry for Japan, without addressing the fundamental problem, which could easily be resurrected, which is their mutual failure to

81 For a full account of MITI, see Johnson, Chalmers A., *Miti and the Japanese Miracle*, (Stanford, California, 1982).

82 Wolf, Marvin, J., *The Japanese Conspiracy: Their Plot to Dominate Industry Worldwide, and How to Deal With It* (London, 1984), p. 3.

83 Masataka Kosaka, 'Containment Jargon' in *Look Japan*, August 1989, pp. 4–5.

84 Editorial, *The Nikkei Weekly*, 13 March 1995.

arrive at agreement over trade. It is more than ever the case that 'the world's most important bilateral relationship' means that 'stable Japan–US ties are vital to the entire Asia–Pacific region'.[85]

The debate about Japan's place in the world, in the late 1990s, is more frenetic than ever, notably whether or not it should regard Asia or America as the area which should have priority in economic or other terms. The view is commonly expressed that the United States interest in Asia is of such concern to Japan that trouble could lie ahead; in this case by a Japanese expert:

> The United States is also aiming to participate aggressively in the emerging markets of East Asia. This means that the central focus of the friction between Japan and the United States will be shifting from the bilateral trade imbalance toward activities in East Asian economies. It is thus to be expected that Japanese industrialists will be looking with renewed interest at Confucianism, Buddhism, and other shared elements of East Asian culture, hoping to put them to use to gain an advantage over Western countries in the scramble to build up a presence in China and other Asian countries.[86]

This comment is an almost perfect illustration of how Japan is so firmly locked into its history.

And so the complex relationships between these two great nations continue, from Perry with his autocratic demands, through to President Lyndon Johnson, who said that the United States should not be 'easy prey to any yellow dwarf with a pocketknife',[87] to the more restrained but several objections to trade restriction. On the Japanese side, there has been accommodation to the west, bitter resentment at western assumptions of Japanese inferiority, and great violence because of it. The Japanese people continue to wrestle with the questions which were asked in 1853. And the important ones are still about the meaning of being Japanese, the place of Japan in the world, and the balance between accommodating and resisting alien cultures.

---

85 Ibid.
86 Noda Nobuo 'The Dangerous Rise of Asianism' in *Japan Echo*, Vol. 22, No. 1, Spring 1995, pp. 6–11. As in many publications of the day, much space is taken up with Japan's search for international orientation.
87 Quoted in Chomsky, Noam, *World Orders Old and New* (London, 1994), p. 20.

Overleaf ▶
Walking forward to the past

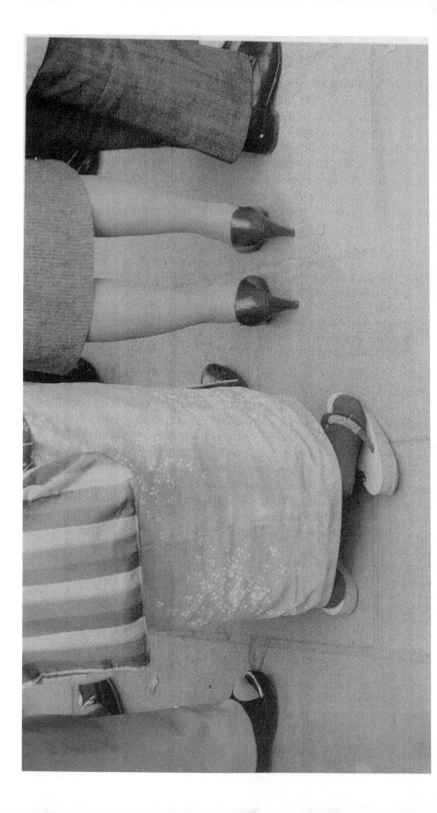

Glossary

Akihito – Present Emperor of Japan, who began his reign in 1989.

Bakufu – Camp government; term used to describe the Shogunal government.

Burakumin – Hamlet dwellers; current official term for outcastes.

Bushido – The Way of the Warrior; the classical military code of honour.

Chijiru – Curly hair – a term of abuse used on Okinawa to describe offspring of local women and American servicemen.

Daimyo – Great name; feudal lords with great authority, ranked next to the Shogun.

Dajokan – Briefly the Grand Council of State in the early part of the Meiji Era.

Danzaemon – The 'ruler' of the outcastes before the Meiji Restoration.

Dowa – Integration. Present-day term used to describe government policy, and attempts to integrate outcastes.

Ebune – Sea-going people; an historical minority.

Edo – The name of Tokyo before 1868. The period of Tokugawa rule from 1603 is called the Edo Era.

Eta – The original abusive term for the outcastes.

Gaijin – Foreigners.

Genro – Original Elders; the oligarchy which ruled Japan during the Meiji Era and much of the Taisho Era.

Genroin – Chamber of Elders, established in 1875 and abolished in 1890. Not to be confused with **genro**.

Heejarmie – Goats' eyes – a term of abuse used on Okinawa to describe offspring of local women and American servicemen.

Hibakusha – A survivor of the atomic bombing.

Hinin – Non-person, applied to beggars, prostitutes and others before the Meiji Restoration.

Hirohito – Posthumously Showa. Emperor from 1926 until 1989. He was both the longest living and the longest reigning emperor.

Ippan – Term used by outcastes to describe non-outcastes.

Jikeidan – Vigilantes who roamed the Kanto area after the earthquake of 1923, killing Koreans.

Junshi – The practice of following a dead lord by suicide. Banned in 1662, there have been examples after an emperor's death in this century. One of the most famous was General Nogi after Meiji's death.

Kamikaze – Wind of heaven. Used to describe the storm which dispersed a Mongol invasion fleet in the thirteenth century. Adopted to describe the 'suicide pilots' in the Pacific War.

Kempei-Tai – Military police, especially feared in Imperial Japan for their notorious brutality, especially towards prisoners of war in the Pacific War.

Kijiya – Woodworkers; an historical minority.

Koban – Police box, widely visible throughout Japan.

Kokugaku – A school of thought which sought to reassert the dominance of Japanese culture.

Kokutai – National polity, the abstract concept which dominated Imperial policy from 1868 until 1945.

Konketsuji – Sometimes '*hafu*', a child of mixed race.

Koseki – Japanese family registers, used as a means of discovering outcaste relationships.

Kurombo – 'Nigger', a term of abuse used on Okinawa to describe offspring of local women and American servicemen.

Kwantung (Liaotung) – Important peninsula in Manchuria. The area also gave its name to the infamous Japanese Kwantung Army.

Kyudojin – Former aborigines, used formally to describe the Ainu.

Manchukuo – Manchuland, the country defined as a replacement for Manchuria by the Japanese in the 1930s.

Matagi – Professional hunters; an historical minority.

Meiji Era – 'Enlightened government' is the term describing the rule of the restored emperor in 1868.

Mikado – Heavenly Gate, a term used in the past to describe the emperor.

Ninja – Literally 'secret person': assassin.

Ronin – Masterless samurai.

Sakoku – Closed country, used to describe the period during the Tokugawa shogunate when Japan isolated itself.

Samurai – One Who Serves, the military caste, notably during the Edo Era. They, and their privileges, were abolished soon after the 1868 Restoration.

Sanka – River workers and dwellers; an historical minority.

Semmin – Base people, collective term for **Hinin** and **Eta** before the Meiji Restoration.

Seppuku – Ritual suicide by disembowelling, often accompanied by decapitation by a comrade. An alternative term is *harakiri*. Generally **Seppuku** is the term used by the Japanese.

SCAP – Supreme Commander for the Allied Powers. He and his office (SCAP is used to refer to both) made policy in the reconstruction of Japan from 1945 until 1952.

Shin Heimin – New Commoners, used to replace the abusive term **Eta** in the Meiji Era.

Shizoku – Former ex-Samurai, when their rank was abolished.

Shogun – The full title means barbarian-subduing generalissimo. Military dictators who ruled Japan for several hundred years before the 1868 Restoration.

Showa – The Era from 1926 to 1989 when Hirohito was emperor.

Shunto – Present day ritual street demonstration by trade unions.

Sokobiki – minority group of fisherpeople.

Taisho – Great Righteousness, the name given to the emperor, and his Era, from 1912 to 1926.

Tatara – Ironworkers; an historical minority.

Tenno – Heavenly Sovereign, the name used by the Japanese for the emperor.

Terakoya – commoner schools in the Edo Era.

Tokugawa – The shogunal family which ruled Japan from 1603 until the Imperial Restoration of 1868.

Tokugawa Ieyasu – The founder of the dynasty which ended the civil wars in the early seventeenth century.

Yakuza – Contemporary organised professional criminal gangs.

Zaibatsu – Wealthy Estate. The huge conglomerates which dominated Japan from the end of the nineteenth century until 1945, and arguably afterwards.

Bibliography

Books

AGAWA HIROYUKI, *The Reluctant Admiral: Yamamoto and the Imperial Navy* (Tokyo, 1979).

AGENCY FOR CULTURAL AFFAIRS, *Japanese Religion: A Survey* (Tokyo, 1981).

ANDERSON, R.S., *Japan: Three Epochs of Modern Education* (Washington, 1959).

BARR, PAT, *The Coming of the Barbarians: a Story of Western Settlement in Japan 1853–1870* (London, 1967).

BEARDSLEY, RICHARD K. (ed.), *Studies in Japanese History and Politics* (Ann Arbor, 1967).

BEASLEY, W.G., *The Meiji Restoration* (Stanford, California, 1972).

BELLAH, ROBERT N., *Tokugawa Religion: the Values of Pre-Industrial Japan* (Glencoe, Illinois, 1957).

BEN-DASAN, ISAIAH, *The Japanese and the Jews* (New York, 1991).

BERGAMINI, DAVID, *Japan's Imperial Conspiracy* (London, 1971).

BERRY, MARY ELIZABETH, *Hideyoshi* (Harvard, 1989).

BRINTON, MARY C., *Women and the Economic Miracle: Gender and Work in Post-War Japan* (California, 1993).

BURUMA, IAN, *The Wages of Guilt: Memories of War in Germany and Japan* (London, 1994).

BUSCH, NOEL F., *The Emperor's Sword: Japan versus Russia in the Battle of Tsushima* (New York, 1969).

BUTOW, ROBERT J.C., *Tojo and the Coming of the War* (Princeton, 1961).

CHECKLAND, OLIVE, *Humanitarianism and the Emperor's Japan 1877–1977* (London, 1944).

CHEKHOV, ANTON, *The Island of Sakhalin* (London, 1989).

CHOMSKY, NOAM, *World Orders Old and New* (London, 1994).

COOX, ALVIN D., *Nomonhan: Japan Against Russia 1939* (Stanford, California, 1985).

DEACON, RICHARD, *A History of the Japanese Secret Service* (London, 1982).

DE VOS, GEORGE AND LEE, CHANGSOO, *Koreans in Japan: Ethnic Conflict and Accommodation* (California, 1981).

DE VOS, GEORGE AND WAGATSUMA HIROSHI, *Japan's Invisible Race: Caste in Culture and Personality* (California, 1966).

DORE, R.P. (ed.), *Aspects of Social Change in Modern Japan* (Princeton, 1967)

DUBRO, A. AND KAPLAN, DAVID E., *Yakuza: The Explosive Account of Japan's Criminal Underworld* (Tokyo, 1987).

DUKE, BENJAMIN C., *Japan's Militant Teachers: A History of the Left-Wing Teachers' Movement* (Hawaii, 1973).

DUKE, BENJAMIN C. (ed.), *Ten Great Educators of Modern Japan: A Japanese Perspective* (Tokyo, 1989)

FOREIGN PRESS CENTRE (ed.), *Facts and Figures of Japan* (Tokyo, 1989).

FURUKI YOSHIKO, *The White Plum: A Biography of Ume Tsuda: Pioneer in the Higher Education of Japanese Women* (New York, 1991).

GRAY, JACK, *Rebellions and Revolutions: China from the 1800s to the 1980s* (Oxford, 1990).

HACKETT, ROGER F., *Yamagata Aritomo in the Rise of Modern Japan, 1838–1922* (Harvard, 1971).

HANE MIKISO, *Peasants, Rebels and Outcastes: The Underside of Modern Japan* (New York, 1982).

HANE MIKISO, *Modern Japan: An Historical Survey* (Colorado, 1986).

HANE MIKISO (ed.), *Reflections on the Way to the Gallows: Rebel Women in Pre-War Japan* (California, 1988).

HARRIS, SHELDON H., *Factories of Death: Japanese Biological Warfare 1932–45 and the American Cover-up* (London, 1995).

HARVEY, ROBERT, *The Undefeated: The Rise, Fall and Rise of Greater Japan* (London, 1994).

HOYT, EDWIN P., *Japan's War: The Great Pacific Conflict* (London, 1986).

HOYT, EDWIN P., *Hirohito: The Emperor and the Man* (New York, 1992).

JOHNSON, CHALMERS A., *MITI and the Japanese Miracle* (Stanford, California, 1982).

KATO SHIDZUE, *A Fight for Women's Happiness: Pioneering the Family Planning Movement in Japan* (Tokyo, 1984).

KAWAHARA TOSHIAKI, *Hirohito and His Times: A Japanese Perspective* (Tokyo, 1990).

KAYANO SHIGERU, *Our Land was a Forest: An Ainu Memoir* (Boulder, Colorado, 1994).

KISHIMOTO KOICHI, *Politics in Modern Japan: Development and Organisation* (Tokyo 1988).

KODANSHA INTERNATIONAL, *Japan: Profile of a Nation* (Tokyo, 1994).

KODANSHA ENCYCLOPEDIA OF JAPAN (Tokyo, 1983).

LAFCADIO, HEARN, *Kokoro: Hints and Echoes of Japanese Inner Life* (Rutland, Vermont, Tokyo, 1972).

LAM, ALICE C.L., *Women and Japanese Management: Discrimination and Reform* (London, 1992).

LEE, K I-BAIK, *A New History of Korea* (Ilchokak, Seoul, 1984).

LIVINGSTON, J., MOORE, J. AND OLDFATHER, F. (eds), *Post-War Japan: 1945 to the Present* (New York, 1973).

LO, JEANNIE, *Office Ladies, Factory Women: Life and Work at a Japanese Company* (Armonk, New York, 1990)

LONE, STUART, *Japan's First Modern War: Army and Society and the Conflict with China 1894–95* (London, 1994).

MANCHESTER, WILLIAM, *American Caesar: Douglas MacArthur 1880–1964* (Boston, 1978).

MAYER, S.L., *The Biography of General of the Army Douglas MacArthur* (Greenwich, Connecticut, 1984).

MILLER, DAVID, *Submarines of the World: a Technical Directory of the Major Submarines from 1888 to the Present Day* (London, 1991).

MINORITY RIGHTS GROUP, *Japan's Minorities: Burakumin, Koreans, Ainu, Okinawans* (London, 1983).

MITCHELL, RICHARD H., *The Korean Minority in Japan* (Berkeley, California, 1967).

MIURA SEIICHIRO *et al.*, *Lifelong Learning in Japan: An Introduction* (Tokyo, 1992).

MORITA AKIO, REINGOLD, E.M. AND SHIMOMURA, M., *Made in Japan: Akio Morita and Sony* (London, 1987).

MULHERN, CHIEKO IRIE, *Heroic with Grace: Legendary Women of Japan* (Armonk, New York, 1991).

MURAKAMI HYOE, *Japan: The Years of Trial 1919–52* (Tokyo, 1982).

NATHAN, JOHN, *Mishima: A Biography* (Tokyo, 1974).

NEWMAN, J.H., *The Idea of a University* (London, 1852).

NISHI TOSHIO, *Unconditional Democracy: Education and Politics in Occupied Japan 1945–1952* (Stanford, California, 1982).

OLSON, LAWRENCE, *Japan in Post-War Asia* (London, 1970).

PEYREFITTE, ALAIN, *The Collision of Two Civilisations: The British Expedition to China in 1792–4* (London, 1993).

PRANGE, GORDON W., GOLDSTEIN, DONALD M. AND DILLON, CATHERINE V., *Miracle at Midway* (New York, 1983).

PRANGE, GORDON W., GOLDSTEIN, DONALD M. AND DILLON,

KATHERINE V., *Pearl Harbor: the Verdict of History* (New York and London, 1986).

RATTI, OSCAR and WESTBROOK, ADÈLE, *Secrets of the Samurai: a Survey of the Martial Arts of Feudal Japan* (Rutland, Vermont, 1973).

SCHOPPA, LEONARD JAMES, *Education Reform in Japan: A Case of Immobilist Politics* (London, 1991).

SHIBATANI MASAYOSHI, *The Languages of Japan* (Cambridge, 1990).

SHIMAZAKI TOSON, *The Broken Commandment*, translated Strong, Kenneth (Tokyo, 1974).

SILBERMAN, BERNARD S. AND HAROOTUNIAN, HARRY D. (eds), *Japan in Crisis: Essays on Taisho Democracy* (Princeton, 1974).

SMETHURST, RICHARD J., *A Social Basis for Pre-War Japanese Militarism* (Berkeley, California, 1974).

SMITH, ROBERT J., *Japanese Society: Tradition, Self and the Social Order* (Cambridge, 1983).

STORRY, RICHARD, *A History of Modern Japan* (London, 1960).

SWINSON, ARTHUR, *Defeat in Malaya: the Fall of Singapore* (London, 1969).

TAKEDA KIYOKO, *The Dual-Image of the Japanese Emperor* (London 1988).

THOMAS, J.E., *Learning Democracy in Japan: the Social Education of Japanese Adults* (London, 1985).

THOMAS, J.E. AND ELSEY, BARRY, *International Biography of Adult Education* (Nottingham, 1985).

THOMAS, J.E. and STEWART, A., *Imprisonment in Western Australia: Evolution, Theory and Practice* (University of Western Australia Press, 1978).

TURNBULL, STEPHEN, *Ninja* (Dorset, 1992).

WEINER, MICHAEL, *Race and Migration in Imperial Japan* (London, 1994).

WHAN, V.E., *A Soldier Speaks: Public Papers and Speeches of General of the Army, Douglas MacArthur* (New York, 1965).

WOLF, MARVIN J., *The Japanese Conspiracy: Their Plot to Dominate Industry Worldwide and How to Deal With It* (London, 1984).

YAMAMOTO TSUNETOMO, *The Book of the Samurai: Hagakure* (Tokyo, 1983).

Journals, Periodicals and Newspapers

Adult Education and Librarianship (University of Tokyo)
Education in Japan: Journal for Overseas

Financial Times
Insight Japan
Japan
Japan Echo
Japan Forum
Japan Pictorial
Mainichi Daily News
National Women's Education Centre Newsletters, Tokyo
Newsletters of the International Movement Against All Forms of Discrimination and Racism
Problems of Communism
The Independent
The Japan Times
The Nikkei Weekly

Reports

Ministry of Education, Science and Culture, *Education in Japan: A Graphic Representation* (Tokyo, 1982).

Ministry of International Trade and Industry, *A Supplement to MITI Handbook: List of MITI Officials* (Tokyo, 1988).

Ministry of Labour, Japan, *Survey on Employment and Management of Women Workers* (Tokyo, 1981).

Report of the United States Education Mission to Japan. Submitted to the Supreme Commander for the Allied Powers (Tokyo, 1946).

Education in Japan, General Headquarters SCAP, Information and Education Section, Education Division (Tokyo, 1946).

Report by the Japanese Commission for UNESCO (1960).

Ministry of Education, *Japan's Modern Education System: A History of the First Hundred Years* (Tokyo, 1980).

Adult Education in Japan, *Bulletin XXX,* World Association for Adult Education (London, 1926).

Education in the New Japan, SCAP CIE Education Division (1948).

Report of the Second United States Education Mission to Japan (Washington, 1950).

National League for the Support of the School Textbook Screening Suit, *Truth in Textbooks, Freedom in Education, and Peace for Children* (Tokyo, 1993).

National Council on Educational Reforms, Government of Japan, *Fourth and Final Report on Educational Reform* (Tokyo, 1987).

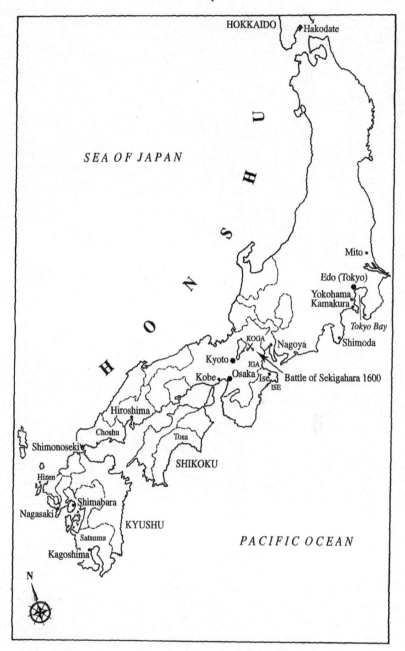

HOKKAIDO • Hakodate

SEA OF JAPAN

H O N S H U

Mito •

Edo (Tokyo)
Yokohama
Kamakura

Tokyo Bay

KOGA
✕

Nagoya

Kyoto •

IGA

• Shimoda

Kobe •

Osaka

Ise •

Battle of Sekigahara 1600

ISE

Hiroshima

Choshu

Tosa

SHIKOKU

Shimonoseki •

Hizen

Shimabara

Nagasaki

KYUSHU

Satsuma

Kagoshima

PACIFIC OCEAN

N

Map 1   *Before the Restoration: Japan in 1860*

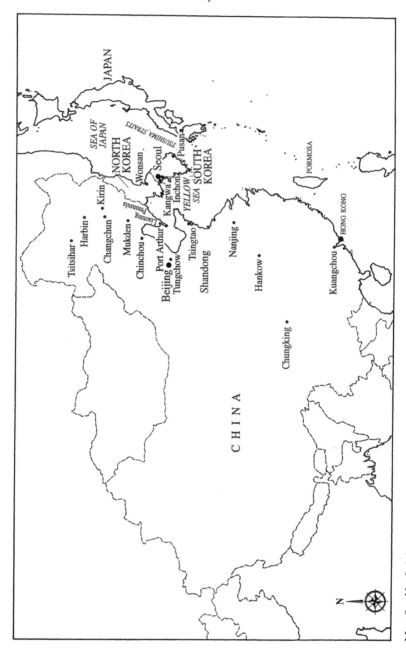

Map 2 *North Asia*

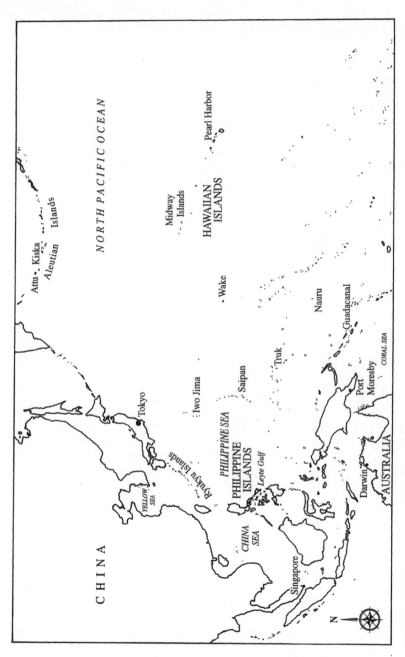

Map 3   *Battlegrounds in the Pacific*

Index